D1546383

FRANKLAND

MANCHESTER
1824

Manchester University Press

FRANKLAND

THE FRANKS AND THE WORLD OF THE EARLY MIDDLE AGES

Essays in honour of Dame Jinty Nelson

edited by

Paul Fouracre *and* David Ganz

Manchester University Press

Manchester and New York

distributed exclusively in the USA by Palgrave Macmillan

Published by Manchester University Press
Oxford Road, Manchester M13 9NR, UK
and Room 400, 175 Fifth Avenue, New York, NY 10010, USA
www.manchesteruniversitypress.co.uk

Distributed exclusively in the USA by
Palgrave Macmillan, 175 Fifth Avenue, New York,
NY 10010, USA

Distributed exclusively in Canada by
UBC Press, University of British Columbia, 2029 West Mall,
Vancouver, BC, Canada V6T 1Z2

British Library Cataloguing-in-Publication Data
A catalogue record for this book is available from the British Library

Library of Congress Cataloging-in-Publication Data applied for

ISBN 978 0 7190 7669 5 *hardback*

First published 2008

16 15 14 13 12 11 10 09 08   10 9 8 7 6 5 4 3 2 1

Typeset
by SNP Best-set Typesetter Ltd., Hong Kong
Printed in Great Britain
by CPI Antony Rowe, Chippenham, Wiltshire

Dame Jinty Nelson

CONTENTS

CONTENTS

TABLES

CONTRIBUTORS

David Bates, Professor of Medieval History, University of East Anglia

Stephen Baxter, Lecturer in Medieval British History, King's College, London

Wendy Davies FBA, Professor Emerita, University College, London

Paul Fouracre, Professor of Medieval History, University of Manchester

David Ganz, Professor of Palaeography, King's College, London

John Gillingham FBA, Emeritus Professor of History, London School of Economics

Sarah Hamilton, Senior Lecturer in Medieval History, University of Exeter

Matthew Innes, Professor of History, Birkbeck College, University of London

Paul Kershaw, Assistant Professor of Medieval History, University of Virginia

C. P. Lewis, Institute of Historical Research, London

Simon MacLean, Lecturer in Medieval History, University of St Andrews

Susan Reynolds FBA, Honorary Research Fellow, Institute of Historical Research, University of London

Theo Riches, Lecturer in History, University of Birmingham

Alice Rio, Sidney Sussex College, Cambridge

Rachel Stone, Lecturer in History, Birkbeck College, University of London

Alan Thacker, Executive Editor, Victoria County History, Institute of Historical Research, University of London

ABBREVIATIONS

Af El.	*Laws of Alfred*
ANS	*Anglo Norman Studies*
ASC	*Anglo-Saxon Chronicle*
ASE	*Anglo-Saxon England*
CCCM	*Corpus Christianorum Continuatio Medievalis*
CCSL	*Corpus Christianorum, series Latina*
CSEL	*Corpus Scriptorum Ecclesiasticorum Latinorum*
DA	*Deutsches Archiv für Erforschung des Mittelalters*
DACL	*Dictionnaire d'archéologie chrétienne et de liturgie*, ed. F. Chabrol and H. Leclercq
DDC	*Dictionnaire de droit canonique*, ed. R. Naz
DHEG	*Dictionnaire d'Histoire et de Géographie ecclésiastiques*
DNB	Oxford Dictionary of National Biography
EHR	*English Historical Review*
EME	*Early Medieval Europe*
HBS	Henry Bradshaw Society
HE	Bede, *Historia Ecclesiastica Gentis Anglorum*
MGH	*Monumenta Germaniae Historica*
AA	*Auctores Antiquissimi*
Poet.	*Poetae Latini Aevi Carolini*
SRG	*Scriptores Rerum Germanicarum in usum Scholarum separatim editi*
SRL	*Scriptores Rerum Langobardicarum et Italicarum*
SRM	*Scriptores Rerum Merovingicarum*
SS	*Scriptores in folio*
MIÖG	*Mitteilung des Instituts für Österreichische Geschichtsforschung*
MS	*manuscript*
NCMH	*New Cambridge Medieval History*
PL	*Patrologica Latina*
PP	*Past and Present*
PRG	*Pontificale Romano-germanique du dixième siècle*

ABBREVIATIONS

Settimane	*Settimane di Studio del Centro Italiano di Studi sull'Alto Medioevo*
SLH	*Scriptores Latini Hiberniae*
TRHS	*Transactions of the Royal Historical Society*
ZRG	*Zeitschrift der Savigny-Stiftung für Rechtsgeschichte*

PREFACE

When it was first suggested that a volume of essays be put together in honour of Jinty Nelson, the editors were inundated with requests from colleagues who wished to be involved. So many people feel a strong sense of gratitude to Jinty for her work, and for the help that she has given them, that we could have filled several volumes, each with a different theme, or even nationality. In the end it seemed most appropriate to give the volume a London basis, with contributions from colleagues and from former students, all of whom have shared with Jinty the rich experience of participating in the Early Middle Ages seminar at the Institute of Historical Research. The editors chose the title 'Frankland. The Franks and the world of the early Middle Ages' to celebrate the way in which Jinty has used her profound understanding of Frankish history as a frame for reflecting upon the nature of early medieval culture and society in general. Each contributor was asked, accordingly, to write an essay on a theme that made connections between the Frankish world and the world beyond, in terms of either time or place, or both.

The volume includes a *tabula gratulatoria* of those very many others who wish to express their appreciation of Jinty's work and their warm personal gratitude to her. The editors recognize that there will be far more who should have been invited. That they were not, merely reflects the fact that Jinty has helped and encouraged more people than anyone can remember. We are grateful to Manchester University Press for supporting this publication from the outset. Jinty has had a long association with the MUP as the series advisor to the *Manchester Medieval Sources* series, which she got off to such a good start with her own *Annals of St Bertin*. Finally, for the record, Jinty likes to be known as Jinty Nelson. She is in fact, Dame Jinty Nelson, but the editors have elected to use 'Janet Nelson' to refer to her in each essay, for they wished to retain a certain academic formality for what is a series of substantial essays which have an importance in their own right. We recognize that this famously unceremonious honorand may be irritated by the formality, but we trust that she will be equally impressed by the substance.

Paul Fouracre and David Ganz, Manchester and London

Introduction: Dame Jinty Nelson . . . An Appreciation

Paul Fouracre and David Ganz

J ANET NELSON (NEÉ MUIR) was born in 1942 and grew up in Black-pool, Lancashire. She studied History at Newnham College, Cambridge and graduated in 1964. In Cambridge she met and in 1965 married Howard Nelson. After graduation she proceeded directly to postgraduate research under Professor Walter Ullmann, completing a PhD in 1967. Her thesis title was 'Rituals of Royal Inauguration in Early Medieval Europe. From *dux populi* to *athleta christi*'. Although she almost never refers to this work, and certainly never sought to publish it, it remains an outstanding treatment of the subject. Importantly, the research gave her an understanding of the political resonance of the liturgy in the early Middle Ages and a thorough grounding in that intellectually rigorous scholarship which is the hallmark of her work. Kathleen Hughes, her college tutor at Newnham, provided a model of generous, supportive and meticulous teaching that has shaped Janet Nelson's care for her own students over the past thirty-seven years.

After the award of the PhD in 1967 she joined her husband in the Hong Kong New Territories. Howard Nelson was engaged in social anthropological fieldwork there, and Janet (or 'Jinty' as she is known to everyone who has ever met her) assisted with enthusiasm. She took the trouble to learn enough written Chinese to analyse the data held in the land registry as a source for the economic history of the village that Howard was studying. The experience of life in a peasant village widened her vision as a historian. Already aware of the importance of understanding ritual a good decade before most historians took this on board, she has always had a keen eye for how families and wider kin groups operated and interacted. It is this insight which has given her such a sharp sense of what was and was not possible for women in the Middle Ages. Her stay in the New Territories also means that Jinty is probably unique among Western medievalists in having some knowledge of Chinese as well as the usual Latin and Greek, and no doubt the only medievalist to have received a genuine Chinese 'white elephant' as a gift expecting a counter-favour. Howard has remained a figure of inspiration to her, as well as an escape valve from the pressures of academia. With their having restored an old farmhouse in the Périgord, for her this became a haven in which summers were spent quietly writing. With Howard she also undertook the pilgrimage to Santiago, a thousand miles walked in sections from 1990 to 1998. It was an exercise in applied medievalism, a demonstration of determined empathy from one with a robustly secular cast of mind.

On their return to the UK, Janet Nelson first worked for the Foreign Office until in 1970 she took up a post as Lecturer in History at King's College, London. She has remained at King's throughout her entire career. Even sabbaticals were spent within a bus-ride of the College. Never short of invitations and enticements to move to other posts, Jinty has always made it clear that she felt that King's and London University was where she wanted to be. Not only did she come to think that History was as exciting and excellent at King's as it could be anywhere, she also became a true Londoner, bringing up a family in South-East London, where her two children Lizzie and Billy were born in 1972 and 1974. Her early career was thus combined with young motherhood, a tough experience that has made her strongly supportive of colleagues trying to balance work and family. At King's, she began to apply the insights of anthropology to her work and to widen her historical interests to include the study of heresy, at the same time building up her understanding of every aspect of Carolingian society. Two early papers, 'Society, theodicy and the origins of heresy' (1971) and 'Royal saints and early medieval kingship' (1973), were seminal. They brought her to the attention of medievalists at large, and they remain widely cited. The reason that they are still required reading is that they cut through myth, romantic assumption, and a certain tendency to exoticize early medieval phenomena. In place of the exotic, they find explanations in the pragmatic needs of people faced with understandable choices. This was not to say that early medieval societies were not in many ways quite different from our own, but that that difference not only should, but also could, be understood. This conviction has underpinned all her work, most recently in thinking about concepts of translation. It was an approach that others immediately appreciated. Janet Nelson quickly became one of the most respected early medievalists around.

Although she continued to write about early medieval inauguration rituals, a new departure came with the 1977 paper 'On the limits of the Carolingian Renaissance', ten pages of crystalline reasoning that challenged her own training in asking whether a cultural programme directed by a government with limited means and little sophistication could have had much meaning on the ground. The Carolingian Renaissance could not, from this angle, be viewed as a decisive moment in European cultural and political development. It was her growing understanding of how early medieval government actually worked, whatever its aspirations, that led her to question whether an assumed widespread revival of culture and learning was a practical proposition. It is a mark of her commitment to understanding the issues, rather than to defending herself, that Janet Nelson has come back to this subject many times. As a result she has built up a growing appreciation of what the Carolingians did actually achieve, and how they managed to do it without much government machinery, but with a certain determination and coherent notion of what they were about. Reasoned debate she values highly, and she continues to treat the question of whether or not the Carolingians did change the course of European development as an open one. One of the editors of this volume spent ten years with her teaching an undergraduate 'special subject' on the reign of Charlemagne and observed how each year Jinty asked this question of the students, not as a teacher who required the 'right' answer, but as a scholar who genuinely values the opinions of others. The students were exhilarated to find themselves treated as serious contributors to the debate, despite, as many admitted, the mental exhaustion that followed a two-hour session in the ring with her.

From the mid-1970s Janet Nelson began to attract a growing number of research students, including several of the contributors to this volume. She built up King's College, London into a magnet for early medieval studies and this fed into a lively research culture at the Institute of Historical Research. Joining John Gillingham and R. Allen Brown as a convenor of the Institute's Early Middle Ages seminar, the latter became extraordinarily successful. Usually packed to the rafters, it hosts papers by the great names in the field, but also encourages postgraduate researchers from across the country to present their work. Under Jinty's influence it became (and remains) famous for a blend of informality and tough discussion. Unforgettable was the 'ten-minute rule' tried in the early 1990s which banned anyone over the age of forty from speaking for the first ten minutes after the end of a paper. There were some painful silences. Given the high level of intellectual exchange and the concentration of like-minded scholars around the Institute at this time, one can see why the prospect of leaving London seemed so unappealing.

Janet Nelson's concern with how ideology, ritual and political thought might be combined in practical action, and with how individuals made choices according to needs and opportunities, led her to work on the reign of Charles the Bald, a figure rather in need of historical rehabilitation. The result was a model of political history that set the pace for a series of studies that rethought the history of the later Carolingians. Whereas in some scholars a concentration on political history might have meant a lowering of horizons around the chosen subject, for Janet Nelson it meant quite the opposite as she applied her understanding of the Latin source material and her grasp of how things worked in detail to a widening array of subjects. For her, the figure of the ruler became the hub from which she moved outward to interrogate every other cultural element. Charles the Bald led to a comparison with King Alfred of Wessex, and this in turn involved wider comparison between England and the Continent, a theme first broached in a Royal Historical Society paper in 1986, but to which she returned in 2002–4 on the four occasions that she addressed that same society as its President. The debunker, and also the optimist, in her, has led back and back to the question of the impact of the Vikings both in England and on the Continent. Her stance can be evinced in the memorable phrase she wrote with Simon Coupland: 'when the Franks looked at Vikings, they saw faces much like their own' (*History Today*, 1988). It is a phrase that voices her humanity as a historian. The same warmth has guided her interest in women's history. This first saw print in 1978, with a characteristic comparative treatment of the careers of two queens, Brunhild and Balthild, which brought to light issues of gender to explain why these women had been treated so harshly by writers both ancient and modern. Subsequent studies have addressed writing and gender more generally, widows and strategies of inheritance, queenship, women and royal courts, and the women in various royal families, not least the daughters of Charlemagne. These studies, which reflect on the nature, purpose and positive attributes, but also the pitfalls, of women's history have brought Janet Nelson's work to a much wider audience than medievalists usually enjoy.

How we access the past has become an issue of increasing importance to her, starting with an analysis of narrative in a notable study of the *Histories* of Nithard (1985) and moving on to a translation of and commentary on the *Annals of St Bertin* (1991). One result has also been an ongoing discussion about the possibility of writing early medieval biography. This is preparatory to a major study on the figure of Charlemagne, prefigured in a 2005 paper 'Charlemagne the man'. Biography, in Janet Nelson's conception, goes to the very root of historical enquiry: can we 'know' people in the distant past in any sense meaningful to our own social and personal experience? It is a question that relates to her long-standing concern with translation – that is, how to capture the essence without simply inscribing ourselves on the text, be it ancient or modern. The modern aspect is significant because few historians are as aware as Janet Nelson of the weight

4

of different national historiographical traditions, and of the importance of understanding what other people are thinking. She has long seen it as her task not just to study European history, but to forge and reinforce links with European colleagues. George Eliot's 'Middlemarch' is one of her favourite books and she is always mindful of the baleful Casaubon whose linguistic deficiency meant that his entire oeuvre could have been pre-empted by the work of some clever German and he would never have known. That it takes a woman, the increasingly perceptive Dorothea, to point this out to him is entirely fitting. We cannot 'know' the past, but the process of trying to understand it should be a collective intellectual effort that not only bridges the difference between past and present, but also serves to translate and reconcile contemporary difference.

Janet Nelson's published output is prodigious. In four volumes of collected essays there are no fewer than sixty-four papers, and to use a typically generous phrase of hers in relation to the work of others, 'not a knocker amongst them'. In addition there are of course her books, edited books, contributions to reference works and surveys, magazine and newspaper articles and, not least, substantial contributions to the on-line prosopography of Anglo-Saxon England. Remarkably, her track record as a 'doer' is as impressive as her publication record. She has been President of the Ecclesiastical History Society, Vice-President of the British Academy, Corresponding Fellow of the Medieval Academy of America, President of the Royal Historical Society, Director of the Centre for Late Antique and Medieval Studies at King's College and on the editorial boards of the journals *Past and Present* and *History Workshop Journal*. For the latter she has put together and edited two special issues. She was a key participant in the European Science Foundation project on the Transformation of the Roman World, and latterly a director of the Anglo-Saxon prosopography project. In 1987 she was made a Reader at King's and 1993 she became Professor of Medieval History, a position that King's College has now made permanent in her honour. In 1996 she was elected a Fellow of the British Academy; in 2004 she received an Honorary degree from the University of East Anglia, and in 2007 another Honorary degree from the University of St Andrews. Janet Nelson has used her growing influence and recognition to advocate the cause of the History, and of Medieval History in particular. As President of the Royal Historical Society she was a tireless ambassador for the subject. When one Minister for Higher Education belittled the profession with the suggestion that the nation could tolerate 'a few ornamental professors of Medieval History' but that the subject was generally not worth taking seriously, she marshalled a powerful response that led to a public retraction. A meddlesome priest she might have been, but her irrefutable achievements and her work for the subject were publicly recognized when she was made a Dame of the British Empire in 2006, a rare honour indeed.

Janet Nelson is held in great affection by all those who have worked with her. Scholars from across Europe and the English-speaking world all know her as 'Jinty' and refer to her with warmth. One reason for this is that she has been unfailingly generous with her time, despite her increasing commitments. The astonishing number of people she has helped with their work, reading their drafts, commenting on their proposals, speaking at their conferences, supplying them with works otherwise unavailable, is revealed in the 'Acknowledgments' sections of a host of books and articles. Determined that the late Tim Reuter's unpublished papers deserved to see the light of day, she put aside her own writing commitments in order to gather together a final volume in his name. This meant retrieving material to turn into the finished article and also translating a great deal of work from German, a wonderful tribute to a deeply missed and highly respected colleague. Likewise she completed the volume of papers planned by the late Patrick Wormald. These are the kinds of task that are enormously time-consuming and carry very little recognition, apart from the admiration of close colleagues. Similarly, she would translate material from French or German or Latin for any student she thought really needed to read it. In short, an abiding of impression of Janet Nelson is of a brilliant mind allied to extraordinary kindness and consideration, and of a scholar and teacher running, it seems, on limitless reserves of energy. It is hard to think of her actually turning down any request for her time and attention, until, that is, she became a grandmother. Since the birth of her grandchildren Elias, Ruth, Martha and Miriam she has dedicated Thursdays to childcare alone, a duty which she relishes. She has, however, been heard to remark that she will probably be able to make up the time on other days. Quite how, it is difficult to imagine.

1

Charters, law codes and formulae: the Franks between theory and practice

Alice Rio

I N HER RECENT third presidential address to the Royal Historical Society, devoted to rights and rituals, Janet Nelson put forward a powerful case for a strong consciousness of rights even among those parts of the Frankish population which we are accustomed to thinking of as powerless.[1] This argument links in with her previous work on records of disputes as evidence for legal practice in the Frankish kingdoms.[2] The purpose of this essay is to see how a different kind of source, the legal formulae, may help bring into sharper focus this view of rights from below. Although formulae do not respond to the same kind of methodological treatment as actual records of dispute settlements, their evidence remains crucial, if only in terms of volume: formulae account for as many as 88 out of the 162 dispute cases listed by Hübner for Francia before 800.[3] Beyond these, a large number of formulae, although they do not give an account of the proceedings and therefore did not make it into Hübner's list, provide models for documents that would have been produced as a result of disputes, to record the terms of the settlement and prevent further litigation.

Formulae are descriptive material turned into normative texts: real cases turned into models for future use. In this sense, they are related both to written laws, on the normative side, and to charters, on the descriptive side.

---

1 J. L. Nelson, 'England and the Continent in the ninth century: III, Rights and rituals', *TRHS* 6th series, 14 (2004), pp. 1–24.
2 J. L. Nelson, 'Dispute settlement in Carolingian West Francia', in W. Davies and P. Fouracre (eds), *The Settlement of Disputes in Early Medieval Europe* (Cambridge, 1986), pp. 45–64.
3 R. Hübner, 'Gerichtsurkunden der fränkischen Zeit', *ZRG Germanistische Abteilung* 12 (1891), appendix, pp. 1–188. See P. Wormald, *The Making of English Law: King Alfred to the Twelfth Century*, vol. 1: *Legislation and its Limits* (Oxford, 1999), p. 73, n. 223, and table 2.2 at p. 74, for a revision of Hübner's list, discounting most formulae.

Historians have interpreted formulary evidence differently according to which of these two approaches was adopted. Written laws and charters yield very different, and sometimes even contradictory, evidence on social relationships in the Frankish kingdoms. They belong to fundamentally distinct historiographical traditions, from which neither has entirely broken free: the positivist tradition of the German *Rechtsschule*, with its strong emphasis on royal power, for laws, and French regional history, preoccupied with the ability of lords to assert their power at a more local level, for charter-collections. As a result, their (admittedly vast) differences have been emphasized more than their common ground. And yet somehow both must be allowed a place in the same early medieval world that produced them: they can, and must, be made sense of together. I will focus here on the different ways in which these sources filter power relationships, and how formulae may help to bridge the gap between them.

The scope of formulae

Legal formulae are in an unusual position among early medieval sources. Their study peaked early. It was begun in earnest by the beginning of the seventeenth century, and formulae elicited fairly steady scholarly interest from then on. The nineteenth century was the golden age of their study: rival editions were published, Eugène de Rozière's work was quickly superseded by Karl Zeumer's *MGH* edition,[4] and there was a flurry of debate and controversy regarding dating and editing work. Fustel de Coulanges relied heavily on formulae as a source in his *Monarchie franque*, and his work can be said to represent the only serious attempt to use them comprehensively in a general history on the same level as, for instance, the law codes or narrative histories.[5] By the 1930s, formulae looked set to become established as a source for the Frankish kingdoms that could not be dispensed with.

Curiously, however, their use declined sharply thereafter. This is especially obvious in the level of attention they receive in textbooks. Until the early twentieth century textbooks on the period always devoted a section to them, typically including an inventory of the evidence and a few words

---

4   E. de Rozière, *Recueil général des formules* (Paris, 1859–71); *Formulae Merowingici et Karolini Aevi*, ed. K. Zeumer, *MGH Legum* V (Hanover, 1886).
5   Fustel de Coulanges, *La Monarchie franque*, Histoire des institutions politiques de l'ancienne France, vol. 3 (Paris, 1888), *passim*, but especially pp. 23–4; see also, for instance, *ibid.* pp. 29, 190, 214, 406, 409, 415–16, 420, 499.

on the genre.[6] Formulae then became an increasingly obscure source as the twentieth century progressed, and they are hardly represented at all in modern textbooks.[7] This rather startling reversal of fortune for a source that had once been considered important partly has its roots in the change in the way we approach our sources. Whereas nineteenth-century scholars had been happy to shape their view of the medieval world to fit the available sources, depending on a relatively straightforward assessment of their reliability or otherwise, the sensitivity to the difficult relationship between text and reality that is the hallmark of modern research places a much heavier demand on our sources. We now view texts as self-conscious reconstructions: where earlier scholars had looked only to evaluate the informative content of a source, we now look for discourse, textual strategies, and power relationships. Historians are now keenly conscious of the need to understand first and foremost what a text is for and how it works: its use, its context of production, what kind of project it was part of. The idea that we should never take anything for granted when it comes to evaluating the purposes and representativeness of a source, even when it purports to be straightforward, had its greatest impact on historians' reading of written law. This was revolutionized in an even more dramatic way than our reading of literary texts, the ulterior motives and deliberate distortions of which had always to some degree been a concern to scholars. The limits imposed

---

6   The classic synthesis on formulae is H. Brunner, *Deutsche Rechtsgeschichte* vol. 1, 2nd edn (Leipzig, 1906), pp. 575–88; see also H. Bresslau, *Handbuch der Urkundenlehre für Deutschland und Italien*, 2nd edn, reedited by H.-W. Klewitz (Berlin/Leipzig, 1931), vol. 2, pp. 225–41. T. Sickel, *Acta regum et imperatorum Karolinorum digesta et enarrata: Die Urkunden der Karolinger*, vol. 1: *Urkundenlehre* (Vienna, 1867) also includes a discussion of some formularies (pp. 112–25). R. Buchner, *Deutschlands Geschichtsquellen im Mittelalter: Vorzeit und Karolinger. Beiheft: Die Rechtsquellen* (Weimar, 1953), pp. 49–55, is still the most recent overview on the subject.

7   There is no index entry for 'formula' or 'formulae' in P. Fouracre (ed.), *NCMH I* (Cambridge, 2005); the whole volume includes only a few footnote references to Marculf. Philippe Depreux, in his *Les Sociétés occidentales du milieu du VIe à la fin du XIe siècle* (Rennes, 2002) does not mention them in his discussion on sources, while R. Le Jan, in *La Société du haut moyen-âge* (Paris, 2003) confines them to a few descriptive lines (p. 17). Formulae are similarly limited to a few passing comments in I. N. Wood, *The Merovingian Kingdoms, 450–751* (London, 1994). In the case of Depreux and Wood, the absence of any substantial discussion is all the more striking since both authors use formulary material elsewhere: P. Depreux, 'La tradition manuscrite des "Formules de Tours" et la diffusion des modèles d'actes aux VIIIe et XIe siècles', in P. Depreux and B. Judic (eds), *Alcuin de York à Tours: Ecriture, pouvoir et réseaux dans l'Europe du Haut Moyen Age* (Rennes/Tours, 2004), pp. 55–71; I. N. Wood, 'Disputes in late fifth- and sixth-century Gaul: some problems', in Davies and Fouracre (eds), *Settlement of Disputes*, pp. 7–22.

by the codes' prescriptive nature are now emphasized, and historians no longer take them as a straightforward reflection of society: they are now examined more in relation to what they can tell us about royal power, or what value system they convey.

This has had a strong impact in the decline of formulae as a source. Their heyday was associated with the deep interest in law and legal texts characteristic of nineteenth-century German scholarship. As a result, formulae have essentially been approached from the angle of legal and institutional history. It is symptomatic in this respect that interest in them should have been curiously concentrated on the problem of the replacement of lost documents and the *apennis* procedure, almost to the exclusion of any other subject.[8] Historians have been most interested in using formulae as evidence for legal structures, or for the information they can give us on those directly involved in the technical aspects of drawing up documents and their level of professionalization, and not for what they can tell us about the stories of the people these documents were drawn for. As far as formulae are concerned, it is assumed, perhaps a little too pessimistically, that these stories are beyond all hope of recovery. The potential of formulae as a source for social history has therefore remained largely untapped.

On the other hand, there is also the angle of the diplomatists, working from the perspective of charters.[9] This approach has only compounded the perceived deficiencies of formulae as a source. It is very rare that a formula can be shown beyond doubt to have been the model of a surviving document, and this has created a level of uncertainty as to whether formulae were used at all. Secure connections between formulae and surviving

---

8   K. Zeumer, 'Über den Ersatz verlorener Urkunden im fränkischen Reiche', *ZRG, Germanistische Abteilung* 1 (1880), pp. 89–123; L. Gobin, 'Notes et documents concernant l'histoire d'Auvergne. Sur un point particulier de la procédure mérovingienne applicable à l'Auvergne: "l'institution d'*apennis*"', *Bulletin historique et scientifique de l'Auvergne* (1894), pp. 145–53; most recently, C. Lauranson-Rosaz and A. Jeannin, 'La Résolution des litiges en justice durant le haut Moyen-Age: l'exemple de l'*apennis* à travers les formules, notamment celles d'Auvergne et d'Angers', in *Le Règlement des conflits au Moyen-Age, XXXIe Congrès de la SHMES (Angers, juin 2000)* (Paris, 2001), pp. 21–33, and W. Brown, 'When documents are destroyed or lost: lay people and archives in the early Middle Ages', *EME* 11 (2002), pp. 337–66.
9   See for instance *Die Urkunden der Merowinger*, ed. T. Kölzer, *MGH Diplomata regum Francorum e stirpe merovingica* (Hanover, 2001); I. Heidrich, 'Titulatur und Urkunden der arnulfingischen Hausmeier', *Archiv für Diplomatik* 11 and 12 (1965–6), pp. 71–279; U. Nonn, 'Merowingische Testamente: Studien zum Fortleben einer römischen Urkundenform im Frankreich', in *Archiv für Diplomatik* 18 (1972), pp. 1–129.

charters are very difficult to establish: the very nature of the genre, and its use of standard expressions, means that two documents of the same type can look very much alike without actually being textually related.[10] As a result, textual similarities which would be considered strong enough evidence to establish a link between two literary texts are insufficient to establish a secure link in the case of documents and formulae. Even if a surviving formula had been used to create a surviving document, the relationship would not be likely to be straightforward: since a formula in its original form obviously could not reflect the different circumstances under which a new document based on it was produced, these differences would have had to be resolved in the process of copying.[11] One should therefore not expect the use of a formula to leap off the page: a degree of adaptation is presupposed by the very nature of the genre.[12] It is thus in practice difficult to distinguish actual examples of the use of formulae from mere coincidences. This does not mean that they were not used: although they hinder the identification of more precise textual relationships, what these widely shared expressions and themes suggest, more positively, is that formulae participated in the same common Frankish legal culture as our surviving documents. This is in itself far more significant and useful than would be the simple discovery of links with individual existing documents, and, as a result, the scarcity of secure textual links need not stop us from exploiting formulae as a fully legitimate source.

What all this does mean, however, is that links with datable surviving charters can rarely help us to pin down the date and place of origin of a

10   The most thorough and detailed attempt at assessing the use of formulae in surviving documents was made by H. Zatschek, 'Die Benutzung der *Formulae Marculfi* und anderer Formularsammlungen in den Privaturkunden des 8. bis 10. Jahrhunderts', *MIÖG* 42 (1927), pp. 165–267. Zatschek was rather too liberal in his identification of textual correlations. In many instances, his links have nothing to support them save the common use of the same biblical quote; in all these cases, the similarity reflects little beyond a common shared knowledge of popular passages of the gospels.

11   It may be telling in this respect that the only cases in which one does find a very close fit between formulae and surviving documents are forgeries, since in their case there were no particular circumstances in the production of the document to necessitate the alteration of the wording of the formula; indeed, a forger would have had a sharpened interest in preserving its style and language, since this would have been the easiest way of ensuring the appearance of authenticity. The description of the objects of these fictional transactions in itself would only have required minimal modifications.

12   See P. Fouracre, '"*Placita*" and the settlement of disputes in later Merovingian Francia', in Davies and Fouracre (eds), *Settlement of Disputes*, pp. 23–43, at p. 30.

collection. The main method of dating formulae has been through the identification of the documents on which they would have been based.[13] The tendency to overstate the relationships between formulae and surviving documents thus affects the reliability of much of the datings suggested for collections, even leaving aside the basic problem that it would be very difficult in any case to be certain of whether the formula would have been based on the document or the document on the formula.

Accordingly, the need to determine context is the most significant obstacle to the use of formulae as a source. In this respect formulae are at a unique disadvantage due to their non-specific nature. A large proportion of what historians usually like to find in a source is simply unobtainable from them because, in a bid to give them general value, scribes removed all names of the persons involved, and most places and dates. Even when the point of origin is securely identified and dated, which is extremely rare, the shelf-life of any collection remains unknown. Although they often reproduce models from the Merovingian period, virtually all of the manuscripts date from the Carolingian period, and it is difficult to judge how relevant these texts may have been by that time. Formulae thus have a loose anchorage in space and time, and historians have been reluctant to rely on them, some even rejecting them entirely, explicitly or in practice.[14]

In a historiographical climate which rightly emphasizes the local diversity of medieval experience, and thus tends to favour regional studies, for which charter collections have proved invaluable, formulae at first sight do not look as if they have much to offer. The highly specific nature of the charter implies a scope that is localized and context-bound, the product of local needs and preoccupations: what could have applied in one village need not have applied in another.[15] Collections of charters can offer an unparalleled *entrée* into local conditions, allowing historians to reconstruct property patterns for particular communities, or create a prosopography

---

13 See among others K. Zeumer, 'Über die älteren fränkischen Formelsammlungen', *Neues Archiv* 6 (1881), pp. 9–115; B. Krusch, 'Ursprung und Text von Marculfs Formelsammlung', in *Nachrichten von der Königlichen Gesellschaft der Wissenschaften zu Göttingen, Phil. hist. Klasse* (Berlin, 1916), pp. 234–74.

14 Robert Fossier's verdict in a recent textbook is particularly severe: '... simples cadres qu'on remplira ensuite, [les formulaires] n'apporteront de données que dans le seul domaine de la diplomatique': R. Fossier, *Sources de l'histoire économique et sociale du Moyen Age occidental: questions, sources, documents commentés* (Turnhout, 1999), p. 44.

15 On the possibilities of charters, see C. Wickham, *Framing the Early Middle Ages* (Oxford, 2005), pp. 384–5.

of the parties and witnesses involved in the transactions. With formulae such opportunities are denied us. If, therefore, one thinks of formulae simply as charters with all of their crucial local information missed out, one will necessarily find them a very uninformative source indeed.

Formulae are thus often treated as poor cousins of charters: the general opinion seems to be that although formulae often contain interesting information, it is made virtually useless because it cannot be tied down to a specific time and place in the way that it can for charters. Formulae are therefore usually approached only as a second-rate source, and have become something historians turn to in the absence of the documents they would have been based on: the *placita* and charters we wish we had, but do not. As a result, despite their continued copying and reworking down to the tenth century, formulae tend to be studied as evidence for the Merovingian period, for which we lack these actual documents almost completely, far more than for the Carolingian period, for which our surviving record is more extensive. The idea that the study of formulae and that of charters should go hand in hand is so dominant in the historiography as to have remained unquestioned, and all in all, it seems fair to say that historians have been less interested in formulae as a distinct genre than in the trace they preserve of their sources.

The methodological adjustment which heralded a new departure in our understanding of so many other medieval sources has thus left formulae in something of a limbo. Like other sources, they have become the object of increased suspicion. Historians, now wary of overconfident generalization and alive to the risks of making assumptions on the meaning and purpose of even the most outwardly utilitarian of early medieval sources, have expressed doubt as to whether they were really used in the way they purported to be, or even whether they were used at all; in addition, no one is quite sure of the context in which they should be considered, whether in terms of when, where, or how.[16] As charters, formulae lack vital information; as legal texts they are exposed to the same suspicion as the law codes when it comes to their application in practice, without giving us much by way of a coherent ideological discourse in exchange. Formulae have thus been rather hard done by, and in most modern work have remained relatively under-exploited.

Taken on their own terms, however, formulae can give us a fuller story. The manuscripts, most of them produced in the course of the ninth century, show a dynamic tradition, obscured by the rigidly *Urtext*-orientated editing work characteristic of the *MGH* series. Formularies found in several

16   Brown, 'When documents', pp. 339–40.

manuscripts, such as those of Marculf, Tours and St-Gall, invariably have a very complex tradition: scribes, it seems, were not so much concerned with reproducing their exemplars word-for-word as with exploiting them as a resource to create a new and highly personalized finished product. As a result, surviving manuscripts often give us vastly different assortments and versions of texts, of which Zeumer's edition only represents the very narrowest view. This may give us an idea of what we are missing of the history of the vast majority of collections which are only known from a single witness. Even in some of those cases, however, the manuscripts show contacts and exchanges, of groups of texts or single texts, between the different collections. Connections and intersections in the manuscript tradition show a very fertile and changing ensemble: the impression is one of a general pool of available material transmitted according to a complex pattern of diffusion, in which collections mattered less than individual texts. The transmission of formulae was a constant and continuous process of modification, selection and reorganization. Since collections never adopted a stable canonical form, they could not have been copied mechanically or merely as a result of tradition: formulae were alive and kicking, and the continued use of these texts as models through to the ninth and tenth centuries therefore seems a fairly safe conclusion.[17]

Given this argument for broad continuity, it is important to consider why these texts survive when and where they do. Despite their apparent descent from Roman documentary traditions, the material evidence for formulae is overwhelmingly Frankish and Carolingian. There is cause to wonder why this should be the case: if they did indeed derive from the Roman legal tradition, which seems highly likely, then why should we find so little of them elsewhere in the areas previously under Roman rule? Why are they so generally absent in Italy, for which the surviving record is usually so much fuller than for Francia?

The issue is not so much one of whether or not documentary models were used in these other areas as one of survival and visibility. The existence of such models outside Francia is attested, despite being very poorly documented: scraps of surviving evidence from Spain and Italy indicate that models similar in function to our Frankish material were indeed being used there, and the degree of standardization of documentary forms in Spanish and Italian documents also suggests that the scribes who drew them up

---

17 See Brown, 'When documents', pp. 358–60, for a similar argument for formulae concerning the loss of documents.

were trained on the basis of earlier documents.[18] The two surviving Italian examples of formulae collections, books VI and VII of Cassiodorus's *Variae* and the *Liber Diurnus*, were both produced in close connection with an especially strong (by early medieval standards) form of centralized government, Cassiodorus with Ostrogothic kingship, the *Liber Diurnus* with the papacy, and are thus admittedly fundamentally different in nature to the Frankish collections, very few of which can be shown to have been created in connection with any royal or imperial court. No collection comparable to the Frankish ones survives for individual Italian monasteries. On the other hand, the *Formulae Visigothicae*, our only evidence for Spain, are resolutely set at a local level, and are very like the Frankish collections; so similar, indeed, as to have led some scholars to hypothesize a link between them and the Angers collection.[19] This example suggests that formulae of much the same type as those we find in Francia were being produced and used in Visigothic Spain, although they were considerably less successful than their Frankish counterparts at leaving a trace in the surviving record.

18   Note that the use of formulae as part of a specialized form of training for scribes does not necessarily imply a very sophisticated documentary style, as can be seen in many of our Frankish examples. Although it is rather more difficult to tell what exactly the production of Latin documents would have involved in Anglo-Saxon England, the consistent use of conventional phrases could suggest that models may have been used there as well. The apparent lack of competence and professionalism of the scribes of early Anglo-Saxon charters does not necessarily mean they were not trained; it simply means they were not under any particular pressure to make their documents conform to strict external standards. These documents were clearly good enough for their users, which implies that scribes were trained just as much as they needed to be. See S. Kelly, 'Anglo-Saxon lay society and the written word', in R. McKitterick (ed.), *The Uses of Literacy in Early Medieval Europe* (Cambridge, 1990), pp. 36–62; P. Wormald, 'The uses of literacy in Anglo-Saxon England and its neighbours', *TRHS* 5th series, 27 (1977), pp. 95–114; M. T. Clanchy, *From Memory to Written Record: England 1066–1307*, 2nd edn (Oxford, 1993).
19   The possibility of a link with the Angers collection, first brought forward by Karl Lehmann, was convincingly discarded by Schwerin, who argued that the resemblance was only superficial, and due to the similar nature of the actions taken rather than to any real textual link. See K. Lehmann, 'Monumenta Germaniae Historica. Legum Sectio V: Formulae Merowingici et Karolini aevi, edidit Karolus Zeumer', *Kritische Vierteljahrschrift für Gesetzburg und Rechtswissenschaft* 29 (1887), pp. 331–46, at p. 336; J. G. O. Biedenweg, *Commentatio ad formulas Visigothicas novissime repertas* (Berlin, 1856), p. 5; J. Beneyto Pérez, *Fuentes de derecho histórico español* (Barcelona, 1931), p. 107; R. Schröder, *Lehrbuch der deutschen Rechtsgeschichte*, 6th edn, ed. E. von Künssberg (Berlin, 1922), p. 294; against the link, see C. von Schwerin, 'Sobre las relaciones entre las Fórmulas visigóticas y las andecavenses', in *Annuario de Historia del Derecho Español* 9 (1932), pp. 177–89.

The question is not why formulae did not survive elsewhere, but why they did, and in such quantity, for Carolingian Francia. To a certain extent, the same question applies to Frankish formulae before the Carolingian period. Although formulae were clearly used in Merovingian Francia, we would not have any of these collections either had it not been for Carolingian manuscripts: a few pages written in early eighth-century cursive inserted at the end of Paris BnF lat. 10756 (fols. 62–64) are our only clear surviving Merovingian example. The evidence clearly indicates that there was a strong new impulse in the production of both manuscripts and new collections during the reigns of Charlemagne and Louis the Pious.[20] This does not mean that these collections were produced as a result of royal initiative: on the whole, collections compiled in the context of the imperial chancery, such as the *Formulae Imperiales* in Paris BnF lat. 2718, do not appear to have been particularly more successful in terms of diffusion than collections compiled outside it. They do not even appear essentially more official: chancery scribes seem to have devised models for their own use in much the same way as local or church scribes, so that, although they often had rather different concerns, their collections were not fundamentally other in nature.[21] The growth in the production of formularies was therefore not the result of imperial initiative, though it is likely that it was the by-product of a more systematically document-minded style of rule and of a renewed pressure to record transactions in correctly written documents.[22] The growing role of ecclesiastical institutions in the production of documents, to record both their own transactions and those of the lay people in their neighbourhood, may have had a more direct impact. Monastic house-scribes could have begun to compile collections in a more accessible

---

20 J. L. Nelson, 'Literacy in Carolingian government', in R. McKitterick (ed.), *The Uses of Literacy*, pp. 258–96, at pp. 261–2.

21 For the *Formulae Imperiales*, see R.-H. Bautier, 'La chancellerie et les actes royaux dans les royaumes carolingiens', *Bibliothèque de l'Ecole des Chartes* 142 (1984), pp. 5–80, at p. 44, and P. Johanek, 'Herrscherdiplom und Empfängerkreis: Die Kanzlei Ludwigs des Frommen in der Schriftlichkeit der Karolingerzeit', in R. Schiffer (ed.), *Schriftkultur und Reichsverwaltung unter den Karolingern*, Abhandlungen der Nordrhein-Westfälichen Akademie der Wissenschaften 97 (1996), pp. 167–88, at p. 186; M. Mersiowsky, 'Saint-Martin de Tours et les chancelleries carolingiennes', in P. Depreux and B. Judic (eds), *Alcuin de York*, pp. 73–90, at pp. 81–4; D. Ganz, 'Paris BN Latin 2718: theological texts in the chapel and the chancery of Louis the Pious', in O. Münsch and T. Zotz (eds), *Scientia veritatis, Festschrift für Hubert Mordek zum 65. Geburstag* (Ostfildern, 2004), pp. 137–52.

22 See Davies and Fouracre (eds), *Settlement of Disputes*, p. 212; M. Innes, *State and Society in the Early Middle Ages: the Middle Rhine Valley (400–1000)* (Cambridge, 2000), p. 117.

state with the design of creating a resource that would outlive their own use, whether for teaching or for the future reference of their peers or successors. Individual users no doubt still picked and chose for themselves what they thought they might need out of earlier collections, but the demand for standardized documents had increased, and with it no doubt also the need to train more scribes and to provide them with more durable reference books.

It is striking that these collections, when their place of origin can be determined (which is not often), almost all seem to have originated in Northern Francia: they are nearly all distributed along or to the North of a rough latitudinal line running along the middle of the Frankish kingdoms through Angers, Tours, Bourges and Salzburg. The only exceptions are a very small fragment from Clermont and the only non-Frankish collection of this kind, the *Formulae Visigothicae*, which is thought to have been produced in Cordoba.[23] Despite the stronger documentary tradition generally attributed by historians to Mediterranean regions, it does look as if formularies had a much harder time surviving in the South than they did in the North. Then again, there could be good reasons why formularies might have been urgently needed in the North: not only were the churches and monasteries situated in the royal heartlands, some of the largest religious houses, and thus perhaps those most in need of an organised system for the training of scribes, they were also those most closely linked to, and aware of, the activities of kings: they were closer to royal centres, were placed on the routes on which kings travelled most regularly, and may thus have had a greater ability, or at least more opportunities, to appeal to the king in cases of disputes. Northern bishops and abbots also tended to have stronger personal or family connections with members of the royal or imperial court, which would again have improved their ability to appeal to the king. All this would have led to a certain pressure for these institutions to keep an appropriate record of transactions and disputes according to external norms of correctness, which in turn would have led to the more systematic development of textbooks as a response.

The large number of manuscripts from the ninth century may therefore be the result of a more systematic way of thinking about these texts, and reflect a move toward a more organized style of transmission. It is even possible that the copying of these collections as full texts in formal manuscripts only began in the Carolingian period: this could explain why so very little manuscript evidence survives from the Merovingian period,

---

23   The most recent edition is by J. Gil, '*Formulae Wisigothicae*', in *Miscellanea Wisigothica* (Seville, 1972), 70–112.

despite the fact that many collections were undoubtedly put together at that time. If most collections in their Merovingian state existed only as casual notes prepared by and intended for only a single user, jotted down at the back or in the margins of books, as can still be seen in a few Carolingian manuscripts, or even kept as loose sheets of parchment, as seems to have been the case with the fragment bound at the end of Paris BnF lat. 10756, they would have had a very slim chance of survival. Religious communities were more likely to develop a systematic approach to the transmission of documentary models than independent notaries. The survival of these texts depends not on *whether* formulae were used, but on *who* used them: the greater the ecclesiastical involvement in the production of documents, the higher their chance of survival, since they then fell into the care of institutions characterized both by an extraordinary longevity and by a strong vested interest in the production and preservation of written records. There would also have been greater opportunities for contacts and exchanges between ecclesiastical institutions than between independent lay notaries: the monk Marculf, in the only surviving preface to such a collection, thus addressed his formulary to a bishop, and may represent an early example of the more organized approach which would allow collections finally to become visible in our manuscript record. Manuscripts of the Carolingian period document continual exchanges between traditions, and the diffusion of these texts from one ecclesiastical institution to another, beyond their original context. This increased diffusion meant that formulae had the chance to generate a lively and fecund manuscript tradition: such exchanges would have ensured a wider distribution for individual collections, and a correspondingly greater number of manuscripts, both of which would have contributed to an increased chance of survival.

If we take them at their origin point, formulae may indeed be said to represent the sub-Roman world of the 'town-clerk' or 'country solicitor';[24] but they only become visible in our surviving evidence after migrating from that world and moving into ecclesiastical archives. These texts are least visible when they remained close to home, in which case they were less likely to be copied and transmitted with as strong a sense of system and accessibility. In times and places in which the Carolingian drive for standardization was not felt, there was no reason for these texts to become formalized on the same scale. This may explain why no Roman texts of this kind survive, why there are so few Spanish and Italian examples, and also why so little manuscript evidence for the Merovingian period survives: in

24 Wormald, *Making of English Law*, p. 37.

all these cases, local scribes may simply have been using their own earlier documents as models, or only keeping models as loose notes, liable to be lost or destroyed. At the opposite end of the chronological scale, precisely such a localization of legal practice may also explain why formulae stopped being copied after the tenth century. Religious houses were still just as much involved in the production of documents, but the absence of external norms may have led to a greater tendency for them to use their own archive as a resource, both for teaching and for the creation of new documents. Less-developed relationships and exchanges between different religious communities would also have given formulae correspondingly fewer opportunities to develop a manuscript tradition. The disappearance of formulae from our record also coincided with a substantial change in documentary practices, with charters becoming replaced by longer, more detailed and less standardized *notitiae*,[25] which were less suited to being derived from a model, and may have led to the emergence of a different style of teaching, relying on memory more than on written models. Such a difference in teaching styles may also be one reason for the near-absence of formularies in the south throughout our period.

The particular set of conditions of transmission of these texts in the Carolingian period allows us a glimpse at texts lost for other times and regions. From the middle of the eighth century to the middle of the tenth, formulae experienced a brief peak of visibility, due to the combination of strong external pressure for correctness in the production of documents, the inclusion of such texts in more durable manuscripts intended for teaching in order to meet the needs of growing monastic communities, and the existence of an empire-wide network of contacts between ecclesiastical institutions.

Formulae thus only become visible in our record when they move beyond a purely local value. For this reason, comparison with charters can only get us so far. It is true that formulae do not provide us with the sense of security associated with knowing that a particular action took place at a particular time and in a particular place, as is possible with charters, and looking for this information in formulae will inevitably prove to be a frustrating exercise. On the other hand, the act of removing details to generalize the content of the text offers possibilities as well as limits: their continued copying and adaptation as a resource for producing new documents suggests that what had happened once was thought likely to happen again. There is something to be said for an approach that would exploit

25   See in particular D. Barthélemy, *La société dans le comté de Vendôme de l'an mil au XIVe siècle* (Paris, 1993), pp. 19–127.

more positively this militant non-specificity, normally seen as their worst weakness, but which is after all what makes them unique as a source. The fact that these texts were produced, copied and reworked over the course of at least four centuries can reveal continuities and changes in the need for specific types of documents, whereas charters, no matter how precise, only give us single events. The fluid shape of formulae, and their capacity to evolve in order to better represent the needs of their users, is the editor's curse, but a stroke of luck for the social historian. To fully appreciate the possibilities of formulae, one needs to move beyond their original context of production: in other words, to take advantage of their capacity to generalize from individual occurrences, and to document expectations for the future as well as isolated cases. Formulae offer a range of possible solutions to particular situations in practice, in a perspective of continuity. This continuity does not contradict the very real and fundamental differences that can be established between the Merovingian and Carolingian periods on the basis of other sources, but formulae do document a certain accepted way of doing things in a day-to-day, practical context, whether for settling disputes or managing one's private property, which could constitute the normally less visible common background uniting the two, and against which more striking shifts may then be offset.

Power relationships in laws, charters and formulae

Having briefly outlined the scope of our formulary evidence, I will now address the question of their perspective, what factors determined and informed their particular take on the Frankish world, and how this compares to law-codes and charters.

Taken at face value, the law codes confirm the worst suspicions associated with the traditional view of this period. Laws were not intended to function as the refuge of the weak against the strong, but rather to institutionalize existing power relationships. The law-codes formally reasserted the legal powerlessness of large groups of the population, such as women or the unfree. This impression is often contradicted by surviving evidence of actual legal practice. Charters and records of dispute offer a more nuanced picture, documenting, for instance, a degree of control by women over their property. The more positive view of social relationships in the early Middle Ages which has come to establish itself in recent years is strongly linked to the discrediting of laws as a source for social history. Historians now prefer to rely on a more anthropological approach, emphasizing local negotiation and diversity, a trend of which the *Settlement of*

Disputes volume was a magnificent and pioneering example.[26] Charters and records of disputes are now seen as more representative, since they constitute evidence for real practice, rather than reflecting a more abstract understanding of how society should function. Since the discrediting of written law as evidence for social practice, charters have thus been seen as the most secure source from which to access the 'real' world.

The question of how far these real cases used written laws as a reference-point at all has been much debated. Rosamond McKitterick, on the basis of a fecund manuscript tradition, has argued that written modes and written law had a wide impact on real practice.[27] Patrick Wormald, on the contrary, inferred both from the strong conservatism and lack of user-friendliness of the law-codes in the manuscript tradition, and from the notable absence of specific references to written law in surviving Frankish records of disputes, that written law did not have much to do with real practice, and instead fulfilled a largely symbolic role.[28] As a result, Wormald proposed a North-South divide in the uses of written law: while the impression in the North is one of a general disregard for written law, the presence of direct references to the law-codes in Italian documents led him to conclude that written law was more profoundly implanted in the South.[29]

Surviving charters and records of disputes deal predominantly with land, since land disputes and transactions were the only ones likely to retain their value beyond the lifetimes of the parties involved, and thus to have any kind of archival longevity. Early medieval kings legislated about people more than they did about land: laws defined rights, obligations and

26 Davies and Fouracre (eds), *Settlement of Disputes*; see also the contributions in J. Bossy (ed.), *Disputes and Settlements: Law and Human Relations in the West* (Cambridge, 1983).

27 R. McKitterick, *The Carolingians and the Written Word* (Cambridge, 1989), pp. 23–75.

28 Wormald, *Making of English Law*, pp. 29–92. On the absence of reference to written law in documents North of the Alps, see P. Wormald, '*Lex Scripta* and *Verbum Regis*: legislation and Germanic kingship from Euric to Cnut', in P. H. Sawyer and I. N. Wood (eds), *Early Medieval Kingship* (Leeds, 1977), pp. 105–38, at pp. 119–23; compare R. McKitterick, 'Some Carolingian law-books and their function', in B. Tierney and P. Linehan (eds), *Authority and Power: Studies on Medieval Law and Government presented to Walter Ullmann on his Seventieth Birthday* (Cambridge, 1980), pp. 13–28. On legal practice in Carolingian Francia, see also J. L. Nelson, 'On the limits of the Carolingian renaissance', *Studies in Church History* 14 (1977), pp. 51–67, reprinted in J. L. Nelson, *Politics and Ritual in Early Medieval Europe* (London, 1986), 49–67; Nelson, 'Dispute settlement'; Nelson, 'Literacy in Carolingian government'.

29 Wormald, *Making of English Law*, pp. 79–83.

punishments for individuals rather than regulating the conduct of private business. Land transactions are therefore less likely to contain references to written law. References in the case of gifts to the Church, for instance, do not tend to refer to legal material, but rather to standard scriptural quotes on the spiritual rewards of Christian charity, apart from occasional references to written law in the case of rules for witnessing, which are found in Frankish documents as well as in Italian ones. Formulae, on the other hand, contain more frequent references to written law. In contrast with the charters, formulae preserve documents not on the basis of their usefulness in entrenching property rights in the long term, but according to what was needed in the here and now, to provide models for situations that might be encountered during the course of a scribe's professional life. Formulae therefore present a more diverse body of evidence than surviving Frankish documents, since they deal not only with people's management of their property, but also with their legal status and law-cases. They contain evidence for disputes of a far more transitory nature than those represented in our surviving body of charters and records of disputes, such as thefts, kidnappings, murders and so on, which would hardly have been worth preserving in the long run. The evidence of formulae could therefore play an important part in allowing us to better appreciate the scope and degree of the influence of written law.

In some cases, reference to a particular piece of written legislation seems fairly straightforward: the text of no. 33 of the *Formulae Imperiales,* in which a church servant is manumitted in order to allow him to become a priest, thus echoes, at some points word-for-word, Louis the Pious's *Capitulare ecclesiasticum* of 818/9, which is found associated with it in the same manuscript.[30] This example at least shows that the compilers of formulae could be well informed as well as up-to-date. Then again, it is not surprising that the *Formulae Imperiales* should give us such an impression, since that collection seems to have been produced by a notary associated with Louis's chancery. Many other formularies refer to known legislation in fairly exact terms, though usually without the same level of textual correspondence as may be observed between *Formulae Imperiales* no. 33 and the *Capitulare ecclesiasticum.* On the other hand, formulae also occasionally cite Salic or Roman law as support for an action when the corresponding clauses never existed so far as we know.[31] Wormald deduced from this that such

---

30 *MGH Capitularia* I and II, ed. A. Boretius (Hanover, 1883), I, no. 138 (*a.* 818/19), c. 6, pp. 276–7.
31 One example is *Formulae Salicae Lindenbrogianae* no. 20.

references corresponded not to the actual text of the law, but to a rather more vague notion of legal custom.[32]

One should certainly not overestimate the extent of scribes' real knowledge of written law from their ability to refer to it in general terms. The same references to written law tend to come up again and again: Louis the Pious's *Capitulare ecclesiasticum* is a case in point. No. 33 of the *Formulae Imperiales*, unlike many of the other texts in that collection, appears to have been a very popular text in the manuscript tradition, and the other manuscripts do not include Louis's legislation alongside it.[33] It is likely that scribes' idea of what written laws contained was derived not from an intimate knowledge of the codes themselves, but precisely from such references found in formulae. This would no doubt have contributed to perpetuating areas of vagueness, as well as resulting in practice in a selection and isolation of those specific laws which were seen as useful for the practical work of legal scribes. Scribes would therefore have been working with a reduced body of legal material, both because their collections only included laws which could be directly used for the production of documents, and because the text of these laws was limited to essential quotes or sound-bites. Scribes do not seem to have been experts in the whole body of written law, but they probably knew as much as they needed to know: perhaps we should envisage a situation in which there was indeed a shared common knowledge of the law, but one that was limited and channelled by the particular needs of different users. Written laws appear in a distorted state in the formulae because they feature there from the perspective of demand, not imposition.[34]

One outcome of this is that the relationship between formulae and written laws was not simply a question of straightforward application:

32 Wormald, *Making of English Law*, p. 79: '. . . it seems that it was the general body of "Salic" custom, not the actual text of the law, that judges and scribes had in mind', and p. 83 on formulae as the main point of contact between documentary practice and written laws. See also Wormald, '*Lex Scripta*', p. 122.

33 Of the manuscripts associated with the *Formulae Imperiales*, Vatican reg. lat. 612, Paris BnF lat. 11379, Vienna 424, St-Paul im Lavanttal 6/1, Leiden Voss. O. 92 and Munich Clm. 19410 only contain no. 33, which seems to have been the only success story from this collection in terms of diffusion.

34 The same goes for canonical legislation: for instance, although divorce was universally condemned by Church authorities in this period, Church and monastic scribes still kept models for divorce documents to accommodate the laity under their lordship. Formulae of divorce survive in ten manuscripts and in five different versions: Marculf II, 30, *Formulae Andecavenses* no. 57, *Formulae Turonenses* no. 19, *Cartae Senonicae* no. 47, *Formulae Salicae Merkelianae* no. 18.

formulae sometimes only referred to written law in order to go against it, if it was not conducive to a satisfactory agreement. A famous example of this is Marculf II, 12, in which a father makes a testament dividing his property equally between his daughter and his sons, thereby contradicting one of the most famous clauses of Salic law, according to which women were not allowed to inherit land:[35]

> To my sweetest daughter X, Y. An ancient but impious custom is held among us, that a sister may not have a portion of her father's land with her brothers. But I, weighing carefully this impiety, say: just as you were all equally given to me by God as children, you should also be loved by me equally, and you should enjoy my property equally after my death.

Marculf II, 10, in which a man makes the children of his dead daughter his heirs jointly with his sons, goes against the same law. It is not particularly surprising to find this sort of solution in practice, since women's ability to inherit land is well documented in other sources: the clause being flouted here is generally thought to have become obsolete very early on, and certainly by the late sixth century.[36] The clause nevertheless remained included in the body of Salic law, even in its later recensions; perhaps it was retained precisely because it could so easily be ignored in practice.

Another explicit, and perhaps rather more surprising, discarding of written laws can be seen again in Marculf II, 29, which records an agreement made after the abduction of a free woman by an unfree man and their subsequent marriage, guaranteeing the woman's own continuing free status as well as that of her future children: although the abductor could have been killed according to the law, the parties involved clearly decided against it, and although the couple's future children could have been classified as unfree, the husband's lord relinquished his claim through this document. This goes against everything we could expect on the basis of legislation from the period regarding this issue, both in Salic law and in later capitularies.[37] It is unclear why such a solution would have been reached in each particular case, and the presence of these formulae does not necessarily mean that it was a common occurrence, but its relative

---

35 *Pactus Legis Salicae*, ed. K. A. Eckhardt, *MGH Legum* I.4.1 (Hanover, 1962), 59. 6, p. 223. Compare *Cartae Senonicae* 42 and 45; *Formulae Salicae Merkelianae* 23 is largely based on this formula.

36 On the possible origins of this clause as relating only to military colonies in the first place, see T. Anderson, 'Roman military colonies in Gaul, Salian ethnogenesis and the forgotten meaning of *Pactus Legis Salicae* 59. 5', *EME* 4 (1995), pp. 129–44.

37 *Pactus Legis Salicae* 13. 8–9, p. 62, and 25. 3–4, p. 94; *Capitularia regum Francorum* 1, no. 142, c. 3, p. 292 (*a.* 819).

success in the manuscript tradition shows it was still worth being prepared for: models of this kind can be found in eleven manuscripts, in eight distinct versions.[38]

Both in the case of women's ability to inherit property and in that of unfreedom, therefore, formulae bring forward an important modifying perspective. Unfreedom is a particularly striking example of this. The law codes all present the unfree as utterly powerless, and the idea of a survival of a 'classical' style of slavery down to the year 1000 is based entirely on this evidence.[39] Formulae, however, show numerous examples of unfree men marrying free women with impunity; they offer glimpses of unfree persons owning land and people,[40] and even one case in which a servant seems to have brought his masters to justice, and was let free when they proved unable to find their deed of ownership for him.[41] Formulae thus give a fundamentally different approach to that of laws, and show a level of negotiating ability even for people who, on the face of it, would be considered at an obvious disadvantage in dealing with a more dominant group or class. The need to conform to a generally accepted notion of what was right may be reflected in the practice of oath-helping, frequently documented in the formulae. Oath-helpers could have been largely instrumental in achieving such a consensus at a local level. Several cases in which oath-helpers were involved led to outcomes which would be very unexpected if the settlement of these disputes had depended exclusively on the coercive ability of the more powerful party. In one such example, *Formulae Andecavenses* no. 10a–b, which dealt with a lord claiming rights over a man, the dispute was resolved, for once, in favour of the accused. We are not likely to find such cases in surviving records of actual disputes: these records survive essentially through ecclesiastical archives, and ecclesiastical

---

38 Marculf II, 29; *Formulae Andecavenses* no. 59; *Cartae Senonicae* no. 6; *Collectio Flaviniacensis* no. 102 (= Marculf II, 29); *Formulae Salicae Merkelianae* no. 31; *Formulae Salicae Bignonianae* no. 11; *Formulae Salicae Lindenbrogianae* no. 20; *Formulae Morbacenses* nos. 18 and 19; *Formulae Augienses Coll.* B no. 41. On the question of marriages between unfree men and free women, see A. Rio, 'Freedom and unfreedom in early medieval Francia: the evidence of the legal formularies', in *PP* 193 (2006), pp. 7–40, at pp. 16–23.

39 P. Bonnassie, 'Survie et extinction du régime esclavagiste dans l'Occident du haut moyen âge (IVe–XIe s.)', in *Cahiers de civilisation médiévale* 28 (1985), pp. 307–43; more recently, see D. Liebs, 'Sklaverei aus Not im germanisch-römischen Recht', in *ZRG, Romanistische Abteilung* 118 (2001), pp. 286–311. See A. Rio, 'Freedom and unfreedom'.

40 *Formulae Salicae Lindenbrogianae* no. 9; Marculf II, 36; *Addenda ad Formulae Senonenses recentiores* nos. 18 and 19.

41 *Formulae Andecavenses* no. 17.

institutions would not have had much interest in preserving records of disputes that had not been resolved to their own advantage. Surviving charters and records of disputes, although they do provide a greater sense of 'reality' than the law codes, have their own distortions due to the conditions of their survival, and are thus unlikely to preserve evidence of successful legal action by the less powerful. By contrast, formulae were preserved according to a different standard of usefulness: they were intended to meet day-to-day, practical needs, and were not selected according to their advantage to a particular party.

Legislating kings put forward a version of legal principles best suited to ensuring the support of the people who mattered on the scale of a kingdom: it is thus hardly surprising that the codes should be so concerned with the imposition of the will and authority of a powerful (and male) ruling elite. This initial statement, however, seems to have been commonly modified according to the local understanding of what was acceptable practice. In this context, perhaps it is not so strange that Salic law was not updated very consistently: an initial conservative statement may have been all that it needed to remain to fulfill its purpose. Where there was a disparity between theory and practice, it was not resolved by changing the law, but in the process of reaching solutions in each particular case, and recording them in documents. That is not to say that written law was merely symbolic, or that it only recorded the efforts of kings at stamping their authority on a resisting population. Formulae and laws do not represent two sides of a struggle between central power and local circumstances. Local agreements did not 'prevail' upon the law: rather, they modified it in order to achieve an appropriate resolution. In this respect, perhaps one should not overstate the contrast in practice between the Carolingian system of public courts and the 'feudal' system generally described as an anarchic attempt at reaching a consensus: the Merovingians and Carolingians were interested in consensus too.[42]

Conclusion

Laws and charters have traditionally been seen in terms of a strict opposition between theory and practice. Formulae, because they took into account

---

42 See Nelson, 'Dispute settlement', pp. 61–3; see also K. Heidecker, 'Communication by written texts in court cases: some charter evidence (*ca.*800–*ca.*1100)', in M. Mostert (ed.), *New Approaches to Medieval Communication* (Turnhout, 1999), pp. 101–26, at p. 118.

the negotiations and concerns of parties involved in specific cases before projecting them into a more normative shape, go a long way toward giving us the missing link between them. Theory and practice make more sense as two ends of a continuum, rather than as two radically opposed spheres. The settlement of disputes was not merely the result of a straightforward assessment of power relationships in any particular instance, but was also profoundly linked to an idea of what was right, and of a right way of doing things; at the other end of the scale, the need to establish consensus in very practical situations was at the origin of much royal and imperial legislation, especially when that legislation was promulgated in the context of assemblies.[43] Written laws constituted a powerful statement of interest, embodying the ability of a king to provide his demanding followers with what they wanted, and to protect their interests. Formulae reflect other interests, and a different demand: where assemblies show us the attempts of kings at establishing consensus among their nobles, formulae, at the other end of the political scale, document these lords' own need to establish consensus when wielding their local power.

Formulae thus show us real users coaxing written law into a shape in which it could be managed and put to good use. Formularies themselves will never tell us the particular local pressures and power relationships which contributed to this process. All that they show is that the scribe who copied them expected to encounter similar situations and similar resolutions in the course of his professional life; but expectation is not such a bad guide. If surviving documents are only the tip of an iceberg, perhaps formulae can at least give us a better idea of its extent and shape. Far from being the dry and lifeless documents one could expect, they give invaluable and diverse insights into the lives of the anonymous Frankish men and women whose stories are recorded in these texts, whether with respect to their rights, their disputes, their status, their gifts, their crimes, their journeys, their marriages, their divorces, or the disposal of their property after their death. They do this with a scope wholly unlike that of any other source for this period: they should be treasured for their eccentricities, not dismissed on account of them.

43 For Charles the Bald in particular, see J. L. Nelson, 'Legislation and consensus in the reign of Charles the Bald', in P. Wormald (ed.), *Ideal and Reality: Studies in Frankish and Anglo-Saxon Society presented to J. M. Wallace-Hadrill* (Oxford, 1983), 202–27. See also T. Reuter, 'Assembly politics in western Europe from the eighth century to the twelfth', in T. Reuter, *Medieval Polities and Modern Mentalities* (ed. J. L. Nelson) (Cambridge, 2006), pp. 193–216.

2

Compulsory purchase in the earlier Middle Ages[1]

Susan Reynolds

T HE PROCEDURE THAT the British call compulsory purchase,
though it is really compulsory sale, and that Americans call
'eminent domain' – also a slightly misleading name, is in the civil-
law tradition simply 'expropriation', or an equivalent word (*espropriazione,*
Enteignung, etc.). Whatever the words modern legal systems use to denote
it, most if not all allow for the taking of land from individuals for what is
seen as the common good, and for the giving of compensation in exchange.
So far as legal historians have been interested in the procedure, they have
generally concentrated on its modern history, since the building of railways,
roads and airports, and the demolition of slums or planning of towns have
made it both common and controversial. Those who have looked for the
origins of the modern law have generally seen them in the recovery of
Roman law and the rise of communal activity in the twelfth century.[2] Their
arguments seem to be predicated on the supposed absence of any sense of
the common good or public spirit, or indeed of any effective law, in the
earlier Middle Ages. No one who has read Janet Nelson on Carolingian
government or on early medieval political ideas in general can accept
this premise as axiomatic. In her words, 'the language of public utility,
the common interest, and so forth . . . expressed not only an ideal but the
reality of political effort' in which, for instance, laymen in Charles the

1 I am grateful to Professor David Ganz for references to discussions of *res publica* and
Professor David Dumville for reading and commenting on a draft of this paper.
2 E.g. Georg Meyer, *Das Recht der Expropriation* (Leipzig, 1868), pp. 70–6; Ugo Nicolini,
*La Proprietà, il principe e l'espropriazione per pubblica utilità: studi sulla dottrina giuridica
intermedia* (Milan, 1952), pp. 93–7, and *Le Limitazioni alla proprietà negli statuti italiani*
(Mantua, 1937), pp. 20–1; R. Waelkens, 'L'Expropriation dans le ius commune
médiéval', *Recueils de la Société Jean Bodin* 66 (1999), pp. 122–31, and other authors
in this volume and *ibid.,* 67 (2000).

Bald's following were personally involved.[3] What she has written about collective judgement and the working of custom at local level suggests that humbler people also took for granted the existence of some kind of common good and the need to find a consensus about it, however often individuals, whether powerful or humble, were seduced by their own selfishness into ignoring it.[4] I am prepared to argue, though with much less evidence than so careful and penetrating a reader of such a wide range of sources would like, that an immanent sense of the common good may have allowed both rulers and local communities to take land from individuals for the sake of that common good even before the Carolingians and outside the kingdoms of the Franks and Anglo-Saxons.

What I am dignifying by the name of evidence of this in the early Middle Ages is at best no more than suggestive. The case still seems worth arguing for two reasons. The first is that the evidence for expropriation for the common good in a variety of traditional societies outside Europe suggests that it might also have been found acceptable and useful in Europe between the fall of the Roman empire and the emergence of learned and professional law after 1100.[5] As far as I can see – and this can at present be no more than a guess – any settled society in which individuals or groups have acknowledged rights in particular pieces of land may find occasions, like the digging of drainage or irrigation channels, the building of roads or fortifications, or the provision of places of assembly or religious ceremonies, in which such individual rights come into conflict with the needs of the community as a whole. Different societies may have different ways of

3   J. L. Nelson, *Politics and Ritual in Early Medieval Europe* (London, 1986), p. 202; cf. *ibid.* pp. 100–11, especially p. 108 nn. 80, 147, 170; *eadem, The Frankish World* (London, 1996), pp. 127, 167, 174–7; *idem,* 'Kingship and Empire', in *Cambridge History of Medieval Political Thought,* ed. J. H. Burns (Cambridge, 1988), pp. 211–51, especially pp. 217–20, 225–7; *idem, Rulers and Ruling Families* (Aldershot, 1999), pp. 129–58; *idem,* 'Kingship and royal government', in R. McKitterick (ed.), *NCMH II* (Cambridge, 1995), pp. 383–430.

4   *The Frankish World,* pp. 51–70.

5   E.g. (though I need many more examples) D. D. Kosambi, 'Origins of feudalism in Kashmir', in *Feudal Social Formation in Early India,* ed. D. N. Jha (Delhi, 1987), pp. 130–44, at p. 141; François, baron de Tott, *Mémoires du baron de Tott sur les Turcs et les Tartares,* 2 vols. (Amsterdam, 1785), 1, 149–53; P. and L. Bohannan, *Tiv Economy* (Evanston, 1968), pp. 82–8; V. Shaddick, *Land Tenure in Basutoland* (London: HMSO, 1954), p. 129; I. Schapera, *Native Land Tenure in Bechuanaland* (Lovedale, 1943), pp. 42, 181–2; M. Gluckman, *The Ideas in Barotse Jurisprudence,* 2nd edn (Manchester, 1972), pp. 80, 141–5: the dialogue in the case Gluckman refers to here does not actually mention compensation: *idem, The Judicial Process among the Barotse of Northern Rhodesia* (Manchester, 1955), pp. 142–5; A. M. Chinhengo, 'Expropriation in Zimbabwe, 1890–1995', *Recueils de la Société Jean Bodin* 67 (2000), pp. 351–95, at 356–8.

reconciling individual and common needs, according to their different economies and legal systems, and some societies may have several different ways of doing so according to the nature of the conflicts. Obvious examples of ways in which land in which individuals had recognized rights has often been subjected to public needs are the taking of taxes, dues and services from the individual holders of the rights. Their land might also be subjected to various kinds of common rights or wayleaves, to control of watercourses, and to the taking of materials from it for building roads, fortifications or other purposes considered to serve the public interest.[6] I am not going to discuss any of these partial subordinations of individual property to public use or service, though some of them were certainly found in early medieval Europe. All I am concerned with is the taking of pieces of land, extinguishing all title, rights or claim the owner or occupier might have, and doing so not as a punishment or to pay the owner's debts but because this piece of land was apparently needed (or said to be needed) for public use or the common good. From now on I shall for brevity refer simply to expropriation when I mean the taking of land for public use or the public good.

The second reason, despite the lack of evidence, for suggesting that early medieval societies made use of expropriation is that, while evidence on most aspects of early medieval society is scarce, there is good reason why it should be even more scarce on this subject. As in other societies where expropriation in the public interest was probably allowed but references to it seem to be rare, pressure from public opinion and the acceptance of social norms may have ensured that only the most awkward or powerful characters objected to surrendering bits of their property to common needs. The difference between a voluntary and compulsory sale may thus be invisible in such records as survive. One example of this uncertainty is a story in the second book of Samuel. When a plague was ravaging Israel the prophet Gad told King David to build an altar on the threshing-floor of Araunah the Jebusite. When David told Araunah he wanted to buy his threshing-floor for an altar, Araunah offered it as a gift, but David insisted on paying for it as he should not give God something that cost himself nothing. The plague stopped.[7] While this is not evidence of a rule of compulsory expropriation it suggests some of the norms that lie behind such a rule: the obligation to give up something for the common good along

6   The boundary between taking materials and taking the land itself could be hard to draw: e.g. 'Querimoniae Normannorum', in *Recueil des historiens des Gaules et de la France*, 24 (Paris, 1904), pp. 1–73, no. 73; London, National Archives, SC 8/326, no. E 731 (transcript given to me by Dr Paul Brand).
7   II Samuel 24:15–25.

with the possibility of being compensated for it. In another biblical story, King Ahab's seizure of Naboth's vineyard does not qualify: though governments through history have often succeeded in passing off their interest as that of the common or public good, Ahab failed to do so. That was perhaps partly because when Naboth refused to sell, Queen Jezebel had him falsely accused and executed, but also because Ahab's wish to turn the vineyard into a herb garden was apparently taken as pure selfishness.[8]

In ancient Greece the evidence of possible expropriation includes legislation for the valuation of non-citizens' property that might be wanted to build temples; the help, with provision for agreeing valuations, that was given by the new regime after a revolution in Athens to those who chose to emigrate to Eleusis, so that they could get consent of the owners of the houses they wanted; and perhaps the laying of drains in private fields in Euboea, with payment to the landowner.[9] In Rome, expropriation was surely accepted by the time that public works began to be recorded in the second century BCE. Apart from the obvious likelihood that Roman roads, fortifications and public buildings would have needed some kind of expropriation, there are later references to actual cases when it took place, and to the need for compensation.[10] According to Justinian, land could be taken even from churches *ad reipublicae utilitatem* provided that equal or greater property was given in exchange.[11] But though emperors might authorize particular expropriations or deal with problems referred to them about compensation, it is not clear that only they could authorize the taking of property anywhere in the empire: local officials or the communities over which they presided seem, I deduce, to have had the right to do it for themselves, simply referring difficult cases to the emperor.

Against this background, I consider the possibility that land was sometimes taken in early medieval Europe, whether by kings or local lords, for what

---

8   I Kings 21. See also the predictions of seizures by kings in I Samuel 8:6, 11, 14.

9   E. Karabélias, 'L'Expropriation en droit grec ancien', *Recueils de la Société Jean Bodin* 66 (1999), 21–54.

10   N. Matthews, 'The valuation of property in the Roman law', *Harvard Law Review* 34 (1921), pp. 229–59; J. Walter Jones, 'Expropriation in Roman law', *Law Quarterly Review* 45 ('1929), 512–27; P. B. H. Birks, 'The Roman law concept of dominium and the idea of absolute ownership', *Acta Juridica 1985*, pp. 1–37; E. L. Corbi, '¿Existió en la época republicana romana el derecho a la expropiación forzoza por causa de utilidad pública?', *Recueils de la Société Jean Bodin* 66 (1999), pp. 115–22; M. Pennitz, 'Die Enteignungsproblematik in Römischen Recht von der Zeit der Republik bis zu Justinian', *ibid.*, pp. 55–114.

11   *Corpus Iuris Civilis*, ed. T. Mommsen and others (Berlin, 1954), 3, p. 53 (*Novellae* 7.2.1).

they claimed was the common good. It seems highly likely that some took it, especially from those too humble to complain, for more or less selfish reasons such as building castles or palaces for themselves or, as the population grew, clearing settlements away from areas in which they wanted to hunt. To assume, however, that any expropriation made by a king or lord before the twelfth or thirteenth century was made for his own purposes and that this was accepted as legal, is clearly unjustified. The assumption, apparently unsupported so far by any evidence from before 1200, is apparently derived from the premise that early medieval government and law lacked any collective element.[12] Nelson and others have provided good evidence to show that that is false.[13] All rulers, whether kings or lesser lords, were supposed to act on behalf of the communities they ruled and consult their subjects, or representatives of them, about what they did.[14] Power tends to corrupt, but even the powerful are at least slightly influenced by the norms of their society and the obligations they have been brought up to think they owe to their subjects. We know that some rulers consulted their subjects and seem to have been concerned about what they saw as their subjects' welfare. Besides, though building palaces or castles may look selfish to modern eyes, later evidence shows that palaces were assumed to serve a public purpose, while castles and other fortifications passed the test even more obviously. In a period of sparse records, like the early Middle Ages, it may therefore be rash to assume that an expropriation apparently done by a king or lord was not thought at the time to be done on behalf of the community he ruled and after consultation with men who spoke on its behalf.

The early medieval law codes do not seem to say anything about expropriation, but one reason for that may be that there was relatively little need for direct, total expropriation, as opposed, for instance, to the collective regulation of arable land and pasture, which is attested. But it may also be that the general principle of giving up land for collective needs in return for compensation was taken for granted, so that the land needed was given up to the local community without fuss or record. Another reason is implied by the character of such legislation as I have found before the nineteenth

---

12 J-L. Mestre, 'Les Origines seigneuriales de l'expropriation', *Recueil des mémoires et travaux publié par la Société d'histoire du droit et des institutions des anciens pays de droit écrit*, 11 (1980), pp. 71–9; J-L. Harouel, 'L'Expropriation dans l'histoire du droit français', *Recueils de la Société Jean Bodin* 67 (2000), 39–77, and *L'Expropriation* (Paris, 2000).

13 Above, nn. 3, 4; below, n. 23.

14 S. Reynolds, *Kingdoms and communities in western Europe, 900–1300*, 2nd edn, (Oxford, 1997), and works cited p. xii, n. 2.

century which directly and explicitly allowed expropriation. Whether in Italian city statutes, English acts of parliament or French royal ordinances, it was chiefly concerned with procedures to follow in particular kinds of case and with ways of assessing the compensation that, it seems, was generally assumed to be due. Even the American constitution, famously made by men who took property rights very seriously, had nothing to say about it, and when the Bill of Rights was added to the constitution a few years later, it dealt only with compensation, apparently assuming the liability of land to expropriation. The absence of references to expropriation for the public good (as opposed to confiscation for crime) in early medieval law codes is therefore not evidence that it was not allowed.

The most striking example in the early Middle Ages of what looks like a modified form of expropriation is what has traditionally been seen as the plundering, spoliation or secularization of Church land by Charles Martel and his descendants, the Carolingian kings and emperors.[15] Although they, like other rulers and lords, sometimes bullied the clergy, ejected bishops and gave their sees to others, and may have taken land from churches for their own selfish purposes, their most famous 'spoliations' seem to have been made for what they claimed were the needs of defence. That Charles Martel had used Church property to support his soldiers is suggested by what his son Karloman told a Church council less than two years after Charles died. According to Boniface, Karloman had at first promised to summon a council for his part of the kingdom in order to reform the Church which, according to Boniface, had long been crushed and despoiled. In the event Karloman told the council that, because of the threat of war from neighbouring peoples, he had decided, with the advice of the clergy and Christian people, to keep for a while the Church property he already had to support his army, on condition that 12d. would be paid every year from each *casata* to the church to which the land belonged. If the holder of the land died the land would go back to the Church, unless the prince (Karloman) was compelled by necessity, in which case he would make a new grant. Churches in real poverty would be exempt.[16] Much the same system of grants of Church land by royal command, though with smaller rents to the churches, was extended by Charlemagne to the kingdom

---

15 P. Fouracre, *The Age of Charles Martel* (Harlow, 2000), pp. 2–3, 121–45, 159–72, discusses both the evidence and the origin of the traditional interpretation.

16 Boniface, *Epistulae*, ed. M. Tangl, *Die Briefe des heiligen Bonifatius und Lullus, MGH Epistolae Selecta.* 1 (Berlin, 1916), no. 50, p. 82 (= Boniface, *Letters*, trans. E. Emerton (New York, 1940), p. 57); *MGH Concilia* II i, ed. A. Werminghoff (Hanover and Leipzig, 1906), no. 2, c. 2: discussed by Fouracre, *Age of Charles Martel*, pp. 139–40.

of Lombardy as well, apparently, as to his other conquests.[17] Not all of the property that found its way into the hands of the followers of kings or mayors of the palace got there because of military needs. Grants made to conciliate rivals or keep powerful subjects happy could nevertheless have been seen at the time as justified by the need to maintain peace within the kingdom: the boundary between the interests of a government and the welfare of its subjects is seldom easy to draw. But if some grants of Church land to laymen look as if they would not have been justifiable by the needs of the kingdom, others were justified, more or less explicitly, at the time and in that way.

According to the formal declarations of kings and councils, none of this ought to count as full expropriation (or secularization), since churches were supposed to retain their ultimate title. This may explain why compensation was made – or supposed to be made – by annual rents rather than lump sums. In practice, though kings periodically made promises to restore what had been taken and some holdings were indeed given back, restoration became politically and legally more difficult when land was left for generations in the hands of one family or passed to people who knew nothing – or could claim to know nothing – of the Church's title.[18] That happened partly because what started as an emergency turned out to last a long time, as tends to happen with powers that governments take in emergencies. It also happened partly because some churches failed, for whatever reason, to collect rents and keep their records up to date, but the most powerful reason of all was perhaps the sheer inertia of customary law in the face of landholders in possession. As a result, much of the land that had been taken from churches to support eighth-century armies was still being held in much the same way in the eleventh century.[19]

Many bishops, abbots and chroniclers no doubt resented what was taken from their own churches, and in the ninth century Archbishop Hincmar generalized their grievances into what became the standard view of the spoliation of the Church.[20] In the eighth century, however, ecclesiastical

---

17 *MGH Capitularia* I, ed. A. Boretius (Hanover, 1883), no. 20 (c. 9).
18 *Capitularia* I, no. 138 (c. 29); W. Goffart, *The Le Mans Forgeries* (Cambridge MA, 1966), pp. 6–20; on restorations, e.g. *MGH Diplomata Karolinorum* III, ed. T. Scheiffer (Berlin, 1966), Lothar I, no. 40; *Diplomi di Berengario I*, ed. L. Schiaparelli (Fonti per la storia d'Italia 35, 1903), nos. 47, 90, 100, 101 *Codice Diplomatico del monasterio di S. Columbano di Bobbio*, 1, ed. C. Cipolla (FSI, 52, 1918), no. 66; É. Lesne, *Histoire de la propriété ecclésiastique en France* (Paris, 1910–43), vol. 2 (1).
19 S. Reynolds, *Fiefs and Vassals: the Medieval Evidence Reinterpreted* (Oxford, 1994), pp. 89–100, 172–6.
20 Fouracre, *Age of Charles Martel*, pp. 123–5.

assemblies seem to have accepted the policy in principle, however reluctantly and as a temporary expedient, because of the needs of the *res publica*.[21] By *res publica* they may have meant only the king's own land and resources, but the words could have wider and more abstract connotations, including Nelson's 'common weal'.[22] Particular words are in any case less important than the ideas behind them: *res publica* was sometimes used as a synonym for *regnum*, which had long had connotations of collectivity and mutual obligations between king and subjects. The more frequent occurrence of words like *res publica* and *communis utilitas* in the writings of learned Carolingian clergy may therefore not mean that the ideas they represent were being revived after a long post-Roman eclipse. Whatever words were used, a king was supposed to use their resources for the defence of his kingdom, which emphatically included the defence of the clergy and their churches. The Merovingian kingdom, however often divided, had remained a single political community partly at least because its great men wanted it to remain, and seems to have been managed by much the same hierarchical but collective institutions and responsibilities as was its Carolingian successor.[23]

Similar assumptions about collective interests and responsibilities, however often overridden by private interests in practice, seem to be discernible in other kingdoms. English kings who took Church lands for themselves or their servants in the ninth and tenth centuries could equally well have justified doing so by needs of defence.[24] Some of what they took they acquired by exchange, which obviated the need to promise that the

---

21 *Concilia* II i, no. 56 (c. 59), of 836: *Monasteria divinis solummodo cultibus dicata non debent et secularibus dari et canonica prodit auctoritas et ipsorum destructio locorum. Sed quia id exigit rei publicae necessitas, saltem conlapsa loca erigi debent et clerici locis, in quibus fuerant, restitui quousque oportunitas id permittit emendari plenius.* W. Wehlen, *Geschichtsschreibung und Staatsauffassung in Zeitalter Ludwigs des Frommen* (Lübeck, 1970), p. 40, interprets this as meaning that monasteries were to be rebuilt *quia id exigit rei publicae necessitas*, but the needs of the *res publica* seem to justify the giving of them to laymen in *Capitularia.* II, no. 227 (c. 5) of 844, and the taking of some land in *Codice Diplomatico del monasterio di S. Colombano di Bobbio*, ed. C. Cipolla (Fonti per la storia d'Italia 52, 1918), no. 66 (877).

22 Nelson, 'Kingship and empire', p. 227. On the range of uses: Wehlen, *Geschichtsschreibung*; H. W. Goetz, 'Regnum: Zum politischen Denken der Karolingerzeit', *ZRG, Germanistische Abteilung* 104 (1987), pp. 110–89.

23 A. C. Murray, 'From Roman to Frankish Gaul: "Centenarii" and "Centenae" in the administration of the Merovingian kingdom', *Traditio* 44 (1988), pp. 59–100; P. Fouracre, 'Carolingian justice: the rhetoric of improvement and contexts of abuse', *Settimane* 42 (1995), pp. 771–803.

24 D. N. Dumville, *Wessex and England from Alfred to Edgar* (Woodbridge, 1992), pp. 29–54.

lands would be returned to the Church. Although churches were not supposed to alienate the property of God and the saints, exchange did not
count as alienation.[25] Some of the many exchanges of land between rulers
and churches may therefore have been made in order to compensate
churches for lands which rulers had taken for what they may have main-
tained was the common good. One example of this could be the grant that
William the Conqueror made to Saint-Benoît-sur-Loire in 1067 in exchange
for what he had apparently taken from them to build a fortification for the
defence of his land (*ob mee terre defensionem*): his land here probably means
the territory he ruled and its inhabitants, rather than his own immediate
property.[26]

If the needs of defence and the public good could justify the taking or
borrowing of Church land, it presumably also justified, and more easily,
the taking of land from laymen. Some new fortifications around existing
settlements followed the line of older defences but others may not have
done, in which case bits of land may have been taken from individuals,
some of whom may have held it as their own by hereditary right. Where
defences already existed, medieval townspeople were given to building on
or next to them and may have established some kind of rights by prescription. All this is unclear, as my use of 'may have' admits. In one case that
must have involved taking land there is slightly more information about
the organization of the work, though not about the acquisition of the land.
A wall was built at Rome around St Peter's and the settlement beside it on
the right side of the Tiber in 848–52. A similar project about fifty years
earlier had been abandoned and the new wall may have run along the same
line, but the growth of the settlement around St Peter's probably meant
that, whether in 800 or 848, part at least of the line may have lain through
private property. The new wall was named the Leonine Wall after pope Leo
IV, who summoned a great assembly of people from inside and outside
Rome to organize the work, but the original initiative had come from King
Lothar. In 846 he ordered money to be collected for the wall from the
whole kingdom, presumably in the first instance from benefice-holders,
since he told the bishops of the kingdom to encourage those with alods or
money to make contributions as those with benefices apparently had to do.
He and his brothers, Charles the Bald and Louis the German, also made
substantial contributions (*non modicas argenti libras*). Surviving inscriptions

25   Lesne, *Histoire de la propriété ecclésiastique*, vol. 1, pp. 290–7.
26   E.g. *Regesta Regum Anglo-Normannorum: The Acta of William I*, ed. D. Bates (Oxford,
     1998), no. 251: Professor Bates gave me this reference.

on the wall imply that different local communities built different sections.[27]

Some of the fortifications ordered by Charles the Bald in 864 *ad defensionem patriae* may have been repairs of old defences but others, or bits of them, may have been built on bits of land that individuals had to give up.[28] The same goes for the defensive works organized by Mercian kings from the eighth century, by kings of Wessex from the ninth, and by Henry the Fowler in Saxony in the tenth. Quite complex systems were prescribed for the *agrarii milites* of Saxony and the owners of specified amounts of land to share the work of building, provisioning and guarding the forts.[29] Where archaeologists find evidence of houses or other buildings underneath the walls or banks of any of these fortifications but apparently dating from not long before them, that suggests that land may have had to be acquired from previous owners or occupiers in order to build at least part of the defences.[30] Nothing, however, seems to be recorded in France, Saxony or England about the way it was acquired, whether for defensive works around existing settlements or for whole forts. Perhaps compensation was not thought to be due. However often individuals evaded their obligations or deserted from armies, the obligation of free men to defend both their local communities and the kingdom, or to provide provisions for those who did, seems to have been more or less taken for granted. Henry the Fowler's instruction to his *agrarii milites* to hold their assemblies and feasts in the forts for which they would be responsible suggests that they already constituted communities of some kind, which may mean that they already shared some responsibilities for policing and local defence. If so, giving up what were probably small bits of land to the forts that were to guard their own neighbourhoods may not have seemed much more onerous or unjust than giving up time and service to the construction and defence of the forts.

27 *Capitularia* II, no. 203; *Liber Pontificalis*, 3 vols., ed. L. Duchesne (Paris, 1886–92), vol. 2. pp. 123–4, 137–8; S. Gibson and B. Ward-Perkins, 'The surviving remains of the Leonine Wall', *Papers of the British School at Rome* 47 (1979), pp. 30–57, 51 (1983), pp. 222–39. My attention was drawn to this episode by Nelson, *Rulers*, p. 148.
28 *Capitularia* II, no. 273.
29 D. Hill and A. Rumble (eds), *The Defence of Wessex: the Burghal Hidage and Anglo-Saxon Fortifications* (Manchester, 1996); Dumville, *Wessex and England*, pp. 24–7, 29–54; N. Brooks, 'The development of military obligations in eighth and ninth century England', in P. Clemoes and K. Hughes (eds), *England before the Conquest* (Cambridge, 1971), pp. 69–84; Widukind, *Rerum Gestarum Saxonicarum Libri Tres*, ed. P. Hirsch, *MGH SRG* (Hanover,1935), pp. 48–9 (I. 35).
30 E.g. at Hereford: P. Rahtz, 'The archaeology of West Mercian towns', in A. Dornier (ed.), *Mercian Studies* (Leicester, 1977), pp. 107–29, at 111, 126.

Privileged churches which had been excused at least some responsibilities may have been more likely to demand, and perhaps receive, compensation for land taken for fortifications. In 915, when a house of the bishop of Pavia had been demolished for a new city wall, king Berengar gave him permission to build one on top of the wall and to have the lines of the wall and a road diverted for his convenience. Other Italian bishops received royal licence to build or repair town defences. In some cases the walls were said to have been hitherto part of the king's *res publica* which now passed to the bishop, so that perhaps no issue arose about compensation.[31] Later in the Middle Ages, when there is more evidence, most of the complaints about the taking of land that I have found came from churches, but their petitions for compensation imply both that the taking of land for public purposes was accepted and that compensation was thought to be due. A few cases show lay landowners also getting compensation.[32] Perhaps some in the earlier Middle Ages had thought it was due, asked for it and even got it, but perhaps collective responsibilities, far from originating with the so-called communal movement of the twelfth century, had been strong enough before then to deter lay landowners from claiming it.

One case in which we can guess why compensation was not made was that recorded in an agreement made in 1058 to build a wall round the north Italian village or town of Nonantola. This was made between the abbot and the men of the town. Since my previous examples, such as they are, look like the result of royal orders, this is my first medieval case of a probable non-royal expropriation: William the Conqueror's exchange with Saint-Benoît-sur-Loire hardly counts as another since his authority in Normandy, even before he had become a king, had been virtually regal.[33] At Nonantola the abbot undertook to build a quarter of the new wall while the inhabitants built the rest. He also gave them as a group all the land around the settlement within stated boundaries for their common good (*ad communem utilitatem suprascripti populi*) and promised not to grant any of it to anyone except for the common profit of the people of Nonantola.[34] Here compensation for any land that was taken from individuals may have seemed inappropriate: everyone was supposed to contribute to the work

---

31 *Diplomi di Guido e di Lamberto*, ed. L. Schiaparelli (Fonti per la storia d'Italia 36, 1906), Guido no. 11; *Diplomi di Berengario I* (FSI 35, 1903), nos. 47, 90, 100, and also 137 (a marquis's fortifications on his own land); *Diplomi di Ugo e di Lotario* (FSI 38, 1924), Ugo no. 11.

32 I hope to deal with the history of compulsory purpose in general elsewhere.

33 Above, n. 26.

34 L. A. Muratori, *Antiquitates Italicae Medii Aevi*, 6 vols. (Milan, 1738–40), vol. 3, cols. 241–3.

and profit from it. The same may apply to other expropriations which I suspect, though without any evidence as yet, could have been made by local communities acting on their own initiative without formal approval from king or lord.

Land was sometimes said to have been taken unjustly, and not only from churches, which casts doubt on the belief that lords before the twelfth century could expropriate at will.[35] I suggest that unjust expropriations were those that were thought to have been made as a result of unjust judgements and not for the common good. The abbot of Nonantola in his 1058 charter gave the men of the town various legal privileges and promised, among other things, not to seize their goods or demolish their houses except as law commanded, saving his jurisdiction (*secundum quod lex precipit salva donnicata justitia*). This suggests that the townspeople thought that he or his predecessors had sometimes demolished houses or taken goods without due judgement. The implication is that the men of Nonantola had an idea about the rights and wrongs of a lord's taking of property from his subjects and that the abbot, whether or not he would have agreed about it in the past, was now prepared to accept it – at least for the time being. Complaints made in tenth- and eleventh-century England about forced sales to churches, or the seizure of land by kings to give to churches, also imply norms that were allegedly being broken.[36] Suggestions of supposedly unlawful expropriations in the past are made in a charter granted by the emperor Henry IV to Lucca in 1081 and, slightly less clearly, in another in the same year to Pisa.[37] A Norman who complained at William the Conqueror's funeral at Caen that William had unjustly seized land on which the church where the funeral was held had been built may not have had a good case. He was nevertheless bought off, presumably to avoid trouble at such an unsuitable time.[38] William had, of course, famously expropriated many important Englishmen, but that was on the ground, however specious, that they were rebels and traitors. As for English townspeople whose houses were demolished to make way for castles after the Conquest, their losses would have been harder to justify, but townspeople who were not

35 Above, n. 12.
36 *Liber Eliensis*, ed. E. O. Blake (Royal Historical Society, Camden Series 3, 92, 1962), pp. 79–80, 83, 91, 109 (II.7, 10, 12, 34).
37 *MGH Diplomata Regum et Imperatorum Germaniae*, ed. T. Sickel (Hanover, 1879–84), *Heinrich IV*, nos. 334, 336.
38 Orderic Vitalis, *Historia Ecclesiastica*, ed. and trans. M. Chibnall 6 vols. (Oxford, 1969–80), vol. 4, p. 106; William of Malmesbury, *De Gestis Regum Anglorum*, ed. and trans. R. A. B. Mynors and others, 2 vols. (Oxford, 1998–99), p. 513 (III.283); *Actes de Guillaume le conquérant et de la reine Mathilde pour les abbayes caennaises*, ed. L. Musset (Caen, 1967), nos. 14 (pp. 106, 107, 109, 110), 20 (127, 128).

important enough to be worth counting as traitors were, presumably, not important enough to object. It was, after all, a violent conquest and they had to keep their heads down.[39] That kind of confiscation, though no doubt it could be represented as done for the common good, lies outside my scope here. According to Henry of Huntingdon, William also had villages in the New Forest demolished and the inhabitants moved out to make hunting grounds, again presumably without compensation. Henry obviously thought this wrong and the story presumably reflects English rumours and resentments, but *Domesday Book* suggests that it was exaggerated: settlement in what became the forest is thought to have been sparse and not all of it, or all arable, is thought to have disappeared.[40]

This meagre and uncertain evidence from between the fifth and the twelfth centuries does not justify any definite conclusions about expropriation for the common good in the period. I nevertheless feel justified in arguing that the ideas about the common good which seem to have been used to justify taking or borrowing land from churches were also probably used to justify the taking of land from individuals for the building of defences. I have found no hint of compensation for land taken except what was paid to churches. I conclude tentatively that, though it is possible that compensation was paid but not recorded, the common good may have been held to outweigh individual rights to the extent that compensation was not thought necessary – except for land taken from God and the saints.

My suspicion that expropriation for the common good, despite the lack of earlier evidence, was not an innovation of the twelfth century that derived from Roman law or new ideas about collective needs is supported by the character of the first cases I have found from then. My first unambiguous case of expropriation with compensation comes from Genoa in 1156, when two men recorded their receipt and sharing of the price of some land in which they both had interests and which the consuls of the city had taken for the towers and walls of the city.[41] At Pisa in 1164 the

39 *Domesday Book* records demolitions but no claims to compensation for them: Robin Fleming, *Domesday Book and the Law* (Cambridge, 1998), index p. 526 (castles).
40 Henry of Huntingdon, *Historia Anglorum*, ed. and trans. D. Greenway (Oxford, 1996), p. 404 (VI. 39); R. Welldon Finn, 'Hampshire', in H. C. Darby and E. M. J. Campbell (eds), *The Domesday Geography of South-East England* (Cambridge, 1962), pp. 287–363, at 324–38.
41 *Historiae Patriae Monumenta* (Turin, Dep. Subalpina di Storia Patria), 6: *Chartarum* 3 vols. (1836–73), vol. 2, nos. 288–9; Jacques Heers, 'Porta aurea à Genes: bourg de réligieux, bourg d'immigrés', in Jacques Heers (ed.), *Fortifications, portes de villes, places publiques dans le monde méditerranéen* (Paris, 1985), pp. 255–76.

incoming consuls had to swear not to make new roads through any alod or other possession except after consultation with all or the greater part of the senators, and to have losses caused by the making of new ditches, walls or roads assessed on oath, taking into account any profit accruing (presumably, e.g., by access to the new roads). Compensation was to be paid to the owner or occupier (*dominus vel possessor*) and assessed by two discreet men, taking into account any profit accruing.[42] The Pisans had by this time started to make extensive and well-informed use of Roman law in their courts,[43] so that they could have got ideas about expropriation from the few references to it in Justinian. But that seems improbable, given the Genoese case just before and given the form of the required consultation which, despite the use of the word 'senator' for those to be consulted, looks entirely traditional, as do the valuations by two discreet men. There is no reference, for instance, to the *reipublicae utilitas* or *communis commoditas* mentioned in Justinian's edict about expropriation.[44] Ideas about the common good could, it seems, be assumed. What was new and/or was now being more carefully recorded was the need to make sure on the one hand that members of the community who now had charge of the affairs of an independent and fast-growing city could be made to do their job honestly and for the common good, rather than for their own profit, and on the other that those who gave up land for the common good received fair but not excessive compensation.

North of the Alps, where Roman law is even less likely to have been influential as yet, German towns were by the thirteenth century taking land from individuals for the needs of defence and giving compensation either in money or other land.[45] In France and England such records as I have found show kings still taking the initiative in building town walls and therefore receiving petitions from landowners for compensation. The first reference to compensation north of the Alps that I have seen does not, however, concern a town. In 1178–80 Henry II of England founded a Carthusian monastery on a royal estate at Witham (Somerset.) so that the peasants there had to be evicted. According to the Life of the new abbot, St Hugh of Lincoln, he interceded for them with the king. As a result, the peasants were offered houses and land on any royal manor they chose or were

---

42 F. Bonaini (ed.), *Statuti inediti della città di Pisa* 3 vols. (Florence, 1854–7), vol. 1, 36, 37, 39.

43 Chris Wickham, *Courts and Conflict in Twelfth-Century Tuscany* (Oxford, 2003), pp. 108–67.

44 *Corpus Iuris Civilis*, 3. 53 (as above, n. 11).

45 H. Planitz, *Die deutsche Stadt im Mittelalter* (Graz, 1954), pp. 321–2, though his Cologne cases seem to be not quite expropriations.

allowed to go where they wanted, absolved from their former services or servitude (*pristine servitutis iugo absoluti*). Hugh also insisted that the king should compensate them for their houses and improvements. The peasants were delighted with this new method of arranging their dealings with the king (*novo negotionis genere exhilarati*).[46] The hagiographical context, together with the reference to novelty, make the contemporary recognition of a norm about expropriation slightly doubtful but not, I suggest, impossible. That Hugh did not object to the taking of the land as such could be because its tenants were unfree, or because he was interested only in the prospects of his monastery. Like Henry and his contemporaries in general, however, he no doubt assumed that monasteries served the public interest. Hugh may have been making the king do something that was generally agreed to be right but which a king could afford to ignore, especially when taking land from people of such low status.

Guillaume le Breton's account of the building of the walls of Paris by Philip Augustus in 1212 may also cast doubt on the acceptance of expropriation with compensation.[47] Although by written law (*iure scripto*) the king could have built walls and ditches on others' property for the public benefit of the kingdom (*propter publicum regni commodum*), he preferred equity to law and compensated out of his own property (*de fisco proprio*) those who suffered loss. Here it is the king's generosity rather than a saint's intercession that is used to explain what is presented as exceptional compensation, though again it may still have been what should have been paid by custom as opposed to written (i.e. Roman) law. That kings of England, or at least king John, were thought to have taken land wrongly and against custom is suggested by clause 39 of Magna Carta 1215 if that clause, like most but not all of the rest of the charter, reflects what was generally thought to be right custom.[48]

What happened or was thought to be right and lawful after 1100 is not evidence of what happened or was thought right before, except insofar as these relatively well attested cases do not give an impression of innovation. Even if compensation to laymen for giving up land for the common good was new, the cases from Italian and German towns do not suggest that it

---

46   *The Life of St Hugh of Lincoln*, ed. and trans. D. L. Douie and H. Farmer (Edinburgh, 1961), pp. 46–7, 60–2. I owe this reference to Professor David Carpenter.

47   Guillaume le Breton, *Gesta Philippi Augusti*, in *Oeuvres de Rigord et de Guillaume le Breton*, ed. H. F. Delaborde (Paris, 1882–5), 1, pp. 193–333, at p. 241; Jean-Louis Harouel, 'L'Expropriation dans l'histoire du droit français', *Recueils de la Société Jean Bodin* 67 (2000), 39–77, at 42.

48   J. C. Holt, *Magna Carta* (Cambridge, 1965), p. 326; cl. 29 in 1225, p. 355.

was seen as needing particular justification. More evidence about both the earlier and later Middle Ages is needed and may even exist in printed sources: one of the difficulties of the subject is that, because historians have paid so little attention to it, it is hard to find references, either in secondary books and their indexes or in the indexes of published sources. I do not claim to have proved that land was taken from individuals in western Europe for the common good in the earlier Middle Ages, but I can, I hope, claim that there is just enough evidence to show that it would be wrong to say that it was not.

3

Gallic or Greek? Archbishops in England from Theodore to Ecgberht*

Alan Thacker

THIS ESSAY WILL argue that in the course of the seventh century, because of its special status as a missionary Church, England developed forms of higher episcopacy unique in the Latin West. To be fully understood, these arrangements must be placed in a much wider context, ranging, as I shall contend, from Gaul at one extreme to the Greek East at the other. Janet Nelson, who has written so tellingly about the Franks and their neighbours, has encouraged us above all to adopt a comparative approach when thinking about early medieval Europe, and this paper is offered in gratitude for her teaching and example.

Our starting point is Pope Gregory the Great's celebrated plan for the English episcopate. Gregory's envoy, Augustine, who had already been ordained bishop on his way to Kent, was to establish London as his episcopal see and consecrate twelve suffragan bishops to be subject to his metropolitan jurisdiction. As an expression of the high and exceptional authority entailed in this commission, Gregory sent him a special vestment, the papal pallium. In addition he was to consecrate a bishop for York, who was also to be a metropolitan presiding over twelve bishops and also to receive the pallium. After Augustine's death the bishop of York was to be totally independent of his colleague in London. Thereafter the two metropolitans were to take counsel together for the well-being of the English Church, the first to be consecrated being reckoned the senior.[1]

Gregory's scheme was never executed. The metropolitan see which Augustine established at Canterbury did not move to London; that of York

---

* The author wishes to acknowledge Thomas Charles-Edwards' seminal discussion of archiepiscopal authority in the British Isles without which this paper would not have been written and which appeared in T. Charles-Edwards, *Early Christian Ireland* (Cambridge, 2000), pp. 416–40.

1 Bede, *Historia Ecclesiastica*, ed. B. Colgrave and R. A. B. Mynors, 2nd edn (Oxford, 1991), I, c. 29.

perished with its patron, the Northumbrian king Edwin, in 633,[2] and even when re-established in the eighth century never acquired its intended complement of suffragans.[3] Nevertheless, the papal plan cast long shadows over the English Church. The product of Gregory's very particular understanding of the role of metropolitans within his own area of authority, the western patriarchate, it was developed – some might say subverted – under the influence of a churchman whose early training had been in a very different world: the Greek East.[4] Theodore indeed was still living as an oriental monk at the time of his appointment to Canterbury, and Bede expressly says that it was deemed prudent to send with him a Latin-trained abbot lest he introduce alien Greek customs.[5] Even so, his intervention brought decisive changes and when, in the early eighth century, the Gregorian plan was revived it was in a form which differed considerably from the original conception.

The early development of higher episcopacy

Isidore of Seville's analysis of the four episcopal orders provides the classic statement. They were headed by the patriarch, *pater principum*, the father of chief prelates, accorded the highest honour and authority because he held the place of an apostle. Second came the archbishop, *princeps episcoporum*, the chief of bishops, who might act as apostolic vicar (*vice apostolica*) and who watched over (*praesidet*) metropolitans as over other bishops. Third was the metropolitan, who took his status from the power and importance of his city but was preeminent over a whole province within which other bishops could do nothing without his authority. On the lowest rung stood the simple bishop, the 'watchman' (*speculator*), thus placed at the base of quite a fearsome hierarchy.[6]

Beneath Isidore's neat scheme lurks a less tidy reality. In particular, the key roles of archbishop and metropolitan were not clearly distinguished.[7] Yet metropolitan authority lay at the heart of higher episcopacy. The title and responsibilities that Gregory conferred on Augustine and his intended

2 *HE* II, cc. 17, 20.
3 See e.g. *HE* V, c. 23.
4 M. Lapidge, 'The career of Archbishop Theodore', in M. Lapidge (ed.), *Archbishop Theodore* (Cambridge, 1995), pp. 1–29.
5 *HE* IV, c.1: *ne quis ille contrarium veritati fidei Graecorum more in ecclesiam cui praeesset introduceret.*
6 Isidore, *Etymologiae*, ed. W. Lindsay, 2 vols. (Oxford, 1911), VII. xii. 4–12.
7 J. Fontaine, *Isidore de Séville: Genèse et originalité de la culture hispanique aux temps des Wisigoths* (Turnhout, 2000), pp. 117–18.

confrère at York originated in the recognition after 312 of the superiority of those sees based on important administrative centres (metropolises). Their holders had jurisdiction over the bishops in the province attached to their metropolis parallel to that of the imperial prefect in secular matters. The authority of metropolitans was defined at the councils of Nicea in 325 and Antioch in 341. They were to summon and manage annual provincial synods and to preside over the election, consecration and disciplining of their suffragan bishops, who were to consult with them on all matters which did not relate directly to their own dioceses.[8]

In general, metropolitans were more numerous and more securely established in the East than in the Latin West. In mainland Italy itself, for example, metropolitan status was initially confined to Rome, which had jurisdiction over the southern or suburbicarian imperial diocese, and Milan, which had jurisdiction over the north. Milan's position declined, however, from the later fifth century, in tandem with its loss of secular status. Its metropolitan authority was assailed first by Aquileia, which claimed apostolic antecedents and eventually indeed the patriarchal style,[9] and later by Ravenna, seat of the Exarchate.[10]

The archiepiscopal title provided a second determining strand in higher episcopacy. In origin, it denoted the holders of the great patriarchal sees – Rome, Antioch and Alexandria – and a few outstandingly important metropolitans, such those of apostolic Ephesus and Caesarea, chief sees of Asia and Pontus.[11] Its continuing quasi-patriarchal implications were especially apparent in Cyprus, where from the late fifth century the metropolitan-archbishop of Constantia's authority was as final as any patriarch's and characterized by particular marks of distinction, such as the right to bear a sceptre in place of the pastoral staff. One factor here may have been geography: Cyprus was an island, and as such the boundaries of its autocephaly could be unambiguously defined.[12]

8   H. Leclercq, 'Métropole', *DACL* XI.1, cols 786–90; F. Claeys Bouuaert, 'Métropolitain', *DDC* I, cols 927–35.

9   G. Fedalto, *Aquileia: Una chiesa, due patriarcati* (Scrittori della chiesa di Aquileia I: Rome, Città Nuova, 1999), pp. 17–167, esp. pp. 62–5, 112–14.

10 R. Markus, *Gregory the Great and His World* (Cambridge, 1997), pp. 143–7; below, p. 47.

11 A. Amanieu, 'Archevêque', in *DDC* I, cols 927–34.

12 G. Downey, 'Claim of Antioch to ecclesiastical jurisdiction over Cyprus', *Proceedings of the American Philosophical Society* 102 (1958), pp. 224–8; C. Karalevskij, 'Antioch', in *Dictionnaire d'histoire et de géographie ecclésiastiques*, ed. A Baudrillart et al. (29 vols., 1912, in progress) III, cols. 579–81; R. Janin, 'Chypre', *DHEG* XII, cols 791–820, esp. 792–5.

Similar, if less complete, elements of independence were apparent in the Emperor Justinian's exploitation of the title.[13] In 535 he transformed his birth-place, Prima Justiniana, into a supra-metropolitan see, whose holder was expressly designated archbishop, holding the place of the pope vis à vis the bishops of Dacia and Pannonia.[14] In the 540s Justinian granted archiepiscopal status to Ravenna, then the seat of imperial government in the West. While, in this case, the new archbishop remained nominally within the province of Rome and could command no metropolitans, the emperor intended that he should at least have the quasi-patriarchal power of performing episcopal ordinations in other provinces in north Italy, then rent by schism.[15]

Archbishops were particularly abundant in Illyricum where senior metropolitans were empowered by imperial favour and by a lack of clarity in their relations with the competing patriarchal jurisdictions of Rome and Constantinople.[16] Already before the elevation of Prima Justiniana, Constantinople had apparently conceded archiepiscopal status to Stephen, metropolitan of Salona (510–27).[17] By the later sixth century, the metropolitans of Thessalonica, the Illyrican capital, and of apostolic Corinth were also in possession of the title.[18] In Sardinia, by contrast, where the papacy had extensive holdings and imperial intervention was fleeting, the pretensions inherent in archiepiscopal rank were curbed. Although the metropolitan of Cagliari seems to have acquired the title when the island came under Byzantine rule in the 530s, by Gregory the Great's time he was

---

13 What follows depends upon R. Markus, 'Carthage – Prima Justiniana – Ravenna: an Aspect of Justinian's *Kirchenpolitik*', *Byzantion* 49 (1979), pp. 277–302. See also T. S. Brown, 'The Church of Ravenna and the Imperial administration', *EHR* 94 (1979), pp. 1–28, esp. p. 8.

14 *Corpus Iuris Civilis*, ed. T. Mommsen, P. Krueger, and W. Kroll, 3 vols. (Berlin, 1911–15), III, pp. 655–6 (Novel 131, cap. 3); J. Zeiller, *Les Origines chrétiennes dans les provinces danubiennes de l'empire romain*, Bibliothèque des Écoles françaises d'Athènes et de Rome 112 (1918), pp. 385–95; and see below.

15 Markus, *Gregory*, p. 146; idem, 'Carthage – Prima Justiniana – Ravenna', pp. 292–9.

16 Illyrican metropolitans were called to councils in Constantinople, an arrangement Rome appears to have accepted: Markus, *Gregory*, pp. 157–61; Gregory the Great, *Registrum epistularum*, ed. D. Norberg, *CCSL* CXL–CXLA (Turnhout, 1982), IX, 157.

17 D. Ch. Segvié, 'Chronologie des êveques de Salone', *Analecta Bollandiana* 33 (1914), pp. 275–73, at p. 268. Cf. E. Dyggve, *History of Salonitan Christianity* (Oslo, 1951), pp. 21, 29; *Registrum*, IX, 196.

18 *Registrum*, I, 26 (Corinth), III, 8 (Thessalonica).

subject to close papal supervision.[19] In Italy itself, the popes discouraged all use of the archiepiscopal style. It was not applied to Ravenna in official correspondence until the mid-seventh century, while in Milan it seems to have been adopted only in the eighth.[20] Elsewhere in the West, the title was scarcely used.[21]

By the early sixth century a new signifier of status was emerging which was to acquire a highly significant role in the development of higher epis-copacy in the West. The Roman pallium could be used either to buttress or – on occasion – to undermine aspirations to supra-episcopal status. Originally granted by the emperor as an emblem of high authority, from an early period it had evolved into a scarf or band of white wool draped over the shoulders and worn at mass to denote superior authority in the Church.[22] In the East, all bishops wore such a vestment, the omophorion, and it is possible, as we shall see, that this may also have been the custom in parts of the West.[23] But by the time that the pallium first appears in the Western record – in the early sixth century – the term was applied primarily to a vestment worn almost exclusively by the pope, the outward sign of his authority, the primary item of which he was despoiled if he was deposed.[24] Its importance as the crucial papal identifier is clear from the prominence that it is given in sixth-century and early seventh-century depictions of popes in Roman mosaics.[25]

The first extension of its use seems to have been in 513, when Pope Symmachus granted Bishop Caesarius of Arles, the exclusive right to wear it throughout Gaul (*per omnes Gallicanas regiones*). In so doing, Symmachus was formalizing Caesarius's role to act as his special agent, in effect his vicar,

---

19 Cf. *Registrum*, I, 60–2, 81; II, 41, IV, 8–10, 24, 26, 29; VIII, 35; IX, 198; X, 17; XI, 13; XIII, 4; A. H. M. Jones, *The Later Roman Empire*, 4 vols. (Oxford, 1964), I, pp. 273–4; 482; A. des Mazis, 'Cagliari', in *DHGE* XI, cols. 167–74.

20 *Registrum*, I, 80; IV, 1–3; XII, 14. *Liber Pontificalis*, ed. L. Duschesne (Bibliothèque des Écoles françaises d'Athènes et de Rome, 2nd edn, 3 vols. (Paris, 1955), vol. 1, pp. 348–9, 360, 391.

21 Below, pp. 50–1.

22 H. Leclercq, 'Pallium', in *DACL* XIII (1), 931–9; G. Bovini, *Ravenna Mosaics* (Oxford, 1978), plates 28, 31.

23 J. A. Eidenschink, *The Election of Bishops in the Letters of Gregory the Great with an Appendix on the Pallium*, Catholic University of America Canon Law Studies, no. 215 (Washington DC 1945), pp. 105–9; H. Leclercq, 'Omophorion', in *DACL* XII, 2, cols 2089–90; below.

24 *Liber Pontificalis*, vol. 1, pp. 202, 282, 293.

25 E.g. the restored image of Felix IV at SS Cosma e Damiano, and those of Pelagius II in S Lorenzo fuori le mura and Symmachus and Honorius I in S Agnese fuori le mura.

taking precedence over other metropolitans in Gaul.[26] This was followed in the 540s by similar (but less effective) grants, generally at the behest of Frankish kings, to Caesarius's immediate successors[27] and, evidently at the emperor's behest, to the new archbishop of Ravenna, Maximian.[28] Later evidence suggests that Justinian had also obliged the pope to grant the same honour to the archbishop of Prima Justiniana.[29] Again the importance of the coveted vestment is demonstrated by the prominence with which it is displayed in episcopal images in the mid-sixth-century churches of Ravenna.[30]

Although few grants of the Roman pallium are recorded before the pontificate of Gregory the Great (590–604), a gradual extension of its use may be discerned. In the later sixth century the popes continued to grant it to the bishops of Arles and – perforce – to the archbishops of Ravenna. By then too (if not before) it was also sent to the metropolitan of Milan, to various leading metropolitans in Illyricum, and (perhaps) to episcopal agents in Sicily.[31] On occasion, however, it was expressly withheld and in certain instances the unfavoured could be threatened with its withdrawal.[32]

Metropolitan status and the vicariate in Spain and Gaul

By the sixth century the role of metropolitans in those parts of Western Europe outside the Later Empire was very different from that of their

---

26   William E. Klingshirn, *Caesarius of Arles: The Making of a Christian Community in Late Antique Gaul* (Cambridge, 1994), pp. 127–32; *Vita Sancti Caesarii*, ed. B. Krusch, *MGH SRM* III (Hanover, 1896), pp. 433–501, I, c. 42; *Epistulae Arelatenses*, ed. W. Grundlach, *MGH, Epistulae* III (Berlin, 1982), p. 40; below, p. 52.

27   *Epistulae Arelatenses*, pp. 59, 62, 66, 74, 75, 454; Eidenschink, *Election of Bishops*, p. 105; Klingshirn, *Caesarius of Arles*, p. 262. In one case, vicarial authority was restricted to the province of Arles.

28   Agnellus of Ravenna, *The Book of the Pontiffs of the Church of Ravenna*, trans. Deborah M. Deliyannis (Washington DC, 2004), c. 70. Ravennate opinion deemed the pallium to be as much in the gift of the emperor as in that of the pope: *ibid.* cc. 40, 110, 113.

29   *Registrum*, V. 10, 16.

30   E.g. at S Vitale and S Apollinare in Classe.

31   *Registrum*, II, 17–19; IX, 177, 234 (Salona); III, 54, 66; V, 11, 15, 61; VI, 31; IX, 167 (Ravenna); IV, 1 (Milan); V. 62–3 (Corinth); VI, 7 (Nicopolis); VI, 8 (Messina); VI, 18 (Syracuse).

32   Eidenschink, *Election of Bishops*, p. 105; Pelagius I, *Epistulae quae supersunt*, ed. P. M. Gasso and C. M. Batlle (Montserrat, 1956), pp. 114–15; *Registrum*, II, 17–19; IX, 221.

counterparts in the East. Ecclesiastical arrangements were much more fluid, largely because the breakdown of imperial authority in the fifth and sixth centuries. In Spain, for example, they were not finalized until the early seventh century and were dominated by the Visigothic kings, who played a leading role in episcopal appointments and in the conduct of conciliar business. Although metropolitans presided over provincial councils, they were appointed by the king and their authority was clearly limited. In 633, for example, the fourth council of Toledo found it necessary to require that episcopal appointments (made in practice by the king) had at least to be confirmed by the local metropolitan.[33] In 683 the thirteenth council of Toledo decreed that the local bishop should not excommunicate members of his clergy who brought contentious matters to their metropolitan before the latter had pronounced judgement.[34] Periodically too the authority of certain bishops was enhanced by their nomination as the pope's personal representative or vicar. Again, this seems to have been *ad hominem* and not necessarily tied to metropolitan status.[35] None of this suggests a highly developed metropolitan system. Significantly, too, the title of archbishop was hardly if ever used in Spain.[36]

The clearest evidence of the limited nature of metropolitan authority in the West comes from Gaul. The breakdown there of stable imperial administration did not allow a clearly defined network of metropolitan sees, and in the fifth century promoted controversy and factionalism over the structure and nature of metropolitan power, a process which encouraged individual episcopal autonomy.[37] Although in the sixth century senior bishops might occasionally experiment with a grand title, such as *episcopus patriarcha*,[38]

---

33 *Concilios Visigoticos*, ed. J. Vives (Barcelona-Madrid, 1963), pp. 136, 198, 222. Cf. E. A. Thompson, *The Goths in Spain* (Oxford, 1969), pp. 34, 180, 296–8; P. D. King, *Law and Society in the Visigothic Kingdom* (Cambridge, 1972), pp. 121–9.

34 Vives, *Concilios Visigoticos*, pp. 430–1.

35 *Epistolae Romanorum pontificum genuinae* I, ed. A. Thiel (Brunsberg, 1848), pp. 213–14, 788, 980; Fontaine, *Isidore*, p. 118.

36 The one exception in the official record occurred at the provincial council of Merida in 666. Although Proficuus subscribed as metropolitan bishop of Merida, his suffragan Sclua, bishop of Egitania, terms him archbishop, perhaps because he was relying upon his support in a dispute with a co-suffragan: Vives, *Concilios Visigoticos*, pp. 331, 343.

37 Ralph W. Mathisen, *Ecclesiastical Factionalism and Religious Controversy in Fifth-Century Gaul* (Washington DC, 1989), *passim*, but esp. pp. 5–6, 22–6, 44–68, 69–74, 173–205, 206–34.

38 E.g. Priscus of Lyon presiding over the council of Macon in 585: *Les Canons des conciles mérovingiens*, ed. J. Gaudemet and B. Basdevant from text of C. de Clercq, 2 vols. (Sources chrétiennes 353, Paris, 1989), p. 454.

this could not disguise the fact that their functions and responsibilities were far less wide-ranging than those of the archbishops of Illyricum and the East. While they had the characteristic metropolitan duty of convening provincial synods once or twice a year, among their provincial fellow bishops (*episcopi conprovinciales*) they seem to have been *primi inter pares* rather than commanding superiors. Gallic metropolitans were elected by their fellow-bishops, and ordained by them or by a metropolitan in their presence; they conducted episcopal ordinations together with their fellow-bishops.[39] They did not count the creation of new sees as part of their responsibilities, since by the sixth century there were plenty of bishoprics in Gaul.[40] Although they were empowered to adjudicate in disputes between their suffragan bishops, the latter could also take their causes to their fellows.[41] In the sixth and early seventh century power was vested above all in episcopal councils, attended by bishops from several provinces and in general convened under royal authority; for like the Visigothic kings the Merovingians kept close control of the Church, and particularly of episcopal appointments.[42] The conciliar records give an overwhelming impression of equality within the episcopate. The subscribers almost invariably use the simple designation *episcopus*, occasionally *metropolitanus*. The principal indication of rank is the fact that metropolitans almost always head the list. None of them, it should be stressed, ever subscribed as archbishop.[43]

One expression of this collegiality was probably the Gallican pallium, which, in a much discussed decree of the first council of Macon (581x3), all bishops were required to wear when celebrating mass.[44] Clearly this must have been a different vestment from that worn by the papal vicars. The suggestion that the council was not referring to a pallium at all, but to the stole, the scarf worn by all celebrants at the Eucharist, has been undermined by the discovery of two pallia among the relics of Caesarius of Arles. Both were of very fine white material, one with a chi-rho ornament, the other plain; the chi-rho, which is of a type current in the lower Rhone valley

---

39 E.g. *Canons*, pp. 198, 232.
40 Cf. episcopal resistance to the creation of the bishopric of Châteaudun in 573: J. M. Wallace-Hadrill, *The Frankish Church* (Oxford, 1983) p. 103; *Concilia Galliae, 511–695*, ed. C. de Clercq, *CCSL* CXLVIIIA (Turnhout, 1963), pp. 211–17.
41 *Canons*, pp. 303, 517 (Orleans, 549, can. 3; Paris, 614, can. 13).
42 Charles-Edwards, *Early Christian Ireland*, p. 418.
43 Although they might be called archbishops by those from areas where the term was in use, e.g. Istria and England: *Gregorii I Papae Registrum epistularum*, ed. P. Ewald and L. Hartmann, *MGH, Epistolae* I–II (Berlin 1891–99), I, 16a; *HE* IV, c. 1; Charles-Edwards, *Early Christian Ireland*, p. 426.
44 *Canons*, p. 430 (can. 6).

in the early sixth century, probably adorned Caesarius's Gallican vestment, while the plain one was that granted by Symmachus in Rome.[45] It would seem, then, that the Gallican Church had an equivalent of the eastern omophorion.

In theory, the principal authority to impinge upon this collegiality was the papal vicariate. By the sixth century, when Caesarius of Arles was granted this office together with the pallium, his role was tightly defined: he was to convene councils on matters of papal concern, refer irreconcilable conflicts to Rome and provide letters of introduction for clerics travelling to the city.[46] The vicariate and pallium were also bestowed upon his three immediate successors,[47] and, unsurprisingly, Gregory the Great regarded the office as established 'according to ancient custom'.[48] Nevertheless, in practice its impact was limited. The bishops of Arles appeared relatively rarely at the great national councils of the Frankish Church, and when they did they did not necessarily subscribe first. Generally at these meetings the senior bishops were the metropolitans of Lyons, Vienne, Rouen and Bourges.[49]

The use of the pallium and the papal vicariates under Gregory the Great

The pontificate of Gregory saw a considerable development in the use and status of the pallium.[50] The pope caused a special niche, immediately above the tomb itself and connected to it by a shaft, to be included in the redesigned Petrine *confessio*, in which were placed pallia before their dispatch to their intended recipients. The vestments were thereby converted into

---

45 Eidenschink, *Election of Bishops*, pp. 106–7; H-I. Marrou, 'Les Deux Palliums de Saint Césaire d'Arles', in H-I. Marrou, *Christiana Tempora*, Collection de l'École française de Rome 35 (1978), pp. 251–2; H. Benoît, 'Les reliques de Saint Césaire, archevêque d'Arles', *Cahiers archéologiques fin de l'antiquité et moyen âge* I (1945), pp. 50–62, esp. pp. 57–8 and pl. VII.

46 Kingshirn, *Caesarius of Arles*, p. 130; *Epistulae Arelatenses*, pp. 41–2.

47 Auxanian (543/5), Aurelius (546), and Sapaudus (557): *Epistulae Arelatenses*, pp. 59, 62, 66, 74, 74; Pelagius I, *Epistulae*, pp. 14–19; Eidenschink, *Election of Bishops*, p. 105; Kingshirn, *Caesarius of Arles*, pp. 131, 262, 264.

48 *iuxta antiquum morem: Registrum*, V, 60.

49 Of the relevant bishops of Arles, Aurelius (in 549) and Florianus (in 614) attest after the bishop of Lyon; Sapaudus sometimes subscribes second, sometimes first: *Canons*, pp. 320, 520; *Concilia Galliae*, pp. 168, 212, 214, 216, 235; *Epistulae Arelatenses*, pp. 66, 454; Charles-Edwards, *Early Christian Ireland*, p. 426.

50 Eidenschink, *Election of Bishops*, pp. 101–43.

contact relics through their incubation on the apostolic tomb.[51] Other evidence confirms this holy status. In particular, in a letter to Leander of Seville, Gregory writes unambiguously that he is sending him the pallium *pro benedictione beati Petri apostolorum principis*.[52] An earlier analogy is provided by the action of Pelagius I (556–61) in sending Eutychius, patriarch of Constantinople, a *tunica* which he had left for three days in the inner part of St Peter's tomb in order that it should be used as a relic ('pro reliquiis vel pro benedictione').[53] Pallia thus made holy signified an authority imbued with a special Petrine quality and enhanced the standing of Gregory's agents and their bonds with the Holy See.[54]

Where Gregory had most authority and where his hands were not tied by established custom, he was generally reluctant to endow sees with any form of enduring superior jurisdiction.[55] That is apparent in his letter of 591 confirming Maximianus, bishop of Syracuse (591–4), as vicar in Sicily. In that, he was careful to stress that the position was a personal one in no way attached to the see of Syracuse.[56] Moreover, although Maximianus received the pallium, he was not alone among Sicilian bishops in being so honoured. For when in 595 Gregory the Great bestowed the pallium upon John, bishop of Syracuse, and Donus, bishop of Messina, he was continuing, according to the wording of both grants, what had been accorded to their predecessors.[57] It seems, then, that the pope generally had more than one agent in the island.[58] In Spain, too, arrangements appear to have remained relatively loosely defined. While Gregory granted the pallium to his friend and representative Leander of Seville, it is not certain that he was formally constituted a vicar.[59]

The most formalized vicariate in the West remained that in Francia. Gregory's commission to Virgilius of Arles (588–610), styled vicar in the

---

51 J. C. M. Toynbee and J. B. Ward-Perkins, *The Shrine of St Peter and the Vatican Excavations* (London, 1956), pp. 220–4.

52 *Registrum*, IX, 228 (p. 804); Eidenschink, *Election of Bishops*, p. 133. Cf. *benedictio* used to mean relic: *Registrum* IX, 229 (p. 810).

53 Pelagius I, *Epistulae*, pp. 62–3.

54 For him it was the crucial element in the special position which the bishops of Arles held in Gaul: *HE* I, c. 27 (resp. VII).

55 E.g. Prima Justiniana: *Registrum*, V, 10, 16. Nevertheless, even in such cases he could still use the grant as a means to intervene: e.g. Ravenna: *Registrum*, III, 54; V, 11, 15; VI, 31; IX, 168; Salona: *Registrum*, II, 17–19.

56 *Registrum*, II, 5.

57 *Registrum*, VI, 8, 18.

58 Cf. the award of the pallium to John, bishop of Palermo in 603: *Registrum*, XIII, 38.

59 *Registrum*, IX, 228; Markus, *Gregory*, p. 167.

kingdom of Childebert (II, d. 596), granted him use of the pallium when celebrating mass. The pope enjoined bishops to attend Virgilius's synods or to send representatives and to seek his permission if they wished to travel long distances. Virgilius was in turn expressly advised to show due honour to the metropolitans of his vicariate. He was to arbitrate in disputes among his bishops with discretion and moderation, and in difficult matters he was to associate a further twelve of his bishops with him or refer them to the Holy See.[60] No conciliar *acta* survive from this period, so it is not clear how operative any of this was. In any case, even in Francia, Gregory's concern to avoid undue reliance on a single agent is apparent. He undercut the bishop of Arles' position in Burgundy by his grant of the pallium to Bishop Syagrius of Autun at the request of Queen Brunhild in 599.[61] Syagrius was not even a metropolitan. The reasons given for the grant were that Syagrius was to convene a council to reform abuses, and that he had been exceptionally helpful to the English mission on its progress through Gaul. When taken with the Sicilian evidence, this suggests that Gregory regarded the pallium primarily as an *ad hominem* distinction honouring exceptionally privileged individuals rather than as systematically attached to the vicariate. That, in Gaul at least, it was not primarily linked with metropolitan authority was made even more apparent when it was denied to Desiderius, bishop of the ancient metropolitan see of Vienne.[62] Gregory in fact seems to have used the pallium principally to strengthen the position of his personal agents, whatever their episcopal or vicarial status.

Unsurprisingly, Gregory was deeply unenthusiastic about archbishops. His use of the title as a form of address in his letters was confined mostly to the earliest year or two of his pontificate and to the leading metropolitans of Illyricum.[63] It is especially significant that even papal vicars with a degree of authority over metropolitans are not styled archbishop. The case of Ravenna provides a particularly clear illustration of his attitude. Although for much of his pontificate it was held by his friends John II and Marinianus, Gregory never addressed either as archbishop (the one exception is generally thought to have been an oversight by the scribe).[64]

This survey of higher episcopacy in the Western patriarchate at the time of the English mission shows that grand and independent archbishops with authority over other metropolitans were imperial promotions, and confined to Illyricum. Where Gregory the Great had his way, authority was

60 *Registrum*, V, 58–9.
61 *Registrum*, VIII, 4, IX, 213, IX, 219, IX, 222.
62 *Registrum*, IX, 221; Markus, *Gregory*, p. 173.
63 *Registrum*, I, 26, 60–2; II, 4; III, 8; IX, 197.
64 *Registrum*, IX, 139.

mediated through a papal agent, whose position was personal and derived primarily from the pallium, a relic-vestment imbued with Petrine power, rather than from occupation of a specific see. Such figures were not necessarily formal vicars, or even metropolitans, and never (except in Illyricum) archbishops. In countries such as Gaul and Spain, where the pope was dealing with well-established secular authorities, the vicariate was granted at royal request and its sphere of action confined largely to matters of direct papal concern. In Gaul in particular, the authority of the metropolitans was a pale shadow of that of their eastern counterparts, and in both Gaul and Spain the archiepiscopal title appears to have been scarcely, if at all, in use. As we shall see, all this has considerable implications for the Gregorian scheme in England.

England in the seventh century

In Britain, as elsewhere, the pope did not choose to rely on a single agent. He was explicit that after Augustine's death the bishops of London and York were to be equal and independent, the first consecrated being the senior. Both were to receive that crucial badge of recognition, the pallium.[65] They were thus neither low-key metropolitans along Gallican lines, nor endowed with supra-metropolitan authority. Their unusual position relates to the missionary status of England: the grant of the pallium was expressly linked by Gregory with their responsibility to create new sees.[66] In areas which already had a full complement of bishops, that was clearly not a normal metropolitan attribute and Gregory seems to have felt the need to afforce his English agents with extra authority for this special responsibility.

Given that their role was (in theory) less than that of the papal vicar at Arles, and given Gregory's evident wariness of the archiepiscopal title by 596, it is almost certain that, despite the repeated references to the contrary in Bede, Augustine and his first four successors never styled themselves archbishop. They are never referred to as such in any letter recorded in Gregory's *Registrum* or in the *Historia Ecclesiastica*. Significantly too, when Theodore held his first council at Hertford in 672 he referred to himself simply as bishop. The grander title came later and as we shall see Theodore (669–90) was the first bishop of Canterbury to adopt it.[67]

65 *Registrum*, XI, 39; *HE* I, c. 29.
66 Cf. Bede's belief that only an archbishop could ordain bishops: *HE* III, c. 29.
67 Charles-Edwards, *Early Christian Ireland*, pp. 429–38, esp. pp. 430–1; *HE* IV, c. 5; below, pp. 57–8.

Theodore arrived in England in 669 in response to an initiative by the kings of Northumbria and Kent to obtain a new bishop for the vacant see of Canterbury; the kings' candidate having died in Rome, he had been chosen by the pope as a replacement.[68] In 669 the English episcopate was at a low ebb. There were few if any canonically ordained bishops, and the second most senior see, York, was in dispute, the initial royal nominee, Wilfrid, having been superseded by another while Wilfrid was abroad seeking consecration.[69] The local situation thus offered the new bishop of Canterbury considerable opportunities of intervention, and Theodore made the most of them. As a Greek, brought up at Tarsus in the patriarchate of Antioch, he was from an ecclesiastical culture which had a maximal view of the role of metropolitans and from the start he was keen to enhance Canterbury's position. One of his first acts was to adjudicate in the disputed see of York, potentially a rival focus of authority.

In 669 Wilfrid needed Theodore's help to regain his see, and in any case probably accepted the superior authority of the new bishop of Canterbury, who came as the pope's agent armed with a special commission.[70] Nevertheless, his biographer Stephen's assertions that as bishops of York both he and his predecessor Colman had been metropolitans are likely to reflect Wilfrid's own position.[71] Such views would explain his splendid Gallic consecration in 664. We know that in Gaul metropolitans had to be consecrated by their own suffragans, preferably with the assistance of one of their peers.[72] Wilfrid, however, lacked suffragans of his own, and at the time of his appointment there was no English metropolitan. The ceremony of 664, held at a Gallic council of twelve bishops, almost certainly presided over by a metropolitan, provided an obvious solution to the problem.[73] Archbishop Berhtwald's consecration in Gaul by Godwin, metropolitan of Lyon, in 693 provides an analogy.[74] Nevertheless, even if Wilfrid did regard himself as a metropolitan, he would have viewed that office in Gallic terms. Never very strong, and never associated with the pallium, Frankish metropolitan authority had become even more low-key in the later seventh

---

68   *HE* III, c. 29; IV, c. 1.
69   Stephen, *Vita Sancti Wilfridi*, cc. 11–12, ed. W. Levison, *MGH SRM* VI (Hanover, 1913), pp. 163–263.
70   Stephen, *Vita Wilfridi*, c. 15: *statuta iudicia apostolicae sedis*.
71   *Vita Wilfridi*, cc. 10, 16.
72   See *Canons*, p. 232.
73   *Vita Wilfridi*, c. 12.
74   *HE* V, c. 8; H. Leclercq, 'Lyon', *DACL* X, cols 1–402, at col. 229.

century with the virtual cessation of conciliar activity.[75] It seems likely therefore that Wilfrid (who may well have worn a Gallican-style pallium at mass)
founded his episcopal identity more upon the princely Gallic diocesan
bishop than upon the ineffectual metropolitan.

By 672 Theodore felt strong enough to hold a provincial council, at
which he described himself as 'bishop of the church of Canterbury sent
from the apostolic see'.[76] The council of Hertford was attended by four
bishops of the southern province, whereas Wilfrid sent legates, almost certainly because he regarded himself as northern metropolitan. Most of the
legislation of the council seems to have been entirely appropriate to a
provincial synod. Attempts were made to regulate the behaviour of bishops
toward each other and towards the monasteries in their dioceses and to
ensure that synods were held twice annually. The only controversial item
was, predictably, the requirement that more sees were to be created – a
subject which Bede or his source expressly says was discussed but which did
not produce an agreed outcome. In this matter, self-interest may well have
been informed by a feeling that this was a subject beyond the authority of
a provincial synod and its metropolitan.[77]

After Hertford, Theodore seems to have assumed a greater authority.
Despite the uncertain response of the synod, he used the illness of Bisi
of East Anglia to consecrate two bishops in his place, thereby dividing
Bisi's see.[78] Shortly afterward, he deposed the recently appointed Winfrith
of Mercia, 'because', says Bede, 'of some act of disobedience.'[79] But
Theodore's greatest test came with the growing quarrel between Wilfrid
and King Ecgfrith of Northumbria. In a deliberate act of provocation, he
was called in to dismember the vast Northumbrian diocese, a decision
taken at a meeting held probably in 678, the synodical authority of which
was later challenged by Wilfrid. At this meeting, Theodore (with royal
backing) took a decision which represented a great extension of his powers.

75 Boniface, *Epistulae*, ed. M. Tangl, *Die Briefe des hieligen Bonifatius und Lullu, MGH,
    Epistulae Selectae* 1 (Berlin 1916), no. 50, p. 82; Wallace-Hadrill, *The Frankish Church*,
    p. 107.
76 *ab apostolica sede destinatus Doruuernensis ecclesiae episcopus: HE* IV, c. 5.
77 Cf. episcopal opposition to the division of the see of Chartres and the assertion
    of the inviolability of existing sees at XII Toledo (681): Wallace-Hadrill, *Frankish
    Church*, p. 103; Vives, *Concilios Visigoticos*, pp. 389–92.
78 *HE* IV, c. 5. Initially perhaps the new bishops were viewed as coadjutors in a single
    a see. Cf. C. Cubitt, 'Wilfrid's usurping bishops: episcopal elections in Anglo-Saxon
    England, *c.*600–600', *Northern History* 25 (1989), pp. 19–38, at pp. 28–30.
79 *HE* IV, c. 6.

On his sole authority, he divided a see with an existing incumbent and in the process deprived a canonically ordained bishop.[80]

Very shortly after these events, at a council held in 679 to condemn the Monothelite heresy, Theodore adopted a new and inflated episcopal style.[81] No longer merely southern metropolitan, he was now 'archbishop by the grace of God of the island of Britain and of the city of Canterbury.[82] Clearly he felt the need to buttress his authority to deal with the challenge of Wilfrid. The decision to deprive Wilfrid of his see without due process and to consecrate three bishops in his place went well beyond the normal competence of a Western metropolitan and papal agent. The assumption of archiepiscopal status was to legitimise his drastic intervention and perhaps forestall appeals to Rome. It is noticeable that the style which he adopted was quasi-patriarchal. In particular, Theodore's association of his authority with the confines of the entire island of Britannia calls to mind the authority of the head of the autocephalous Cypriot Church.

That Theodore had papal approval for this great enhancement of his episcopal style and authority is clear from the fact that Wilfrid never contested his right to consecrate bishops in Northumbria. The most likely occasion for the confirmation of the new dignity is a council held by Pope Agatho in Rome in October 679 to settle the divisions within the English Church, in which it was decreed that the Church in the island of Britannia should be governed by twelve bishops, of whom one would receive the pallium and rule as archbishop.[83] This appears to have been a compromise. While Theodore's position was enhanced (he received the title of archbishop and was granted or confirmed in possession of the pallium), and while his division of the Northumbrian diocese was allowed, no further new sees were envisaged.[84] In all this, the Gregorian scheme was quietly disregarded.

---

80 *Vita Wilfridi*, c. 24; *HE* IV, c. 12.
81 C. R. E. Cubitt, *Anglo-Saxon Church Councils, c.650–850* (Leicester, 1995), pp. 250–8.
82 *gratia dei archiepiscopus Brittaniae insulae et civitatis Doruuernis*: *HE* IV, c. 17.
83 A. W. Haddan and W. Stubbs, *Councils and Ecclesiastical Documents*, 3 vols. (Oxford, 1869–78), III, pp. 131–5; *Sacrorum Conciliorum Nova et Amplissima Collectio*, ed. J. D. Mansi et al., 15 vols. (reprinted 1960), XI, cols 179–82; W. Levison, 'Die Akten', *ZRG* 37, *Kanonistische Abteilung* II (1912), pp. 249–82; N. Brooks, *The Early History of the Church of Canterbury* (Leicester, 1984), pp. 74–5.
84 The addition of the two new Northumbrian sees brought the number of English bishops to twelve.

Wilfrid lodged his appeal at this same council.[85] In his disputes with Theodore, he has not in general had a good press. He has been viewed as litigious and disruptive, a worldly prelate who stood in the way of progress, resisting the reforming ideology advanced by Bede and above all the rational and necessary division of his enormous see. Nevertheless, from a Gallican perspective, his attitude was not unreasonable. As Katy Cubitt has pointed out, his objections as recorded by Stephen were not necessarily to the creation of new sees, nor to Theodore's undoubted right as archbishop to be the agent of this.[86] Wilfrid's main arguments at the Roman council were threefold. First, he had been wrongfully deprived since no offence had been alleged against him. Secondly, that deprivation and the elevation of the new bishops were in themselves conducted uncanonically; these matters had been decided in his absence and upon Theodore's own authority, at a 'meeting' (*conventus*) and not in full council (*synodus*) with his fellow bishops.[87] Lastly, and most importantly, those so created were not drawn from his own diocese (*parrochia*). All this makes sense in terms of the accepted conventions in governing Gallican metropolitans, who were expected to ordain bishops in council with their co-provincials and to handle all episcopal disputes with great circumspection. It also accords with the preoccupations of those Gallic bishops who at Clichy in 626 insisted that that a bishop's successor should come from the same see-centre (*locus*).[88]

The fact that in making his case Wilfrid did not refer explicitly to his own position as metropolitan is not particularly surprising. Given his low-key perception of such status, he may not have seen it as offering much help, especially since he had no suffragans. Nevertheless, his insistence that those ordained to sees in Northumbria should be appointed with his consent may derive from his understanding of metropolitan status. Stephen, indeed, makes him refer to the plurality of dioceses (*pristinae parrochiae*) over which he formerly presided and of provinces (*provinciae*) into which his fellow-bishops were organized.[89]

Pope Agatho appears largely to have accepted these arguments. Wilfrid was to be restored to his see, the intruding bishops were to be expelled,

---

85 The only record is Stephen, *Vita Wilfridi*, c. 29–31. Stubbs treats it as a separate meeting: *Councils* III, p. 135.

86 Cubitt, 'Wilfrid's usurping bishops', pp. 18–28.

87 Wilfrid demanded that the new bishops be chosen *in synodo . . . congregatis episcopis*: *Vita Wilfridi*, c. 30.

88 *Canons*, p. 542.

89 *Vita Wilfridi*, c. 30.

and he was to choose new 'assistant bishops' (*episcopi adjutores*) who were to be confirmed in council by his fellow bishops, and consecrated by Theodore. That sounds like a confirmation of Wilfrid's authority over the northern bishops, *de facto* of a degree of metropolitan authority, not unlike that allowed by the popes themselves to the contemporary archbishops of Cagliari.[90]

Agatho's judgement perhaps encouraged Wilfrid to harbour grandiose new ambitions. According to Stephen, in 680, after it had been delivered, he made confession of the orthodox faith along with 124 other bishops, on behalf of the northern part of Britain and the islands of Hibernia, inhabited by English, British, Scots and Picts.[91] Stephen's account tallies with the records of a Roman synod of 125 bishops held in preparation for the third Ecumenical Council, in which Wilfrid attests in fiftieth place as 'bishop of the holy church of York of the island of Britain and legate of the venerable synod established through Britain'.[92] It would seem that he nurtured grand plans which marched in tandem with the Northumbrian kings' recent military successes, and perhaps sought supra-metropolitan – even archiepiscopal – authority extending as far as Scotland, Ireland and the Isles.[93]

The new archbishopric

The Roman council of 679 enjoined a compromise that was doomed to failure. The victim was Wilfrid, forced into exile when Ecgfrith and Theodore rejected the synod's ruling. He was never again to possess the authority he held in the 670s, even after his restoration to the see of York in the later 680s following his reconciliation with the archbishop.[94] Theodore by contrast emerged from the council with his assumption of quasi-patriarchal status over the whole island of Britannia confirmed. The position thus acquired had the support of two of the most important English rulers, the kings of Northumbria and Kent. By then, however, it was wholly exceptional in the Latin West. At Salona the archbishopric had collapsed under the

90 *Vita Wilfridi*, c. 32; *Liber Pontificalis*, I, p. 366.
91 *Vita Wilfridi*, c. 53: *pro omni aquilonali parte Britanniae et Hiberniae insulisque quae ab Anglorum et Brittonum necnon Scottorum et Pictorum gentibus colebantur*; Charles-Edwards, *Early Christian Ireland*, pp. 432–5.
92 *humilis episcopus sanctae ecclesiae Eboracenae insulae Britannicae, legatus venerabilis synodi per Britanniam constituae. Conciliorum . . . Collectio*, ed. Mansi, XI, col. 306.
93 Charles-Edwards, *Early Christian Ireland*, pp. 432–3.
94 *Vita Wilfridi*, cc. 34–40, 43–5.

assaults of the Avars, while in Sardinia, the archbishop continued to lack full metropolitan rights, in particular over the appointment of suffragans.[95] Nearer home, in Gaul, the vicarial role of Arles had long since faded (although Pope Vitalian commended Theodore himself en route to England to be its bishop), while in Italy Aquileia remained divided through schism.[96] Indeed, the only other fully-functioning Latin archbishopric was anomalous Ravenna, then after a period of full autocephaly (666–82) on the point of returning to obedience to Rome.[97]

Perhaps the nearest comparison is with Iberia. Very shortly after these events, in 681, the new Visigothic king, Erwig, at the prompting of Julian, his senior bishop, enacted that henceforth the king would nominate, and Julian as metropolitan of Toledo, the *urbs regia*, would approve, all appointments to Spanish bishoprics. The traditional rights of the local metropolitan were overridden and henceforth he would simply receive a new bishop at Julian's instruction.[98] The see of Toledo, whose own metropolitan authority over Carthaginiensis had been acquired only in 610, had thus established for itself powers (albeit under royal authority) as extensive as those of the patriarch of Constantinople, and may even have been contemplating independence from Rome.[99] Of course, these events cannot be directly connected with those in England. Julian never assumed the title archbishop, and in any case his political situation was very different. Nevertheless, it may be significant that both Iberia and Britannia saw a strong-minded prelate with royal support strengthen supra-metropolitan authority over a regional Church at much the same time.

One other crucial comparator is Ireland, where in the 680s the competing primatial claims of Kildare and Armagh, the one to be the seat of the archbishop of the bishops of Ireland (*archiepiscopus episcoporum Hibernensium*), the other of the archbishop of the Irish (*archiepiscopus Hibernensium*), were probably directly inspired by Theodore. The island of Ireland like Britannia was to have its own quasi patriarchal figure. Clearly Theodore brought with him ideas which found a ready acceptance in an Insular context.[100] But while the titles and claims to authority were clearly closely

95 Duval et al., *Salona III*, p. 1; Segvié, 'Chronologie', pp. 269–70; *Liber Pontificalis*, I, pp. 366–7.

96 *HE* IV, c. 1; Fedalto, *Aquileia*, pp. 120–72, esp. p. 136. Only resolved under Sergius (687–701): *Liber Pontificalis* I, p. 376.

97 Agnellus, *Book of Pontiffs*, pp. 5, 229–30, 245–6; *Liber Pontificalis*, I, pp. 360–1.

98 Vives, *Concilios Visigoticos*, pp. 393–4.

99 Cf. Thompson, *Goths in Spain* pp. 275–7; King, *Law and Society*, pp. 123–4.

100 Charles-Edwards, *Early Christian Ireland*, pp. 421–9; Cogitosus, *Vita Sanctae Brigidae*, in *Acta Sanctorum* III (Antwerp, 1658), p. XXX; *The Patrician Texts in the Book of Armagh*, ed. L. Bieler, *SLH* X (Dublin, 1979), p. 188.

related, the realities of power were quite different. The Irish archbishops never exercised the extraordinary authority wielded briefly by Theodore and his immediate successor.

One of the principal qualifications for autocephalous, quasi-patriarchal status of the kind implicit in Theodore's new title was apostolic origins. Thus the emergence of Cyprus from the shadow of Antioch had undoubtedly been facilitated by the *inventio* of the apostle Barnabas.[101] Ravenna too had sought to enhance its position by first soliciting and then planning to steal relics of St Andrew from Constantinople.[102] It is in Theodore's similar need that we find the origins of the cult of Gregory as apostle of England. This reaches its most extreme expression in the Whitby *Life of Gregory*, composed at a monastery where Northumbrian and Kentish royal traditions intermingled, and which thus provided a fruitful milieu for the promotion of the new archbishopric. Theodore was the founding impresario of the cult of Gregory, who conveniently provided the new arrangements with a sponsor he could present as patron of all the English (albeit primarily the Northumbrians and men of Kent), not tied exclusively to Canterbury.[103]

Theodore's vigorous development of the high authority of his office ensured that for a while the archiepiscopal see had remarkable power and standing. Theodore's successor, Berhtwald, who may have been challenged initially by Wilfrid, secured his position by papal confirmation and the grant of the pallium. He adopted the style 'archbishop of the Church of Kent and all Britain' and used his authority with considerable success to force through the creation of new bishoprics.[104] Canterbury's high view of its prerogatives at this time is clearly expressed in Theodore's epitaph, in which the late archbishop was described as *princeps episcoporum*, a phrase which evokes Isidore's definition of the archiepiscopal office.[105] Nicholas Brooks has commented upon Berhtwald's extraordinary ascendancy over the English episcopate and the slavish nature of Bishop Wealdhere of London's profession of obedience to his metropolitan archbishop in his letter of 704/5.[106] Wealdhere fulsomely styles Berhtwald 'most reverend lord, to be blessed by the proclamations of the catholic fathers, ruler of

---

101 Karelevskij, 'Antioch', *DHGE* III, cols 580–1.
102 Markus, *Gregory*, pp. 145–6; Agnellus, *Book of Pontiffs*, p. 190.
103 A. Thacker, 'Memorializing Gregory the Great: the origin and transmission of a papal cult', *EME* 7 (1998), pp. 59–84, at pp. 75–8.
104 *Vita Wilfridi*, cc. 43, 53, 60; *Liber Pontificalis*, I, p. 376; Haddan and Stubbs, *Councils*, III, pp. 229–3; Brooks, *Church of Canterbury*, pp. 76–8.
105 *HE* V, c. 8.
106 Brooks, *Church of Canterbury*, pp. 79–80.

the government of all Britain', and addresses him variously as 'your Holiness' or 'your Grace'. He begs the archbishop's permission to attend a council to settle disputes between his own king (of the East Saxons) and the king of the West Saxons, and seeks his instructions upon how to deal with the latter who has failed to comply with Berhtwald's requirement to divide the West Saxon see. He ends with a declaration of obedience which can only be described as grovelling: 'I choose what you may choose, refuse what you may refuse, and hold the same view as you in all things.'[107]

The implications of Berhtwald's claims to obedience are illustrated by his attempt, a little before the penning of this letter, to resolve the increasingly anomalous position of Wilfrid, who, once again deposed, had been an exile in Mercia for some ten years. According to Stephen's (admittedly partisan) account, at the instance of King Aldfrith (686–705) Berhtwald set up a council in Northumbria to degrade Wilfrid from his episcopal rank and take control of his remaining possessions. He demanded that Wilfrid submit not to the authority of the synod as a whole (whose bishops in the event appear to have been unreliable) but to his judgement as archbishop alone. Wilfrid, made of sterner stuff than Wealdhere, pronounced himself prepared to submit to the archbishop's decrees only if they were in accordance with the earlier papal judgements. Stephen relates that Aldfrith was prepared to use force but that at the instance of his fellow bishops Wilfrid was allowed to return to Mercia. Wilfrid's insistence on appealing once again to Rome issued in excommunication, presumably promulgated by the English Church's quasi-patriarchal ruler.[108] Interestingly, the entire contentious episode is not mentioned by Bede.

At Rome, Wilfrid based himself upon the judgements of Pope Agatho and the uncanonical nature of the demand to submit himself to the archbishop's sole judgement.[109] Berhtwald's envoys in turn accused him of contumaciously defying the archbishop's authority, as confirmed by the Holy See. But whatever ambitions he may once have entertained, the ageing bishop was now primarily concerned to retain his privileged control over his two great monasteries. He acquiesced in the papal judgement that Archbishop Bertwald should convene a synod to determine the matter and that if that failed the case should be referred to Rome. Berhtwald, clearly unwilling to have a further appeal from his authority, sought reconciliation, a process facilitated by the death of the implacable Aldfrith in 705. Wilfrid

---

107 *elego quae elegeris, renuo quae renueris, et idipsum in omnibus tecum sapiam:* Haddan and Stubbs, *Councils*, III, pp. 274–5 (trans. Brooks).
108 *Vita Wilfridi*, cc. 45–9.
109 *Vita Wilfridi*, c. 53: *ipsius solummodo archiepiscopi iudicium consentire.*

was allowed his episcopal rank and restored to Ripon and Hexham. Four years later he was dead.[110]

Bede and the northern archbishopric

Theodore had created a new model of episcopal power, unique in the West in its melding of metropolitan authority, archiepiscopal status and papal delegation confirmed by the pallium. He bequeathed this to his successors. In England, however, such power could not in the long run be sustained in its full plentitude, dependent as it was upon special political and eccle-siastical circumstances and the personal standing of Theodore himself, a forceful outsider. In the early eighth century Wilfrid's dream of a northern archbishopric was to be partly realized, albeit in a reduced form. The Gregorian plan had relevance once more.

Bede's later writings, especially the *Historia Ecclesiastica*, illustrate the development of new sentiments. Like Stephen, he habitually styles the early occupants of the see of Canterbury archbishop.[111] There is probably nothing disingenuous in this. Augustine's epitaph, quoted in the *History*, indicates that at the time of its composition that was the tradition of Canterbury itself.[112] So by the early eighth century Gregory's grant of the pallium and of metropolitan authority to Augustine had been interpreted in terms of the quasi-patriarchal role assumed by the see of Canterbury under Theo-dore and his successors. This anachronism had its attractions for both Stephen and Bede. For Stephen, it justified Theodore's crucial interven-tion in 664, otherwise improper if York was, as the Wilfridians contended, a metropolitan see.[113] For Bede, it emphasized the Roman Church's author-ity over the British and ultimately the Irish hierarchies. At the ill-fated council held at Bangor Iscoyd between the British bishops and Augustine, one of the main issues was that the British should accept the latter as arch-bishop.[114] Indeed Bede even expressly styles Augustine as archbishop of Britain. Significantly this unique designation occurs immediately after his account of that episode and in the context of the new sees of London and Rochester.[115] The assumption that archiepiscopal status was inherent in the

110 *Vita Wilfridi*, cc. 50–66.
111 E.g. *HE*, II, cc. 2, 3, 4, 6, 7, 8, 9, 18; III, cc. 20, 28, 29; IV, c. 1.
112 *HE* II, c. 3. Rome apparently held the same the view in the time of Sergius (867–70): Haddan and Stubbs, *Councils*, III, p. 231.
113 Charles-Edwards, *Early Christian Ireland*, pp. 429–30.
114 *HE* II, c. 2.
115 *HE* II, c. 3.

Gregorian plan had implications for York as well as for Canterbury. Bede carefully includes Pope Honorius's letters of the 630s granting the pallium to both metropolitans (Honorius and Paulinus) and requiring that the survivor should consecrate the other's successor. Indeed he expressly ascribes Paulinus's consecration of Honorius to the fact that he was of the same rank.[116] The implications are clear, although curiously Bede never actually styles Paulinus archbishop.

What then did Bede, a patriotic Northumbrian and a firm believer in the apostolic authority of Gregory the Great, make of Theodore's subversion of the Gregorian plan for two metropolitans? The plain fact is he passed over it without comment, with the simple statement that 'he was the first of the archbishops whom the whole English Church consented to obey.' Bede clearly approved of Theodore.[117] His were happy and fortunate times; he introduced new learning; he travelled everywhere to set up bishops in 'suitable places'. He was in fact a model exponent of the programme of Church reform which we know that Bede had in mind throughout his later years and increasingly during the period that he was writing the *History*.[118] Indeed, Bede seems to have regarded the kind of quasi-patriarchal authority which he epitomized as essential for the promotion of this work. In his late commentary on Ezra, for example, the prophet's reforming role is incapsulated in the appellation *pontifex*, a rank expressly equated with that of archbishop and clearly crucial to Bede's notion of reform.[119] That appellation is expressly applied to Theodore at the reforming council of Hertford. There Bede depicts him charging the assembled bishops to observe all that is conducive to the unity and peace of the Church, 'as becomes an archbishop'.[120]

---

116 *HE* II, cc. 17, 18.
117 Yet he restricts himself to quoting only 8 of the 34 lines of Theodore's epitaph, whereas in Wilfrid's case he quotes all 20 and in Caedwall's all 24. Did it make claims likely to conflict with the creation of a northern archbishop and metropolitan? *HE* V, cc. 7, 8, 19.
118 A. T. Thacker, 'Bede's ideal of reform', in P. Wormald (ed.), *Ideal and Reality in Frankish and Anglo-Saxon Society* (Oxford, 1983), pp. 130–53; S. DeGregorio, '*Nostrorum socordiam temporum*: the reforming impulse of Bede's later exegesis', *EME* 11 (2002), pp. 107–22; *idem*, 'Bede's *In Ezram and Neemiam* and the reform of the Northumbrian church', *Speculum* 79 (2004), pp. 1–25.
119 Bede, *In Ezra et Neemiam*, ed. D. Hurst, *CCSL* CXIX A, II, p. 327 (line 1587). On this see S. DeGregorio, esp his translation, Bede, *On Ezra and Nehemiah* (Translated Texts for Historians, Liverpool, 2006), pp. xxxiii–xxxvi, 113; *idem*, 'Bede's *In Ezram et Neemiam*', esp. pp. 18–20.
120 *eo quo pontificem decebat*: *HE* IV, c. 5.

By the early eighth century the circumstances which made Theodore's dominant role possible were changing. The Northumbrian-Kentish axis which had provided its main secular backing had been weakened by the rising power of Mercia, by 731 overlord of all the kingdoms south of the Humber. The Northumbrian dynasty which had been a prime mover in the alliance with Kent had been extinguished by 729, perhaps as early as 716, and the last of the fully independent Kentish kings, Wihtred, died in 725. As Mercian power increased, Northumbria withdrew from intervention in the south. A final turning point, rendering the creation of a Northern archbishopric especially urgent, may have been the appointment of a Mercian, Tatwine, to the see of Canterbury in 731.[121]

Bede's *History* makes it clear that by 731 the revival of the Gregorian plan or something like it was on its author's mind, especially as he wrote the later chapters. Clearly, Bede did not admire Berhtwald. He describes him as learned in the scriptures and ecclesiastical discipline, but in no way to be compared with Theodore.[122] His death in 731 is recorded without comment, and his tomb-epitaph is not included, although it was certainly known in eighth-century Worcester.[123] Berhtwald is described simply as archbishop, never as archbishop of Britain, although we know from other sources he used the title and was regarded as such in Rome.[124] Even more significantly, in a concluding chapter of the *History*, Bede described Berhtwald's successor the Mercian Tatwine (731–4) merely as presiding with his suffragan, Ealdwulf, bishop of Rochester, over the churches of Kent. The archbishop and the twelve sees[125] of the southern province are listed separately from the four bishops of Northumbria in what looks like a deliberate evocation of the Gregorian scheme.[126]

The year 731 was climactic. Not only did Tatwine succeed Berhtwald as archbishop of Canterbury, but there was turmoil in Northumbria, where King Ceolwulf was temporarily deposed and Bede's diocesan Acca permanently excluded from his see; shortly afterward, Wilfrid II was replaced at York by Ecgberht, Ceolwulf's cousin and the brother of his ultimate successor.[127] It must be significant that Bede chose to end the

---

121 Except to note that Cf. *HE* V, c. 23.
122 *HE* V, c. 8: *vir et ipse scientia scripturarum inbutus, sed et ecclesiasticis simul ac monasterialibus disciplinis summe instructus, tametsi prodecessori suo minime comparandus.*
123 *HE* V, c. 23; M. Lapidge, *Anglo-Latin Literature* (London, 1996), pp. 369–70.
124 E.g. *Vita Wilfridi*, c. 60; *Liber Pontificalis*, I, p. 376. Cf. Brooks, *Early History*, pp. 78, 79–80, 343.
125 The insertion of the bishopric of Wight looks like a deliberate attempt to reach the Gregorian number.
126 *HE* V, c. 23.
127 *HE*, 'Continuations', p. 572.

Historia at this point. In the aftermath of this crucial period, it becomes clear that the plan to establish a Northumbrian archbishopric was in place. Bede's letter to Ecgberht, written in 734, is incontrovertible evidence that he was then being groomed for archiepiscopal power. Indeed, Bede expressly predicts that Ecgberht would easily secure metropolitan status and the pallium from the Holy See, provided he ordained new bishops in accordance with the Gregorian plan. The new Ezra was, like the original, to have a secular helper in reform. King Ceolwulf was to be Ecgberht's Nehemiah, and the creation of new sees was to be by archiepiscopal and royal decree.[128]

In his late writings, then, the question of the Northumbrian archbishopric was never far from Bede's mind. The new archbishop, with his authority to convoke councils, create new sees and discipline bishops, was to be the key player in his plans to reform the Northumbrian Church. Whether Bede knew that the crucial title and the concomitant enhancement of power, which he traced back to Augustine of Canterbury, was in fact the achievement of Theodore cannot now be determined. What is clear is that he lost no opportunity in his narrative to enhance archiepiscopal authority and to link it with the creation of new sees and with the achievement of reform. Wilfrid, with his conservative Gallic notions of the scope of metropolitan and episcopal power, forced Bede to present Theodore's single archbishopric as inevitable and necessary. By the 720s, however, it was redundant. What was needed by then was the appropriation of the authority which Theodore had shaped so crucially over England as a whole for local deployment in the service of the Northumbrian Church.

Conclusions

By the early eighth century the new understanding of the role of archbishops was deeply embedded among the English. It not only coloured their understanding of Canterbury's past, it affected their view of neighbouring hierarchies. For Stephen of Ripon, Wilfrid's first Gallic patron was archbishop of Lyon;[129] for Bede, the pastor of Arles was an archbishop,[130]

---

128 *pontificali simul et regali edicto: Epistola Ecgberhti*, ed. C. Plummer, *Baedae Opera Historica*, 2 vols. (Oxford, 1896), I, pp. 405–23, para 9, 10. Cf. *HE*, 'Continuations', p. 572.

129 *Vita Wilfridi*, cc. 4, 6.

130 Note that the Gregorian *Libellus* for which Bede is the only source refers (*HE* I, c. 27, resp. 7) only to the bishop of Arles.

while the consecrator of Berhtwald was metropolitan not of Lyon but of all Gaul.[131] In many ways England and Francia stood at twin poles in the development of episcopacy in the seventh-century Latin West. In conservative Gaul, the core figure remained the individual bishop. By the later seventh century there was little by way of superior jurisdiction and there were certainly no archbishops.[132] The contrast with England where for most of that period there had been one supremely powerful archbishop, beyond whose authority there lay only appeal to the pope himself, could scarcely have been greater.

As Levison pointed out, the English model was taken across the Channel by English missionaries to Frisia and Germany. In Frisia, Willibrord,[133] as Bede expressly noted, was consecrated 'archbishop of the Frisian people' by Pope Sergius at Pippin II's request.[134] Alcuin relates that he was consecrated archbishop and invested with the pallium by the pope.[135] Willibrord, however, failed to develop a Frisian province. The archiepiscopal title and the special jurisdiction which it implied died with him. His near contemporary Wynfrith (Boniface) was more successful.[136] From the start Boniface established close links with Rome. Consecrated bishop in 722, he received the pallium and with it the title archbishop of the new province of Germany in 732, just in fact as Northumbria was preparing to revive the archbishopric of York.[137] Clearly, by the time of Pope Gregory III (731–41), the papacy had adopted the English model as the norm for missionary activity in western Europe. From 739 Boniface acquired suffragan bishops, including Willibrord's successor in Frisia, and finally in the 740s his own see, eventually established at Mainz.[138] By then archbishops had been introduced into the Frankish Church at Rheims, Sens, and Rouen, although after some confusion only one, Rouen, received the pallium.[139]

131 *HE* I, cc. 24, 27; IV, c. 1.
132 See his statement in 742 that the Franks had not held a synod for more than 80 years nor had had an archbishop: Boniface, *Epistulae*, no. 50, p. 82.
133 W. Levison, *England and the Continent* (Oxford, 1946), pp. 53–69; Wallace-Hadrill, *Frankish Church*, pp. 144–7.
134 *HE* V, c. 11.
135 Alcuin, *Vita S. Willibrordi*, ed. W. Levison, *MGH SRM* VII (Hanover, 1920), c. 7, p. 122. Cf. *Liber Pontificalis* I, p. 376.
136 Levison, *England and the Continent*, pp. 70–93; Wallace-Hadrill, *Frankish Church*, pp. 150–61.
137 Boniface, *Epistulae*, no. 28, p. 49: *hinc iure tibi sacri pallei direximus munus, quod beati Petri apostoli auctoritate suscipiens induaris atque inter archiepiscopos unus Deo auctore precipimus censearis* Cf. nos. 46, 59, pp. 74, 109.
138 *Ibid.*, nos. 80, 88, pp. 180, 201–2.
139 *Ibid.*, no. 58, p. 106.

Janet Nelson has reflected often on the potent and diverse interaction between England and the Continent in the early Middle Ages. Her message is that this was not a simple matter of exchange but that each side took what was useful. Archiepiscopal authority, which had developed in a highly exceptional way in seventh-century England, was adopted in Frankia in that singular form because it suited the Frankish rulers in their desire to control and reform their Church. Probably neither side understood the origins of that authority even though it was to be the means by which changes of great importance were effected.

4

Forgetting and remembering Dagobert II:
the English connection

Paul Fouracre

D AGOBERT II WAS a Merovingian king who ruled for about four years in Austrasia, the Frankish kingdom which included north-eastern France, Belgium and the Rhineland. His reign probably began in late 675 or early 676. Very little is known about him, but he has been the subject of attention on two counts. First, as a child he was prevented from succeeding his father as king. He was exiled to Ireland by an ancestor of the Carolingians, one Grimoald, who placed his own son on the throne. But then Grimoald was attacked and executed for this crime. About twenty years after his disappearance, Dagobert apparently returned to Francia and ruled briefly in Austrasia, as we have just seen. Modern historians, concerned with the rise of the Carolingians to European dominance, have been interested in what looks like their premature bid for power in deposing Dagobert. The so-called 'Grimoald coup' has an impressive bibliography, much stimulated by the great Bruno Krusch's conviction that Dagobert ruled twice – i.e., that he had a short reign before Grimoald drove him out. Disproving Krusch has been a set piece of scholarship in the field of Merovingian history, for it is an exercise that tests the ability to get chronology and sense out of what are fragmentary and laconic sources.[1]

The second reason for interest in Dagobert II is that he became the focus of a martyr cult. A very low-key cult, to be sure, for as we shall find, its adherents had basically no idea of who he was. But it was a cult that survived long enough to be somewhat revived after seventeenth-century scholars believed that they had discovered the identity of the saint, and were able to give the cult a historical basis. The survival of the cult encouraged Baigent, Leigh and Lincoln to imagine that there was some kind of memory of Dagobert's special qualities, and they made him an important link figure

---

1 For the most recent contribution, with bibliography, M. Becher, 'Der sogenannte Staatsstreich Grimoalds: Versuch einer Neubewertung', in J. Jarnut, U. Nonn and M. Richter (eds), *Karl Martell in seiner Zeit*, Beihefte der *Francia* (Sigmaringen, 1994), pp. 119–47.

in their controversial work *The Holy Blood and the Holy Grail*, published in 1982. Here they claimed that Dagobert was a descendant of Christ, and that he passed on the holy blood through a son, Sigisbert, whose descendants still carry it.[2] This fantastical hypothesis became the basis of a highly successful novel, Dan Brown's *The Da Vinci Code*,[3] and together these works have done more than all the efforts of modern historians combined to bring the Merovingians, and Dagobert II in particular, to the popular imagination. Their picture of Dagobert relied on a text known as the *Vita Dagoberti*, edited by Krusch in the *MGH, SRM*.[4] It takes only a glance, however, to see that this 'Life' actually has nothing to do with Dagobert II. Ironically, in purporting to uncover a historical memory, Baigent, Leigh and Lincoln in fact start with a plainly fabricated account. It is nevertheless valuable to see how the account was made up. It is also instructive to see how the picture of a little-documented figure like Dagobert can change dramatically with the addition, or loss, of just a little information.

The *Vita Dagoberti* is a text composed sometime between the end of the ninth century and the later eleventh century in which a commissioned author tried to construct a 'Life' of someone called 'Dagobert' by drawing on some well known – i.e., frequently copied – works of the Merovingian and Carolingian periods.[5] The selection and interpretation of these texts is very revealing of what an author could find out when set the task of researching the life of a distant figure, and of what sense he or she could make of earlier times. The author was writing at what Patrick Geary has characterized as a 'time of oblivion' in which distant traditions, or institutionalized memories, no longer made sense.[6] It will be the thrust of this essay that whenever only meagre information was available (which was often the case in the early Middle Ages), it was impossible to make sense of the past, that is, to take a prosaic approach to Geary's sense of oblivion

2 M. Baigent, R. Leigh, H. Lincoln, *The Holy Blood and the Holy Grail*, rev. edn (London, 1996 [1982]), pp. 257–71, 328–9.

3 D. Brown, *The Da Vinci Code* (London, 2003). In February 2006 Brown was sued by Baigent and Leigh for plagiarism but the case was unsuccessful. In a review of the *Holy Blood and Holy Grail* the novelist Anthony Burgess had remarked 'It is typical of my unregenerable soul that I can only see this as a marvellous theme for a novel'.

4 *Vita Dagoberti III Regis Francorum*, ed. B. Krusch, *MGH SRM* II (Hanover, 1888), pp. 511–24. It was Krusch who added the ordinal 'III' to the title on circumstantial grounds.

5 It is because there is so little verifiable historical detail in the work that it so difficult to date. See C. Carozzi, 'La Vie de Saint Dagobert de Stenay: histoire et hagiographie', *Revue Belge de Philologie et d'Histoire* 62 (1984), pp. 225–58, at p. 225.

6 P. Geary, *Phantoms of Remembrance: Memory and Oblivion at the End of the First Millennium* (Princeton, 1994). See for instance the 'Conclusions', pp. 177–81.

and also to generalize it. In this case it can be demonstrated that without access to one key text, Stephen of Ripon's *Life of St Wilfrid*, it is scarcely possible to know that Dagobert II ruled in the later seventh century, and that he died violently.[7] Hence the need to fabricate, for the *Life of Wilfrid* was not known on the Continent before the seventeenth century. Although Bede in his *Ecclesiastical History*, a work that was of course well known on the Continent, did give a précis of Bishop Wilfrid's career that seems to have been based on Stephen's *Life*, he left out the section that mentioned Dagobert.[8] So it was not so much that Dagobert II had been forgotten as that no one had ever heard of him. Let us first review what we know of Dagobert and next examine the *Vita Dagoberti*. We will then look at how Dagobert II was rediscovered via the *Life of Wilfrid* in the seventeenth century, and was subsequently re-inscribed in the history of the period. This will lead us to an evaluation of the *Life of Wilfred* as a source, to reflections on the significance of Wilfrid himself, and finally to further thoughts on the relationship between memory and tradition.

We know of four Merovingian Dagoberts. Dagobert I. d. 638 is the best known. He has a coinage, figured in chronicles, charters and Saints Lives and there is also a ninth-century *Gesta Dagoberti*.[9] Dagobert I is the best remembered Merovingian king after Clovis. Dagobert III, who ruled from 711 to 716 is also known through narrative sources and charters, and the *Vita Dagoberti* is loosely about him, rather than about Dagobert II. There was an infant Dagobert whom the *Vita Lantberti Fontanellensis*, which is a fairly well informed text of the mid-eighth century, tells us was the son of King Childeric II and Queen Bilichild.[10] All three were murdered in 675, and a later version of the 'Life' of Audoin of Rouen says that they were buried in Rouen, as, it claims, Dagobert II had been too.[11] Finally we have

---

7 Stephen of Ripon, *The Life of Bishop Wilfrid by Eddius Stephanus*, ed. and trans. B. Colgrave (Cambridge, 1927, reprinted New York, 1985).

8 Bede's précis comes in *HE* V, c. 19. He does not refer to Francia at all in his account of Wilfrid's second journey to Rome.

9 *Gesta Dagoberti I Regis Francorum*, ed. B. Krusch, *MGH SRM* II (Hanover, 1888), pp. 399–425.

10 *Vita Lantberti abbatis Fontanellensis et episcopi Lugdunensis*, ed. W. Levison, *MGH SRM* V (Hanover, 1910), pp. 608–12. Most of this work has been lost and the reference to the infant Dagobert comes in chapter 5 just as the manuscript breaks off.

11 *Vita Audoini episcopi Rotomagensis*, ed. W. Levison, *MGH SRM* V, pp. 563–7, *Alter biographus* c. 41, quoted at p. 565, n. 6. This tells us that in St Peter's Rouen were buried the two wives of King Clothar II, Dagobert 'whom Grimoald tonsured', Childeric, Bilichild and their son. The text does not name the infant as the *Vita Lantberti* does, but otherwise draws on the latter's text at the point just before it breaks off. It seems likely that the author saw the name 'Dagobert' and assumed that this must have been Dagobert II, hence the omission of the name for the infant.

the latter, Dagobert II, identifiable in four other texts. Medieval and modern people have been prone to getting their Dagoberts mixed up, especially as both at the time of Dagobert II's exile and during Dagobert III's reign there were 'mayors of the palace' – prime-ministerial figures – called by the same name: Grimoald. This is where Krusch went wrong in mixing up his Dagoberts and Grimoalds.

It is from the *Liber Historiae Francorum*, a Neustrian chronicle completed by the year 727, that we learn of Dagobert II's birth and exile, the latter being the consequence of the 'Grimoald-coup' which we mentioned earlier.[12] It tells of how Dagobert II was the son of Sigibert king of Austrasia, himself the son of Dagobert I. Sigibert ruled in Austrasia from 632 to 656. When Sigibert died in 656, the 'mayor of the palace' Grimoald tonsured the young Dagobert, giving him over to Dido bishop of Poitiers who had him conducted to Ireland. Grimoald then placed his own son on the throne of Austrasia. But the Neustrians, that is, the Franks of what is now north-west France, rose up against Grimoald and took him to Paris where was executed 'because he had acted against his lord'. We hear no more about Dagobert from this source. Meanwhile, since the Merovingian line in Austrasia had disappeared, the Neustrian branch of the dynasty ruled in Austrasia too, the first of these kings being Childeric II who was sent to Austrasia in 662 after Grimoald's demise. Childeric, as we have just seen, was assassinated along with wife and infant in 675. He was eventually replaced by his younger brother, Theuderic III. Between the rule of these two brothers in Austrasia there was the brief reign of Dagobert II. We can detect it in only one Merovingian source, the *Vita Sadalbergae*, which as Hans Hummer has recently demonstrated, is very probably a seventh-century work.[13] It merely says that Sadalberga moved her convent from northern Burgundy to Laon following 'recent fighting between Kings Dagobert and Theuderic'.[14] We cannot find any other pairing of a Dagobert

12   *Liber Historiae Francorum*, ed. B. Krusch, *MGH SRM* II (Hanover, 1888), pp. 238–328. Chapters 43–53 are translated with commentary in P. Fouracre and R. Gerberding, *Late Merovingian France: History and Hagiography* (Manchester, 1996), pp. 79–96. It is c. 43 that concerns Dagobert II and this is the only narrative of his exile. The work is seminal for all subsequent histories of the later Merovingian period. On its composition and interpretation, see R. Gerberding, *The Rise of the Carolingians and the* Liber Historiae Francorum (Oxford, 1987).

13   *Vita Sadalbergae abbatissae Laudunensi*, ed. B. Krusch, *MGH SRM* V, pp. 49–66; H. Hummer, 'Die merowingische Herkunft der Vita Sadalbergae', *DA* 59 (2003), pp. 459–93.

14   *Vita Sadalbergae*, c. 13, p. 57.

and a Theuderic, so this must be a reference to Theuderic III and Dagobert II. A second, but more problematic, reference is from Paul the Deacon's *Historia Langobardorum*, composed in the later eighth century. Following on from the mention of a comet that we know appeared in 676, Paul says that 'at that time' Dagobert was ruling the kingdom of the Franks or Gauls and with him King Grimoald drew up a *foedus . . . pacis firmissimae*.[15] One is naturally suspicious of the Dagobert/Grimoald pairing, and since King Grimoald of the Lombards died in 671, whereas Dagobert returned to Francia only after the death of Childeric in 675, and the comet appeared in 676, if there was a peace treaty it must have been one made between Grimoald's successor Pectarit and Dagobert. It therefore looks as if Paul the Deacon knew of Dagobert II's rule, but may have got his Lombard kings mixed up. So, the one source that tells us that Dagobert II was exiled to Ireland seems not to have noticed (or chose not to disclose) that he ever returned, and the two sources which may refer to him after his return show no signs of being aware that he had ever been away.

It is the *Life of Wilfrid* alone which allows us to make some sense of all this. The *Life of Wilfrid* was written shortly after Wilfrid's death in 709, and being composed by Eddius Stephanus/Stephen of Ripon who knew his subject personally, it is regarded a source of great historical value. Stephen relates how in 679 when Wilfrid was travelling on the Continent on his way Rome he met and stayed with Dagobert 'king of the Franks'. Dagobert was very grateful to Wilfrid because it was Wilfrid who had facilitated his return to Francia from Ireland. Having been exiled to Ireland 'in his youth', Dagobert's friends and relatives hearing that he was still alive, asked Wilfrid to get him to come from Ireland to England, and from there to send him to Francia. This Wilfrid did in style, providing Dagobert with arms and companions. Now Dagobert offered Wilfrid Strasbourg, the 'chief bishopric of his realm'.[16] Wilfrid declined and continued on his way to Rome, next staying with King Pectarit in Campania. Interestingly, the theme of exile and return is again voiced through Pectarit, who tells Wilfrid that as a youth he had had to seek refuge with the king of the Huns. The story of Pectarit's refuge with the Huns – i.e., the Avars – does in fact figure in Paul the Deacon's *Historia Langobardorum*, and this offers a rare confirmation of information Stephen provides in relation to Wilfrid on the Conti-

---

15 Paul the Deacon, *Historia Langobardorum*, ed. L. Bethman and G. Waitz, MGH SRL (Hanover, 1878), pp. 7–242, V, c. 32, pp. 197–8.
16 *Life of Wilfrid*, c. 28, pp. 55–7.

nent.[17] In 680, after attending a Council in Rome, Wilfrid returned to Francia, only to find that Dagobert had recently been assassinated by some 'treacherous dukes' with, even worse, the consent of the bishops. People were angry with Wilfrid because he had brought Dagobert back, and Dagobert had turned out to be a rotten king, or, in the eyes of modern historians (who prefer their Merovingians to be active) an effective king.[18] He had laid waste cities, spurned advice, imposed tribute on the people and despised the Church of God. Stephen has Wilfrid reply that he had only been doing his duty in sending Dagobert back, and could not have predicted how things would turn out.[19] Given that the *Life of Wilfrid* and the *Liber Historiae Francorum* are independent of each other, each confirms the other's account of the exile, and the *Life of Wifrid* confirms the evidence of the *Vita Sadalbergae* and the *Historia Langobardorum* that Dagobert II was indeed ruling in Francia, – i.e., in Austrasia – in the later 670s.

It is only the *Life of Wilfrid* that says that Dagobert II died violently, but a King Dagobert was being venerated as a martyr in the Ardennes region by the end of the ninth century.[20] According to the *Vita Dagoberti*, this Dagobert was buried in the church of St Remigius at Stenay in the Ardennes. King Charles the Bald came and translated his relics to a newly built basilica which was dedicated to Dagobert as martyr and staffed with canons.[21] A charter in the cartulary of the monastery of Gorze says that this happened in the year 872.[22] That the cult was in existence by the late tenth century and thus probably before the *Vita Dagoberti* was written is confirmed by an

---

17 *Historia Langobardorum* V, c. 2, p. 180. There is, however, a significant difference between the two accounts. In the *Life of Wilfrid* it was said the 'king of the Huns' was offered a barrel full of gold to betray Pectarit but refused. The story is the second of two concerned with the theme of attempted bribery by Christian ruler and honourable refusal by pagan chief. In chapter 27, pp. 53–5, the 'mayor of the palace' Ebroin similarly offered Adalgsil 'king of the Frisians' a barrel full of gold to deliver up or kill Wilfrid. In the *Historia Langobardorum* the *caganus* (i.e., khan) of the Avars was threatened with war by King Grimoald if he continued to harbour Pectarit, who was then in effect asked to leave.

18 For a positive view of Dagobert II, based on an optimisitic reading of every possible reference to him including the *Vita Dagoberti*, J. Semmler, 'Spätmerowingischer Herrscher: Theuderich III und Dagobert II', *DA* 55 (1999), pp. 1–28, esp. pp. 19–28.

19 *Life of Wilfrid*, c. 33, pp. 68–9.

20 For an account of how the cult developed, R. Folz, 'Tradition hagiographicque et culte de Saint Dagobert, roi des Francs', *Le Moyen Age* 69 (1963), pp. 17–35.

21 *Vita Dagoberti*, c. 14, pp. 520–1.

22 *Vita Dagoberti*, p. 521, n. 1.

entry in the now lost Calendar of Queen Emma, wife of Lothar IV which refers to a St Dagobert king and martyr whose festival was 23 December.[23] The martyrology of Usuard for Belgium, also gives 23 December as the festival of a *Dagoberti Regis Francorum*, as does the *Vita Dagoberti*, although a Brussels addition to Usuard gives the day as 11 September.[24] One might surmise that Stenay was indeed the burial place of Dagobert II, as it lay by the Meuse at the heart of his kingdom. It must have been known that a King Dagobert who died violently was buried there, but the cult was effectively brought to life by Charles the Bald's decision to dedicate and endow the basilica.[25] What he seems to have been doing here was stressing the ancient and venerable nature of Frankish kingship that the name Dagobert evoked, and his patronage of the cult also provided an entrée into the newly acquired region of western Lotharingia.

In 1069, Godfrey the Bearded, duke of Lorraine, donated the *basilica Sancti Dagoberti* to the monastery of Gorze and it became a Benedictine priory. The canons were said to have grown lax and were replaced by monks.[26] The prologue to the *Vita Dagoberti* tells us that the author composed the work for the brothers of Stenay to have something to read on 23 December. They said that they wanted to know more about their patron saint because nothing was known of his glorious martyrdom, and the memory of him was slipping away from the living.[27] The work survives in just two manuscripts, one twelfth-, the other thirteenth-century. The earlier manuscript contains only the *Vita Dagoberti*. On folio two a later hand has added *scripta a monacho Satanaco* (i.e., Stenay). It would therefore seem reasonable to date the 'Life' to a time after Gorze's acquisition of Stenay.

23　Folz, 'Tradition hagiographique', p. 19.
24　*Martyrologium Usuardi*, ed. J. de Sollier, *Acta Sanctorum* June VI and VII (Antwerp, 1715). Usuard's entry for 23 December does not mention Dagobert, but reads *Basilicae in honore Sanctae Crucis et Vincentii martyris et depositio domni Childeberti Regis*. J. Dubois, *Le Martyrologe d'Usuard: Texte et Commentaire* (Brussels, 1965), p. 364 comments that Usuard closed his work with the Holy Cross, Vincent and Childebert in honour of his own abbey of St Germain des Prés of which Childebert I (d. 23 December 558) was the founder. The *auctaria* (local additions from the tenth century onward) add *eodem die, Sancti Dagoberti regis Francorum*: de Sollier, p. 760, and for the 11 September variant, p. 528.
25　On the endowment, which was transferred to the monks of Gorze in 1069, *Cartulaire de l'Abbaye de Gorze*, ed. A. D'Hebomez (Paris, 1898), no. 148, pp. 258–61, a charter of 1124. The property had passed into the hands of Beatrice, wife of Godfrey the Bearded, duke of Lorraine.
26　*Vita Dagoberti*, p. 509.
27　*Vita Dagoberti*, p. 512: his deeds *a memoria viventium modo hominum penitus recesserunt.*

Claude Carozzi, who originally agreed with an eleventh-century date, has, however, set out a well-worked hypothesis that it was in fact composed in the time, and at the behest, of Fulk, archbishop of Rheims (d. 900). This is on the basis of the work's concern with the monastery of St Wandrille and the possible influence of works produced in the monastery of St Bertin, of which Fulk had been abbot.[28] The hypothesis is that the *Vita* served as a kind of manifesto for the establishment of Charles the Simple, crowned at Reims in 893, the backing of Stenay serving also as political route into the Meuse area, just as it had done for Charles the Bald. According to this reading, the *Vita Dagoberti* is a delicately crafted work that responded to political conditions in the 890s. For all this there is no clear evidence, and if this was Fulk's *testament politique*, as Carozzi puts, it was a very vague one. One could, in fact, accept Carozzi's reading and the point would remain: the author of the *Vita Dagoberti* clearly had no knowledge of Dagobert II. He used the *Gesta Dagoberti* of Dagobert I and so must have known that this king was buried at St Denis, not Stenay. So to his eyes the only Dagobert who could have been buried at Stenay was the person known to us as Dagobert III, attested as ruling 711–716. Our author therefore made an attempt to turn this king into a martyr. Let us now see what he did.

He took his cue from the *Liber Historiae Francorum*, and drew also on the *First Continuation of the Chronicle of Fredegar*,[29] the *Gesta* of the abbey of St Wandrille,[30] the *Gesta Dagoberti* and Paul the Deacon's *Historia Langobardorum*. In addition Krusch identified use of Einhard's *Life of Charlemagne*,[31] the *Annales Mettenses Priores*,[32] Alcuin's *Vita Willibrordi*[33] and Willibald's *Vita Bonifatii*.[34] In these cases, however, identification is based on probable sources of information rather that demonstrable textual borrowing. The author was, to put it mildly, cavalier with his material. He began with Dagobert's ancestry, concentrating on his father Childebert III who ruled 694–711, and built on the *Liber Historiae Francorum*'s very favourable but

28 Carozzi, 'La Vie de Saint Dagobert'.
29 *The Fourth Book of Fredegar and its Continuations*, ed. and trans. J. M. Wallace-Hadrill (London, 1960).
30 *Gesta Sanctorum Patrum Fontanellensis Ceonobii*, ed. and French trans., P. Pradié, *Chronique des Abbés de Fontenelle* (Paris, 1999).
31 Einhard, *Life of Charlemagne*, trans. P. Dutton, *Charlemagne's Courtier: The Complete Einhard* (Ontario, 1999), pp. 15–39.
32 *Annales Mettenses Priores*, ed. B. von Simson, *MGH SRG* (Hanover and Leipzig, 1905), first section trans. with commentary, Fouracre and Gerberding, pp. 330–70.
33 Alcuin, *Vita Willibrordi Archiepiscopi Traeiectensis*, ed. W. Levison, *MGH SRM* VII (Hanover and Leipzig, 1920), pp. 113–41.
34 Willibald, *Vita Bonifatii*, ed. W. Levison, *MGH SRG* (Hanover, 1905).

brief remarks about this king, making him *fortissimus,* a builder of churches who enjoyed innumerable triumphs.[35] But he then ignored his source when it said that after ruling for a few years his son Dagobert 'took ill and died'.[36] Dagobert, he claimed, was brought up by his 'grandmother' Balthild in the monastery of Chelles. Balthild was in fact his great-grandmother and had died long before he was born. Chosen king for his illustrious lineage, piety, vigour, wisdom and beauty, he was crowned king at Reims (a detail that betrays the later origin of this work). A long section extols his peace-making abilities,[37] and this could have been inspired by Paul the Deacon's report of the *pax firmissima* supposedly made between Dagobert and Grimoald. The *Liber Historiae Francorum,* on the other hand, made it very clear that Dagobert III's reign was precisely the time that terrible fighting erupted amongst the Franks.[38] As king, Dagobert sowed some wheat that grew miraculously,[39] he made a grant to St Denis,[40] and decided in favour of St Wandrille and its abbot Hugo over the disputed foundation of Fleury in Vexin, taken from the monastery by the 'mayor of the palace' Childeric.[41] In reality, Hugo did not become abbot until 723. The 'mayor of the palace Childeric' must be king Childeric II, mentioned retrospectively in the section on Hugo in the St Wandrille *Gesta.*[42]

35 *Vita Dagoberti* c. 3, p. 513, building on *Liber Historiae Francorum* cc. 49, 50 which described Childebert as *vir inclytus,* and . . . *bonae memoriae . . . rex iustus.* One wonders whether the focus on Childebert was also influenced by the fact that for 23 December Usuard commemorated Childebert I, who was more certainly a Church founder. See note 22 above.

36 *Liber Historiae Francorum,* c. 52: *Dagobertus rex aegrotans mortuus est regnavit annis 5.* Apart from recording his accession, this is all that this source says about Dagobert III.

37 *Vita Dagoberti,* c. 4, pp. 514–15.

38 *Liber Historiae Francorum,* c. 51: *In illis diebus, instigante diabulo, Franci denuo Cocia silva in Francos invicem inruunt ac sese mutuo dirissima cede prosternunt.*

39 *Vita Dagoberti,* c. 5, p. 515.

40 *Vita Dagoberti,* c. 6, pp. 515–16.

41 *Vita Dagoberti* c. 8, p. 516.

42 The author seems to have been reading the *Gesta Patrum Fontanellensis* here, but made little sense of it. This is not surprising because the work tends to jump around chronologically. It tells of the grant of Fleury by Pippin in c.II.1, pp. 26–8, but returns to Pippin in c.IV.2, pp. 62–5, in tracing Hugh's ancestry, and then tells of a grant Hugh had made in the time of Dagobert III (in 713), before moving on to a grant he made as abbot, thus after 723. It then refers to a grant he made in 717, and finally to grants from a layman, all of which was confirmed by Theuderic IV 'the father of Childeric, the very last of the race of Merovingian kings'. The confusion of the author of the *Vita Dagoberti* is matched by that of Pradié, the work's most recent modern editor who mistranslates Childeric as Theuderic's father (p. 65). Carozzi, 'La Vie de Saint Dagobert', p. 250 thought that the author was not at all confused,

Next, in the company of Charles Martel, Dagobert went to Frisia in support of the missionary Willibrord. There he miraculously freed some prisoners through the agency of his *archicapellanus*, one Boniface who went on, we are told, to become archbishop of Mainz and a martyr.[43] The author drew on Paul the Deacon for an account of Dagobert's death. Paul related a strange tale of the later sixth-century King Guntramn and his out-of-body experience. Our author basically substituted Dagobert in place of Guntramn.[44] Dagobert was out hunting in the Ardennes. Separated from the rest of his companions, with just his godson in attendance, he lay down to sleep. He dreamed that he was in a meadow with a stream, across which there was a marvellous iron bridge. This he crossed and came to a beautiful building which he found was full of treasure. He then returned to the meadow, where he woke up and told his godson of the dream. The godson replied that while the king was asleep he had seen a small reptile emerge from his mouth. The reptile came to the stream but was unable to cross. So Dagobert's companion laid his sword across the stream and the reptile made its way to the opposite bank where it scurried in and out of an oak tree before returning across this iron bridge and re-entering Dagobert's mouth. After hearing this story, Dagobert went back to sleep. His godson then became deranged by the thought of all the treasure and stabbed his master with a spear. He then crossed the stream but could find no way into the oak tree. While walking round and round it in vain, he was struck down and died an agonising death.[45] In the Guntramn story, of course, the treasure was buried under a hill, the king woke up and went and got it.

It should be clear by now that our author had nothing to say about any Dagobert. Very roughly what he seems to have done in having Dagobert restore Fleury to St Wandrille, and having him visit Willibrord in Frisia, making a journey to the eastern part of his kingdom, bringing peace and in supporting the Church and caring for the weak and for orphans, was to substitute Dagobert for the figure of Pippin of Herstal who also did all of these things. It was on this basis that Krusch thought that the *Vita Dagoberti* owed much to the *Annales Mettenses Priores* which has an encomium on Pippin. The *Annales Mettenses Priores*, for its part, does mention Dagobert

---

and substituted the 'mayor of the palace' Childeric for Ebroin, a mayor with a villainous reputation, because Elibert, one of the people in Fulk's circle, had a father named Ebroin. Since the 'mayor of the palace' Ebroin does not figure in the *Gesta* at all, it seems too convoluted to speculate that the author of the *Vita Dagoberti* would have wanted to bring him in, but had to come up with another name.

43 *Vita Dagoberti*, cc. 9–10, pp. 516–18.
44 Paul the Deacon, *Historia Langobardorum* III, c. 34, pp. 138–40.
45 *Vita Dagoberti*, c. 12, pp. 518–20.

III, but in a context that showed that Pippin was the real ruler: after Childebert's death, 'Pippin in his usual faithfulness appointed his son Dagobert king'.[46] On Childebert, the *Annales* say that he was established on the throne by Pippin. 'Giving to these men the name of kings, he kept the reins of the whole realm and governed with the highest glory and honour'.[47] We read the *Annales Mettenses Priores*, completed in 805, as part of a remarkably sustained effort on behalf of the Carolingians to justify their seizure of power from the Merovingians in 751. This section of the *Annales* can be seen as contesting the favourable account of Childebert and the Neustrians presented in the *Liber Historiae Francorum*, the first step toward which had been taken in the first *Continuation of the Chronicle of Fredegar* which copied the *Liber* but cut out the praise for Childebert.[48] The image of weak Merovingians and vigorously powerful Carolingians is further articulated in the *Royal Frankish Annals*, and then it is given the flesh of historical detail in the *Annales Mettenses Priores*. The image culminates in the famous opening chapter of Einhard's *Vita Karoli* in which the Merovingians are portrayed as on the ropes, drained of energy and owning but one *villa*.[49]

Recent work has been impressed by the sheer persistence of the Carolingians in rewriting history, for they did so with a consistency that left no alternative view possible.[50] It is therefore striking to see that the author of the *Vita Dagoberti* understood or cared nothing for all this. Or, if Carozzi is right and the work is a piece of propaganda for a Carolingian king, Charles the Simple, it is even more striking that by the year 900 memories of the early Carolingians has receded to such an extent that it was possible to make free with an image of a potent late Merovingian. The *Vita* is, in other words, a decidedly post-Carolingian work. Take, for instance, the term used to describe the Merovingians, a *gens robustissima*. Theuderic, Dagobert's grandfather was *strenuissimus*. Childebert's qualities we have already mentioned. Dagobert himself was *genere clarissimus, omni bonitate mentis strenuus, corporis virtute robustus, consiliis providus, nulli pietate secundus, moribus modestus*. Is this insistence on the robust energy of the Merovingians, and the downplaying of Pippin's role a deliberate refutation of the Carolingian

---

46 Fouracre and Gerberding, p. 364.
47 Fouracre and Gerberding, p. 362.
48 P. Fouracre, 'Observations on the outgrowth of Pippinid influence in the "Regnum Francorum" after the battle of Tertry (687–715)', *Medieval Prosopography* 5 (1984), pp. 1–31.
49 P. Fouracre, 'The Long Shadow of the Merovingians', in J. Story (ed.), *Charlemagne: Empire and Society* (Manchester, 2005), pp. 5–21, here, pp. 6–9.
50 See for instance R. McKitterick, 'The illusion of royal power in the Carolingian annals', *EHR* 115 (2000), pp. 1–20.

version of history? Certainly, if we date the work late, it concerns a region in which there may have been some hostility to the Carolingians after the shenanigans of Charles of Lorraine in the dying days of the dynasty. But clear as the Carolingian viewpoint might seem to us today, it is surely likely that after the dynasty's decline their discourse of self-justification would have been very hard to comprehend. Would anyone have been moved to contest it? We have seen that our author had no trouble in making this Dagobert into a martyr whereas one source that we know he used, the *Liber Historiae Francorum*, said that he died naturally. Such disregard suggests that he was hardly likely to be troubled by the fact that some texts he was reading had an anti-Merovingian line, even if he could have recognized it as such. So what we are seeing in the apparent reversal of the Einhard picture is a hagiographer doing his job in heaping unrestrained praise on his subject. Sometimes he deliberately ignored inconvenient information, but one can argue that more often he simply did not understand the detail before his eyes.

If we believe the Prologue of the *Vita Dagoberti*, it is not surprising that the cult of St Dagobert never really took off. The monks (or, in Carozzi's scenario, the canons) at Stenay, had no idea of who their patron saint was, and if they indeed hoped to find out something by commissioning this 'Life', what they got was a few hagiographical commonplaces about the pious king, mixed with a bit of folklore, accompanied by the praise of a long-gone dynasty, praise that utilized what one might term 'cut and paste' conventions of kingly virtue. It is the generic nature of these conventions that makes it hard to see the work as a political manifesto. Perhaps more to the point, the monks got only one post-mortem miracle, and a long-winded low-key miracle at that: a woman was spinning on the day of his festival and got her hand stuck to the distaff.[51] There was clearly not a lot going on at Dagobert's shrine. By the sixteenth century the cult was nevertheless still going. Dagobert's festival was being celebrated at Verdun, and he became the patron of two other local churches. But Stenay itself was secularized in 1580 and the claustral buildings demolished. In 1591 it was sacked by the Hugenots and Dagobert's relics were dispersed, some ending up at St-Ghislain de Mons. Where the cult did spread beyond Stenay, this seems invariably to have been to places in which there was some association with Dagobert I.[52] In the seventeenth century people were still getting their Dagoberts mixed up. The Bollandist Godfrey Henschen then attempted to

---

51 *Vita Dagoberti*, c. 16, pp. 522–3.
52 Folz, 'Tradition hagiographique', pp. 30–2.

sort out the Dagobert problem in a book published in 1655 and entitled
De Tribus Dagobertis Francorum Regibus Diatriba.[53]

What set Henschen off was the discovery made ten years earlier by Adrian
de Valois that Dagobert II had returned from Ireland to Francia. This discovery came not from a reading of the *Life of Wilfrid*, but from William of
Malmesbury's early twelfth-century *Gesta Pontificum Anglorum* in which
William included excerpts from the *Life*. William copied from Stephen of
Ripon the passage on Wilfrid going to the Continent in 679 and meeting
the grateful Dagobert, and so we get the story of the exile and return. And
we also hear of how Dagobert offered Wilfrid the bishopric of Strasbourg,
the chief bishopric of his land.[54] But William did not include the section
on Wilfrid's return from Rome through Francia and his encounter with
the angry bishop who told him of Dagobert's assassination and blamed
Wilfrid for inflicting the king upon the Franks. So Henschen now, as it
were, had half the story. He still had not read the *Life of Wilfrid* and so did
not know how Dagobert had died, but he was aware of the martyr cult,
which he ascribed to Dagobert II as the only one of the three Dagoberts
not known to have met a natural end. He had read the *Vita Dagoberti*, but
while accepting that the Dagobert cult was associated with Stenay, he
rejected the *Life* as a source – one look at the *Liber Historiae Francorum* told
him that this Dagobert son of Childebert was not a martyr, and he comprehensively demolished the work in terms of its historical content.[55] In his
search for more evidence for Dagobert II as king, Henschen looked at
material from Strasbourg because William of Malmesbury had quoted
Stephen in saying that this was the chief bishopric of his land, and William
had referred to Dagobert as king of the Franks beyond the Rhine, which
would just about fit Strasbourg. Two works in particular caught his eye.
These were the *Vita Arbogasti* and the *Vita Florentii*, the lives of two bishops
of Strasbourg.[56] Although bishops lists for Strasbourg variously put Florentius in the sixth century, Arbogast in the time of Dagobert I, and both
before a bishop Ansoald who was attested as the Council of Paris which
took place in 614,[57] Henschen placed them in the time of Dagobert II. This

53 G. Henschenius, *De Tribus Dagobertis Francorum Regibus Diatriba* (Antwerp, 1655).
54 William of Malmesbury, *The Deeds of the Bishops of England (Gesta Pontificum Anglorum)*, trans. D. Preest (Woodbridge, 2002), III, c.100, p. 148.
55 Henschen, *De Tribus Dagobertis*, pp. 187–92.
56 *Vita Arbogasti*, ed. J. Pinius, *Acta Sanctorum* July V (Antwerp, 1727), pp. 177–9. This
  work was said to have been written by Utho bishop of Strasbourg 950–65, but survives only in an early printed edition; *Vita Florentii*, ed. A. Poncelet, *Acta Sanctorum*
  Nov. III (Brussels, 1910), pp. 400–2, said to have been composed in the twelfth
  century at the earliest.
57 L. Duchesne, *Fastes Episcopaux de l'Ancienne Gaule* (Paris, 1915), vol. 3, p. 171.

was because he noted that the *Vita Deodati*, another Alsatian work, eleventh-century at the earliest, said that Arbogast and Florentius were colleagues (*comites*) of Deodatus, who supposedly died in 679.[58] Seeing that Arbogast preceded Florentius in the lists of Strasbourg bishops, Henschen imagined that Arbogast was installed as bishop on Dagobert's return to Francia and that Florentius was made bishop when Wilfrid turned down Dagobert's offer of the bishopric.

Both works are built around miracles concerning the children of Dagobert. Eight out of the ten chapters of the *Vita Arbogasti* tell of how Dagobert's only son – named as Sigibert in later Alsatian tradition – fell from his horse while hunting. The boy died but Arbogast brought him back to life. The *Vita Florentii* had Florentius cure Dagobert's daughter of deafness and blindness. The thirteenth century *Annales Argentinenses* changed this to the casting out of devils and put a rough date to it: 673. This in turn influenced the *Annales Marbacenses* which had Dagobert dying in 674 and leaving two sons, Sigibert and Clovis.[59] From the latter, is clear that again the Dagoberts were getting mixed up – i.e., that the king in all these narratives was Dagobert I, for it was he who had two sons named Sigibert and Clovis. But because the *Vita Arbogasti* mentioned an only son, Henschen reasoned that the father must have been Dagobert II. He also gave a name to two daughters, Irmina of Oeren and Adela of Pfalzel, known to us through a charter and a will. They were once thought to be daughters of Dagobert I, but were almost certainly affines, or more probably relatives, of the Pippinid family.[60]

Convinced that Dagobert had a son old enough to go hunting in the early 670s, Henschen argued that Dagobert must have returned to Francia before Childeric II's assassination in 675. So why not in 662, when Childeric became king of Austrasia following the disappearance of Grimoald's son? The solution was to imagine that Dagobert ruled for some time in a trans-Rhenish subkingdom based on Strasbourg until Childeric's death in 675, at which point he became king of all Austrasia.[61] Henschen could only guess at who the mother of these children might have been – he went for a Saxon duchess. As for Dagobert's death, which, remember, had to be a violent

58 Henschen, *De Tribus Dagobertis*, pp. 76–7. *Vita Deodati*, ed. D. Paperbroch, *Acta Sanctorum* June III (Antwerp, 1701), pp. 872–4, c. 4. p. 873.

59 *Annales Argentinenses*, ed. P. Jaffé, *MGH SS* XVII (Hanover, 1861), pp. 86–90; *Annales Marbacenses*, ed. R. Wilmans, *MHG SS* XVII pp. 146–80, here p. 146.

60 M. Werner, *Adelsfamilien in Umkreis der frühen Karolinger: Die Verwandtschaft Irminas von Oeren und Adelas von Pfalzel*, Vorträge und Forschungen 28 (Sigmaringen, 1982).

61 Henschen, *De Tribus Dagobertis*, pp. 72–3.

one, he picked up on the reference in the *Vita Sadalbergae* to 'recent fighting between Theuderic and Dagobert' and imagined that Theuderic and his 'mayor of the palace' Ebroin had captured Dagobert and then executed him. Reading the later version of the *Vita Audoini* which says that a king Dagobert ('the tonsured one'), as well as Childeric, Bilichild and infant, was buried in Rouen, he believed Rouen to be the burial place of Dagobert II. How Dagobert's remains then got to Stenay left Henschen baffled.[62]

Henschen's account of Dagobert II's career stood for just over twenty years, until, finally, the great Dom Jean Mabillon read the whole of Stephen of Ripon's *Life of St Wilfrid*. He edited and printed the work in 1677.[63] Now it was clear that Dagobert had not been in Austrasia very long before Wilfrid met him in 679, so that it was likely that he returned only after the death of Childeric in 675. How, and roughly where and when he died, was now also clear. The fact that Theuderic took over in Austrasia after his death suggests that he did not have descendants. This, with minor amendments, has remained the accepted version – accepted, that is, among academic historians. Yet in *The Holy Blood and the Holy Grail*, Baigent et al. preferred Henschen's reconstruction because this gave Dagobert a family, and they wished to have Dagobert as the conduit for the blood of Christ. In fact to their credit they did reference the *De Tribus Dagobertis*, albeit at second hand.[64] But with a disregard for their source that would have impressed the author of the *Vita Dagoberti*, they parked Dagobert in waiting in the foothills of the Pyrenees, the land of Cathars and Templars and mysterious treasure, rather than in boring old Alsace. They also give him a different wife, from the Visigothic royal line. The rest is phantasy, or fraud, and not worthy of serious attention. It is amusing, however, to see how what purports to be a secret memory passed down the generations can be clearly shown to be based on an uninformed reading of the work of a seventeenth-century scholar who was struggling to piece together a narrative from incomplete sources which had themselves confused earlier traditions.

Let us now turn to the figure of Wilfrid, because so much hangs on him.

---

62 Henschen, *De Tribus Dagobertis* pp. 132–3, 185. He suggested that Dagobert was buried in Rouen but then moved to Stenay as part of a peace deal between Neustria and Austrasia.

63 *Vita Wilfridi* ed. J. Mabillon, *Acta Sanctorum Ordinis S. Benedicti*, saec. IV, pt 1 (Paris, 1677), pp. 676–722.

64 Baigent, Leigh and Lincoln, *Holy Blood*, p. 537, n. 26. The authors seem to have got the Henschen reference from Folz, 'Tradition hagiographique', p. 33. Folz was not concerned to show the obvious shortcomings of Henschen's reconstruction.

Take out the *Life of Wilfrid* and not only is there scarcely a trace of Dagobert II in Francia, but also there is virtually no evidence for Wilfrid's presence on the Continent. Only Wilfrid's attestation of the Council of Rome in 680 indicates that he was ever there. His supposed continental experiences nevertheless play a large part in historians' reconstructions of the early Anglo-Saxon Church. Wilfrid is said to have learned from the Franks how to be a princely bishop. It was only the heroic archbishop of Canterbury, Theodore, who cut Wilfrid down to size and prevented him becoming prince-bishop of all of Northumbria. Walter Goffart went so far as to think that the *Life of Cuthbert*, the Whitby *Life of Gregory* and much of Bede's *Ecclesiastical History* were all produced to contest Wilfrid's vision of how the Church should be.[65] But we can only summon up that vision, and thus understand the contest, through a rather nuanced reading of Stephen's *Life of Wilfrid*. Try re-reading Bede without it. His account is surely by no means as hostile to Wilfrid as Goffart thinks. As Thomas Pickles has observed, Bede does actually acknowledge Wilfrid's achievements in what is an obituary précis in Gregorian fashion.[66] One cannot obviously see here a clash between two principles of ecclesiastical organization. These may be inferred by the modern reader with a wide-ranging knowledge of Church history, but would contemporaries have made the inference, especially as there is no evidence for any other author or commentator having read Stephen's *Life*? If there is any coolness toward Wilfrid in Bede, this could simply come from the fact that Wilfrid fell out with Benedict Biscop, the founder of Bede's own monastery, although this is something else we can find out only from Stephen's *Life*. Drawing on Paul's discordant parting from Barnabas in *Acts*, Stephen tells of how Wilfrid and Biscop parted when on Wilfrid's first trip to Rome he decided to stay on in the city of Lyons and enjoy the hospitality of its powerful bishop, Dalfinus.[67] It is in fact the Lyons episode which is held to have turned Wilfrid's head toward the notion of the powerful rather than the pastoral bishop. On his return from Rome, Wilfrid was said to have stayed for three years in Lyons, leaving only when Dalfinus was executed on the orders of the malevolent queen Balthild, 'a second Jezabel' who had no fewer than nine bishops killed.[68] But as Janet

---

65 W. Goffart, *The Narrators of Barbarian History* (Princeton, 1988), IV 'Bede and the Ghost of Bishop Wilfrid', pp. 235–328.

66 T. Pickles, 'Gregory the Great's *Regula Pastoralis* and Bede's *historiae*', paper read at Institute of Historical Research 'Early Middle Ages' seminar, 1 November 2006. Nick Higham likewise reads Bede as treating Wilfrid with great approval. N. J. Higham *(Re-) Reading Bede: The Ecclesiastical History in Context* (London, 2006), pp. 64–5.

67 *Life of Wilfrid*, c. 3, pp. 8–9.

68 *Life of Wilfrid*, c. 6, pp. 12–15.

Nelson showed nearly thirty years ago, Stephen's account is problematic.[69] An inscription, charters and later *Acta* all show that the bishop of Lyons was called Aunemundus, not Dalphinus. The *Acta Aunemundi* say that it was Aunemund's brother, the count of Lyons, who was called Dalphinus, a name which, unsettlingly, means 'brother' in Greek. There is no mention of Wilfrid at Lyons. Furthermore, we can work out that Aunemund was killed in 660, by which time Wilfrid was back in England, and cannot, therefore, have been prepared to die alongside his patron as Stephen claimed.[70] It is interesting to note that neither Bede nor Stephen seemed to know that this Balthild was regarded as a saint (and certainly not as a serial killer of bishops), that she was actually English, and founder and latterly inmate of the monastery of Chelles, even though Bede knew of her husband King Clovis, and reported that English princesses entered Chelles and other Neustrian Frankish monasteries at this time.[71] Just as the *Life of Wilfrid* did not circulate on the Continent, there is no indication that any Frankish 'Lives' from this period were known in England, and one of these lives was a *Life of Balthild*, which we know must have been in existence by the year 691.[72] There is circumstantial evidence, largely from name forms, to suggest fairly close contacts between southern and eastern England and Francia in this period. Balthild's move to Francia should be understood in that context. Indeed, the argument that at one time Frankish kings even exercised some kind of hegemony in southern England is taken seriously.[73] But our only textual evidence for contacts comes from Stephen and Bede. No continental writer says anything about England. There was, in other words, very little basis on which to construct a memory of contacts between England and Francia in the later seventh century, hence our reliance on circumstantial evidence. We can only begin to guess at how it might have been possible for Wilfrid to find, equip and return Dagobert II to Francia.

Stephen, and Bede in his précis of Stephen, tell us that on his second journey to Rome – i.e., the journey on which he met Dagobert – Wilfrid

69   J. L. Nelson, 'Queens as Jezabels: the careers of Brunhild and Balthild in Merovingian History', *Studies in Church History*, subsidia I (1978), pp. 31–77, reprinted, J. L. Nelson, *Politics and Ritual in Early Medieval Europe* (London, 1986), pp. 1–48.

70   *Acta Aunemundi*, trans. with commentary, Fouracre and Gerberding, pp. 166–92; pp. 172–6 for the difficulties in reconciling Stephen's account with the information from Lyons itself.

71   Bede, *HE* III, c.19 for Clovis; III, c. 8 for the entry of English princesses into Frankish monasteries.

72   *Life of Balthild*, trans. with commentary, Fouracre and Gerberding, pp. 97–132.

73   The argument was put forward by Ian Wood: I. N. Wood, *The Merovingian North Sea*, Occasional Papers on Medieval Topics 1 (Alingsås, 1983).

spent the winter preaching in Frisia.[74] Bede goes on to say that the conversion of the Frisians was later achieved by Willibrord. It is curious that the *Calendar of Willibrord*, a contemporary document that commemorates several Anglo-Saxon Churchmen, does not include Wilfrid, even though Willibrord had been an oblate at Wilfrid's monastery of Ripon.[75] In his *Vita Willibrordi*, Alcuin likewise did not mention Wilfrid. He did include him in his poem on York, but here he was drawing on Bede, not Stephen.[76] It seems to have been Bede, rather than Stephen, who was responsible for preserving the memory of Wifrid, for there is no evidence of anyone drawing on the *Life of Wilfrid* before the tenth century. Although Wilfrid does figure in calendars from the ninth century, one again suspects that it was Bede rather than Stephen who inspired the commemoration.

It was King Eadred of Wessex who rescued Wilfrid from growing obscurity by raiding Ripon in 948 and bringing his body and Stephen's *Life* back to the south. The *Life* then inspired a poetic account of Wilfrid's career by the scholar Frithegod, completed by 958. Frithegod's poem actually embellished Stephen's story of Wilfrid's relations with Dagobert, expanding the section in which Wilfrid heard of Dagobert's death.[77] No doubt he chose to do this to honour his patron Oda archbishop of Canterbury who in 936 had played a part in the return to Francia of another royal exile, Louis d'Outremer, a returnee who, like Dagobert, provoked the Franks. Michael Lapidge has argued strongly that Frithegod was a Frank, his name being an Anglicization of the Frankish Fredegaud.[78] After Oda's death in 958, he apparently took manuscripts of the poem back to Francia, one of which Mabillon read at Corbie and edited and published in 1672.[79] Henschen seems to have come tantalizingly close to reading it too, because he quoted two lines of a now lost metrical 'Life' of Audoin of Rouen, also by Frithegod.[80] A revival of interest in Wilfrid thus came from Canterbury

74   *Life of Wilfrid* c. 26, pp. 52–3; Bede, *HE* V, c. 19.
75   *The Calendar of St Willibrord*, ed. H. A. Wilson (HBS, 1918, reprinted Woodbridge, 1998). On Willibrord in Ripon, *Life of Wilfrid* c. 26, pp. 52–3.
76   Alcuin, *De Pontificibus et Sanctis Ecclesiae Eboracensis*, trans. P. Godman, *Alcuin, The Kings, Bishops and Saints of York* (Oxford, 1982), lines 577–646, pp. 48–55.
77   *Frithegodi monachi Brevilogium Vitae Beati Wifridi*, ed. A. Campbell (Zurich, 1950), lines 694–715, 780–99, pp. 33–4, 36–7. Possibly in deference to Oda, Frithegod changed the bishop who told of Dagobert's death and threatened Wilfrid into the leader of a band of *latrones*. He added the detail, presumably imagined, that Dagobert was stabbed in the groin.
78   M. Lapidge, 'A Frankish scholar in tenth-century England: Frithegod of Canterbury/Fredegaud of Brioude', *ASE* 17 (1988), pp. 45–65.
79   Lapidge, 'A Frankish scholar', pp. 54–5.
80   Henschen, *De Tribus Dagobertis*, p. 133. He quoted Frithegod to show that more than one king was buried in Rouen.

after Stephen's *Life* had been acquired from Ripon. First we have Frithe-god's poem, then Eadmer's *Life of Wilfrid*,[81] which relied heavily on Frithe-god as well as on Stephen, and finally William of Malmesbury who used Eadmer to supplement Stephen. The earliest surviving manuscripts of Stephen's *Life* are late eleventh-century and from Canterbury. It was these, presumably, that Eadmer and William used. So, a memory of Wilfrid as a hugely important figure can only be a later medieval and modern one if it is derived from the *Life*. Hagiographers tried to set up positive memories that secured the reputation of their subjects for all time, but if their writing did not circulate, that memory could not become part of a wider consciousness.

The *Life of Wilfrid* is therefore a text that is to us vital for historical research, but not one of which more than a handful of early medieval people were aware. In the *Historian's Craft* Marc Bloch argued that with the multi-disciplinary tools at our disposal we can find out more about the pattern of the medieval past than the people living in it could ever have under-stood.[82] He was right in the sense that over the centuries we have gathered together information that was originally disparate and unconnected. This is precisely what we have been doing in piecing together the history of Dagobert II. What we have seen is that that history cannot be written without reference to the *Life of Wilfrid*. As the author of the *Vita Dagoberti* demonstrates all too clearly, it is simply impossible to identify Dagobert II unless one has access to the *Life of Wilfrid*. Henschen's researches show what happens when new information becomes available. Because he had half the story of Dagobert from Willliam of Malmesbury, Henschen was able to describe his return to Francia, but because he did not know what happened to Dagobert after his return, he relied too heavily on the one piece of information he did have, namely that the chief bishopric of Dagobert's kingdom was Strasbourg. What William chose to include, and to omit, thus determined the direction of Henschen's speculation, and we have seen how this wrong-footed him. The engagement with the *Life of Wilfrid* in two stages, as it were, provides an excellent illustration of how the inclusion of new information radically changes the picture when we are dealing with subjects for which there is very little source material. The difficulty of trying to reconstruct the presence of Wilfrid on the Continent without reference to the *Life*, and also in trying to estimate his importance in England itself,

---

81 *Vita Sancti Wilfridi auctore Eadmero*, ed. and trans., B. Muir and A. Turner, *The Life of St Wilfrid by Eadmer* (Exeter, 1998).

82 M. Bloch, *The Historian's Craft*, trans. P. Putnam (Manchester, 1954), pp. 48–78.

points us to numerous *lacunae* in what evidence we do have. Bede's apparent ignorance of the nationality and career of Balthild, despite the good circumstantial evidence of contacts between Balthild's circle and the English, reminds us that we cannot assume that information that is available to us now was widely shared then. The point is that these are not just silences which hinder our understanding of the past: they stopped people shortly after the time, or even contemporaries, understanding events and situations.

In the prologue to the *Vita Dagoberti*, the author says that he is writing because the deeds of Dagobert had 'slipped away from the memory of the living'. Creating such a memory was an institutional and religious necessity, but as Fentress and Wickham suggest, memory constructed through narrative tends to be devoid of historical meaning and context.[83] Our author may have succeeded in making people more aware of a martyr King Dagobert, but the subject had become thoroughly de-historicized in the process – witness the strange of the story of his death. The author's fabrications show how it was simply not possible to access any historical memory of the king who had actually been murdered, Dagobert II. What we term the construction of 'memory', and there is quite an industry of memory studies, refers to the process of finding out, or creating, both by research and by the use of fiction. Henschen was not recovering the memory of the forgotten Dagobert II, he was doing historical research. Did research get harder after the year 1000 as Geary implies? No, surely, fragmented information and breaks in tradition meant that at all times it was difficult. The foreshortening of historical perspective characteristic of early medieval writing may owe as much to gaps in information as it does to a mentality that painted people of different times in the same Christian colours. The difference, as Geary also implies in what is a very suggestive but also rather elusive essay, is that in the mid-eleventh century people were doing this research for the first time. It was not just families and institutions (like Stenay) which were trying to invent a past, but also a newly important intellectual elite, people like Eadmer and William of Malmesbury, who were retrieving and co-ordinating information to open up new perspectives on the past. Far from being a time of oblivion, this was precisely the time that people began to look into the more distant past to recover what had been lost long before.

83 J. Fentress and C. Wickham, Social Memory (Oxford, 1992), pp. 9–10.

5

Some Carolingian questions from Charlemagne's days

David Ganz

P ARIS, BNF LATIN 4629, is a manuscript containing Frankish law-codes, capitularies of Charlemagne and formulae, most probably copied in Bourges at the start of the ninth century.[1] It has been linked with the court of Charlemagne by Donald Bullough.[2] Amid the legal texts it contains a dialogue that offers insights into some of the questions Charlemagne's subjects sought to answer.

Texts like this are rarely edited; they do not offer original thoughts, and often attest to the poor Latin and poor spelling of the scribes who copied them. They occur quite often among more substantial materials assembled in Carolingian manuscripts. By offering a transcription and a translation I hope first to provide a teaching source for those who want to understand Frankish thoughts, especially about religion and ethics, and then to explore where these questions and answers may have come from, and why they might have been copied here. That exploration is, of course, an exercise in what some call historical imagination and others call guesswork. As such, it stands as a tribute to the scholar who has given me the strongest support for guessing how Carolingians thought and acted.

---

1 The manuscript is most fully described in H. Mordek, *Bibliotheca capitularium regum Francorum manuscripta Überlieferung und Traditionszusammenhang der fränkischen Herrschererlasse, MGH* Hilfsmittel 15 (Munich, 1995), pp. 502–7. I cannot accept Mordek and Bischoff's view that it was originally bound with Leiden BPL 114, though the two manuscripts are coeval and are both linked to Bourges. I am grateful to the members of a workshop which met in Leiden to discuss both manuscripts, and especially to Pat Geary and Andre Bouwman. For sage council I thank Jan Ziolkowski, whose forthcoming edition of the 'Salomon und Marcolf' dialogue texts will explore lay dialogues.

Paris BNF Latin 4629 ff 15v–18v

Principles of this edition

The following edition is a transcription that keeps the orthography of the manuscript and does not add punctuation. The capitals of the manuscript have been retained. Italics are used for passages which seem direct quotations, while footnotes identify passages which seem closely related. In searching for sources and parallels I have consulted the electronic versions of the *Patrologia Latina* and the Brepols Library of Latin texts.

The text

INCIPIT QUESTIO DE TRInitate Quomodo credis Deum Rep Trinum et unum INT Quomodo trinum et quomodo unum RS Trinum in personis et unum in deitatem[3] INT Quomodo credis patrem RS Patrem nec factus nec natum esse credo. filium natum non factum spiritum vero sanctum nec genitum nec creatum sed ex patrem et filiumque procedens unum deum esse confiteor[4] INT fuit trinitas antequam Cristus naceretur aut non RS fuit INT Dic mihi quo ordine RS *Ante collet ego parturiebar adhuc terram non fecerat quando parabat caelos adheram dum vallaret terminus (16 r) et lege poneret aquis ego eram*[5] INT Tota trinitas de caelo commota est aut non R Tota commota est sed non tota adsumpsit carnem sed non admisit divinitatem homo erat et deus erat. Secundum dicta sancti hysidori *Christus in formam servi servos et in forma servi non servos: In forma quippe servi Domini servus et in forma servi omnium dominus*[6] et iterum *Christus deus et homo totum ergo Christum non diligit qui homine odit.*[7] INT homo quantas substantias habere in te R *Homo ex duobus constat substantiis corporis adque anime*[8] sed triplex actum id est corporis anime et spiritus.[9] Spiritus non alias ab anime in substantia sed actum

---

2   D. A. Bullough, 'Charlemagne's Court Library Revisited', *EME* 12 (2004), pp. 339–63 at p. 358.

3   Cf. Isidore, *De fide catholica*, I. 4.

4   Cf. Paris BN Lat 2718 f 138r an excerpt from Isidore, *de ecclesiasticis officiis*, 2. 24. Compare the Carolingian text from Passau text edited by F. Brunhölzl, *Studien zum geistigen Leben in Passau im achten und neuntem Jahrhundert, Abhandlungen der Marburger Gelehrten Gesellschaft 26* (Munich, 2000), p. 53. I am very grateful to Helmut Reimitz for providing me with a copy of this monograph.

5   *Proverbia* VIII 24.

6   Isidore, *Sententiae*, I, c. 14.

7   Isidore, *Sententiae*, II, c. 3.

8   Cf. Brunhölzl, *Studien*, p. 52.

9   Cf. M. Förster, 'Das älteste mittellateinische Gesprächsbüchlein', *Romanische Forschungen* 27 (1910), pp. 342–8 at p. 344 *triplex est in actio, hoc est corpus et animam et spiritus.*

discretus[10] est ut anima eo quod agit hominem anima proprie nunccupetur et secundum spiritum suum flatus spiritus advertatur sed singulis substantiis id est duabus in unum coniunctis quattuor rebus ex his *ossibus nervis venis et carnem*[11] Natura eiusdem vivificantem substantiae *quattuor in se gerit diversitatis ut esuriat siciat concupescat soporetur.*[12] INT Quod sunt genera litterarum R Septem INT Quot R. Hebraee Athice Latine Syre Caldaice Egyptiae et Getiche INT Quis quales invenit R. Moyses ebreas Fenices Athias Nicostras Latinas Abraam Syras et Caldaycas Ysis Egypticas Gulfila Ieticas Amen (f 16v)

INCIPIT FILOSOPHIA IKUDITIO cum
INT Quid est initio virtutis R Non facere malum INT Quid est profectus virtutis R Agere bona IN Quid est consummatio virtutis R. Permanere in bonum INT Que ethimologia virtutis R Iustus ordo amoris[13] IN Que est iusticia amoris R Ut Deum diligas propter semetipsum super omnia te propter eum, proximum sicut te,[14] universa vero que sunt quoniam ad haec sunt facta pro laudem Domini diligatur. Haec est iusticia amoris.

INT Ergo corpori pulchritude diligenda erit R Sic a te oportet diligi ut Deum cuius creatura es conlaudes INT Ego pro dilectione corporis ago R Perversus est talis amor quia bonum pessime amas unde te potius odis cum id amas quo te perimas[15] INT Potest aliquis natus semper vivere R Qui potest ab inmortale nasci IN Potest aliquis non peccare R Qui potest sine peccatum nasci INT Quid est peccatum R Contemtus precepti divini INT Quid est proprietas contemti R Supervia Omnis namque superbus dispicit iussione Domini sui et quicquid pretera fecerit peccat[16] (17r) INT Bonum est mori quam peccare R Melius est vivere et non peccare quam seipsum interiri si non peccet peccat quam se occidit INT Quomodo non peccavimus R Si praeceptis Domini Dei nostri obediamus que ei iussit fieri libenter

10 Cf. Augustine, *de Anima* I, xvii *PL* 44, col. 491.
11 Cf. M. Förster 'Gesprächsbüchlein', p. 344 *quattuor septies in corpore esse videmus, hoc est, ossibus, nervis, et venis adque carnem.* The passage from '*homo ex duobus*' to '*soporetur*' is also found in a group of manuscripts, including Cologne Dombibl. 15, and Karlsruhe Aug. 229.
12 Cf. M. Förster 'Gesprächsbüchlein', p. 344 *quattuor in se gerit diversitates, hoc est, ut esuriet, et sitiat ut concupiscat et somnum capiat.*
13 Cf. Augustine, *de Civitate Dei*, 15. 22 *definitio brevis et vera virtutis ordo est amoris.* I have not found this quoted in later texts.
14 Cf. Mattheus XXII 37.
15 Cf. Augustine, *De Disciplina Christiana*, c. 4–5: *PL* 40, cols. 671–2.
16 Cf. Augustine, *De Natura et Gratia*, c. 29.

faciamus eaque proibuerit. fieri non fecerimus si hoc modo agamus non peccamus. INT Quare turbamur R Quia deo non vacamus Nam si ei nos occuparemus ab universis perturbationis alieni efficeremur INT Quomodo poterimus quieti esse. R Si semper per divinis eloquiis meditemur et curas temporales reppulerimus INT Amo contentionem R Quia ignoras ratio-nem Omnis namque contemtio discordia generat Ratio vero et scientia tribuit et pacem conservat. INT Amo mulierem R Ergo amas mortem Dixit quidam *adulter est in sua uxore amator ardentior In aliena autem omnis amor turpis est sive grandis sive parvus*[17] INT Ergo mulier mors est R Non quia ipsa est mors seo causa est mortis[18] quia per eam venimus in mortem. Memento illam sententiam veram *A muliere initium factum est peccati et per illa omnes moriemur*[19] INT Ergo odio abendum est mulier R Propter peccatum non propter natura. Odi igitur vitium ama creaturam quoniam et ipsa homo est et Dei opus est bonum INT Infirmus sum R Gaude si animo vales (17v) INT Sanus sum R Opta potius anima quam corpore INT Oculos doleo R Si cordis oculosque aegritat geras non magni ducas corporis damnum Nam et animalia et raptilia corporales oculos habent Tu vero si hos habes gaudes quia angelis similes es non animalibus INT Surdus sum R Letare quia non audis superflua INT Alioquin pro pulcritudinem corporis placent R Atque utinam ex animi virtutibus perserverentia Corporis pulchritudo aut senec-tute succedente deperit aut morvo intercedente subtrahitur et novissimo morte finitur INT Nonulli bene locuntur R Si ita agunt ut finiantur et sibi sunt utiles et auditoribus si vero dissonant facta verbis sibi nihil prosunt sed potius utiunt quia sitientes quod est bonum contemnunt INT Felices sunt qui suas abent facultates R Multos his feliciores illis qui eas perparum necessitates ad sempiternam hereditatem permiserunt ubi eas cum magno fenore reccepturi sunt INT Ergo qui meas facultates abeo felix non sum R Non quid est secundum tuam opinionem felicis tibi esse videris si eas aut serves aut augeas Socrastes (*sic*) vero suas in mare dimersit (18r) dicens eis Ego vos potius mergam ne ipse mergat a vobis[20] Si hoc esse vos quod fuit et iste filosophus aut hoc facio quod ille aut aliquid melius. Nonne utilius est ut eas indigentibus largiaris cum magnus per divini precepti et subplan-tes cupiditatem quam in mari eas proicias sine ulla divina repromissionem aut Christianus dat pauperibus aut filosophus proieciet in mare IN Nihil orum facio R Ideo nec perfectus Christianus es nec certus filosophus Nest-erorum es. *Quur mihi facis iniuriam*[21] R Veritas non est convitium. Omnis

---

17 Jerome, *Adversus Iovinianum,* I, c. 49.
18 *Mulier causa mortis* is discussed in Petrus Chrysologus *Sermo* 64.
19 Ecclesiastes XXV 33.
20 Jerome, *Adversus Iovinianum,* II, c. 9.
21 2 Regum XIX 43.

iniuria convitium est *Ego quippe veritatem locutus sum*[22] non convitium inrogavi. In Quae sunt bona cogitationes R De virtutibus cogitare sine cessationem IN Quae sunt principales virtutes NOM meministi filosophorum sententiam in qua generaliter omnes consonant quattuor dicentes arcites esse virtutes id est temperantia fortitudo iusticia et prudentia de quibus magnis fontibus cetera virtutum decurrere flumina[23] IN Cum facto non sit quomodo oranti Ezechie XV anni quasi ad praesentem vitae tempus adduntur R Quia utique arguebatur Ezechias extremis non faci decreto sed diei vocationem adiutio (18v) in tantum aut vite anni prius non fuerant constituti ut per supplicationem videantur adiecti[24] INT Que causa scribitur in die illa magna tribulationis nemo liberabitur nisi Noe Danihel et Iob[25] Cum utique quando Ezechiel ista dicebat solus forsitan Danihel in corpore fuerit duabus aliis iam tunc in pace vel carnis nexibus absoluti.[26] FINIUNT

Translation

Here begins questions on the Trinity. Question How do you believe in God? Answer Three and one. Question How three and how one? Answer Three in persons and one in deity. Question How do you believe in the Father? Answer I believe that the Father was neither created nor begotten, I believe that the Son was born but not made, I believe the Spirit was neither begotten nor created but proceeding from the father and the Son I confess one God. Question Was there a Trinity before the Spirit was born or not? Answer There was. Question Tell me in what order. Answer *Before the hills I gave birth he had not made the earth when he prepared the heavens, the aether when he prepared a boundary and set a law for the waters I was.* Question Is the whole Trinity moved from heaven or not? Answer It all moved but not all put on flesh but it did not loose his divinity, he was man and God. According to the words of Saint Isidore *Christ was a servant in the form of a servant and in the form of a servant he was not a servant. In the form of a servant servant of the Lord and in the form of a servant Lord of all* and again *Christ God and man so he does not love Christ who hates man.* Question How many substances does

---

22 John VIII 40.
23 This order of the virtues is found in Julianus Pomerius *De Vita Contemplativa, PL* 59, col. 501. The ordering of the virtues in Late Antiquity and the Early Middle Ages is discussed by S. Mähl, *Quadriga Virtutum Die Kardinaltugenden in der Geistesgeschichte der Karolingerzeit* (Cologne/Vienna, 1969), pp. 101–3.
24 Eucherius Lugdunensis *Instructionum ad Salonium de Regnum* VI *CSEL* 31 (1894), p. 83 reading *non fati decreto sed Dei evocationem.*
25 *Collectanea Pseudo-Bedae*, ed. M. Bayless and M. Lapidge, *SLH* 14 (Dublin, 1998), no. 234.
26 Eucherius in Ezechielem *CSEL* 31, p. 87 reading *nexibus absolutis.*

man have? Answer Man is made of two substances body and soul but three in act that is body mind and soul. Spirit is not different from soul in substance but it is different in act just as the soul is called anima because it moves man and according to his spirit the breath of the soul but to these substances, that is two in one are joined four things, bones, nerves, veins and flesh. The nature of the living substance contains four differences, that is hunger, thirst, desire and sleep.

Question How many kinds of letters are there? Answer Seven. Question What are they? Answer Hebrew, Attic, Latin, Syrian, Chaldean, Egyptian and Gothic. Question Who found which one? Answer Moyses Hebrew, Fenicas [Phoenices] Attic, Nicostras [Nicostratas] Latin, Abraham Syrian and Chaldean, Isis Egyptian and Ulfilas Gothic. Amen.

Here begins philosophical erudition.

Question What is the beginning of virtue? Answer Not to do evil. Question What is the advance of virtue? Answer To do good. Question What is the fullness of virtue? Answer To persist in good. Question What is the etymology of virtue? Answer The just order of love. Question What is the justice of love? Answer To love God for himself above all things, yourself because of Him, your neighbour as yourself, all things which are are loved because they are made for this for the praise of the Lord. This is the justice of love. Question So should beautiful bodies be loved? Answer They should be loved by you so that you praise God whose creation you are. Question I act for love of the body. Answer Such love is perverse for you love the good badly so that you rather hate yourself when you love that by which you perish. Question Can someone born live for ever? Answer Who can be born from someone immortal? Question Can someone not sin? Answer He who can be born without sin. Question What is sin? Answer Contempt for divine precepts. Question What is the nature of contempt? Answer Pride Every proud person despises the command of his Lord and whatever else he does he sins. Question Is it better to die than to sin? Answer It is better to live and not to sin than to to kill oneself if he doesn't sin, he sins by killing himself. Question How do we not sin? Answer If we obey the commands of our Lord God and do freely what he orders and do not do what he prohibits if we act in this way we do not sin. Question Why are we troubled? Answer Because we do not wait on God. For if we busy ourselves for Him we are made remote from all trouble. Question How can we be at rest? Answer If we always contemplate divine scripture and drive away temporal cares. Question I love strife. Answer Because you are ignorant of reason. All strife gives rise to discord. Reason pays tribute to learning and preserves peace. Question I love a woman. Answer Therefore you love death. For as someone says 'The more ardent lover of his own wife is an adulterery. Love of another woman is always shameful, whether great or small. Question So woman is death? Answer Not because she is death but she is the cause of death for through her we enter into death. Remember this true opinion. By a woman was made the beginning of sin and through her we all die. Question So woman should be hated? Answer Because of sin not because of nature. Therefore I hate vice I love the creature for she is man and the work of God is good. Question I am weak. Answer Rejoice if your soul is well. Question I am healthy. Answer Wish rather in soul than in body. Question I suffer in my eyes. Answer If the eyes of the heart are sick you risk no small loss in your body. For beasts and reptiles have bodily eyes. But you if you have them rejoice for you are like angels and not like beasts. Question I am deaf. Answer Rejoice that you do not hear vainness. Question Some things delight because of the beauty of the body. Answer But would that they had persisted because of the virtues of the soul. The beauty of the body either perishes with the coming of old age or is removed by illness and finishes in a new death. Question Some speak well. Answer If they do this so that they are restrained they profit themselves and their hearers, but if their deeds differ from their words they do not advance themselves but rather they despise what is good. Question Are they happy who have their faculties. Answer Much happier than them are those who come to an eternal reward where they will be received with great fervor. Question So because I have my faculties I am not happy. Answer Not as you think that you will be happy if you keep them or increase them. Socrates threw his possessions into the sea saying to them, 'Better that I drown you than that I am drowned by you.' If you want to be like that philosopher, either I do what he did or something better. Isn't it more useful that you give them to the needy by divine command and uproot desire than that you throw them into the sea without any divine reward? Either the Christian gives them to the poor or the philosopher throws them in the sea. Question I do neither of these. Answer Then you are neither a perfect Christian nor a sure philosopher.[27] Question Why do you do me wrong? Answer Truth is not a reproach. All wrong is a reproach. I spoke the truth and did not ask for reproach. Question What are good thoughts? Answer To think of the virtues unceasingly. Question What are the principal virtues? Answer Do you not remember the opinion of the philosophers in which all agree saying there are four chief virtues, that is, temperance, fortitude, justice and prudence, from which great founts the rivers of the other virtues flow.

---

27 I avoid the problem of translating *Nesterorum*, which I can make nothing of. Perhaps we should read *ne* and then some term contrasted with a sure philosopher?

Discussion

Question-and-answer texts like this one were used for teaching. Frequently they draw on and simplify more complex material.[28] For instance, the opening sections on the Trinity and on the soul and body bear a close resemblance to the opening of a dialogue found in Sélestadt MS 1, a Merovingian manuscript, in Vat. Reg. Lat. 846, a ninth-century manuscript copied at Tours in the time of Fredugis, and also in Cologne Dombibl. 15 and Karlsruhe Aug CCXXIX.[29] Similar texts on the principle sins, faith, baptism and Christ are found in El Escorial L III 8 ff 77–79v, Laon 288 f 16v–17 and 55–59, and Orleans BM 116 f 63.

Sources and ideas

The text is unique among Carolingian texts known to me in quoting two passages from Jerome's *Adversus Jovinianum*, a treatise against matrimony. The story of Crates, originally found by Jerome in the *Sentences* of Sextus, is transmitted in a corrupt form which may suggest that our text does not derive directly from Jerome, but I have been unable to discover any author who uses the work and might have served as an intermediary.[30]

The discussion of the cardinal virtues in this text is very elementary: the virtues were first discussed by Cicero, and among Christian authors by Ambrose, who was the first to use the expression *principales virtutes*. The fullest Carolingian discussion is found in Alcuin's *de Rhetorica et Virtutibus*.[31] Our text sees them both as the subject of discussion by philosophers and as the source of other virtues. The suggestion that they should always be thought about is unusual and may be unique.

The very garbled list of inventors of alphabets includes Ulfilas, the inventor of the Gothic alphabet, and is paralleled in a poem *de Inventoribus*

---

28 For a survey of religious and secular teaching dialogues see L. W. Daly and W. Suchier, *Altercatio Hadriani Augusti et epicteti Philosophi*, Illinois Studies in Language and Literature xxiv/1–2 (Urbana, 1939), pp. 25–44.

29 For the Selestadt and Karlsruhe manuscripts M. Gorman, 'The Carolingian miscellany of exegetical texts in Albi 39 and Paris Lat. 2175', *Scriptorium* LI (1997), pp. 336–54 at pp. 351–2. For the Vatican manuscript Wilhelm Schmitz, *Miscellanea Tironiana: Aus dem Codex Vaticanus Latinus Reginae Christinae 846 (Fol. 99–114)* (Leipzig, 1896).

30 Walahfrid Strabo's personal anthology, St Gallen, Stiftsbibliothek MS 878 includes on page 335, under the heading *de Conflictu*, the quotation *Abite pessum male cupiditates, ego vos mergam ne merger a vobis*. It may be viewed online at http://www.cesg. unifr.ch/virt_bib/manuscripts.htm

31 Alcuin *De Rhetorica et Virtutibus*, ed. K. Halm, Rhetores Latini Minores (Leipzig, 1863), pp. 522–50.

Litterarum by Eugenius of Toledo, composed before 657,[32] which adds Ulfilas to the list of inventors found in the first book of Isidore's *Etymologiae*. Eugenius also spells Ulfilas Gulfila, although the spelling with a consonant as the first letter is too common for this fact to be a clear determinant. The list is also used by Julian of Toledo in his *Ars Grammatica*.[33] Whether this suggests a Spanish source for our text is less certain. The same passage about alphabets is found in Cologne MS 85 on fol. 103v and in several other related manuscripts.[34]

Most interesting is the discussion of bodily beauty, sin and women. I have not found any comparable investigation of whether women are to be hated, with the distinction of *vitium* and *creatura*, and the assertion that as a work of God woman must be good. The list of bodily ills and their spiritual counterparts is likewise without clear parallels, and the eyes of the soul which make man akin to the angels also seem unique. The final section (which I have not translated) combines two passages from Eucherius's *Instructiones*, though in so garbled a form that they cannot have made much sense.

This brief text shows some engagement with questions of ethics and particularly with how earthly goods are to be used. The discussion of earthly goods, of women and of adultery, and the relatively simple theological instruction offered, might both suggest that the answers relate to lay concerns, but goods, women and even law codes occupied the thoughts of monks: the distinction between lay and clerical was a permeable boundary.[35] The dialogue form used here may suggest that the answers were to be learned by heart.

There has been much speculation about how the Carolingians tried to instruct the laity.[36] Many simple dialogue texts seem to have been designed first and foremost for priests, or for monastic schools. Because this text is less concerned with elementary instruction in dogma, and because it can be dated palaeographically to the reign of the emperor Charlemagne, it is worth consideration as a reminder of some of the things that some Carolingians were worried about. But the quality of the spelling must raise the question of how far this text could have been understood by anyone. Were

---

32   Eugenius of Toledo, *MGH AA* XIV, p. 257.

33   *Ars Iuliani Toletani Episcopi*, ed. M. Maestre Yenes (Toledo, 1973), p. 115.

34   Gorman, as note 29.

35   See Patrick Wormald and Janet L. Nelson (eds), *Lay Intellectuals in the Carolingian World* (Cambridge, 2007).

36   For a helpful recent discussion cf. D. A. Bullough, 'Alcuin and lay virtue', in L. Gaffuri and R. Quinto (eds), *Predicazione e società nel Medioevo: riflessione etica, valori e modelli di comportamento* (Padua, 2002), pp. 71–91, and the pieces by Rachel Stone cited in her contribution to this volume.

words such as *supervia*, showing 'b'/'v' confusion, *naceretur*, *Ikuditio* for *Eruditio*, *Raptalia* for *reptilia* and phrases like *aut hoc facio quod ille aut melius* readily understood? Do they represent an attempt to transcribe the sounds of daily speech? The poor orthography would seem to provide substantial problems for any reader of the text, and must raise the question of what the scribe thought he was copying. It is distinctly worse than that of most of the other texts copied in this manuscript. The letter H is frequently omitted, *Locuntur* is spelled with 'c' instead of 'q', and 'u' and 'o' and 'b' and 'v' are confused.[37] Cases are confused, so that prepositions govern unfamiliar cases as *ex patrem, ab anime* and the curious *ossibus nervis venis et carnem* where an accusative follows a set of ablatives. The question *Quid est initio* corresponds to the accusative ablative confusion related to the loss of final m[38] But the sentence *Bonum est mori quam peccare* with its use of infinitives and of *quam* as a comparative conjunction after *bonum* rather than *melior* is harder to explain.

Current discussion of the differences between Merovingian and Carolingian Latin has spent little time investigating the evidence of orthography and syntax in our manuscript sources, preferring sociolinguistic interpretations.[39] This strange text shows what an accomplished scribe thought acceptable Latin. The strangeness of that Latin, and of the way this text was slipped into a law book, may confirm Janet Nelson's reflections on the 'limits of the Carolingian Renaissance': how did the court instruct the laity, and how did it develop an effective European Latin? If Donald Bullough is right to suggest that our text may reflect 'the instruction in "higher

---

37 On Merovingian orthography cf. Els Rose in her edition of *Missale Gothicum, CCSL* 159 D (Turnhout, 2005), pp. 37–66, and the earlier studies which she cites there. Omitted 'h' is treated on p. 61, and 'b'/'v' confusion on p. 56.

38 Rose, pp. 70–83 is a fine survey of changes of case.

39 For a series of articles which combine linguistic and historical approaches R. Wright (ed.), *Latin and the Romance Languages in the Early Middle Ages* (London, 1991). The best survey remains J. Herman, *Le Latin vulgaire*, 3rd edn (Paris, 1975). Specific features of Merovingian Latin are treated by J. Herman, 'Sur quelques aspects du latin mérovingien: langue écrite et langue parlée', in *Latin vulgaire-Latin tardif III* (Tübingen, 1992), pp. 173–86, Marc van Uytfanghe, 'Histoire du latin, protohistoire des langues romanes et histoire de la communication', *Francia* 11 (1983), pp. 579–613, and M. Banniard, 'Latin tardif et latin mérovingien: communication et modèles langagiers', *Revue des études latines*, 73 (1995), pp. 213–30. For more linguistic studies the volume edited by J. Herman, *La transizione dal latino alle lingue romanze: atti della Tavola rotonda di linguistica storica, Università Ca' Foscari di Venezia, 14–15 giugno 1996* (Tubingen 1998). The finest account of Merovingian Latinity, with a full bibliography, is by Els Rose in her introduxtion to her edition of the *Missale Gothicum, CCSL* 159 D (Turnhout 2005), pp. 23–187.

things" of older *pueri* and the less talented younger *adolescentes*,[40] we have here a trace of the conversations of the court, and it is right that they are 'not without a sense of humour.' As such, they do honour to a scholar who makes us all feel less talented.

40   Bullough 'Court library', p. 358.

6

'Immune from heresy': defining the boundaries of Carolingian Christianity[1]

Matthew Innes

I N 763-4, A RENEWED version of the oldest Frankish law-code, *Lex Salica*, was issued in the name of the first Carolingian king, Pippin. A verse prologue celebrated the achievements of 'the invincible race of the Franks', among whose many qualities, it was claimed, was that they were 'immune from heresy'.[2] As Pippin's reign is beginning to emerge from the historiographical shadow cast by the smooth narrative of '751 and all that' carefully elaborated under Charlemagne, the contours of his kingship are becoming clearer.[3] The revision of *Lex Salica* offers priceless testimony to the representation of a new regime, to be placed alongside Pippin's efforts at 'renewal' in other legislative genres – capitularies and conciliar acts – and the royal image promoted on coins and documents.[4] Claims about Frankish 'invincibility' like those voiced in 763-4 articulated the forging of new

---

1   I should thank Paul Fouracre for his editorial skill and help with the Fredegar *Continuations*, Rachel Stone for her invaluable assistance with capitularies and councils, Tehmina Goskar for help with Mediterranean itineraries and the cult of Michael, and John Arnold and Caroline Humfress for advice on the definition of heresy.

2   *Lex Salica*, ed. K. Eckhardt, *MGH Leges* IV ii (Hanover, 1962), Prologue, pp. 22–9, lines 1, 10.

3   See the inspiring start provided by M. Garrison, 'The Franks as the new Israel? Education for an identity from Pippin to Charlemagne', in Y. Hen and M. Innes (eds), *The Uses of the Past in the Early Middle Ages* (Cambridge, 2000), pp. 114–60, esp. pp. 129–34; for '751 and all that' see R. McKitterick, 'The illusion of royal power in the Frankish annals', *EHR* 115 (2000), pp. 11–20, revised in her *History and Memory in the Carolingian World* (Cambridge, 2004). See also the essays in M. Becher and J. Jarnut (eds), *Der Dynastiewechsel von 751: Vorgeschichte, Legitimationsstratagien und Erinnerung* (Münster, 2004), a collection, which, in spite of its continued focus on 751, also begins to right the strange neglect of Pippin's innovative reign. Compare J. Semmler, *Die Dynastiewechsel von 751 und die fränkische Königsalbung* (Düsseldorf, 2003).

4   Pippin's kingship, and the politics of his reign, still lack proper study, but in addition to the essays in Becher and Jarnut (eds), *Dynastiewechsel von 751*, see those in *Francia* 2 (1974), and for the vital familial political context of the first decade of Pippin's reign, P. Fouracre, *The Age of Charles Martel* (London, 2000), pp. 155–74.

aristocratic coalitions around the new ruler: this much is well known.[5] But what of the identification of Frankish rule with Christian orthodoxy, and the denigration and denial of the Christian credentials of the Franks' opponents, claims which constitute a secondary but all too easily over-looked theme of the royal ideology of the *Lex Salica* revision?

This essay will argue that such claims were rooted in the debates staged at the Church councils of the 740s, and the development of a programme of religious 'correction'. It argues that if we are to understand Carolingian notions of ecclesiastical order and Christian renewal as they were to emerge by the end of the eighth century, we must take seriously the strident accusa-tions about heresy that animated relations between the Franks and their neighbours under Pippin. Looking at the uses of the rhetoric of heresy in Pippin's reign inevitably involves focusing on the career of Boniface. The horizon of our sources for the debate about religious order in the first decade of Pippin's rule is, after all, effectively defined by the career of the Anglo-Saxon missionary and Papal legate. The letter-collection and 'Life' compiled posthumously by Boniface's disciples provide the fullest picture of these years, while Boniface himself was the driving force behind the conciliar legislation of this period. This material graphically illustrates Boniface's attempts to delegitimize his opponents as heretics and schismat-ics, who spread error and overturned right order. But, as we shall see, it needs carefully contextualizing. Boniface's claims were made in a wide-ranging conversation which involved the Papal court in Rome, and the entourages of not only Pippin but also a number of other Carolingian princes in Francia. A close reading of the material indicates that Boniface's stridency did not carry all parties. It also enables us to place the activities of Boniface's opponents – above all, the Neustrian bishop Adalbert – in the context of religious practices with deep roots in the late antique and Merovingian Gallic Church, and of contacts with the sacred topographies of Italy and the Holy Land.

Pippin's prologue to the revised *Lex Salica* essayed a history in which the Frankish kingdom in Gaul and Germany was the historical result of God's backing, and a judgement on the Romans who were former persecutors of Christian martyrs. Hence the opening celebration of Frankish 'invincibility' was intimately linked to claims about the Franks' steadfast and orthodox Christian faith. As the prologue makes clear, this claim to a special religious role rested on a reading of early Frankish history shared by Pippin and his

5 On the underlying social process, see the still-seminal T. Reuter, 'Plunder and tribute in the Carolingian Empire', *TRHS* 5th series, 35 (1985), pp. 75–94.

circle. Long-established historiographical traditions presented Merovingian success under Clovis as a result of his alignment with the mainstream Gallic episcopate, in contrast to the Arianism associated with the other barbarian courts of the post-Roman West. Carefully constructed at the end of the sixth century by Gregory of Tours, the equation of the Franks' political success with their 'firm conversion' to the Catholic faith was the cornerstone of the claims voiced in the *Lex Salica* prologue.[6]

The prologue's evocation of the distant past invites comparison with the historical account of Pippin's kingship in the 750s and 760s commissioned by Pippin's cousin Count Nibelung in the final *Continuation* of the *Chronicle of Fredegar*.[7] Here, Pippin's campaigning south of the Loire was explicitly tied to the exploitation suffered by the southern Gallic Church at the hands of the rulers of Aquitaine who were cultivating a 'Roman' identity. This accusation stands out from those levelled at Pippin's other opponents in the *Continuations of Fredgar*. Whereas the other victims of the Carolingian juggernaut were presented as 'rebels' who deserved roundly smacking into line, the Aquitainians were vilified for offending the purity of the Church. In a catalogue rehearsed at the very end of the text, under the year 768, the Aquitainians' Christian credentials are blackened: they had oppressed and expropriated ecclesiastical property, ignoring ancient liberties granted 'under the name of immunity'.[8] For Pippin's advisors 'immunity' stood at the heart of attempts to safeguard right order in the Church; both capitulary legislation and royal diplomas promote immunity as necessary to ensure that the Church enjoyed proper royal protection and was safeguarded from the

6　For the complexities obscured by Gregory's account, see I. Wood, 'Gregory of Tours and Clovis', *Revue Belge de Philologie et d'Histoire* 58 (1985), pp. 249–72, which demonstrates *inter alia* how much more we need to think about the nature of 'Catholic' and 'Arian' alignment in the fifth and sixth centuries; for concerns about the Arian heresy underpinning Gregory's ecclesiology and so shaping his historiography, M. Heinzelmann, *Gregory of Tours: History and Society in Sixth-Century Gaul* (Cambridge, 2001) and his 'Heresy in Books I and II of Gregory of Tours' Historiae', in A. C. Murray (ed.), *After Rome's Fall: Sources and Narrators of Barbarian History dedicated to Walter Goffart* (Toronto, 1998), pp. 67–82. For Carolingian receptions of Gregory see now H. Reimitz, 'Social networks and identities in Frankish historiography: new aspects of the textual history of Gregory of Tours', in H. Reimitz, R. Corradini and M. Diesenberger (eds), *Texts and Identities in the Early Middle Ages: Texts, Resources and Artefacts* (Leiden, 2003), pp. 229–68.

7　J. M. Wallace-Hadrill (ed.), *The Fourth Book of the Chronicle of Fredegar with its Continuations* (Oxford, 1960), *Continuations* c. 34, for the roles of Pippin's uncle Childebrand, and Childebrand's son Nibelung, as patrons. For the possible occasions of Childebrand and Nibelung's commissions, see R. Collins, *Fredegar* (Aldershot, 1996), but note McKitterick, 'Illusion', pp. 44–7.

8　Fredegar, *Continuations*, c. 41.

polluting stains of secularity. The major crime of the Aquitainians in the *Continuations* is precisely their failure to observe these norms: Frankish intervention was necessary for the restoration of proper order in the Church.

It is intriguing to find echoes of this same vocabulary of immunity in the *Lex Salica* prologue, written in the same circles only four years or so earlier.[9] While rooted in the narrative of Clovis' reign inherited from Gregory, the Frankish identity thus articulated was not solely backward-looking. It provided a powerful template for Pippin's own campaigns south of the Loire, which could be represented as being waged to safeguard proper Christian faith. In celebrating the care shown by the Franks for those Christians martyred by the Romans whose cults had been previously neglected, Pippin's prologue alluded to the avid interest of the Frankish elite in the relics of Roman martyrs, and his own particular involvement in the cult of Petronilla, St Peter's daughter.[10] The prologue thus grafts a sense of historical mission, in which Frankish arms guarantee proper order in religious doctrine and practice, onto the traditional celebrations of shared martial valour and God-given victory that defined the public collective action of the Frankish elite. In doing so, it imbued this act of secular legislation with concerns that had emerged in conciliar acts in a very different context, in the first, fraught and contested years of Pippin's rule: in 744, the 23 bishops brought together at Soissons under Pippin's auspices as 'mayor of the palace' had resolved to hold annual synods so as to ensure that heresy did not arise again among the populace, who had in the recent past been seduced by 'false priests' who had now been deposed.[11]

9 This is no accident, given that Baddilo, a scribe involved in drafting diplomata and legislation, wrote the prologue; see the discussion of his activities by Garrison, 'Franks as new Israel?', pp. 129–34. For contemporary understandings of immunity, see B. Rosenwein, *Negotiating Space: Privileges of Immunity in Early Medieval Europe* (Ithaca, 1999) and, for the material aspects, P. Fouracre, 'Eternal light and earthly needs: practical aspects of the development of Frankish immunities', in W. Davies and P. Fouracre (eds), *Property and Power in the Early Middle Ages* (Cambridge, 1995), pp. 53–81.

10 See in general J. Smith, 'Old saints, new cults: Roman relics in Carolingian Francia', in J. Smith (ed.), *Early Medieval Rome and the Christian West: Essays for Donald Bullough* (Leiden, 2001), pp. 317–39. On the cult of Petronilla, whose body was translated by Pope Paul shortly after his election in 757 in a new oratory next to St Peter's, where the baptismal shawl of Pippin's daughter Gisela was placed in 758, see, *Liber Pontificalis* vol. 1, ed. L. Duchesne (Paris, 1884), 'Life of Paul' c. 3, and *Codex Carolinus*, ed. W. Gundlach, *MGH Epistolae* III, *Epistolae Karolini aevi* 1 (Berlin, 1892), no. 14; and see A. Angendent, 'Das geistliche Bündnis der Päpste mit den Karolingern (754–96)', *Historisches Jahrbuch* 100 (1980), pp. 11–94, esp. p. 48 for links with the prologue.

11 *MGH Capitularia* vols. I and II, ed. A. Boretius (Hanover, 1883–1901), I, no. 12, c. 2, p. 29.

The fears expressed by the bishops assembled at Soissons in 744 were couched in terms of the potentially polluting spread of heresy. Their response was the holding of regular Church councils to ensure that the Frankish Church adhered to canonical norms and to guard against such the seduction of the populace by those who propagated error. This agenda was, shaped by the activities of the Anglo-Saxon Churchman Boniface.[12] In the hands of the young princes Carloman and Pippin, the calling of 'reform'[13] councils became a mechanism to legitimate a family power which sat ill with accepted idioms of authority focusing on Merovingian kingship. The revival of conciliar activity under Carloman and Boniface in 742 was thus rapidly followed by Pippin at Estinnes in 743.[14] As a result, Boniface's influence expanded beyond his initial mission-field across the Rhine, where he had previously operated with Papal licence, and into Francia proper, where he was now able to direct synodal activity which reshaped the Frankish Church; in 744 he received a fresh papal licence confirming this new focus of activity, reforming the Church of Gaul and Bavaria.[15] As patrons of this initiative, Carloman and Pippin were thus acting as 'protectors of the Church' in a new, active, manner and aligning themselves with the authority of Rome to do so.

Examining the canons agreed by the bishops assembled at Soissons underlines the complexity of 'correction'. The process created a sense of corporate leadership within the Church, and encouraged a debate about the right ordering of Christian society informed by regular exchanges with Rome and a search for authoritative norms: in other words, it nurtured a sense of an 'orthodox' ecclesiastical tradition encompassing and unifying the Churches of the Frankish realms. Few modern commentators have noted the extent to which, at least for Boniface and his circle, these developments could be consistently represented in terms of an age-old struggle between the canonical norms of God's holy and apostolic catholic Church,

12 The seminal studies of Boniface's career and influence remain those of T. Schieffer, *Winfrid-Bonfatius und die christliche Grundlegung Europas* (Freiburg, 1954) and W. Levison, *England and the Continent in the Eighth Century* (Oxford, 1946).

13 For the problems of our usage of this concept in this period, see T. Reuter, ' "Kirchenreform" und "Kirchenpolitik" im Zeitalter Karl Martells: Begriffe und Wirklichkeit', in J. Jarnut et al. (eds), *Karl Martell in seiner Zeit* (Sigmaringen, 1994), pp. 35–59; I have used 'correction' as corresponding more precisely with contemporary understandings of what was at stake.

14 For the *acta* see *MGH Concilia* II i, ed. A. Werminghoff (Hanover and Leipzig, 1906), nos. 1, 2.

15 Boniface, *Epistulae*, ed. M. Tangl, *Die Briefe des heiligen Bonifatius und Lullus, MGH Epistolae Selectae* 1 (Berlin, 1916), no. 58.

and the attempts of apostates, heretics, schismatics, ultimately inspired by the devil, to subvert the true faith and seduce the populace into error.[16]

Of course, such a self-representation was useful for Boniface and his followers, in that it flattened the complexities of the present, mapping them onto a typological template familiar from Biblical and hagiographical narrative. In Willibald's *Life of Boniface*, completed in the very last years of Pippin's reign – that is, around a decade after its hero's death in Frisia in 754 – now obscure political struggles east of the Rhine are thus presented in terms of the holy man's struggle against such timeless enemies.[17] This interpretative scheme meant that the syncretic religious cultures Boniface encountered were understood as deviations from universal norms, the result of the agency of evil men determined to wean those who had professed Christianity away from the true faith, 'false brethren who perverted the minds of the people and introduced among them under the guise of religion dangerous heretical sects'.[18] Willibald went on to depict Boniface's activities in Thuringia, Bavaria and Francia in turn as resting on the expulsion of heretics and the institution of canonical norms underwritten by an infrastructure of regular councils and bishops. In Thuringia, Willibald thus names four otherwise unattested figures – Torchtwine, Zeretheve, Eaubercht and Hunraed – 'the devil's disciples and insidious seducers of the people', whom Boniface had banished from Thuringia, and whose work was undone by the preaching and Church foundation of Boniface and his followers. In Bavaria under Duke Hugobert, 'a certain schismatic named Eremwulf, who has imbued with heretical opinions' was 'expelled in accordance with canonical decrees', while a subsequent invitation from Duke Odilo saw Boniface's preaching 'restoring the sacraments of the faith to their primitive purity': deceitful and immoral bishops and priests who had propagated 'evil, false and heretical doctrines' were expelled and replaced with four bishops consecrated by Boniface. In Francia, the renewal of

---

16 Though one aspect of Boniface's vocabulary of approbation is studied, alongside much else, by M. Glatthaar, *Bonifatius und das Sakrileg: Zur politischen Dimension eines Rechtsbegriffs* (Frankfurt, 2004).

17 On the representation of Boniface and his circle, see I. Wood, *The Missionary Life: Saints and the Conversion of Europe* (London, 2001), pp. 57–78, esp pp. 61–64 on Willibald. On Boniface's cult and commemoration, P. Kehl, *Kult und Nachleben des heiligen Bonifatius im Mittelalter (754–1200)* (Fulda, 1994).

18 Willibald, *Vita Bonifatii*, ed. W. Levison, *MGH SRG* (Hanover, 1905), c. 6; the logic is already present in c. 5: the Thuringians had once been true Christians but bad priests who transgressed canonical norms by fornicating – i.e., marrying – polluted the true faith and so led the people into error. The most accessible English translation of this source is that in T. Head and T. Noble, *Soldiers of Christ* (London, 1998).

conciliar activity not only meant that 'abuses were redressed and corrected in accordance with canonical authority', but also that 'a dark impenetrable gloom of error' created by the 'insidious doctrines of heretics' was lifted.[19]

Immediately on Boniface's death, Lull, his successor as bishop of Mainz, had written a long letter committing his memory, as a holy man and martyr, to Archbishop Cuthbert of Canterbury: in it, Boniface as a model bishop upholding the true faith and the canonical norms of the holy Church had fought ceaselessly against 'persecutors, pagans, heretics, schismatics and seducers', fighting 'all enemies of the true faith, heretics, schismatics and men of bad living'.[20] Lull's collecting and preserving a selection of Boniface's correspondence itself was just as much an act of cult and commemoration as the prayers requested from Cuthbert and the writing of Willibald's 'Life'. It is striking that Lull himself was able to include a number of letters in which Boniface himself was able to present his work as a campaign against heretics and schismatics, such as a request for the prayers of three Anglo-Saxon holy women, Leobgytha, Tecla and Cynehilde.[21] In promoting Boniface's cult as that of a martyr who had died preaching to pagans, but much of whose life had been spent defending the correct norms of the faith against those whose doctrines or practices led to schism and error, Lull and his circle were building on Boniface's self-representation. Of most of the rogues' gallery of defeated opponents listed by Willibald, we know little more than the names. But of two – Adalbert and Clement, both mentioned by Willibald as being removed by Boniface from the communion of the bishops of Francia under Carloman and Pippin – a fuller account of the basis for Willibald's claims of heretic perversions survives, thanks to the transmission of the acts of a Roman synod convened in October 745 to hear their case.[22]

The chronology of the condemnation and deposition of these two archenemies of Boniface is convoluted. Adalbert had already been condemned

---

19 Willibald, *Vita Bonifatii*, cc. 6, 7. As Willibald and other sources make clear, in the context of these sources Thuringia here denotes everything east of the Rhine between Alemannia and Saxony; for the possible political range of the Thuringian *duces* see M. Innes, *State and Society in the Early Middle Ages: the Middle Rhine Valley 400–1000* (Cambridge, 2000), pp. 171–2.

20 Boniface, *Epistulae*, no. 111, pp. 238–43. An English translation of the collection, with different numbering, is available in E. Emerton, *The Letters of Boniface* (New York, 1940).

21 Boniface, *Epistulae*, no. 67, pp. 139–40.

22 Boniface, *Epistulae*, no. 59. Note that this is only transmitted via Boniface's letter collection, and was presumably available to Willibald.

by the Neustrian churchmen assembled at Soissons in 744. The acts of Soissons record little of the basis for the deposition: the heretic Adalbert was a 'false priest' who had deceived the populace, and so was publicly condemned by bishops and priests, with the consent of prince and people. The hearing at Rome in 745, on the other hand, rested on a written dossier sent by Boniface in the person of his emissary Denehard, along with supporting documents. Clement was not mentioned at Soissons, nor in the surviving acts of the earlier councils convened by Boniface in Germany in 742 and at Estinnes in 743, but was also the subject of extended report in the written dossier presented at Rome in 745, albeit without supporting documentation.[23] The condemnation of 'pseudo-prophets' guilty of 'the heresy of simony' had already been relayed to Zacharias in 744 in letters requesting that the insignia of metropolitan status be forwarded to those bishops newly advanced as archbishops by the councils convened by Boniface.[24] But by 745 it was necessary to write to Zacharias again, naming both Adalbert and Clement. Although both had been deprived of their offices and placed in the custody of the Frankish princes, they were refusing to accept the penances to which they had been condemned, and continuing to lead the people astray; hence the necessity of Papal intervention.[25] Although the Roman synod convened to hear their cases confirmed their deposition and the need for penance, their fate was still not fully closed: in January 747 Pope Zacharias, writing to Boniface about a further Frankish council, acknowledged continuing fears about the activities of Adalbert and Clement.[26] Boniface's correspondence with Zacharias makes it clear that Adalbert and Clement were not the only Frankish bishops deposed in these years. In 747 Zacharias linked the cases of Adalbert and Clement with that of another, otherwise unknown, 'ex-bishop', Godescalus.[27] Similarly, in

---

23 That Boniface does not claim in his letter to Zacharias that Clement had been condemned by bishops in council suggests that he had here acted alone, perhaps brandishing his papal mandate to 'correct' the Frankish Church, and was seeking papal approval for his actions. Much earlier scholarship, however, agonized over the chronology of hypothetical Church councils for which there is no direct evidence, simply because additional synods were felt necessary to account for the deposition of both Clement and Gewilib before autumn 745, when Zacharias alluded to both in his letter to Boniface, *Epistulae*, no. 60.

24 Boniface, *Epistulae*, nos. 57, 58.

25 See the report to the Roman synod of 745, Boniface, *Epistulae*, no. 59.

26 Boniface, *Epistulae*, no. 77. The context here is the heightened political uncertainty in Francia following Carloman's 'abdication' and journey to Rome and Grifo's 'escape' and bid for power: precisely the kind of circumstances in which the deposed bishops and their supporters might manoeuvre for factional support.

27 Boniface, *Epistulae*, no. 77.

October 745 when Zacharias wrote to Boniface confirming the Roman synod's condemnation of Adalbert and Clement, he also encouraged action against bishops whose adultery or homicides made them ineligible for holy office, and upheld Boniface's letter of complaint against Bishop Gewilib of Mainz.[28]

The process was long-drawn-out, not least because Adalbert and Clement evidently enjoyed significant levels of support among their peers even after their formal condemnation. In the uncertain political conditions that prevailed right up to 754, when long-running conflicts within Pippin's family were at last settled by the death of Grifo and the final removal of Carloman and his offspring from the scene, such support had to be taken seriously. In this atmosphere, Boniface's attempt to reshape the Frankish episcopate in the 740s was a tortuous one. The depositions of Adalbert and Clement are likely, therefore, to have fitted into the contours of factional politics. Adalbert's deposition at Soissons in 744 certainly came in the aftermath of a bitter internal struggle which ended with Pippin prevailing in Neustria.[29] It is difficult not to link Boniface's ability to move on enmities which dated back to Charles Martel's reign to the shaking out of the Neustrian establishment which inevitably followed. While the context of Adalbert's deposition places him firmly within the Neustrian episcopate, Clement seems to have been active within Carloman's Austrasian realm.[30] Boniface seems to have felt able to move on his case, like that of Gewilib, at some point in 744 or 745, presumably drawing on his newly confirmed mandate to act as papal legate within the Frankish Church as a whole.

The acts of the synod convened by Zacharias at Rome to hear Boniface's case against Adalbert and Clement preserve a blow-by-blow account replete with *oratio recta*. Boniface's letter makes detailed charges against both Adalbert and Clement, urging the Pope to confirm the former's deposition as agreed under Pippin at Soissons, and to write to Carloman ordering the latter's imprisonment to prevent his teachings from spreading. Boniface takes particular care to establish not only the uncanonical status of his opponents' ministries, but also the heterodoxy of their teaching. His categories of approbation are elastic: Adalbert and Clement are lambasted as

---

28 Boniface, *Epistulae*, no. 60. Note that Boniface's actual letter of complaint against Gewilib is not transmitted, and our understanding of the case and the basis of action against him rests primarily on this indirect testimony. Boniface was still hoping to be granted the see of Cologne after this date, so the deposition preceded any plan to make Boniface bishop of Mainz, politically far more peripheral at this date.

29 For the politics, Fouracre, *Age of Charles Martel*, pp. 161–8.

30 This seems to me the implication of the account offered the Roman synod of 745, in which it is Carloman who has Clement in custody.

'false priests, heretics and schismatics'. But he is at pains to show that their contravention of established norms was not simply confined to the irregular nature of the ordination and improper conduct, but also encompassed the promulgation of 'fables, false miracles and prophecies' which subverted the true doctrine of the Church.

The doctrinal element in the accusations of heresy levelled by Boniface is clearest in the case of Clement, which received far less discussion than that of Adalbert. Clement – who was of Irish origin – was accused of holding opinions on a number of matters which stood contrary to the traditions of the Church as established in synodal decrees and the writings of Jerome, Augustine and Gregory the Great. Boniface claimed that Clement had fathered two children while exercising the office of bishop, which left him open to the accusation that he refused to acknowledge the sacred canons and despised synodal decrees. Further, Boniface condemned Clement's teachings on Christian marriage, in particular his argument from Old Testament precedent that it was legitimate for a man to marry his brother's widow. Finally, Clement was accused of teaching that at the Last Judgement Christ would deliver all 'believers and unbelievers, servants of Christ as well as worshippers of idols' from damnation in Hell.

Eighth-century Austrasia was a region undergoing the final stages of Christianization and in many areas the fate of pagan ancestors must have been a live and emotive issue. Frankish missionaries in Frisia, for example, were faced with potential converts fearful that their forebears would be condemned to eternal torment by the new faith.[31] Clement's response, in presenting Christianity as a means of saving dead kin as well as living converts, spoke to these concerns. Likewise, his teaching on marriage may have been designed to accommodate local practice, in accordance with a long-standing Papal policy of gradualism and toleration. On the specific point of taking the Old Testament as a literal statement of binding law, Clement was following a line of interpretation common in his native Ireland, and which had enjoyed some popularity in Merovingian Gaul.[32] But for Boniface, just as Clement's sexual activity was presented as a wilful deviation from the canons, so his teachings constituted a rejection of correct doctrine as enshrined in the writings of Jerome, Augustine and Gregory. Boniface

---

31 See the *Vita Wulframni*, ed. W. Levison, *MGH SRM* V (Hanover, 1910), pp. 661–73, c. 9, p. 668, and for further parallels R. Fletcher, *The Conversion of Europe* (London, 1997), p. 406.

32 See the discussion of R. Meens, 'The uses of the Old Testament in early medieval canon law: the Collectio Hibernensis and the Collectio Vetus Gallica', in Hen and Innes (eds), *Uses of the Past*, pp. 67–77.

was clear, then, that Clement was consciously deviating from authoritative norms. The specific points raised by Boniface could thus be seen as collectively constituting 'damnable opinions which are contrary to Catholic belief', and his teachings on the Last Judgement specifically constituted suspect doctrines on the issue of predestination. Hence the possibility of describing Clement as a heretic.

The 'heretification' of Adalbert was a more complex affair. As we saw, the surviving record of the council of Soissons in 744 simply records Adalbert's deposition as a 'false priest' who had 'deceived the people'. Boniface's subsequent reports to Zacharias, while they do not identify Adalbert by name, clearly allude to his deposition, but continue to level fairly general accusations against 'pseudo-prophets' who had obtained episcopal office by simony and so were heretics following in the footsteps of Simon Magus.[33] The evidence submitted to the Roman synod of October 745, however, presents a far more detailed case designed to cast Adalbert as the devil's agent in seducing the people of Gaul from correct Christianity.[34]

Adalbert's offence was to act the holy man, with sufficient success to command enough support to oppose Boniface's 'correction' of the Frankish Church. He was thus identified as the ringleader among the 'false bishops, adulterous priests and vicious clerics' who were persecuting Boniface. Boniface's case is that, although Adalbert's followers claimed that he was 'a saintly apostle . . . a patron and intercessor, a doer of good deeds and a worker of miracles', in fact he was a wolf in sheep's clothing, whose dress, bearing and behaviour recalled that of the hypocrites in Holy Scripture. Adalbert's early career, according to Boniface, rested on deception: he had build up a following among the 'simple folk', particularly 'captivating weak women' whose households he visited, carrying relics of 'extraordinary but rather suspect holiness' which he claimed had been brought from the other end of the world by an angel disguised as a man. He was then consecrated as a bishop by his peers, an elevation which Boniface is at pains to present as uncanonical, carried out by 'ill-instructed bishops' whom Adalbert had bribed: this smear was the thrust of the earlier condemnation of Adalbert as guilty of the 'heresy of simony' in Boniface's letters to Zacharias. Adalbert's conduct as a bishop, as presented by Boniface, proved that he was a vainglorious deceiver, who claimed to intercede directly with God, on account of his own merits. Boniface claimed that Adalbert erected crosses and oratories in the countryside but refused to

33 Boniface, *Epistulae*, nos. 57, 58.
34 For what follows Boniface, *Epistulae*, no. 59.

dedicate them to martyrs and apostles, instead distributing his own hair and fingernails, which were carried around in procession with the relics of St Peter. Most shocking of all, Adalbert received penitents seeking to confess their sins with the claim that: 'I know all your sins: your secret deeds are open to my gaze. There is no need to confess, since your past sins are forgiven. Go home in peace: you are absolved'. For Boniface, these accusations demonstrated that Adalbert was claiming equal status to that of the Apostles. Three pieces of written evidence as to Adalbert's conduct were further produced and discussed to confirm this diagnosis: a 'Life' written to establish Adalbert's sanctity while he still lived; a letter allegedly sent from Jesus in Heaven to Jerusalem, where it was discovered by the archangel Michael and thence had found its way via Rome to Adalbert; and a prayer composed by Adalbert which invoked the names of eight angels who, Michael excepted, were not recognized by the Pope and were seen as demons whose invocation confirmed that Adalbert was an agent of the Devil.

In Boniface's account, the resulting clash appears to pit the charismatic leader of a popular cult against the authoritative voice of the hierarchical structures of the institutional Church. Adalbert has thus become a figure of interest for modern historians wishing to trace a strain of social protest against ecclesiastical institutions, or to find a popular religion which stood outside of, and separate from, the formal Church.[35] Certainly Adalbert's representation as a living exemplar of holiness has much in common with that of other self-styled holy men, such as the sixth-century 'pseudo-Christ' described by Gregory of Tours as building up a following of three thousand 'not only the commoners but also some clergy'.[36] Adalbert's portrayal as a charismatic cult-leader rests on the apparent all-embracing enthusiasm of his followers – denigrated using gender and class stereotypes as 'weak women' and 'common folk' easily seduced by emotive appeals – who believed, according to Boniface, that their patron offered them direct access to the divine. Adalbert is thus presented as something like a living relic, and contact with him offers automatic absolution regardless of the

---

35 For the former tendency, see J. C. Russell, 'St Boniface and the Eccentrics', *Church History* 33 (1964), pp. 235–48; for the latter, A. Gurevich, *Medieval Popular Culture: Problems of Perception and Belief* (Cambridge, 1989), pp. 63–73, and N. Zeddies, 'Bonifatius und zwei nützliche Rebellen: die Häretiker Aldebert und Clemens', in M.-T. Fögen (ed.), *Ordnung und Aufruhr im Mittelalter* (Frankfurt 1995, Ius Commune Sonderheft 70), pp. 217–69 (the best, and fullest, analysis).

36 The comparison with Gregory of Tours, *Decem Libri Historiarum*, eds W. Levison and B. Krusch, *MGH SRM* I, i (Hanover, 1937), X, c. 25, is Gurevich's.

formalities of confession and penance. For Boniface, this made Adalbert a pseudo-prophet, who presented himself as equal to the apostles and thus encouraged his followers to bypass the formal hierarchies of descending divine power controlled by the institutional Church. The dossier presented at Rome certainly contains material that supports such an accusation. Adalbert is accused of venerating his own hair and fingernails as relics alongside those of the apostles. Likewise the 'Life' allegedly circulated by Adalbert's followers offers the hagiography of a living figure, and so claims sanctity before the grave. Moreover, the surviving fragment, preserved in the acts of the synod, seems to compare Adalbert with Christ: it explains that 'while he [Adalbert] was in his mother's womb the grace of God came upon him, and before his birth his mother saw, as in a vision, a calf issuing from her right side', in clear imitation of Christ.[37]

Nonetheless, care needs to be taken before taking this rhetoric at face value and analysing the conflict as one between the hierarchical authority of bishops and cultic 'popular religion'. Adalbert may have embodied some of the enthusiastic hopes of his followers for direct and unmediated contact with the holy, and in embracing these hopes crossed a line which allowed Boniface's castigation of his as a 'pseudo-prophet'. But even Boniface's dossier makes it clear that Adalbert was also very much a part of the Church establishment. Take Boniface's claim that the crosses and oratories founded by Adalbert were so popular that 'throngs of people absented themselves from the established churches, flouted the injunctions of the bishops and held their services in those places, saying, "The merits of St Adalbert will help us"'. This sits uneasily with the fact that Adalbert had been raised to the episcopal dignity by his fellow bishops: his network of churches can scarcely be seen as an attempt to create a dissenting counter-Church outside of regular hierarchies. In fact, in creating a personal constellation of rural churches Adalbert was acting exactly as did many other late Merovingian bishops. The destruction of this network – at Soissons in 744, it was ordered that the buildings be burned – was justified by Boniface's claims about the subversive nature of Adalbert's ministry. In fact, Boniface's attack on Adalbert's activity may rest on tensions over diocesan boundaries and episcopal spheres of influence of a kind which were endemic in the late seventh and early eighth centuries and, indeed, marked Boniface's own career. In a Church which rested more on personal constellations of holy

37 As pointed out by Russell, 'Eccentrics', p. 438. Note that the surviving fragment of text, preserved in the Rome *acta*, says that what follows is an account of Adalbert's *gesta* – i.e., it does not claim to be a formal *vita* on a traditional post mortem model.

foundations than territorially defined episcopal jurisdiction such conflicts were inevitable.[38]

Boniface's claims that Adalbert had refused to consecrate oratories to the relics of martyrs and apostles, and discouraged his flock from pilgrimage to Rome, were clearly designed to horrify Papal ears. But Boniface's detailed account of his opponent's activities hints at several points that relics and Rome lay at the heart of Adalbert's ministry. Adalbert's career was based on his miraculous acquisition of relics, and the popularity of his chapels and churches rested on his processing between them with holy relics, including the relics of St Peter, perhaps here incorporating the liturgical processions which defined the city of Rome into his native Gallic landscape.[39] Boniface does not specify whose relics 'of extraordinary but suspect holiness' Adalbert claimed to possess, although he does see their acquisition as the basis of Adalbert's entire career. According to Boniface, Adalbert claimed these relics had been brought 'from the ends of the earth' by 'an angel disguised as a man'. The acts of the Roman synod preserve the first part of the 'letter from Heaven' also possessed by Adalbert. This text claims that it was written by Jesus, and fell from Heaven to Jerusalem, where it was found by the Gate of Ephraim by the Archangel Michael; the copy possessed by Adalbert was then passed on to a priest named Icore, who read it and sent it to another priest in the 'city of Jeremiah', who in turn passed it to another priest in a 'city of Arabia', and so on to a further priest at an unidentified 'city', possibly Bethany, thence to 'the mount of the holy archangel Michael' and, via an angel, to Rome and the tombs of the Apostles. The notary compiling the synodal acts ends there, omitting the remainder of the text of the letter, so the substantive claims advanced in it are lost.

'Letters from Heaven' might seem outlandish to us, but they are a recurrent and little-understood aspect of early medieval religious history, and cannot be seen as inherently heterodox. 'False noxious letters' which 'fell from heaven' were first condemned in the *Admonitio Generalis* of 789, in a clause probably inspired by the memory of Adalbert's career. But even Charlemagne's insistence that letters from heaven be burned did not prevent their continuation as a central aspect of Carolingian culture. Indeed, in the *Admonitio* what was at issue was the identity of the owners of

38 For the relatively fluid and personal nature of late Merovingian Church organization see e.g. K. Heinemeyer, *Das Erzbistum Mainz im römischer und fränkischer Zeit*, vol. 1 (Marburg, 1979).

39 Compare Chrodegang's 'translation' of the Roman stational liturgy to his see at Metz: M. Claussen, *Chrodegang of Metz and the Reform of the Frankish Church and the Regula Canonicorum in the Eighth Century* (Cambridge, 2005).

such letters, and the potential unorthodoxy of their contents; hence it should be no surprise to find that such epistles, when in approved hands, were accepted as valid objects of interpretation.[40] Adalbert's letter, as is clear, rehearsed an itinerary from Jerusalem to Rome and thence, presumably, to Francia; by placing Adalbert at the end of a chain of angels and priests passing this text on, it validated his possession of a sacred text originating in Jerusalem and discovered by the archangel Michael. Boniface, remember, claimed that Adalbert's career rested on the appeal of 'extraordinary but suspect' relics acquired 'from the ends of the earth' by 'an angel disguised as a man'. The letter from heaven, then, is best seen as extraterrestrial authentication of Adalbert's relics.

If the letter is linked to a now lost relic-collection, the details of the letter's itinerary from Jerusalem become all the more interesting. The Gate of Ephraim, where the letter was allegedly found, was a genuine site in Jerusalem. While the names of the various priests responsible for passing the text on have no obvious source or parallels, the places with which they are linked are best explained as a somewhat garbled evocation of the sacred topography of the Holy Land: hence the 'city of Jeremiah', the 'city of Arabia' and probably the 'city of Bethany'.[41] The desire for contact with the land of the Bible evident here is similar to that which inspired Frankish churches to prize 'soil from the Jordan' or 'stone from the walls of Jerusalem' as holy relics.[42] The next step in the itinerary of Adalbert's letter may similarly be rooted in contemporary interest in the Holy Land as a potential site of pilgrimage. The letter travelled, thanks to an angel, to 'the mount of the holy archangel Michael'. This is normally identified with modern Mont St Michel, off the north-eastern French coast, where Michael had appeared to Bishop Autbert of Avranches in 708 at a prehistoric site on an island which was subsequently dedicated to the archangel's cult. However, the primary site identified with the Archangel Michael in this period remained the cave-grotto on the rocky promontory of Monte Sant'Angelo

---

40 I am grateful to Mayke de Jong for discussion of this phenomenon, which deserves proper study; Russell, 'Eccentrics', pp. 239–40, also notes the ubiquity of letters from heaven, citing the still-fundamental study of H. Delahaye. For the *Admonitio*, see *MGH Capitularia* I, no. 22, c. 78, p. 60.

41 The text has *civitas Wetfaniam*, but I accept Russell's suggestion of Bethany ('Eccentrics', p. 239) as that which makes most sense, the text is clearly of a site in the Holy Land.

42 On Frankish relic-collecting see M. McCormick, *Origins of the European Economy: Communications and Commerce, 300–900* (Cambridge, 2001) pp. 283–318, analysing the surviving relic tags from Sens (*Chartae Latinae Antiquiores* 18 no. 682) and Chelles (*Chartae Latines Antiquiores* 18 no. 669). See also J. P. Laporte, *Le trésor des saints de Chelles* (Chelles, 1988).

sul Gargano on Italy's Adriatic coast; Autbert's Gallic site imitated, and was profoundly influenced by, the Italian cult centre.[43] Adalbert's letter was taken to the mount of Michael en route from Jerusalem to Rome, and the major pilgrimage routes linking the Frankish world, Italy and the Holy Land likewise passed from Rome via Monte Sant'Angelo to the Adriatic and eastern Mediterranean shipping lanes. The journey of an anonymous eighth-century pilgrim from Autun to Rome, Monte Sant'Angelo, by ship to Constantinople and thence to Jerusalem is recorded on an eighth-century relic tag preserved at Sens, while the late eighth-century Bishop of Verdun, Peter, travelled to Rome, Monte Sant'Angelo and thence Constantinople, Jaffa and Jerusalem.[44]

Against this background, the case for seeing Adalbert's 'letter from Heaven' as validating a collection of relics which encompassed the transcendent power of the most sought-after sites in Italy and the Holy Land is compelling. Boniface himself, moreover, admits that Adalbert possessed relics of St Peter: Adalbert was accused of presenting himself as equal to the Apostles because he had his hair and fingernails carried alongside Peter's remains in processions. The bishops of Rome operated strict controls over the distribution of relics of their own peculiar patron and predecessor, making grants of contact-relics only (that is, precious objects which had been pushed into contact with the Apostle's tomb), and those only sparingly.[45] Given that the transmitted text of Adalbert's letter from heaven ends with an angelic journey to Rome, it is tempting to see it as legitimating the acquisition of relics of Peter through inevitably illicit channels, such as we know developed in response to Frankish demand in the ninth century.[46] Adalbert's association with authoritative sources of supernatural power thus threatened Boniface's own claims to be Rome's chosen representative in Francia, by offering direct and tangible access to the numinous source of Papal authority, Peter.

Adalbert's appeal rested on more than his possession of relics, and his ability to offer his followers contact with the cults of the apostles at Rome

---

43 On the sites and the cult, see most recently P. Bouet et al. (eds), *Culte et pèlerinage à Saint Michel en occident: les trois monts dédiés à l'archange*, Collection de l'École française de Rome 316 (Rome, 2003).

44 See McCormick, *Origins*, pp. 134–6, 304–5, 310–11.

45 See J. McCulloh, 'From Antiquity to the Middle Ages: continuity and change in papal relic policy from the 6th to the 8th century', in E. Dassmann and K. Frank (eds), *Pietas: Festschrift für Bernhard Kötting, Jahrbuch für Antike und Christentum*, Ergänzungsband 8 (1980), pp. 313–24.

46 For the ninth-century relic trade see P. Geary, *Furta Sacra: Thefts of Relics in the Central Middle Ages* (Princeton, 1978).

and the Biblical landscape of the Holy Land. Central to his career is a fascination with angels in general, and a personal devotion to the archangel Michael in particular. Angelic visitations mark the surviving fragment of his 'Life', and punctuate the letter from heaven – which, remember, was discovered by Michael and arrived in Europe via Michael's shrine. The prayer composed by Adalbert and recited by his followers, indeed, invokes nine angels in particular: Uriel, Raguel, Tubuel, Michael, Adinus, Tubuas, Saboak and Simiel. Of these, Michael was universally recognized as a genuine angel. The remaining eight names, however, enraged Zacharias and the Italian bishops assembled at Rome. These were not true angels, but demons in disguise, confirming that Adalbert was an agent of the devil; in any case, the names of the angels were not known to men, and Adalbert's prayer, in supplying these names, confirmed his status as a vainglorious deceiver. In fact, none of these angelic names is unique to Adalbert. Raguel is surely a mistake for the unambiguously orthodox, Biblically-attested, Raphael, while others originate in apocryphal Biblical books, and still others in confusions around human Biblical characters. There are attestations to the currency of similar angelic nomenclatures in Merovingian and Carolingian Gaul in a range of inscriptions and litanies.[47] Adalbert's prayer therefore should not be seen as the work of a learned fraudster claiming to know the unknowable, so much as a reflection of the bewildering variety of traditions current in the churches of Gaul, and the unsettled nature of late antique angelology. It was once again Charlemagne, in the *Admonitio Generalis*, who forbad the naming of angels other than Michael, Raphael and Gabriel, warning against prayers to 'unknown angels' as well as 'false saints' and 'dubious martyrs'; but angelology remained, and remains, a complex matter.[48] The cult of the archangel Michael, moreover, which lay at the heart of Adalbert's angelology, was, as we have seen, a popular recent arrival in Neustria. Adalbert's devotion here rode the most fashionable current trends and, as with his interest in Roman relics and the Holy Land, rested on changing patterns of Frankish contact with the Mediterranean world.

Boniface's case against Adalbert and Clement, needless to say, was accepted, with both stripped of episcopal office, Adalbert condemned to penance and his writings held in the papal archive to warn future generations, and Clement excommunicated. In presenting these opponents as heretics, consciously deviating from canonical norms enshrined

47 See the discussion of Russell, 'Eccentrics', pp. 237–8.
48 *Admonitio Generalis*, c. 16, *MGH Capitularia* I, no. 22, p. 55; and see in general D. Keck, *Angels and Angelology in the Middle Ages* (Oxford, 1998).

in authoritative texts, Boniface was following the letter of his initial licence.[49] But the condemnation of Adalbert and Clement drafted by the papal notary and subscribed by the central Italian bishops who heard the charges studiously avoided the language of heresy, instead railing against the 'sacrilegious teachings' of these 'delinquents'. Likewise, in Boniface's subsequent correspondence there is a disjuncture between his self-representation as a hammer of heretics, and the congratulations offered by his contacts at the Papal court on his work in stamping out blasphemy, schism and sacrilegious practices among the Franks, which eschew the terminology of heresy.[50]

These divergent perceptions were to come into sharp focus in Boniface's next attempt to use Papal authority to remove an opponent. In 746 Boniface – perhaps buoyed up by his success in having Adalbert and Clement removed – sent to Rome a letter condemning an unnamed Bavarian priest. Boniface's full case here is hard to reconstruct, for only Pope Zacharias' reply to his initial letter survives. But at its heart lay the formula used by the unnamed priest in baptizing his flock: his poor Latinity meant that he had been invoking not 'the name of the father, the son and the holy spirit' but 'the fatherland, the son and the holy spirit'. In the Christological disputes so typical of late antiquity, such formulae had played a central role in marking the boundaries between rival theological dispensations, and the issue of the validity of baptisms performed by heretics and false priests were matters of intense debate. Judging from Zacharias' pointed response, Boniface had similarly seen the mistake in the baptismal formula as constituting a sign of doctrinal heterodoxy. For Zacharias, however, 'a slip in Latin introduced neither error nor heresy'.[51]

Boniface's case here looks thin, but we should remember that we have only Zacharias' reply, and do not know whether Boniface had attempted to link the baptismal formula to other indices of deviation from canonical norms, in the manner in which he had so cleverly constructed cases against Adalbert and Clement. What is clear is that for Boniface and his contemporaries, the dangers posed by Christological mistakes in baptismal formulae were neither academic nor idle. An insistence on following the proper form of the baptismal rite lay at the heart of these initial efforts at Christian renewal, and the need to establish and follow canonical teaching on baptism and marriage lay at the heart of Pippin's legislation both secular and

49 Boniface, *Epistulae*, no. 44.
50 Boniface, *Epistulae*, nos. 60, 61, 62, 85. NB no. 84 does use the term but in 748, and in generic not specific terms.
51 Boniface, *Epistulae* no. 68.

synodal. This was not a matter of unthinking 'formalism', for the performance of the baptismal rite was understood as articulating adherence to the true faith; Boniface's sensitivity to the importance of correctly performed baptism, and his fear that error in baptismal ritual might lead to error in belief and develop into full-blown heresy, were thus far from isolated.[52] Quite how much was at stake is revealed by a very long letter by Zacharias in 748, dealing with Boniface's continued fears about the dangers of baptism performed incorrectly, or by false priests or heretics, and collecting canonical authorities on the baptismal rite and the circumstances in which rebaptism was necessary.[53]

The implication of Zacharias' sharp rejoinder to Boniface in 746 was that heresy involved an element of conscious, wilful, deviation: ignorant errors such as those of the unnamed Bavarian priest did not make their author a heretic. Ultimately, however, it is difficult to avoid the impression that in his attempt to intervene in Bavaria, Boniface had grown over-confident of his ability to attract Papal support against his opponents thanks to the success of 745. In 746 Boniface was not acting with Pippin and Carloman's backing against rivals in Francia proper, but attempting to intervene in Bavaria, whose political alignment remained delicate. The priests Virgil – an Irish monk who had found the favour of first Pippin, then Odilo of Bavaria[54] – and Sidonius thus were able to defend their colleague to Zacharias, earning Boniface's enmity as a result. Boniface thus proceeded to turn his fire on Virgil, claiming that he was stirring up Odilo's hostility and boasting that he had been promised one of the Bavarian bishoprics which Boniface himself had created in 739.[55] As in his heretification of Adalbert, Boniface combined personal and political smears – behind which lurk the 'heresy of simony' – with accusations about uncanonical teaching. Virgil, he claimed, taught that there was another world, populated with men and women, beneath this one.[56] Virgil, however, was to defend and

52 On baptism in this period see A. Angendendt, 'Der Taufritus im frühen Mittelalter', *Settimane* 33 (1985), pp. 275–336 and, on the relationship between 'form' and belief, P. Cramer, *Baptism and Change in the Early Middle Ages, c.200–c.1150* (Cambridge, 1993), pp. 130–220.
53 Boniface, *Epistulae*, no. 80.
54 On Virgil's career see H. Wolfram, 'Virgil of St Peter's at Salzburg', in P. Ni Chathain and M. Richter (eds), *Irland und die Christenheit* (Stuttgart, 1987), pp. 415–20.
55 These accusations are only known through Zacharias' reply, Boniface, *Epistulae*, no. 80.
56 For folkloric and mythological parallels in Virgil's native Ireland, see J. Carey, 'Ireland and the antipodes', *Speculum* 64 (1989), pp. 1–10, and note P. Brown, *The Rise of Western Christendom: Triumph and Diversity, AD 200–1000* (Oxford, 1996), p. 421.

clear himself in Rome, shortly afterward being made bishop of Salzburg. In this different context, the strategies of heretification which Boniface had used so successfully against Adalbert failed.[57]

The differences between Boniface, eager to use the language of heresy against his opponents, and the Roman Church, more chary in accepting such charges, turned primarily on different experiences and identities, not on different understandings of heresy itself. Boniface's English background, and the controversies over Easter and similar matters that had enjoyed such a high profile in the insular Churches of the seventh century, may have played a role here, although even in their virulent phases these conflicts had not led to the wholesale heretification of rival parties. Surely more important was Boniface's continental experience of reshaping the micro-Christendoms of the Frankish world through the establishment of hierarchical episcopal leadership and a tradition of collective synodal activity. Anxious to portray his own role in the black-and-white terms that befitted a holy man, and mindful of his Papal licence to convert the pagans and lead the peoples of Germany from error, the notion of a campaign against opponents who were sacrilegious and, when prepared to defend their teachings, heretical, came easily.

Rome, on the other hand, although functioning as the leader of a western, Latin, Christianity which was increasingly distinct from the Imperial Church in the east, continued to see itself as a spiritual leader within the Christian Church as a whole. Roman attitudes toward accusations of heresy thus remained profoundly influenced by late antique attempts to maintain the integrity of the universal Church, and potentially divisive charges were treated with caution.[58] It was primarily in the 750s, when Zacharias' successor Stephen, and his brother and successor Paul were desperate to secure Pippin's support against the Lombards, that religious invective crept into Papal correspondence with the Franks. Letters rehearsing the barbarity and impiety of Lombard leaders encouraged an escalating

---

57 Boniface's involvement in the complex Frankish politics of the late 740s and early 750s is unclear, but his impotency in his moves against Virgil, and the tone of his letters, may point to a waning star, one important context for his eventually renewed mission in Frisia.

58 On the political situation of the eighth century Roman Church, the best study remains T. Noble, *The Republic of St Peter* (Philadelphia, 1984), but we should not see Papal policy as monolithic nor change in Papal policy as overly dramatic: see M. Costambeys, 'Property, ideology and territorial power of the papacy in the Early Middle Ages', *EME* 9 (2000), pp. 367–96 and on papal views of kingship C. Azzara, *L'ideologia del potere regio nel papato altomedievale (secoli VI–VIII)* (Spoleto 1997).

rhetoric of ethnic degeneracy which eventually allowed the reactivation of long-dormant slurs about the heretical past of the Lombards.[59]

What is less clear is the attitude of Pippin and his circle to claims about heresy. As his capitularies, charters and coins make clear, Pippin understood his kingship as a divinely granted ministry to provide care for the Church and protection for the poor.[60] Within this ideology of Christian kingship, the Franks' special role as guardians of orthodoxy could play an important role. Boniface's insistence on the need for 'correction' to safeguard 'true religion' against the threat of heresy in the 740s here prepared the way for the Papal enlisting of Frankish power to safeguard Rome itself – the fount of apostolic authority – from Lombard opponents whose Christian credentials could be blackened. Hence by the time of the *Lex Salica* prologue, notaries working at Pippin's court could trumpet Frankish immunity from heresy. Hence by the end of his reign, the author commissioned by Pippin's kinsman Nibelung could blacken the Christian credentials of the rulers of Aquitaine, the main object of Frankish military attention in the last decade of the reign. Hence shortly after Pippin's death, in 770 when Rome was faced with a potentially dangerous marriage alliance between a Frankish princess and the Lombard king, the Pope felt that the Franks might be moved by a reminder of the polluting heretical past of a 'leprous race', surely unsuitable allies for St Peter's special people.[61]

This conjunction of Boniface's views on 'correction' in the 740s with the necessities of Papal diplomacy in the 750s suggests the possibility of justifying Carolingian expansion by the wholesale heretification of its victims. Certainly, one striking aspect of Carolingian historiography as it was established under Charlemagne was the writing out of the Christian credentials of opponents like the Aquitainians. But ultimately the representation of

59 See the correspondence collected in *Codex Carolinus*, and for a careful reappraisal of relations between Pippin, Pavia and Rome, see W. Pohl, 'Das Papsttum und die Langobarden', in Becher and Jarnut (eds), *Dynastiewechsel von 751*, pp. 145–61; the conjunction of interests between Pippin, anxious about rivals within his own family, and Stephen and Paul, anxious to use the Franks to cow the Lombards and silence rival factions in Rome, seems to mark a crucial shift.

60 The familial traditions allegedly reported to Charlemagne by Paul the Deacon in the 780s may be relevant here, hitting these same notes to provide justification for the family's rise for kingship and the eventual triumph of one line within the family: *Gesta episcoporum Mettensium*, ed. G. H. Pertz, *MGH SS* II (Hanover, 1829), pp. 260–8.

61 Compare *Codex Carolinus*, no. 45; on the context of this latter see J. L. Nelson, 'Making a difference in the eighth century: the daughters of Desiderius', in Murray (ed.), *After Rome's Fall*, pp. 171–90, and on the rhetoric, compare W. Pohl, 'Zur Bedeutung ethnischer Unterscheidungen in der frühen Karolingerzeit', *Studien zur Sachsenforschung* 12 (1999), pp. 193–208.

the past developed by Carolingian historiographers did not develop such themes, nor did it draw on notions of deviance or orthodoxy.[62] In part, this was simply because of the fact that the major victims of the Carolingian juggernaut under Charlemagne, at the formative stage in court historiography, were pagans. The Franks' archetypical enemies, after all, were the Saxons, and so Frankish conquest was ultimately read in terms of the expansion of Christianity full stop. Frankish agency in bringing a people out of the pagan past created a shared Christian present. But the rhetoric of heretification, staining entire groups by rehearsing histories polluted by diabolic aberration, had no place in a political system whose logic was inclusive, not divisive. By the last decades of the eighth century, and in the first of the ninth, Carolingian rulers could, of course, represent themselves as guardians of orthodoxy, particularly when discussing Greek 'error', but such claims were not politically live, in that they did not condition relationships with Constantinople nor shape the practice of kingship within the Empire.[63] Ultimately, it is no accident that the Boniface who was celebrated as a founding father of Carolingian Christianity was a missionary combating pristine paganism. Here, Boniface's final decision to seek red martyrdom in Frisia following the waning of his political star was vital in shaping his subsequent cult.

Boniface's fears of heresy, however, have been tacitly ignored, the implication being that his terminology is intemperate, inappropriately adopted to label cultural oddities which were only to be expected in a region of new converts and ill-defined ecclesiastical structures. This is typical of attitudes toward claims about heresy in the early Middle Ages more generally. Campaigns against heresy may be less evident in the early medieval centuries than in late antiquity and the high Middle Ages, but the language of heresy in the surviving sources should not simply be ignored because it fails to comply with expectations rooted in our more sophisticated understanding of the preceeding and succeeding periods.[64] The refusal to take talk like

62 On these issues, see now R. McKitterick, *History and Memory in the Carolingian World* (Cambridge, 2004).

63 See for example T. Noble, 'Tradition and learning in search of ideology: the *Libri Carolini*', in R. Sullivan (ed.), *The Gentle Voice of Teachers: Aspects of Learning in the Carolingian Age* (Columbus, OH, 1995), pp. 227–60, but note, for the status of the *Libri Carolini* and the priority of fears about the teaching of Felix of Urgell, A. Freeman, 'Carolingian orthodoxy and the fate of the *Libri Carolini*', *Viator* 16 (1985), pp. 65–108.

64 For a rare exception see M. de Jong, 'Religion', in R. McKitterick, ed., *Short Oxford History of the Early Middle Ages* (Oxford, 2001), pp. 131–64, at pp. 142–4, discussing heretics as 'imaginary others'; my approach here differs in specifics but is complementary.

Boniface's seriously ultimately rests on a backward projection of the increasingly tight definitions of heresy that were developed by the canon lawyers of the twelfth and thirteenth centuries. In fact, while Boniface and his contemporaries – like other early medieval thinkers – did not cite a single authoritative or canonical definition of heresy, their discussions rested on a common implicit understanding of what was involved: conscious deviation from canonical norms.[65]

Once we do take Boniface's fears about heresy seriously, it becomes clear that they are far from isolated. Not only did they animate the first stages of the process of 'correction', they also continued as a central but easily missed strand running through Carolingian legislation. Concerns about 'the heresy of simony', which began with Boniface's criticisms of the worldly networking of the Frankish episcopate and were central to the first stages of his campaign against Adalbert, were taken up at Ver in 755, in the *Admonitio Generalis* of 789 and through a rich seam of ninth-century material.[66] Fears about the spread of aberrant belief were also a constant, and bad ritual was seen as the first step on the path that led to error: Charlemagne himself worried that mispronunciation or miscopying of words might introduce deviant ideas.[67] In response, baptismal rites – understood as a pact with God to avoid infidelity, heresy or error – became a vital mechanism for the articulation of theological orthodoxy to the populace.[68] Similar concerns also animated other areas of the liturgy: Walahfrid Strabo explained that fears about the spread of teaching of Felix of Urgell had resulted in the practice of reciting the Creed more widely

---

65 Note that even Gratian, as the beginning of the process of high medieval legal definition, cites no single or coherent canonical definition, but deals with specific issues such as the status of priests ordained by heretical bishops: A. Winroth, *The Making of Gratian's Decretum* (Cambridge, 2000), pp. 34–76. On Carolingian perceptions see D. Ganz, 'Theology and the organization of thought', in R. McKitterick (ed.), *NCMH* II (Cambridge, 1995), pp. 758–85 and NB Alcuin's succinct definition, quoted p. 758.

66 *MGH Capitularia* I, no. 14, c. 24, p. 37; no. 22, c. 21, p. 55; no. 175, c. 6, p. 358; no. 177, c. 12, p. 364; *MHG Capitularia* II, no. 196, c. 1, pp. 29–30; no. 227, c. 2, p. 114; no. 252, p. 206; no. 257, c. 12, p. 262; no. 275, c. 9, p. 335; no. 293, c. 8, p. 399, and c. 43, pp. 408–9; *MGH Concilia* II, no. 37, c. 43, p. 282; no. 42, c. 6, p. 472; np. 50D, c. 11, pp. 617–8; NB this represents only a limited survey. These injunctions deserve fuller study in the wider context of Carolingian attempts to regulate gift-exchange around officials and priests. For a framework for such study, T. Reuter, 'Gifts and simony', in E. Cohen et al. (eds), *Medieval Transformation: Texts, Power and Gifts in Context* (Leiden, 2000), pp. 157–68.

67 *MGH Capitularia* I, no. 29, p. 79.

68 See now S. Keefe, *Water and the Word: Baptism and the Education of the Clergy in the Carolingian World* (Notre Dame, 2002).

and frequently in the offices of the Mass as 'medicine against the poison of heretics'.[69]

Walahfrid's example serves as a reminder that the complex debates around difficult theological points which punctuate the late eighth and ninth centuries – the attack on Felix's 'Adoptionism', the debate on images and on Claudius of Turin's extreme repudiation of them, the discussions on the meaning of the Mass following Amalarius' interpretation, and the controversy on predestination inaugurated by Gottschalk's teaching – all intersected ultimately with issues of practice. Such controversies were not solely intellectual affairs.[70] In fact, while positions in such debates might define factions within the clerical elite,[71] it was primarily isolated outsiders who could be branded trouble-makers and who were pursued and punished as a result. Politically motivated smears against insiders concerning heresy were correspondingly rare.[72] For an ecclesiastical and political establishment whose authority rested on its ability to meld together and unite diverse communities, open dissent over such issues was a spectre too awful to contemplate. In the Roman world of the fourth and fifth centuries, and again in the ferment of the twelfth and thirteenth, ecclesiastical leaders, by identifying as heretics groups who threatened or resisted their control, created orthodox authority for themselves.[73] In Carolingian Europe, the dynamics of authority were different and, despite Boniface's attempts to

---

69 Walahfrid Strabo, *Libellus de exordiis et incrementis quarundam in observationibus ecclesiasticis rerum*, ed. and trans. A. Harting-Côrrea (Leiden, 1995) c. 23.

70 The best introduction to the theology is Ganz, 'Theology' See also C. Chazelle, *The Crucified God in the Carolingian Era* (Cambridge, 2001), and the sympathetic re-contextualization of Felix's teaching by J. Cavadini, *The Last Christology of the West: Adoptionism in Spain and Gaul 785–820* (Philadelphia, 1993). Exemplary in looking at how high theology interacted with political and social imperatives is D. Ganz, 'The Debate on Predestination', in M. Gibson and J. L. Nelson (eds), *Charles the Bald: Court and Kingdom* (Aldershot, 1990), pp. 283–302.

71 As Ganz, 'Predestination', p. 355, memorably put it.

72 The example that springs to mind are the attacks on Charles the Fat's advisor Liutward of Vercelli reported in the *Annals of Fulda*, trans. T. Reuter (Manchester, 1991) sa. 887, the theology of which is nonsensical, making it clear that this is a political put-up. See also the bizarre smear of which the congregation of St Medard's at Soissons clears itself, in the context of Pippin of Aquitaine's attempted escape from custody there in 853, in *MGH Capitularia* II, no. 258, c. 5, p. 265.

73 This is the fundamental insight of the landmark work on the high medieval period, R. I. Moore, *The Formation of a Persecuting Society, 950–1250* (Oxford, 1987); for heretification as a process of authority see now J. Arnold, *Inquisition and Power: Catharism and the Confessing Subject in Medieval Languedoc* (Philadelphia, 2001), chapter 6.

make it so, heretification was not a viable strategy, for it potentially threatened the integrity and identity of Church and kingdom. Anxieties about the boundaries of true Christianity were ever present, but controversy over wrong belief was avoided wherever possible. The Franks had indeed become immune from heresy.

7

English history and Irish readers in the Frankish world*

Paul Kershaw

EXEGETE, HAGIOGRAPHER, HISTORIAN, poet, grammarian and, most fundamentally by his own reckoning, *famulus Christi*, Bede was a man of many parts.[1] By the standards of eighth-century Northumbria, however, he was not much of a traveller. Others – Benedict Biscop, Ceolfrid – were. Such travellers and their entourages bound Northumbria to a wider and rapidly changing world. It was their knowledge, the craftsmen they hired and, above all, the books that Biscop, in particular, acquired that laid the foundations for the high creations of Bede's own sedentary scholarship.[2] His famous portrait of the peace and order that prevailed in Edwin's reign – that rare moment when mother and child might journey freely from sea to sea – carried echoes not only of Bede's reading and Northumbrian sense of self, but perhaps traces also of its

* In the preparation of this paper I have accumulated many debts which I am delighted to acknowledge here: Cullen Chandler, John Contreni, Scott DeGregorio, Mary Garrison, David Ganz, Alan Thacker and Joshua Westgard all shared their knowledge and research with me, and their incisive comments have improved this paper considerably. My heartfelt thanks to them all. The errors that remain are my own. The editors have also shown exceptional patience, for which I thank them.

1 For this self-description see, among other occurrences, *HE* I, *praef.* I quote from B. Colgrave and R. Mynors, *Bede's Ecclesiastical History of the English People* (Oxford, 1969), and English translations are from J. McClure and R. Collins, *Bede, The Ecclesiastical History of the English People, The Greater Chronicle, Bede's Letter to Egbert* (Oxford, 1994) with occasional alterations.

2 As Bede himself acknowledged in his reflections upon Biscop's travels in his Homily on his Feast Day, see D. Hurst (ed.), *Homiliae Evangelia*, CCSL 122 (Turnhout, 1955), I. 13, pp. 91–2: see L. Martin, 'Homily on the Feast of St Benedict Biscop by the Venerable Bede', *Vox Benedictina* 4 (1987), pp. 81–92. For Biscop's contribution see M. Lapidge, *The Anglo-Saxon Library* (Cambridge, 2006), pp. 26–30, 34–7; E. Fletcher, *Benedict Biscop,* Jarrow Lecture (Jarrow, 1981). For Ceolfrid see I. Wood, *The Most Holy Abbot, Ceolfrid,* Jarrow Lecture (Jarrow, 1995).

author's anxieties about travel beyond the secure precincts of Wearmouth and Jarrow, his home since the age of seven.[3]

If we have little evidence that Bede travelled, we have bountiful evidence that his works achieved far-reaching and sustained popularity.[4] The paradoxical coexistence of Bede's own stability with the far-reaching influence of his works is familiar to early medievalists. So, too, is the general course by which the *Historia ecclesiastica* – my particular focus here – made its way into the wider culture of the early medieval West.[5] Bede's *Historia* found transmitters. It also found translators. In the later ninth century it was recast into Old English by an unidentified Mercian scholar working, perhaps, in the ambit of Alfred's court.[6] In the later ninth or tenth century it was partially and idiosyncratically recast into Old Irish.[7]

Compilations and other excerpts from Bede's text have received much less attention.[8] Recent years have witnessed a growing willingness to identify

---

3 *HE* II, c. 16. For an explicit example of travel anxiety in Bede's work see *Vita Cuthberti*, ed. B. Colgrave, *Two Lives of Saint Cuthbert* (Cambridge, 1940), c. 12.

4 On general issues of Bedan reception and perceived authority: J. Hill, 'Carolingian Perspectives on the Authority of Bede', in S. DeGregorio (ed.), *Innovation and Tradition in the Writings of the Venerable Bede* (Morgantown, 2006), pp. 227–49; G. Brown, 'The preservation and transmission of Northumbrian culture on the Continent: Alcuin's debt to Bede', in P. E. Szarmach and J. T. Rosenthal (eds), *Sources of Anglo-Saxon Literary Culture* (Kalamazoo, 1997), pp. 159–75.

5 For the reception of the *Historia ecclesiastica* the starting point remains D. Whitelock, *After Bede*, Jarrow Lecture (Jarrow, 1961). Recent comments on the *HE*'s continental popularity include J. Hill, 'Carolingian Perspectives on the Authority of Bede', in DeGregorio (ed.), *Innovation*, pp. 227–250, at 239–40. M. L. W. Laistner and H. H. King, *A Handlist of Bede Manuscripts* (Ithaca, 1943), supplemented by K. W. Humphreys and A. C. Ross, 'Further manuscripts of Bede's "Historia ecclesiastica", of the "Epistola Cuthberti de obitu Bedae", and further Anglo-Saxon texts of "Cædmon's Hymn" and "Bede's Death Song", *Notes and Queries* 220 (1975), pp. 50–5. For an overview of these and other assessments of the transmission of Bede's works see now the major contribution of J. Westgard, 'Dissemination and reception of Bede's *Historia ecclesiastica* in Germany, *c.*731–1500: the manuscript evidence' (unpublished thesis, University of North Carolina, Chapel Hill, 2005). I must thank Dr Westgard for offering me his own valuable views on the Bern Bede manuscript.

6 *The Old English Version of Bede's Ecclesiastical History of the English People*, ed. T. Miller, *EETS* o.s. 95, 96, 110, 111 (London, 1890–8), on which see J. Bately, 'The Alfredian canon revisited', in T. Reuter (ed.), *Alfred the Great, Papers from the Eleventh-Centenary Conferences* (Aldershot, 2003), pp. 107–20, at 108–10, D. Whitelock, 'The Old English Bede', *Proceedings of the British Academy* 48 (1962), pp. 57–90.

7 P. Ní Chatháin, 'Bede's Ecclesiastical History in Irish', *Peritia* 3 (1984), pp. 115–30; *eadem*, 'Aspects of [the] Irish treatment of some works of Bede', in S. Lebecq, M. Perrin and O. Szerwiniack (eds), *Bède le Vénérable entre Tradition et Postérité/The Venerable Bede: Tradition and Posterity* (Lille, 2005), pp. 283–7.

8 A phenomenon noted by Laistner and King, *Handlist*, p. 94.

sophisticated 'authorial' intent beyond the traditional textual categories.[9] Coupled with this has been a realization that, often concealed in the notes of editions from the Monumentists (and others), there exists a range of idiosyncratic reworkings of key historical works – the result of purposive excerption, reworking, reaggregation: careful recasting not careless recopying.[10] These versions might betray something of the range of responses such works evinced in later readers: 'subaltern' responses to the master narratives of barbarian history. The question of particularity in reception raises a final issue. Studies of individual responses to Bede's thought remain rare, those of responses to his historical writings even more so.[11]

Having started the hares of reception, reinterpretation and reuse, my intention in the remainder of this paper is to pursue them through a limited landscape: the relationship between the *Historia* of the influential but resolutely static Bede and a set of scholars whose physical movement defined them as *peregrini*, the ninth-century Irish expatriate scholars who made their careers in the Carolingian world. Within that community, I will focus upon one in particular, Sedulius Scottus.[12] The lives of such men – '*scotti* who die in foreign lands' in the self-conscious words of a marginal comment found in the ninth-century manuscript Bern 363 – are a reminder

---

9   P. Geary, '*Auctor et auctoritas* dans les cartulaires du haut moyen âge', in M. Zimmerman (ed.), "Auctor" *et* "Auctoritas": *Invention et conformisme dans l'écriture médiévale, Actes du colloque de Saint-Quentin-en-Yvelines (14–16 juin 1999), Mémoires et documents de l'École des Chartes* 59 (Paris, 2001), pp. 61–71; W. Pohl, 'History in fragments: Montecassino's politics of memory', *EME* 10 (2001), pp. 343–74, esp. pp. 344–6; 350.

10 See for example R. McKitterick, 'Carolingian history books', in her *History and Memory in the Carolingian World* (Cambridge, 2004), pp. 28–59 and works cited by her.

11 John Contreni's work on Eriugena's engagement with Bede has set the standard for such studies, 'John Scottus and Bede', in J. McEvoy and M. Dunne (eds), *History and Eschatology in John Scottus Eriugena and His Time* (Leuven, 2002), pp. 91–140; idem, 'Bede's scientific works in the Carolingian age', *Bède*, pp. 247–60, and the study of Claudius of Turin's use of Bede's commentaries, G. Italiani, 'Il "De templo Salomonis" di Beda e il commento ai re di Claudio di Torino', *Immagini del Medioevo: saggi di cultura mediolatina* (Spoleto, 1994), pp. 179–90. On the treatment of Bede's historical work by Notker and Frecculf see the important study of M. I. Allen, 'Bede and Frecculf at medieval St. Gallen', in L. A. J. R. Houwen and A. A. MacDonald (eds), *Beda Venerabilis*, pp. 61–80.

12 D. Ó Cróinín, 'Hiberno-Latin Literature to 1169', in F. X. Martin, R. T. W. Moody and F. J. Byrne (eds), *New History of Ireland* (Oxford, 2005), pp. 371–404, at 393–401. Scholarship on the Irish contribution to Carolingian culture is substantial. A key entry points is J. Contreni, *Carolingian Learning, Masters and Manuscripts* (Aldershot, 1982).

that Bede's monastic *stabilitas* was not the only mode of early medieval scholarly life.[13]

Like Bede, Sedulius Scottus was exegete, grammarian, teacher and poet.[14] Both wrote for royalty: Bede for Ceolwulf, and Sedulius for several members of the Carolingian royal family (and their relatives by marriage), turning out panegyric, occasional verse and a single political tract, his prosimetric *Liber de rectoribus Christianis*, written for Charles the Bald in late 869. For his part, Sedulius seems to have seen in Bede something of himself. At the *Historia*'s close Bede, famously, sketched a self-portrait: 'I have spent all my life in this same monastery, applying myself entirely to the study of Scripture, and, amid the observance of the discipline of the Rule and the daily task of singing in church, I always found it sweet to learn, or to teach or to write'.[15] When Sedulius came to compose his own six-line verse *confessio* he offered a self-portrait close to Bede's own.[16]

> *Aut lego vel scribo, doceo scrutorve sophian.*
> *Obsecro celsithronum nocte dieque meum.*[17]

The lines that followed reflect the influences of Horace and Martial and Sedulius' own efforts to craft the poetic persona of a man navigating the pleasures and the pitfalls of earthly life, balancing, like several of his more powerful contemporaries, earthly appetites with pious humility.[18]

---

13 Folio 138r: *de scottis qui moriuntur in aliena regione.*

14 Sedulius' career and writings are well surveyed by L. Davies, DNB, 'Sedulius Scottus (fl. 840x51–860x74)'.

15 *HE* V, c. 24: *cunctumque ex eo tempus uitae in eiusdem monasterii habitatione peragens, omnem meditandis scripturis operam dedi; atque inter obseruantiam disciplinae regularis, et cotidianam cantandi in ecclesia curam, semper aut discere, aut docere, aut scribere dulce habui.'* On this passage see S. DeGregorio, 'Bede the Monk, as Exegete: evidence from the Commentary on Ezra-Nehemiah', *Revue bénédictine* 115 (2005), pp. 343–68, at 346–7.

16 R. Düchting, *Sedulius Scottus: Seine Dichtungen* (Munich, 1968), p. 194, noting the relationship between Bede's 'meditandis scripturis', 'cotidianam' and Sedulius' 'scrutor sophian', 'nocte dieque', among other parallels, and asking 'Ob Sedulius die gewichtigen Sätze Bedas im Gedächtnis hatte?' Clearly he did.

17 'I read or I write, I teach or study wisdom / Both night and day I beseech my Highthroned One': *Sedulius Scottus: Carmina*, ed. I. Meyer, *CCCM* 117 (Turnhout, 1991), no. 74, lines 1–2. cf. Düchting, *Sedulius Scottus*, pp. 193–4.

18 For Sedulius' use of Martial, Düchting, *Sedulius*, p. 194. For Sedulius' Horatian self-image see F. Stella, 'Carolingi, scrittori', in S. Mariotti (ed.), *Orazio: Enciclopedia oraziana* (Rome. 1998), III, pp. 159–67.

Vescor, poto libens, rithmizans invoco Musas,
Dormisco stertens, oro deum vigilans.
Conscia mens scelerum deflet peccamina vitae:
Parcite vos misero, Christe Maria, viro.[19]

If the *Historia*'s closing author portrait served as an influence upon Sedulius' poetic self-representation, what can be said about the impact of the work as a whole? To understand Sedulius' engagement with Bede the historian, let us turn to two of Sedulius' works, first, his florilegium, the so-called *Collectaneum miscellaneum*, and, second, the *Liber de rectoribus Christianis* itself.

I begin with the *Collectaneum*.[20] This is a substantial work, containing as it does some 3,500 individual excerpts of varying lengths and running, in its *CCCM* edition, to some 367 pages of printed text.[21] It has sometimes been seen as Sedulius' 'notebook', serving as a distillation of his reading, a compendium of ideas, imagery and aphorisms to be used in the classroom context or to serve as raw material for more polished works.[22] It is indeed true that several of the excerpts contained in the *Collectaneum* occur elsewhere in Sedulius' writings, in particular the *Liber de rectoribus Christianis*.[23] However, the relationship between florilegium and political tract is not so simple, characterized more by complementarity than by strict stemmatic dependence, for as we have it, Sedulius' *Collectaneum miscellaneum* is far from a scrappy vademecum.[24] The sections amount to florilegia within florilegia, incorporated wholesale in the larger

---

19 *Carmina* no. 74, lines 3–6. 'I eat, I gladly drink. Rhyming, I invoke the Muses. / Snoringly, I sleep. Vigilantly, I pray to God. / My conscience mourns for the sins of my life. / O Christ, O Mary, spare your miserable man'.

20 Sedulius Scottus, *Collectaneum Miscellaneum*, ed. D. Simpson, *CCCM* 67 (Turnhout, 1988), best approached with the additional indices of F. Dolbeau, *Supplementum, CCCM* 67 (Turnhout, 1990), and see Dolbeau's comments in 'Recherches sur le *Collectaneum Miscellaneum* de Sedulius Scottus', *Archivium Latinitatis Medii Aevi (Bulletin Du Cange)*, 48–9 (1990), pp. 47–84.

21 B. Löfstedt, 'Zum *Collectaneum* des Sedulius Scottus', *Acta Classica: Verhandelinge van die Klassieke Vereniging van Suid-Afrika* 32 (1989), pp. 111–17.

22 Simpson, *Collectaneum*, p. xxii; xx–xxiv.

23 S. Hellmann, *Sedulius Scottus* [hereafter *LdRC*], pp. 109–17; L. Davies, 'Sedulius Scottus: *Liber de rectoribus Christianis*, a Carolingian or Hibernian mirror for princes?', *Studia Celtica* 26 (1991), pp. 34–50, pp. 36, 40.

24 For a discussion of the actual logistics of assembling excerpts and the nature of actual early medieval notebooks rather than formally assembled commonplace collections, see M. Lapidge, 'The origin of the *Collectanea*', in M. Bayless and M. Lapidge (eds), *Collectanea Pseudo-Bedae, Scriptores Latini Hiberniae* 14 (Dublin, 1998), pp. 1–12, at 6 n. 13.

work.[25] Sources, but perhaps also models, for Sedulius include other collections: Defensor of Ligugé's *Liber scintillarum* and the *Collectio canonum Hibernensis*.[26] Alongside *sententiae* ordered by subject – 'On Human Life', 'On Death', 'On Judgment Day' – or by established categories such as virtues and vices, Sedulius devoted numerous discrete sections to extracts drawn from the specific works of a wide range of classical and patristic authors.

Among their number we find Bede. It is a testament to his authority as a scholar (and perhaps as stylist) in Sedulius' eyes that Bede, almost uniquely among post-Roman authors, received a separate section.[27] Beneath the title 'from the Deeds of the English' (*ex gestis Anglorum*) Sedulius extracted forty-one excerpts from the *Historia* drawn from all five books. All but two passages are in the order in which they occur in the *Historia*.[28] Most run to between one and three lines in their modern edition and consist of specific comments or observations by Bede, cut from their immediate context and reshaped into generalized statements or dicta. A few, however, are longer, and maintain some internal narrative coherence.[29]

Sedulius began his compilation with two brief statements about Diocletian's persecutions (nos. 1–2) and a further two about the Anglo-Saxon invasions (nos. 3–4), before moving on to two passages describing the qualities of Germanus of Auxerre and his fellow missionaries and then abridging Bede's account of the 'Alleluia' victory (nos. 5–6). Following a single extract from the ninth and final reply in Gregory's *Libellus responsionum* on the nature of sin (no. 7), a sequence of brief phrases follow sharing a focus in a king's ideal relationship to God (nos. 8–18), drawing from Boniface V's letter to Ethelberga (cited in *HE* II, c. 11) and Bede's accounts of Edwin and Oswald. Nos. 19–24 are a sequence of extracts from Bede's account of Áedán, concentrating in particular upon his saintly qualities (mildness, humility, self-control) and two of his miracles, *HE* II, cc. 15, 16). A short

25 Simpson, *Collectaneum*, XXV, pp. 157–89; LXXX, pp. 314–56; M. Garrison, 'The *Collectania* and medieval florilegia', in M. Bayless and M. Lapidge (eds), *Collectanea Pseudo-Bedae*, pp. 42–83.
26 *Liber Scintillarum*, ed. H. M. Rochais, *CC* 117 (Turnhout, 1957).
27 Simpson, *Collectaneum*, LXXII, pp. 292–6.
28 In the discussion that follows I use the numbering provided by Simpson.
29 For example no. 6, an extract from Bede's account of the 'Alleluia' victory of Germanus of Auxerre, and no. 20, the longest extract in the collection, an abbreviated version of Bede's account of Áedán giving away the gift of a horse from Oswine, and no. 25, an extract drawn from that early medieval favourite, Fursey's vision of Hell. See Simpson, *Collectaneum*, LXXII nos 6, 20, 25, pp. 293–5.

excerpt from Fursey's vision of Hell, listing the fires of sin glimpsed by the saint (no. 25) is followed by a sequence addressing Judgement Day (nos. 26–7), and by a return to excerpts treating holy virtues, in this case those of Tortgyth and Putta (nos. 28–9). The final extracts consist of apothegmata and imagery drawn from Bede's account of Wilfrid, addressing those who fell short of the ideals of the Christian life (nos. 31–35), closing with a sequence of passages that, like the earlier section on Áedán, excerpt some of Bede's description of Wilfrid's qualities.

These extracted passages reveal something of Sedulius' interest in the political imagery, ideas and examples of Bede's *Historia*. They also shed light upon the figures in the *Historia* that engaged Sedulius' interests: Germanus, Oswald, Áedán and Wilfrid, and their qualities. Certain extracts seem to have been selected for their arresting turn of phrase and metaphor. After all, Sedulius was – as his verse reveals – a stylist. From the *Historia* he drew several striking agricultural images:

Tum hostes caedunt omnia, et quasi maturam segetem obuia quaeque metunt, calcant, transeunt.[30]
[Then the enemy hosts cut down everything; they reaped, trampled down, and passed through whatsoever was in their way as if it were ripe corn].

Omnis inimici zezania penitus est expurganda.[31]
[Every tare of the enemy must be absolutely rooted out.]

Aratra eorum nec recte incedunt.[32]
[Nor do their ploughs run straight.]

Bede's earthy one-liners clearly caught Sedulius' eye. At least one phrase, however, might be said to have struck a more personal chord. Sedulius' pen-portrait offered an image of a scholar capable of moving from watchful prayer to gleeful drinking. It ought not to surprise us then that he took from Bede's account the mutual delight Cuthbert and the hermit Herbert found in each other's company:

Tunc sese alterutrum caelestis uitae poculis debriarunt.[33]
[Then each made the other drunk with the cups of the heavenly life.]

---

30 Simpson, *Collectaneum*, LXXII no. 3, p. 292, drawing from *HE* I, c. 12.
31 Simpson, *Collectaneum*, LXXII no. 26, p. 295, drawing from *HE* III, c. 29.
32 Simpson, *Collectaneum*, LXXII no. 34, p. 295, drawing from *HE* V, c. 9.
33 Simpson, *Collectaneum*, LXXII no. 33, p. 295, drawing from *HE* V, c. 27.

Sedulius possessed a sustained interest in wisdom literature and *sapientia* in its manifold forms. The first section in Sedulius' *Collectaneum* consists of the so-called *Proverbia Grecorum*, a sequence of quasi-scriptural maxims whose smattering of Greek terms and title mask a work probably composed in seventh-century Ireland.[34] A second set of extracts from the *Historia* suggest that Sedulius saw Bede's writings as a source of *sapientia*: presented as free-standing statements, they offered universal truths.

Gemina pestis est acerbissima: odium ueritatis et amor mendatii.[35]
[These twin plagues are the bitterest: hatred of truth and the love of lies.]

Nullus fidem bonam, quae omnibus ornamentis preciosior est, amore pecuniae perdere debet.[36]
[No one should lose good faith, which is more precious than every valuable, for the love of money.]

Caminus diutinae tribulationis multos electos decoquit.[37]
[The forge of prolonged tribulation refines many of the elect.]

Grande uulnus grandioris curam medelae desiderat.[38]
[A great wound calls for a greater cure.]

Qui non uult aecclesiae ianuam sponte humilitatis ingredi, necesse habet ianuam inferni non sponte dampnatus introduci.[39]
[He who will not enter willingly the gate of the church of humility has of necessity to be brought unwillingly through the gate of Hell.]

In these extracts Bede, commentator on Proverbs and a scholar who hymned others for their wisdom, found himself mined for *sapientia*.[40]

---

34   D. Simpson, '*The Proverbia Grecorum*', *Traditio* 43 (1982), pp. 1–22; B. Bischoff, 'Nachlese zu den *Proverbia Graecorum* (sechstes Jahrhundert?)', *Anecdota novissima* (Stuttgart, 1984), pp. 98–100; B. Taylor, 'Medieval proverb collections: the West European tradition', *Journal of the Courtauld and Warburg Institute* 55 (1992), pp. 19–35.

35   Simpson, *Collectaneum*, LXXII no. 4, p. 292, drawing from *HE* I, c. 14.

36   Simpson, *Collectaneum*, LXXII no. 14, p. 293, drawing from *HE* II, c. 12.

37   Simpson, *Collectaneum*, LXXII no. 29, p. 295, drawing from *HE* IV, c. 9.

38   Simpson, *Collectaneum*, LXXII no. 32, p. 295, drawing from *HE* IV, c. 23.

39   Simpson, *Collectaneum*, LXXII no. 36, p. 295, drawing from *HE* V, c. 14.

40   Bede, *Super parabolas Salomonis*, ed. D. Hurst, *CCCM* 119B (Turnhout, 1983), pp. 20–163. On florilegia and wisdom see Garrison, 'Florilegia', pp. 53–7.

What of the individuals who captured Sedulius' eye? In the cases of Wilfrid and Áedán, Sedulius was clearly interested in Bede's assessment of their virtues, excerpting for both the *Historia*'s brief descriptions of their character and qualities. Their humility, in particular, caught his eye.[41] It was in this context that he copied Bede's famous account of Áedán's decision to give away the horse that King Oswin had given him. With Germanus and Oswald, the fact that saint and king had both ensured victory over their enemies by prayer rather than through force of arms sparked Sedulius' interest:

Osuald rex dixit: Flectamus omnes genua, et Deum omnipotentem uiuum ac uerum in commune deprecemur, ut nos ab hoste superbo ac feroce sua miseratione defendat.[42]
[King Oswald said: 'Let us all kneel and together beseech the almighty, living and true God to defend us in his mercy from a proud and fierce enemy'.]

With immediate consequences:

Hinc ipse cum pauco exercitum uictor exstitit.[43]
[Hence he, together with a small army, emerged the victor.]

To these excerpts Sedulius added a number that focused upon Oswald's constancy in faith, and the benefits that his subjects enjoyed as the result of a ruler standing in right relation to God. These same images informed his own formulation of ideal kingship.

Taken as a whole the resonances of such an idiosyncratic set of extracts with both Sedulius' formally projected persona and what we can see of his interests and opinions elsewhere in his work leaves lingering suspicions that what we see here is very much Sedulius' individual response to the *Historia*: a ninth-century Irish scholar plucking what appealed from the writings of an eighth-century Northumbrian.[44] Might Bede's image of

---

41 Simpson, *Collectaneum*, LXXII no. 19, p. 293 (Áedán's general qualities), drawing from *HE* III, c. 3; no. 20, pp. 293–4 (Áedán's *humilitas maxima* and his giving away of Oswine's gift of a horse to a poor man), drawing on *HE* III, c. 14.

42 Simpson, *Collectaneum*, LXXII no. 17, p. 293, drawing from *HE* III, c. 2.

43 Simpson, *Collectaneum*, LXXII no. 18, p. 293, drawing from *HE* II, c. 9.

44 In time the wheel would, appropriately, turn again. In the later tenth century Ælfric borrowed from Sedulius' *Liber de Rectoribus Christianis* at several points: J. C. Pope, *Homilies of Ælfric: A Supplementary Collection* 2 vols., EETS o.s. 259, 260 (London, 1967–68), pp. 375–6, 378–9 and 727.

Áedán also have struck a chord with Sedulius? Áedán was, after all, an expatriate Irish churchman setting forth examples of humility and correct Christian behaviour to a king, though it is doubtful, bearing in mind the frequency with which alimentary anxieties surface in Sedulius' verse, that he would have been as selfless as Áedán in giving away a royal feast, and the silver upon which it was served, to the poor.[45] Nor is it easy to imagine Sedulius as shocked as his countryman when faced, as Áedán was, by the novelty of a humble king. By the time Sedulius set foot on Frankish soil, humility was well on its way to a central position in the ideology of Frankish kingship.[46] It was a quality he himself would praise, although Sedulius' kings, of course, exercised humility within a single context, their relationship with God.[47]

The role of guide to the exercise of Christian rule is implicit in his numerous poems on kingship. It reached its fullest flowering, however, in Sedulius' composition of the *Liber de rectoribus Christianis*. This *Fürstenspiegel*, was composed around 869, almost certainly for Charles the Bald on the occasion of his accession to the Lotharingian throne.[48] Across twenty chapters of prose and verse Sedulius outlined his view of Christian kingship, revealing in the process the breadth of his historical knowledge, as he paraded a number of figures from the scriptural and classical past from David and Solomon through to Constantine, Theodosius II and Theoderic, and including on the way some less frequently encountered presences in ninth-century Western political thought: Xerxes, Leonidas, Alexander the Great.[49] In

---

45 *HE* III, c. 6.

46 P. E. Dutton and H. L. Kessler, *The Poetry and Paintings of the First Bible of Charles the Bald* (Michigan, 1995), pp. 81–4; R. Deshman, 'The exalted servant: the ruler theology of the Prayer book of Charles the Bald', *Viator* 2 (1980), pp. 385–417.

47 *LdRC* c. 12, pp. 53–7.

48 N. Staubach, *Rex Christianus: Hofkultur und Herrschaftspropaganda im Reich Karls des Kahlen, II. Die Grundlegung der 'religion royale'* (Cologne, 1993), pp. 200–10. For earlier arguments for the work's recipient, Davies, 'Sedulius'.

49 *LdRC*, c. 1, pp. 21–5 (Solomon), c. 3, pp. 27–30 (Saul), c. 4, pp. 30–3 (Solomon), c. 5, pp. 34–7 (Theodosius and Placilla), c. 8, pp. 43–6 (Antiochus, Herod, Pontius Pilate, Pharaoh, Nero, Julian the Apostate, Theoderic), c. 9, pp. 46–9 (Solomon, the Antonines, Constantine, the Theodosii), c. 11, pp. 50–3, (Constantine, Valentinian, Jovian), c. 12, pp. 54–8 (David, Theodosius, Solomon), c. 14, pp. 62–6 (Leonidas, Xerxes), c. 14, pp. 62–6 (Antoninus Pius, Saul, Solomon, David), c. 15, pp. 66–72 (Moses, Hezekiah, Josephat, the Maccabees, the Theodosii, St Germanus), c. 16, pp. 72–7 (Constantine), c. 17, pp. 77–80 (Amaziah, Jeohoaz, Julian the Apostate, David), c. 18, pp. 80–4 (David, Constantine, Alexander). Greek history, like Greek letters, fascinated Sedulius: B. M. Kaczynski, *Greek in the Carolingian Age: The St Gall Manuscripts*. Speculum Anniversary Mongraphs 13 (Cambridge, MA, 1988), pp. 5, 85, 91, 115.

addition to Bede Sedulius deployed lessons drawn from the *Scriptores Historiae Augustae*, Orosius and the *Historia Tripartita* ascribed to Cassiodorus.[50] Structurally, the *Liber*'s prosimetric form betrays Boethius' influence, as does Sedulius' use of the image of the wheel.[51] While not a historical work in the strictest sense, the *Liber* shares with the *Historia* a vision of the past as a repository of exemplars, good and bad, which taught their royal recipients how to live and rule, teaching, as Bede put it, how they might 'learn to pursue those things which they learned to be good and pleasing in God's sight'.[52] The *Liber* begins with a striking image, the accession of the Christian ruler:

Postquam regale sceptrum regnique gubernacula rector Christianus susceperit, primum quidem gratiarum actiones atque condignos Omnipotenti sanctaeque ecclesiae honores oportet ut rependat.[53]
[As soon as a Christian ruler has taken up the royal sceptre and the government of the kingdom, it is fitting that he first should repay acts of thanksgiving and suitable honours to God].

The image – as Hellman noted – echoed Bede's own account of Oswald's accession and no. 9 in the *Collectaneum*'s Bedan section.

Tunc regale sceptrum regni que gubernacula Osuald suscepit.[54]
[Then the royal sceptre and the rulership of the kingdoms were taken up by Oswald.]

Oswald offers the specific case that Sedulius, working in a fashion very similar to that which he displayed when turning Bede's specific phrases

---

50 For the *Scriptores* in the *Collectaneum*, LXXVIII, pp. 305–13, Orosius, *Collectaneum* XXII, pp. 147–52; for the *Historia Tripartita' Collectaneum* XXVI, pp. 190–200. On the *Scriptores* see L. W. Gurney and P. J. Gurney, 'The *Scriptores Historiae Augustae*: history and controversy', *Literary and Linguistic Computing* 13.3 (1998), pp. 105–9, with references to earlier studies.

51 A. Scharer, 'The writing of history at King Alfred's court', *EME* 5 (1996), pp. 177–206.

52 *HE, Praef.*: *Siue enim historia de bonis bona referat, ad imitandum bonum auditor sollicitus instigatur; seu mala commemoret de prauis, nihilominus religiosus ac pius auditor siue lector deuitando quod noxium est ac peruersum, ipse sollertius ad exsequenda ea, quae bona ac Deo digna esse cognouerit, accenditur.*

53 *LdRC* c. 1, pp. 21–2.

54 Simpson, *Collectaneum*, LXXII no. 9, p. 293. This excerpt is unique in that it draws from both *HE* II, c. 5's account of Eadbald's accession (*Eadbald regni gubernacula suscepisset*) and *HE* III, c. 3's account Oswald's (*Oswald . . . suscepit regnum*). For this excerpt's debts see Hellmann, *Sedulius*, p. 21.

into generalized proverbs, universalized into the ideal *rector Christianus*.[55] In 869 Oswald was, in some ways, a plausible model on which to base an ideal of rulership intended for Charles the Bald. Oswald had, after all, reunited Bernicia and Deira, and Charles, following Lothar's death, was poised in 869 to extend his authority into Lotharingia: a peaceful ruler presiding, like Oswald, over two realms.[56] This fusion was to be sealed by Charles' coronation in the basilica of St Stephen in Metz, an occasion at which Sedulius was present and at which he composed verses in Charles' honour.[57]

One of the strongest themes in the *Collectaneum* extracts is that drawn from Bede's instances in which victory was won through God's aid, the result of prayer before battle and thanksgiving after.[58] 'The Christian leader should trust neither in his own strength nor in that of his followers, but in the Lord', runs the title of chapter 14.[59] In the following chapter ('Why divine assistance should be implored against rumbles of hostile wars') Sedulius built upon this idea, working out at some length and with numerous examples the lesson of Oswald's victory and offering a substantial account of Germanus' victory, drawing extensively from Bede.[60] Other key elements in Sedulius' *Liber* carry strong Bedan resonances. Equally important to Sedulius was the sense for a ruler to be wise, to rule well through *sapientia* and, like Oswine faced with Áedán, to acknowledge the authority of the Church and its agents. 'It is glorious', announces the title of the *Liber*'s twelfth chapter, 'for a pious ruler to submit to the most beneficial admonitions and reproofs of priests'.[61] A virtuous ruler, Sedulius explained

---

55   For attitudes to Oswald on the Continent see A. Jansen, 'The development of the St Oswald legends on the Continent', and D. Ó Riain-Raedel, 'Edith, Judith, Matilda: the role of royal ladies in the propagation of the Continental cult', in C. Stancliffe and E. Cambridge (eds), *Oswald: Northumbrian King to European Saint* (Stamford, 1995), pp. 210–29 and 230–41.

56   On the importance of Charles's ruling two kingdoms, see *Annales Fuldenses*, ed. F. Kurze, *MGH SRG* 7 (Hanover, 1891), *s.a.* 869, and Nelson, *Charles*, pp. 219–20.

57   *Carmina* no. 12, pp. 28–9. For commentary see Staubach, *Rex Christianus*, pp. 200–10; R. Düchting, *Sedulius Scottus*, pp. 60–4.

58   Simpson, *Collectaneum*, LXXII no. 6, drawing from *HE* I, c. 2 (Germanus' 'Alleluia' victory), p. 293; no. 12, drawing from *HE* II, c. 11 (Pope Boniface advises Æthelburga to give thanks to God for her husband's conversion and that of his subjects), p. 293; nos. 17–18, drawing upon *HE* III, c. 2; II, c. 9 (Oswald's prayer before battle and the victory that came about as a direct result), p. 293.

59   Hellmann, *Sedulius*, p. 21: XIV. *De duce Christiano, non in sua nec in suorum fortitudine, sed in Domino confidat.*

60   Hellmann, *Sedulius*, p. 21: XV. *De eo quod imminentibus hostilium bellorum fragoribus divinum sit implorandum auxilium. LdRC* c. 15, pp. 66–72, at 68–70.

61   Hellmann, *Sedulius*, p. 21: XII. *De eo quod saluberrimis antistitum admonitionibus et correptionibus pio rectori obtemperare sit gloriosum.*

in the chapter's opening, echoing Bede's description of Wilfrid excerpted in the *Collectaneum*, ought to possess the virtues he expected in his subjects: humility and obedience.[62] Sedulius went on illustrate royal obedience not with the image of Áedán with Oswine at his feet, but rather with the classic image of a ruler kneeling before the authority of a priest, Theodosius' penance before Ambrose in Milan.[63] Nor did Sedulius ignore the damage wrought by bad kings. What made kings evil? Bad advisors, Sedulius explained. What characterized bad advisors? 'A twofold disease', he explained, 'love of falsity and hatred of the truth': the disease that had plagued post-Roman Britain at a time when bad counsel – the decision to invite the Saxons in as defenders – paved the way to its undoing.[64]

The *Collectaneum's* Bede extracts, with their focus upon the dangers of deceitfulness, the repeated notion that victory came from God not human agency and the overwhelming notion that prayer was the means by which God's aid might be enlisted, together with a repeated sense of the importance of humility amount to a blueprint for the face of kingship to be found in the *Liber de rectoribus Christianis*.

Might they have been selected from the *Historia* because they resonated with Sedulius' own pre-existing vision of rulership? This is doubtful, not least because of the overwhelmingly textual relationship between the *Historia*, the *Collectaneum* and the *Liber*. The *Historia* influenced Sedulius' political thought, rather more than any indigenous tradition of Irish kingship tracts had.[65] Sedulius, after all, was a scholar, to some degree 'for hire', and the intellectual culture he encountered in high Carolingian circles had been shaped by Alcuin and was, until his death in 856, being shaped by Hrabanus. Association with Bede offered scholarly credibility, and status, as Notker would recall some decades later.[66] And so, perhaps, it mattered

---

62 *LdRC* c. 12, p. 54: *Oportet autem modestum dominatorem pondere humilitatis et oboedientiae virtute fieri praeditum, ut virtutes, humilitatem videlicet atque oboedientiam, quas ipse in subiectis diligit, in se ipso recognoscat.* Compare with Simpson, *Collectaneum*, LXXII, no. 37, p. 296, drawing from *HE* V, c. 19: *Vir humilitatis et oboedientiae uirtutibus, non mediocriter insignitus.*

63 S. Hamilton, 'A new model for royal penance? Helgaud of Fleury's Life of Robert the Pious', *EME* 6 (1997), pp. 189–200; R. Schieffer, ' "Von Mailand nach Canossa", Ein Beitrag zur Geschichte der christlichen Herrscherbusse von Theodosius nach Canossa: Heinrich IV', *DA* 28 (1972), pp. 333–70.

64 *LdRC* c. 7, pp. 41–2 at 42: *Hinc saepe tumultuosa indisciplinatione et Dei cultrix pietas et veritas opprimitur, cum multum derogatio praevaleat quando derogatores creduntur fide digni, quos gemina pestis corrumpit acerbissima, amor videlicet falsitatis et odium veritatis.*

65 Davies, 'Sedulius'.

66 Notker claimed that Alcuin's pre-eminence at Charlemagne's court rested largely on his being a *discipulus* of Bede, *Gesta*, I. 1, p. 3. Notker was, in fact if not in spirit,

to Sedulius, whose use of Bede may be a reflection of his authority in the Frankish world as much as it is a manifestation of it.

General lessons and specific phrases from the *Historia* can be found in Sedulius' *Liber*. The only named figure found in both is St Germanus: a Gallic churchman with a thriving cult in Francia in large part due to the energies of Sedulius' immediate contemporary Heiric of Auxerre. Sedulius clearly considered kings from the Achæmenid, Macedonian, Maccabean and Theodosian houses appropriate models for Charles the Bald. Charles was after all, a scholar, a pupil of Walahfrid.[67] In his *Historiae*, Freculf of Lisieux had taught the young prince early lessons about some of the same rulers whom Sedulius, four decades later, would evoke for an experienced king in his mid-forties.[68]

Sedulius' *Collectaneum* and *Liber de rectoribus Christianis* reveal something of an individual ninth-century scholar's response to the *Historia*, and the very particular lessons it taught when harnessed to a set of ideals of ruler-ship. A different perspective is offered by the Irish scholars who excerpted Bede in Bern, Bürgerbibliothek 363. This manuscript, also known also as the 'Bern Horace', is familiar to classicists and early medievalists alike.[69] It

wrong; see M. Lapidge, 'Aediluuf and the School of York', in A. Lehner and W. Berschin (eds), *Lateinischen Kultur im VIII. Jahrhundert: Traube-Gedenkschrift* (St Ottilien, 1990), pp. 161–78 [reprinted in M. Lapidge, *Anglo-Latin Literature, 600–899* (London, 1996), pp. 381–98, with addenda at 513.] For Notker's appraisal of 'our Bede' (*Beda noster*) as a new sun in the west (*novum solem ab occidente*) see E. Raumer, 'Notker des Stammlers '*Notatio de illustribus uiris*'; kritische edition', *Mittellateinisches Jahrbuch* 21 (1986), pp. 34–69, with text at 58–69.

67 Nelson, *Charles*, pp. 82–6; R. McKitterick, 'Charles the Bald (823–877) and his Library: the Patronage of Learning', *EHR* 95 (1980), pp. 28–47. For Walahfrid's role as Charles' tutor, and for arguments that he was not, see C. Booker, 'A new Prologue for Walafrid Strabo', *Viator* 36 (2005), pp. 83–105 at pp. 83–4.

68 Freculf, *Frechulfi Lexoviensis episcopi opera omnia*, ed. M. I. Allen, *CCSL* 169A (Turnhout, 2004). A. Knaepen, 'L'Histoire gréco-romaine dans les sources littéraires latines de la première moitié du IXe siècle: quelques conclusions provisoires', *Revue belge de philologie et d'histoire* 79 (2001), pp. 341–72.

69 H. Hagen, *Catalogus codicum bernensium, bibliotheca Bongarsiana* (Bern, 1875), pp. 347–50; idem, *Codex Bernensis 363 phototypice editus, Codices graeci et latini photographice depicti* 2 (Leiden, 1897). Studies of the manuscript as a whole include S. Gavinelli, 'Per un'enciclopedia Carolingia (codex Bernese 363)', *Italia Medioevale e Umanistica* 26 (1983), pp. 1–25; J. Contreni, 'The Irish in the Western Carolingian Empire (According to James F. Kenney and Bern, Bürgerbibliothek 363)', in H. Löwe (ed.), *Die Iren und Europa im früheren Mittelalter* (Stuttgart, 1982), pp. 758–98. Kenney, *Early History*, pp. 559–60. Specific studies of the OI glosses: W. Stokes, *Goidelica* (1872), pp. 54–5; C. Nigra, 'Les gloses irlandaises du manuscrit de Berne', *Revue Celtique* 2 (1873–75), pp. 446–52.

copies the text and copious accompanying marginalia from an earlier manuscript, an indication of the scholarly value assigned to the comments, cross-references and annotations of the so-called 'Bern master'. The identities of those named in the margins, their collective association with northern Italy, and the additional evidence of a sequence of poems once ascribed to Sedulius, and dedicated to Tado, Archbishop of Milan (860–8), all point strongly to its production in or around Milan, probably within the general orbit of the episcopal *familia* of St Ambrogio, and the 860s as the likeliest date for the assembly of the exemplar.[70] Among other texts it contains together with extracts from Dioscorides' *materia medica*, most of Servius' Vergilian commentaries, works on rhetoric and dialectic by Atilius Fortunatianus and Augustine, and a selection of verse, mostly classical, and including excerpts from Ovid and the Odes of Horace.[71]

Recently characterized as a 'rhetorical-poetical miscellany', Bern 363 is almost certainly a teaching collection with wide pedagogic application: a guide to grammar, metrics, rhetoric and medicine, among other subjects.[72] Bern 363's marginalia are a roll-call of ninth-century intellectuals. Sedulius Scottus and Eriugena both figure prominently, the former's presence leading many to conclude that the original manuscript emerged from what Traube called the *Sedulius Kreise* ('the Circle of Sedulius'), but so do figures like Angelberga, wife of Louis II, Gottschalk, Ratramnus and Hincmar, together with a number of unidentified figures.[73] These marginal names served as cross-references: points where the example, writings or known opinions of the named individual might be raised in discussion, in order

70 Gavinelli, 'un'enciclopedia'. For the poems see N. Staubach, 'Sedulius Scottus und die Gedichte des Codex Bernensis 363', *Frühmittelalterliche Studien* 20 (1986), pp. 549–89. Many of these issues are addressed by C. Chandler (Lycoming College, PA) in his unpublished paper '*Codex Bernensis 363*: the Italian connection'. I thank Dr Chandler for generously sharing his many insights with me.
71 Gavinelli, 'un'enciclopedia', pp. 3–4.
72 Contreni, 'Irish', p. 769. In an unpublished paper, 'Codex Bernensis 363: Reading Horace in the Ninth Century', delivered at the 2002 Annual Meeting of the Classical Association of New England, Dr John Higgins added support to Bern 363's purpose as a teaching collection by arguing that the arrangement of the poems was by metre rather than conventional order. I draw from the abstract printed in *Classical Association of New England Annual Bulletin* (2003), p. 17.
73 For identifications of many of the names see Hagen, *Codex Bernensis*, pp. xliii–lxviii, and the comments of Contreni, 'Irish', pp. 766–8; Kenney, *Sources*, p. 560; Chandler, '*Codex*'.

to illustrate or elucidate particular points (or when a particular passage, in turn, might illuminate another issue), or to remind the reader of a relevant contemporary event or figure.[74] Other marginal notes, such as the frequent occurrence of the sigla 'q' (*quaestio, quaerere*) and 'p'. (*praedicare*), often embellished with an x-shaped cross on the descender much resembling a chrismon, and frequent injunctions to *lege semper* ('*l.s.*'), together with the Bern Master's occasional habit of adding enumerations beside passages of texts (a reflex to which I shall shortly return) provided a framework for ordered exposition. A further aid was the expansion of certain words and short phrases in the text's main body, fitting the book for classroom consultation and easy reference. These were aids for the eye.[75] Taken as a whole, Bern 363 not only sheds powerful light on the transmission of key texts but also hints at the far more intangible processes of explicating texts in the ninth century.

Folios 188v to 194r of Bern 363 contain a substantial portion of the *Historia ecclesiastica*'s first book, which for present purposes I will refer to as the Bern Bede. It begins with a highly abbreviated version of Bede's prefatory dedication to Ceolwulf in *HE* I, c. 27 and ends toward the close of Gregory's *Libellus responsionum*, in its question-and-answer form. It follows a selection of passages drawn from the first three books of the *Metamorphoses*, an abrupt break midway through Cadmus' battle with the water serpent at the Castalian spring, and is itself followed by a sequence of three poems dedicated to Tado of Milan, which starts at the top of folio 194v, the text ending, in mid-thought, at the bottom of folio 194r (. . . *quae est in membris meis*) toward the close of Gregory's reply to Augustine's query about nocturnal emissions. From the position of Bede's final request for prayers (*Praeterea omnes . . .*) it is clear that it belongs, albeit perhaps in the capacity of a 'quite eccentric' cousin – to the family of the Moore Bede once in Charlemagne's collection.[76]

What was a partial text of the *Historia* doing rubbing shoulders with Augustan verse, Hellenistic pharmacopeia and late antique grammars in that ninth-century classroom, with its (probably) Irish master and Italian students?

---

74 Contreni, 'Irish', pp. 766–8, to whose discussion my comments here are heavily indebted.
75 Contreni, 'Irish', p. 767.
76 The phrase is from Colgrave and Mynors, *Bede*. p. xlvi Facsimile: P. Hunter Blair, *The Moore Bede: Cambridge University Library Kk. 5. 16. With a contribution by R. A. B. Mynors, Early English Manuscripts in Facsimile*, 9 (Copenhagen, 1959).

Before answering these questions it is necessary to take a closer look at the Bern Bede's actual text. The first point to make is that the Bern Bede is the product of heavy editing: whole passages were cut, and the surviving text restitched into continuous prose. Beneath the rubric *Incipit liber I historie gentis aeclesiastici a beda presbytero. Numero. V. libri* at the base of the first column of folio 188v, Bede's preface is reproduced in highly compressed form. The title's lack of an identifying genitive (*anglorum*) may well be a simple scribal slip rather than intentional excision – the opening of the preface does after all retain Bede's reference to his work as the *historia gentis Anglorum* – but it is an emblematic omission. In treatment of text and, as we shall shortly see, marginal apparatus, the Bern Bede reveals a scholarly milieu in which the English element of the *Historia* evinced far less interest or understanding than the information it offered about Britain, about Ireland and about the Irish.[77] In this respect the Bern Bede has parallels with the Old Irish versions of the *Historia*, vernacular reworkings that themselves excised elements of no 'especial interest for the Irish in the ninth and tenth centuries'.[78]

The Bern Bede's preface, drops many of the specifics of the work's composition and presentation, omitting the reference, for example, that the preface formed part of a second attempt to present the work to Ceolwulf (*et nunc ad transscribendum ac plenius ex tempore meditandum retransmitto*).[79] The king's interest in the sayings and deeds of 'the famous men of our own people' (*nostrae gentis virorum inlustrium*), together with his hope not only that Ceolwulf would be edified by the work but also that it would educate those over whom he ruled, were both dropped, leaving the Northumbrian ruler with an altogether blander interest in just 'sayings and deeds'. Similarly, Bede's closing request for prayers with its pointed reference to his work as *historia nostrae nationis* was cut, and replaced instead with a rather more neutral request for remembrance and prayer.[80] The Bern Bede also condensed much of Bede's account of information-gathering, excisions not without parallel in the Carolingian reception of

---

77 For Bede's treatment of the physical world of Britain and Ireland see A. Merrills, *History and Geography in Late Antiquity* (Cambridge, 2005), pp. 259–81, 287–9.
78 Ní Chatháin, 'Aspects', pp. 284–5, with the quotation from 285, and particularly the treatment of the first thirteen chapters of the *HE* attached to the *Lebor Bretnach*, on which see. Ní Chatháin, 'Bede's Ecclesiastical History in Irish'.
79 Folios 188v–189r.
80 Folio 119r: ... *per meis infirmitibus et mentis et corporibus apud supernam clementiam saepius intervenire meminerint ut apud dominum fructum piae intercessionis inveniam.* Compare with the full text *HE*, Preface, p. 8.

the *Historia*.[81] A mistaken reference to 'the West Saxons' where the *Historia*'s original text talked of 'the East Saxons' was a cue for the addition of a corrective gloss: *orientalium* added above the erroneous *occidentalium*, a slip best explained by eye-skip by a copyist faced with a sequence of references to West and East Saxons, ethnic groups with which he may have had no great familiarity.[82]

A series of chapter headings immediately follow the preface. Listed as I through to XXIIII, the focus of these titles actually corresponds to the titles for *HE* I, cc. 1–34. The reduced numbering in the Bern Bede is the result of some substantial omissions. That said, the actual body of the subsequent text fails to cover all the subjects mentioned by the capitula, breaking off toward the end of *HE* I, c. 27, a chapter listed as I, c. 21 in the text's own capitula list (see table 7.1).

Several chapter titles were abbreviated, and often reworded. Few, though, were recast as radically as that for *HE* I. c. 15 (I, c. 13 in the Bern capitula list). Here the original chapter heading was given new twist: the Saxons who were invited to come to assist in the British defence travelled by means of three boats, 'that is by trireme' (*triremibus id est*).[83] Bede's original chapter title made no mention of the precise means of conveyance, though the main text of *HE* I, c. 15 offers the information that they travelled in three long boats (*Britanniam tribus longis nauibus aduehitur*), a detail ultimately derived from Gildas' account of the Saxons' 'three keels'.[84] Three ships became 'three-ships' or 'threefold' ships. It gives some pause for thought to consider that within the scholarly circles that produced Bern 363 the *adventus Saxonum* could be thought of in terms of the navies of the ancient Mediterranean rather than of navies in the sub-Roman North Sea.[85] In this light, it is perhaps not surprising that the author of the Bern Bede displayed little understanding of the distant Saxon past. His account of Hengist and Horsa's ancestry was as idiosyncratic as his description of their transportation. The *Historia*'s genealogy – 'they were the sons of Wihtgisl, whose father was Witta, whose father was Wecta . . .' was recast as family history. Witta and Wecta became one generation: wife and husband.

---

81   Westgard, 'Bede', pp. 31–3.

82   Folio 189r.

83   Folio 189r: *Ut inuitata Britanniam gens Anglorum in adiutorium cum tribus tantum triremibus id est nauibus . . .*

84   *HE* I, c. 15: '*Tunc Anglorum siue Saxonum gens, inuitata a rege praefato, Britanniam tribus longis nauibus aduehitur, et in orientali parte insulae, iubente eodem rege, locum manendi, quasi pro patria pugnatura, re autem uera hanc expugnatura, suscipit*'. On this account see P. Sims-Williams, 'The settlement of England in Bede and the *Chronicle*', *ASE* 12 (1983), pp. 11–41.

85   On *triremes* and *trieris* see Isidore, *Etymologiae*. XIX, i, 10 and 23.

Table 7.1 Capitula numbering in the Bern Bede, fols. 189r–189v

Historia ecclesiastica	Bern Bede
1	1
2	2
3	3
4	4
5	5
6	6
7	7
8	–
9	–
10	8
11	9
12	10
13	11
14	12
15	13
16	14
17	15
18	16
19	–
20	–
21	–
22	17
23	18
24	19
25	20
28–30	21
31	–
32	22
33	23
34	24

What of the chapters that follow? Bede's account of Britain's five languages (*HE* I, c. 1) was cut.[86] Similarly, Bede's dating clauses were often dropped. Omitted too were Bede's occasional asides, such as when discussing the OE name *Reptoncaestir* or, in *HE* I, c. 15, the names for places and

---

86   Folio 189v.

peoples in Bede's day, intended for a specifically English audience.[87]
Bede's account of Claudius' invasion (*HE* I, c. 3), Septimius Severus' refor-
tification of Britannia (*HE* I, c. 5), the reigns Constantine and Constantius
(*HE* I, c. 8) and Maximus' usurpation (*HE* I, c. 9) and the passages addressing the British request for help (*HE* I, c. 12) were all cut. So also was Bede's
substantial account of St Germanus' victory over the Pelagians in debate
and over the Saxons and Picts by battlefield prayer, the 'Alleluia' victory
we have already encountered (*HE* I. cc. 17–21). This stands in stark contrast
to Sedulius' own evident interest documented in the *Collectaneum* and the
Liber. It may not be wholly coincidental that Pelagius' commentaries on St
Paul were in circulation and in use by Irish scholars in Carolingian schools
– not least by Sedulius Scottus himself – though as we have seen, he had
no qualms about redeploying Bede's account of Germanus' victory for his
own purposes.[88] In marked contrast to the treatment of Germanus, however,
Bede's account of St Alban, that rare example of a culted British martyr,
survived largely intact in Bern 363.[89]

Experienced as a continuous piece of prose, the Bern Bede offers a
compressed account of British history from Caesar to Augustine's mission,
with a noticeable slackening of interest in late imperial history and a sustained moment of collapse in interest when dealing with the life and career
of St Germanus. Specific changes to the text – Saxon triremes, Witta's
gender reassignment – suggest little awareness of or concern with the early
English past. But if this is the material, what can we say about how it was
read and reused? What do the marginalia and surrounding apparatus
reveal about the Bern master's responses to the *Historia*?

---

87 An etymology that clearly engaged at least one reader at St-Gall in the mid-ninth
    century, see Westgard, 'Bede', pp. 103–4, discussing the ethnographic annotations
    in the mid-ninth century St Gall, Stiftsbibliothek MS 247.

88 E. Bertola, 'Il commento paolino di Sedulio Scoto: un caso di Pelagianesimo nel
    secolo nono?', *Divinitas* 39(1) (1995), pp. 41–54; H. J. Frede, *Pelagius, der Irische
    Paulustext, Sedulius Scottus* (*Vetus Latina: Aus der Geschichte der lateinischen Bibel* 3
    (Freiburg, 1961).

89 R. Sharpe, 'The late antique Passion of St Alban', in M. Henig and P. Lindley (eds),
    St Alban and St Albans, Roman and Medieval Architecture, Art and Archaeology, The
    British Archaeological Association Conference Transactions 24 (Leeds, 2001), pp.
    30–7. For Alban's *Passio* among the martyrs of Rome, Francia and Milan in at least
    one Legendary in ninth-century Italy, Turin, Biblioteca Nazionale, D.V.3 see P. A.
    Hayward, 'The Cult of St Alban, *Anglorum protomartyr*, in Anglo-Saxon and Anglo-
    Norman England', in J. Leemans (ed.), *More than a Memory: The Discourse of Martyr-
    dom and the Construction of Christian Identity in the History of Christianity* (Louvain,
    2005), pp. 169–99 at 178–9.

As noted earlier, certain words throughout Bern 363 were written in enlarged letters.[90] A number of words from the Bern Bede were enlarged in just this fashion: ALBBION (fol. 189v), ALD CLUD (fol. 190r), ALBANU(M) EGREGIU(M) FECUNDA BRITANNIA PROFERT (fol. 193v), CARACALLA (fol. 193v), accompanied by a 'q', a reference to Alban's cloak rather than the emperor, and GILDAS SERMONE FLEBILI SERMONE (fol. 194v). Similarly, several words from the *Libellus responsionum* were also strikingly enlarged, INTEROGATIO and RESPONSIO, for example (fol 193v), and a number of key terms in Gregory's treatment of sin's threefold character, SUGGESTIO and DELECTATIO featuring prominently.[91] Notions of sin aside, the majority of such enlargements within passages were references to aspects of late British history, its saints, sites and, in Gildas, its historian and critic.[92] Alcluith – 'ALDCLUD' was Strathclyde's capital.[93] In Bern 363 an Irish etymology has been added to Bede's text, so that the name's origins came from *Ail Cluaide*, 'the rock of the Clyde', replacing Bede's own Latin explanation (*Alcluith quod lingua eorum significat Petram Cluith*).[94] Later, the name of the kingdom of which Alcluith was the capital, Dál Riata, was also explicated, the editor replacing Bede's Latin explanation with one drawn from the original Irish. Bede's original words: 'They are still called Dál Riata after this leader, *daal* in their language signifying a part' (*a quo uidelicet duce usque hodie Dalreudini uocantur, nam lingua eorum daal partem significat*).[95] The Bern editor substituted a definition of his own, 'Dail, that is the house or subdivision of the lord Riaddai' (*dail id est progenies vel curia. riaddai dominus*). Not only did the Bern Bede's editor replace Bede's *daal* and *reuda* with their orthographically accurate Old Irish forms, he also offered a more detailed etymology, replacing Bede's '*partem*' ('a part') with the alternatives *progenies* and (once again) the classical-sounding *curia* ('tribe' or 'house sub-division'), terms with different fields of meaning, but which suggest that the editor of the Bern Bede

---

90 Contreni, 'Irish', p. 773.
91 Folio 194r. This also caught Sedulius's eye; Simpson, *Collectaneum* LXXII no. 7, p. 293, drawing from *HE* I.27.
92 Folio 194v. The reference to Gildas seems also to reflect the Bern master's interest in *Quellenforschung*, Bede's quotation from Prosper at the close of *HE* I.10 produced a marginal comment identifying the source, f.194r.
93 T. M. Charles-Edwards, *Early Christian Ireland* (Oxford, 2001), p. 228.
94 Folio 190r: '*ald clud. id est. ail. cluaide*'. On Alt Clut see L. Alcock, 'A multi-disciplinary chronology for Alt Clut, Castle Rock, Dumbarton', *Proceedings of the Society of Antiquaries of Scotland* 107 (1975–6), pp. 103–13.
95 T. M. Charles-Edwards, 'Bede, the Irish and the Britons', *Celtica* 15 (1983), pp. 42–52.

was a native Irish speaker, well able to supplement Bede's information with understanding of his own.[96] Can it be a coincidence that Alcluith, in the Irish kingdom of Dál Riata, was the birthplace of St Patrick, or that Reuda, the kingdom's founder, was a *scottus* himself?[97]

The Bern Bede's margins cast further light on the text's place in the ninth-century classroom. What is immediately apparent is that certain passages of the Bern Bede excited substantially greater interest than others. Unlike the case of Sedulius, where we saw such engagement manifest itself in excision and copying, in Bern 363 we see it displayed in marginal additions. Of all, the margins of the *Libellus* (fols. 192–4) in particular were subject to intense marking up, frequent marginal enumerations, and the addition at apposite points of $\overline{GG}$ (*Gregorius*) and $\overline{RS}$ (*responsio*), intended once again to guide the eye through the thickets of Gregory's words.[98] As elsewhere in Bern 363 there are repeated entries of '*c.s.*', for example by Bede's account of pearl-bearing mussels, in *HE* I.1, hinting at a reference to the *Sanas Cormaic* (Cormac's Glossary).[99]

By far the majority of marginal annotations in these folios, however, are the 'q' and 'p', identifying moments where questions were to be asked, or specifics elucidated. Such sigla occur, for example, beside Bede's observation that there were twenty cities in the province of *Britannia*,[100] or that the Picts, upon arrival, demanded wives of the Irish.[101] The Bern master took particular interest in information about Ireland. The very first occurrence of the 'q' siglum in the Bern Bede, for example, occurs beside the description of Britain's rivers and their abundance of salmon and eels.[102] On occasion such interest was made explicit. Beside Bede's account of Palladius'

96 A. A. Duncan, 'Bede, Iona and the Picts', in J. M. Wallace-Hadrill (ed.), *Writing of History in the Middle Ages: Essays Presented to Richard William Southern* (Oxford, 1981), pp. 1–42, for this passage and possible Ionan sources for Bede's etymology.

97 M. Nieke and A. A. Duncan, 'Dalriada: the establishment and maintenance of an Early Historic Kingdom in Northern Britain', in S. Driscoll and M. Nieke (eds), *Power and Politics in Early Medieval Britain and Ireland* (Edinburgh, 1988), pp. 6–21; J. W. Bannerman, 'The Dál Riata and Northern Ireland in the sixth and seventh centuries', in J. Carney and D. Greene (eds), *Celtic Studies: Essays in Memory of Angus Matheson, 1912–1962* (London, 1968), pp. 1–11.

98 A striking contrast with the treatment of the *Libellus* in the OI translations: see Ni Chathain, 'Bede'.

99 Contreni, 'The Irish', p. 773. K. Meyer (ed.), *Sanas Cormaic: Cormac's Glossary* (Halle, 1913); P. Russell, 'The sound of silence: the growth of Cormac's Glossary', *Cambridge Medieval Celtic Studies* 15 (1988), pp. 1–30.

100 Folio 189v, *HE* I, c. 1.

101 Folio 190r, *HE* I, c. 1.

102 Folio 189v, *HE* I, c. 1.

Irish mission the Master added '*de scottorum fide*', one of three direct references to *scotti* in Bern 363's margins.[103] Similarly, Bede's observation that even scrapings from an Irish codex were sufficient to combat snake bites demanded class room exposition:

> p Denique vidimus quibusdam a serpen
> te percussis rasa folia codicum qui
> de hibernia fuerit[n] et ipsam rasuram
> aquae in missam ac potatam talibus.[104]

In the same vein, the *Historia*'s account of the Reuda's Irish settlement 'by treaty or the sword' was accompanied by the letters *l* (*lege*) and *s* (*semper*). It was always to be read out when taught:

> procedentes autem tempore Brittania post
> l. britones et pictos tertiam scottorum
> natonem in pictorum partes suscepit.[recaepitt]
> .s. qui duce reudda de hibernia progressi vel
> amicitia vel ferro inter eos habi
> tarent Nam lingua eorum dail. id est
> progenies vel curia. riaddai dominus.[105]

Similar marginal enumerations were added alongside other parts of the *Libellus*, such as Gregory's detailing of what the Bern master saw as the obligations of married clergy in minor orders (to live a moral life, to attend to the chanting of the psalms, and to keep heart, tongue and body from all things unlawful) and his influential tripartite characterization of sin ('All sin is committed in three ways . . .'), a passage, as we have already seen, that was already emphasized by enlargement, and caught Sedulius' eye, too.[106]

At points the marginalia to the *Libellus* become more dense. Augustine's eighth question, 'Should a pregnant woman be baptized?' had no fewer than eleven 'q''s added alongside its thirteen lines of text. Gregory's response, in its turn, warranted some 15 marginal 'S''s ('always, always, always . . .'), and the rare addition of an individual name in the margins, that of Ermenfrid. On one level this is a telling indication of Gregory's authority within the circle of the Bern master.[107] Simultaneously it hints

---

103 Folio 194r. See also f. 104r (*de flexu genuum ut scotti faci*); f. 138r (*de scottis qui moriuntur in aliena regione*).

104 Folio 190r, *HE* I, c. 1 (with changes).

105 Folio 190r, HE I, c. 1 (with changes).

106 Folio 194r, *HE* I, c. 27 (with changes).

107 R. Meens, 'The influence of Gregory the Great's answers to Augustine's queries about childbirth, menstruation and sexuality', in R. Gameson (ed.), *St Augustine and the Conversion of England* (Stroud, 1999), pp. 174–86.

that the world of the Bern master shared concerns with other parts of the Carolingian world. It was in the ninth century's middle decades that this same passage was copied into the Pseudo-Isidorian decretals, and, subsequently, several other episcopal capitulary collections.[108]

In contrast to other sections of Bern 363 the margins of the Bede text contains the names of only two contemporary figures: 'Ermenfrid' and 'Giso'. The most frequent names in Bern 363's margins, those of Sedulius Scottus and John Eriugena, are wholly absent. Ermenfrid we have already encountered, his name entered beside Gregory's views on pregnancy and purity. His name occurs, in various orthographic permutations including once with a final *eth*, 'hermenfrið', besides several passages of the *Libellus responsionum*.[109] He might be plausibly identified as Ermenfrid, Bishop of Tortona, who subscribed together with Hagan of Bergamo and others at the synod of Milan convened by Bishop Angilbert II in 842.[110] All three men appear in Bern 363's margins – pointing to the fact that the manuscript's marginal roster attests as much to the political as to the intellectual circuits of Carolingian northern Italy. Not only had Ermenfrid done duty as Lothar's chancellor, Tortona itself was not unimportant. It occurs, alongside other north Italian centres, in Lothar's Olona capitulary of 825. Bobbio fell within its diocesan limits, and in 833 Judith was imprisoned there during Lothar's abortive rebellion. In the years in which Bern 363 was copied it seems also to have been a centre of intellectual engagement. In 862, for example, a copy of Claudius of Turin's commentary on Paul's letters was produced there.[111] Ermenfrid was invoked on four occasions, all of which refer to him within the context of issues raised by Gregory's *Libellus*.

Giso's, however, is the only name to appear elsewhere in the manuscript. The first occurrence is alongside *Metamorphoses* I. 104, Ovid's account of

108 Meens, 'Influence', p. 179.
109 Might he also be the figure listed as 'herem' on f. 55v in the company of John and Dodo alongside *Georgics* IV.225–6 on the primal cause? See Contreni, 'Irish', pp. 774–5.
110 *MGH Concilia* II, ii, ed. A. Werminghoff (Hanover and Leipzig, 1908) pp. 814–15. See W. Hartmann, *Die Synoden der Karolingerzeit im Frankenreich und in Italien* (Paderborn, 1989), p. 244. On Tortona in the early Middle Ages see E. Cau, 'Ricerche su scrittura carolina e cultura a Tortona nel IX e X secolo', *Rivisita di storia della chiesa in Italia* 26 (1972), pp. 79–100; D. Bullough, 'Le scuole cattedrali e la cultura dell'Italia settentrionale prima dei Comuni', *Atti del II Convegno di Storia della Chiesa in Italia, Italia Sacra* 5 (Padua, 1964), pp. 111–43.
111 M. Gorman, 'The commentary on Genesis of Claudius of Turin and Biblical studies under Louis the Pious', *Speculum* 72 (1997), pp. 279–329.

the Golden Age when, among other delights, wild strawberries could be freely gathered. The 'Bern master' appended a cryptic remark: *magistus dixit gisoni manduca arbuta*.[112] Giso's relationship to the wild strawberries of a lost golden age will likely always remain obscure. Hagen thought it was a joke.[113] Giso's views, however, on the fauna of Britain were considered of value by his contempories, his name appearing repeatedly alongside Bede's description of Ireland:

dives lactis

p   *de mellis insula. Nec vinear(um)*

Γ   *expers piscium uolucr(u)mque, sed et cer*

Γiso *vorum cap(r)ea(um) q(ue) uenatus insignis*

Γiso *Est autem propriae patria scottorum est*

giso *est autem sinus maris permaximus qui ubi civitas munitissima est*

ALD CLUD ID EST AIL CLUIADE

Who was Giso, and why might he come to mind when the Bern master read Bede's words on Ireland's stags and roe deer of Britain, 'the true *patria* of the Scotti'? Since Traube, he has been identified, not implausibly, with Iso of St Gall, *doctor nominatissimus*, sometime master of St Gall's so-called 'external' school and teacher of Notker Balbulus, among others.[114] Giso is a presence, also, in another manuscript's margins with connections to the world of the *peregrini,* the bilingual Psalter now in Dresden, the so-called 'Codex Boernerianus' (Dresden, Sachsiche Landesbibliothek, MS A. 145b) where, unlike in the margins of Bern 363, his name occurs wholly transliterated into Greek 'ΓΥϹΩ'.[115] Mindful of the strong episcopal presence in Bern 363's margins a second and, on balance, a likelier candidate may well be Giso, bishop of Modena.[116]

More significant than finding an answer to the question of Giso's identity is the very existence of the question itself. Viewed from one perspective Ermenfrid and Giso are dead ends: we can know no more about their engagement with Bede's thought. From another, however, they are crucial reminders that Bede's writings engaged scholars well beyond the Carolingian heartlands, and well beyond the scholarly genealogy that linked

---

112 Folio 187v.

113 Hagen, *praefatio*, p. xlvi: *De ioco monachali agi videtur.*

114 M. de Jong, 'Pollution, penance and sanctity: Ekkehard's Life of Iso of St Gall', in J. Hill and M. Swan (eds), *The Community, the Family and the Saint: Patterns of Power in Early Medieval Europe* (Turnhout, 1998), pp. 145–58.

115 Kaczynski, *Greek in the Carolingian Age*, p. 17, n. 40.

116 D. Bullough, 'Le scuole cattedrali', pp. 111–43. I must thank Professor John Contreni for directing my attention to Giso of Modena.

Hrabanus' Fulda, through Alcuin, to Bede's Jarrow, and which was still inspiring admiration in the reign of Charles the Fat.[117]

The Bern Bede offers an important counterpoint to the ninth-century Old English translation of the *Historia*.[118] While the ninth-century Mercian translator excised references to Rome and papal authority, his continental near-contemporary ignored the English, cutting down Bede's original text, garbling issues of Saxon descent and arrival but taking care with matters of geography and issues related to the presence of the Irish in Britain.

The ninth-century Mercian scholar behind the Old English translation of Bede left a portrait of the Abbess Hild as someone famed in her day as one who both oversaw those in her charge *swiðe geornfull* ('very diligently') and whose *micel snytro ond wisdomes* ('great prudence and wisdom') led her to be sought out by high and low alike for counsel and advice.[119] The same might well be said of Janet Nelson, a more recent northern *magistra*. Her King's College office, between the Strand and the Thames, sits above what was once a thriving Middle Saxon *wic* that linked southern England to a wider world: Dorestadt, Quentovic, Byzantium, Fustat.[120] The nameless men and women who worked on that same site some twelve centuries ago would have recognized her vision of their age. So too would the scholars I have looked at here, for whom seventh-century English kings and Irish holy men served as models for the construction of an image of an ideal ruler for a ninth-century Frankish king, and for whom Bede's *Historia* was a school book for teaching northern Italians about British toponymy, Ireland's absence of snakes and Gregory the Great's notions of sin and pollution. It is an international vision.

---

117 Notker, *Gesta*, I. 2, p. 3.
118 N. Guenther Discenza, 'The Old English Bede and the construction of Anglo-Saxon authority', *Anglo-Saxon England* 31 (2002), pp. 69–80.
119 *The Old English Version of Bede's Ecclesiastical History of the English People*, ed. T. A. Miller, EETS o.s. 95–6 (London, 1890–91), III. 23. On Hild see A. T. Thacker, DNB, 'Hild (614–680)'.
120 G. Malcolm and D. Bowsher with R. Cowie, *Middle Saxon London: Excavations at the Royal Opera House, 1989–99* (London, 2003).

8

In search of the Carolingian 'dear lord'*

Rachel Stone

T HE CLOSE PARALLELS between Janet Nelson's biography of
Charles the Bald and Richard Abels' biography of Alfred the Great
are clear.[1] Both authors investigate their subjects' role as rulers,
intellectuals and fighters against the Vikings; both books raise issues as to
the extent to which early medieval biography is possible. Yet one notewor-
thy distinction between the books centres on their treatment of lordship.
Lordship is at the centre of Abels' discussions both of the social structures
of Wessex and of Alfred's political thought.[2] In contrast, lordship occupies
a far more peripheral role in Nelson's book. Does this different treatment
of similar social structures simply reflect divergent historiographical traditions or is it more significant? In this paper I want to make some comparisons between lordship in Francia and England, focusing less on the
institution itself than on contemporary depictions of the relationship, in
particular in literary sources, and the moral norms associated with it.

Although there have been many discussions of the practice of 'Herrschaft'
in the Carolingian world, especially in regional studies, analysis of the ethos
of the lord-man relationship has largely relied on 'Germanic' texts.[3]

---

* This paper develops one of the themes of the PhD I wrote under Janet Nelson's
   supervision in 1999–2005. Her breadth of scholarly knowledge and enthusiastic
   support were invaluable in helping me shape and complete my dissertation and her
   values continue to inform my research.
1 R. Abels, *Alfred the Great: War, Kingship and Culture in Anglo-Saxon England* (Harlow,
   1998); J. L. Nelson, *Charles the Bald* (London, 1992).
2 Abels, *Alfred*, pp. 34–44, 249–55. See also now on this topic D. Pratt, *The Political
   Thought of King Alfred the Great* (Cambridge, 2007).
3 Some particularly influential works include W. Schlesinger, 'Herrschaft und Gefolgschaft in der germanisch-deutschen Verfassungsgeschichte', *Historische Zeitschrift* 176
   (1953), pp. 225–75, partially translated as W. Schlesinger, 'Lord and follower in
   Germanic institutional history', in F. L. Cheyette (ed.), *Lordship and Community in
   Medieval Europe* (New York, 1968), pp. 64–99; H. Kuhn, 'Die Grenzen der ger-
   manischen Gefolgschaft', *ZRG, Germanistische Abteilung* 73 (1956), pp. 1–83; F. Graus,

Lordship in Anglo-Saxon England has attracted far more scholarly attention, with the 'dear lord' widely seen as a key theme in Old English literature.[4] Discussions of the ethos of Old English secular poetry have frequently used the comparative method. Parallels for particular moral norms in poems such as *Beowulf* and *The Battle of Maldon* have been found in Roman descriptions of barbarians,[5] Scandinavian and Celtic texts,[6] French *chansons de geste*[7] and even wider afield.[8] Yet the sources of Carolingian Francia have rarely been used in this way.[9] This is surprising, since more Carolingian secular poetry survives than Old English,[10] although it has been relatively

'Über die sogenannte germanische Treue', *Historica* 1 (1959), pp. 71–121; D. Green, *The Carolingian Lord: Semantic Studies on Four Old High German Words: Balder, Frô, Truhtin, Hêrro* (Cambridge, 1965).

4 'Dear lord' is a translation of the Old English words *freawine* and *winedryhten*, used in several poems, including *Beowulf*, *The Wanderer*, and *Guthlac*. See J. Bosworth, *An Anglo-Saxon Dictionary: Based on the Manuscript Collections of the late Joseph Bosworth* (Oxford, 1882), pp. 331, 1233. I have so far found only one use of the Latin equivalent *dominus carus* in Carolingian literature: *Poeta Saxo, MGH Poet*. I, book 4, v. 373–4, p. 55 where the *proceres* return home after Charlemagne's coronation of Louis the Pious in 813: *sibimet iam conicientes, / Cari conspectu domini hunc esse supremum*. On the perceived importance of Anglo-Saxon lordship see e.g., M. Cherniss, *Ingeld and Christ: Heroic Concepts and Values in Old English Christian Poetry* (The Hague, 1972), p. 34: 'The relationship between lord and retainer is the central one in Old English verse'; K. O'Brien O'Keefe, 'Heroic values and Christian ethics', in M. Godden and M. Lapidge (eds), *The Cambridge Companion to Old English Literature* (Cambridge, 1991), pp. 107–25 at p. 107: 'The ethos of heroic life pervades Old English literature . . . The touchstone of that life – as represented in Old English literature at least – is the vital relationship between retainer and lord.'

5 Tacitus' *Germania* is by far the most prominent source used, but other comparisons are visible in e.g., R. Woolf, 'The ideal of men dying with their lord in the *Germania* and in *The Battle of Maldon*', *ASE* 5 (1976), pp. 63–81.

6 See e.g., S. Evans, *The Lords of Battle: Image and Reality of the Comitatus in Dark-Age Britain* (Woodbridge, 1997).

7 See e.g., E. Irving, 'Heroic role models: Beowulf and others', in H. Damico and J. Leyerle (eds), *Heroic Poetry in the Anglo-Saxon Period: Studies in Honor of Jess B. Bessinger Jr* (Kalamazoo, 1993), pp. 347–72 at pp. 348–51.

8 R. Frank, '*The Battle of Maldon* and heroic literature', in D. Scragg (ed.), *The Battle of Maldon, AD 991* (Oxford, 1991), pp. 196–207 at p. 197: '*The Battle of Maldon* marshals and reviews the ranks of familiar but deeply held ideas that shape not only Old English heroic poetry but battle narratives from Greenland to Japan.'

9 One of the few sustained comparisons is P. E. Szarmach, 'The (sub-) genre of *The Battle of Maldon*', in J. Cooper (ed.), *The Battle of Maldon* (London, 1993), pp. 43–61.

10 Substantial Carolingian secular poems include Abbo of St Germain-des-Prés, *Bella Parisiacae urbis*: ed. and trans. H. Waquet, *Abbon: Le siège de Paris par les Normands, Les classiques de l'histoire de France au moyen âge* 20 (Paris, 1942); Ermoldus

little studied.[11] There is also a substantial corpus of Carolingian normative texts and historical writing. My question in this paper is: where is the Carolingian *Battle of Maldon*? More generally, where are the Carolingian texts that extol the loyalty and emotional ties of man and lord in the way that many Anglo-Saxon ones do?

One immediate objection to the comparison might be that the majority of Carolingian texts are in Latin, not the vernacular.[12] Yet the language of these texts need not have a decisive influence on their content and concepts.[13] Lay nobles formed part of the audience for Carolingian Latin poetry and historical writing; a few lay people even wrote such texts themselves.[14] Discussions of 'Germanic' values have often drawn heavily on Latin texts, from Tacitus' *Germania* onward. The existence of both Carolingian Latin and Old English versions of the story of Walter of Aquitaine[15] also implies a shared poetic tradition.

Nigellus, *In honorem Hludovicii Pii* ed. and trans. E. Faral, *Ermold le Noir: Poème sur Louis le Pieux et épitres au roi Pépin*, Les classiques de l'histoire de France au moyen âge 14 (Paris, 1932), pp. 2–201 [hereafter *In honorem*] and Theodulf, *Paraenesis ad iudices*, MGH *Poet.* I., pp. 493–517. Following P. Dronke, 'Waltharius-Gaiferos', in U. Dronke and P. Dronke (eds), *Barbara et antiquissima carmina* (Barcelona, 1977), pp. 27–79 and others, I also see *Waltharius* as a ninth-century poem: *Waltharius and Ruodlieb*, ed. and trans. D. M. Kratz (New York, 1984), 2–71. There are also a number of shorter secular poems, most of which are translated in P. Godman, *Poetry of the Carolingian Renaissance* (London, 1985) and Sedulius Scottus, *On Christian Rulers and the Poems*, ed. E. G. Doyle, Medieval and Renaissance Texts and Studies (Binghamton, NY, 1983).

11 The two most detailed modern works on Carolingian Latin poetry are A. Ebenbauer, *Carmen Historicum: Untersuchungen zur historischen Dichtung im Karolingischen Europa* (Vienna, 1978) and P. Godman, *Poets and Emperors: Frankish Politics and Carolingian Poetry* (Oxford, 1987).

12 I omit discussions here of Old High German and Old Saxon texts from the Carolingian period. The ninth-century poetry is largely religious, with the exception of the *Hildebrandslied* and *Ludwigslied*.

13 M. Innes, 'Teutons or Trojans? The Carolingians and the Germanic past', in Y. Hen and M. Innes (eds), *The Uses of the Past in the Early Middle Ages* (Cambridge, 2000), pp. 227–49 at p. 245: 'it would be a mistake to think in terms of two distinct, hermetically sealed traditions [learned, Christian, Latin and written versus popular, Germanic, vernacular and oral] with widely variant values and foundations. We need to think in terms of interaction between written accounts and oral legends' (p. 246): 'the language of recitation or transmission did not determine the content of traditions.'

14 R. McKitterick, *The Carolingians and the Written Word* (Cambridge, 1989), pp. 227–41.

15 *Waldere*, ed. E. van Kirk Dobbie, *The Anglo-Saxon Minor Poems* (New York, 1942), pp. 4–6.

Timothy Reuter commented that it was an illusion to see Carolingian Francia as 'after the heroic age'.[16] Warbands, for example, still played an important role in Carolingian military life.[17] Equally, some of the most significant Old English texts date from a relatively 'unheroic' period.[18] There are some obvious parallels between Carolingian and Old English poems: Paul Szarmach showed how *The Battle of Maldon* fits into a tradition of poetry discussing warfare between Christians and Vikings.[19] There are also similarities in the use of poetry as royal propaganda: John Hill's description of the author of the 'Battle of Brunanburh' as 'the exultant poet of absolute victory over rightly savaged foes'[20] is equally applicable to a number of Carolingian poems.

The dear dead lord

My search for the emotional aspects of the lord-retainer relationship begins with the most extreme example: the willingness of the follower to die with his lord. Anglo-Saxonists still debate whether such an ideal was common (or existed at all) within Old English literature.[21] One significant problem has been deciding what examples are relevant. There are relatively few early medieval texts (in Old English or other languages) that clearly show a situation in which retainers outlive their lord on the battlefield and yet have no hope left of victory. In contrast, there are a number of texts which show men either avenging their lords or dying to protect

16 T. Reuter, 'Plunder and tribute in the Carolingian empire', *TRHS*, 5th series, 35 (1985), pp. 75–94 at p. 91.

17 Reuter, 'Plunder', pp. 81–4.

18 O'Brien O'Keefe, 'Heroic values', p. 113: 'The divergence between the literary representations of warrior life and the social realities of both kingship and military life are usefully illustrated by the activities of Alfred the Great.' F. C. Robinson, 'God, death and loyalty in *The Battle of Maldon*', in M. Salu and R. T. Farrell (eds), *J. R. R. Tolkien, Scholar and Storyteller: Essays in Memoriam* (Ithaca, 1979), pp. 76–98 at p. 77: 'The battle of Maldon was fought and the poem about it was written at a time when the Heroic Age of England . . . lay in the distant past.'

19 Szarmach, 'Subgenre'.

20 J. Hill, *The Anglo-Saxon Warrior Ethic: Reconstructing Lordship in Early English Literature* (Gainesville, 2000), p. 138.

21 There is the further question of whether any such norms were adhered to in practice, but the mere existence of the concept as an ideal is significant in itself.

them.[22] *The Battle of Maldon* is one of the few texts definitely presenting the ideal of dying with one's lord, although even this has been disputed.[23] Commentators on the poem have stressed that such an ideal is not 'sensible, worldly, or rational'.[24] As a military strategy, a refusal to outlive one's lord is foolish.[25] As an ideal, however, it can provide an inspirational message of heroism, loyalty and love.[26]

As Roberta Frank noted,[27] one of the few other examples of a refusal to outlive one's lord comes from a Carolingian source. The original version of the Royal Frankish Annals for 782 reports a successful battle in the Süntel Mountains. The revised version describes a Frankish defeat, due to a premature and badly planned attack. Although some of the Franks escaped, a number of nobles were killed, along with some of their men 'who preferred to die with them rather than live after them.'[28] The annalist

---

22 Woolf, 'Ideal'; R. Frank, 'The ideal of men dying with their lord in *The Battle of Maldon*: anachronism or *nouvelle vague*', in I. Wood and N. Lund (eds), *People and Places in Northern Europe, 500–1600: Essays in Honour of Peter Hayes Sawyer* (Woodbridge, 1991), pp. 95–106; S. Fanning, 'Tacitus, *Beowulf* and the *comitatus*', *Haskins Society Journal* 9 (1997), pp. 17–38 at pp. 17–29.

23 J. Niles, 'Maldon and mythopoesis', *Mediaevalia* 17 (1994), pp. 89–21 at pp. 106–10 correctly points out that Byrhtnoth's followers seek revenge for their lord, rather than death. Yet his suggestion that the situation was not hopeless and that some of the warriors may in reality have survived (p. 108) is not reflected in the tone of the poem. The author at several points deliberately emphasizes the inevitability of defeat for the Anglo-Saxons. There is no dominant Viking figure on whom Byrhtnoth's death can be avenged (Woolf, 'Ideal', p. 76); the rhetoric of the retainers' individual speeches includes what Ute Schwab, '*The Battle of Maldon*: a memorial poem', in J. Cooper (ed.) *The Battle of Maldon: Fiction and Fact* (London, 1993), pp. 63–85 at p. 83 describes as 'auto-epitaphs' and the outcome is clearly foreshadowed in Byrhtwold's famous couplet near the end of the poem (Dobbie, *The Anglo-Saxon Minor Poems*, p. 16, v 312–13): *Hige sceal þe heardra, heorte þe cenre, / mod sceal þe mare, þe ure mægen lytlað* ('Thought must be the fiercer, heart the greater, courage the greater as our strength grows less').

24 Frank, 'Ideal', p. 105.

25 Woolf, 'Ideal', p. 71.

26 See e.g., Woolf, 'Ideal', p. 81: 'There are some scenes in literature . . . which neither exemplify nor deny a moral commandment but rather illustrate the heroic dimensions of the human will'; E. B. Irving, 'The heroic style in *The Battle of Maldon*', *Studies in Philology* 58 (1961), pp. 457–67 at p. 466: 'The naked sinews of loyalty . . . are exposed here'; Frank, 'Ideal', p. 105: 'The theme of men dying with their lord can be adapted to many different contexts and purposes . . . Only its affective value seems constant.'

27 Frank, 'Ideal', p. 99.

28 *Annales regni Francorum* s.a. 782, ed. F. Kurze, *MGH SRG* (Hanover, 1895), p. 63: *Sed maior Francis quam pro numero iactura fuit, quia legatorum duo, Adalgisus et Geilo, comitum quattuor aliorumque clarorum atque nobilium usque ad viginti interfecti, praeter ceteros, qui hos secuti potius cum eis perire quam post eos vivere maluerunt.*

says nothing further about these men; there is no attempt to glorify them or to present the battle as anything but a disaster, quickly avenged by Charlemagne himself. This passing mention of such devoted behaviour suggests that the emotional attachment to a lord could be just as strong for Frankish warriors as for Anglo-Saxons. The literary depiction of lordship, however, is noticeably different in the two cultures, as an overview of Carolingian texts on lordship makes clear.

Carolingian lords

References to lords and the concept of lordship are pervasive in Carolingian texts, although relatively little explicit detail is given on the relationship between lord and man.[29] Carolingian legislation tends to stress the use of lordship to aid royal government, for example in levying hosts,[30] or preventing disorder.[31] This utilitarian view of lordship is reflected in a capitulary that allowed a man to swear oaths of fidelity only to the ruler and his own lord *ad nostram utilitatem et sui senioris*.[32] When legal sources refer to the moral aspects of lordship, the focus is firmly on the subordinate's loyalty. The analogy of lordship was often used, for example, in the texts of oaths to rulers.[33] Men were forbidden to leave their lords except

---

29 S. Reynolds, *Fiefs and Vassals: the Medieval Evidence Reinterpreted* (Oxford, 1994), p. 88: Most descriptions of Carolingian 'vassalage' rely on a relatively small body of evidence relating largely to royal *vassi*. A more extended discussion of the Carolingian evidence is in R. Stone, 'Masculinity, nobility and the moral instruction of the Carolingian lay elite' (PhD, King's College London, 2005), pp. 103–14.

30 See e.g., *Capitulare missorum de exercitu promovendo 808*, c. 1, *MGH Capitularia* I, ed. A. Boretius (Hanover and Leipzig, 1883), no. 50, p. 137. For a detailed discussion of the role of lords in the Anglo-Saxon *fyrd* see R. Abels, *Lordship and Military Obligation in Anglo-Saxon England* (Berkeley, 1988).

31 See e.g., *Capitulare missorum Aquisgranense primum 808*, c. 7, 17, *MGH Capitularia* I, no. 64, p. 153.

32 *Capitulare missorum in Theodonis villa datum secundum, generale 805*, c. 9, *MGH Capitularia* I, no. 44, p. 124. Cf. *Hlotharii, Hludowici et Karoli conventus apud Marsnam primus 847, Adnuntiatio Karoli* c. 3, *MGH Capitularia* I, no. 204, p. 71.

33 M. Becher, *Eid und Herrschaft: Untersuchungen zum Herrscherethos Karls des Großen* (Sigmaringen, 1993), pp. 145–63 shows that this analogy was used in the general oath of 789 even though there is no definite evidence that vassals had previously sworn oaths. Cf. the profession of faith by the bishops in *Capitula electionis Hludowici Balbi Compendii facta 877, MGH Capitularia* II, ed. V. Krause and A. Boretius (Hanover and Leipzig, 1897), no. 283E, p. 365*): isti seniori et regi meo Hlodowico . . . secundum meum scire et posse et meum ministerium et auxilio et consilio fidelis et adiutor ero, sicut episcopus recte seniori suo debitor est.*

in extreme cases.[34] A few texts impose additional penalties for the homicide of a lord by his man.[35]

A few of the numerous moral treatises written for kings and other laymen provide more details. Dhuoda, writing to her teenage son William at Charles the Bald's court, describes Charles as the lord given by God to William.[36] William must therefore serve him with 'pure and certain faith'. He must be without 'annoyance, half-heartedness and laziness', 'truthful, vigilant, useful and distinguished.'[37] Yet although Dhuoda's work is full of maternal emotion,[38] her passing references to the emotional bonds of lordship are noticeable for their conventional form. Repeatedly, William is told simply that he must 'love and fear' his superiors, including his father Bernard, the *optimates* at court and Charles the Bald and his relatives.[39] Her only mention of any more passionate emotions in lordship is in a description of how David wept for the dead Saul and Jonathan.[40]

---

34 *Capitulare Aquisgranense*, c. 16, *MGH Capitularia* I, no. 77, p. 172 (if lord wants to kill him, beat him with a staff, pollute his wife or daughter or take his inheritance); *Capitula francica* c. 8, *MGH Capiularia* I, no. 104, p. 215 (if lord unjustly wants to reduce him to *servitium*, commits adultery with his wife, tries to kill him, or if the lord can defend him and does not do so).

35 *Capitulatio de partibus Saxoniae*, c. 12, 13, *MGH Capitularia* I., no. 26, p. 69: death for someone carrying out the *raptus* of his lord's daughter or killing his lord or lady; *Praeceptum Karoli III*, *MGH Capitularia* II, no. 237, pp. 142–3: exile for the *nefarium malum* of killing one's lord. There is, however, no Carolingian equivalent to Alfred's declaration that no mercy may be shown to a man killing his lord (see Af El. 49,7, *Die Gesetze der Angelsachsen*, ed. F. Liebermann (Halle, 1903–16), pp. 44–7. One actual Carolingian judgement, describing a particularly nasty case, where a man had a slave kill his two *domini*, both children (*MGH Capitularia* I, no. 129, p. 257) does not show any special outrage; the punishment, as normal, is a fine.

36 Dhuoda, *Handbook for her Warrior Son: Liber manualis*, ed. and trans. M. Thiebaux (Cambridge 1998 [hereafter LM], 3–4: *Seniorem quem habes Karolum, quando Deus, ut credo, et genitor tuus Bernardus . . . tibi ad serviendum elegit*. Cf. Alcuin's letter to Count Maginhar, *MGH Epistolae* IV, no. 33, p. 75: *Fidelis esto ad dominos, quos dedit tibi Deus*.

37 LM 3–4: *puram et certam illi in omnibus tene utilitatis fidem . . . sine molestia et tepiditate atque pigritia, fideliter est serviendum . . . sis verax, vigil utilisque atque praecipuus*.

38 See P. Dronke, 'Dhuoda', *Women Writers of the Middle Ages: a Critical Study of Texts from Perpetua (d. 203) to Marguerite Porete (d. 1310)* (Cambridge, 1984), pp. 36–54; J. L. Nelson, 'Dhuoda', in P. Wormald and J. L. Nelson (eds), *Lay Intellectuals in the Carolingian World* (Cambridge, 2007 pp. 106–20).

39 See e.g., LM 3–1: *Qualiter domno et genitori tuo Bernardo . . . timere, amare atque fidelis in omnibus esse debeas*; 3–8: *time, ama, venera et dilige eos* [Charles the Bald's relatives]; 3–9: *Optimates ducum et consiliarios illorum . . . ama, dilige et servi frequenter*; 4–4: *Si timorem et amorem, ex fidelitatis industria, circa genitorem et seniorem tuum, vel circa optimates ducem et cunctos pares tuos, maiorunque sive et iuniorum, tenens*.

40 LM 3–8.

The same linking of love and fear is seen in the only sustained discussion in Carolingian texts of the moral attributes of a lord. The seventh-century Irish writer Pseudo-Cyprian has, as the sixth of his twelve 'abuses of the world', the *dominus sine virtute*.[41] Extracts from this chapter were quoted several times by Hincmar, who saw it as applying not only to kings, but to all who 'dominated':[42]

> Three things are necessary for those who rule, namely fear, obedience and love; for unless the lord is equally loved and feared, his commands will avail little. Through favours and friendliness, let him seek to be loved, and through just punishments, not for injury to himself, but violations of the law of God, let him strive to be feared.[43]

Few normative texts go beyond this emotionally ambivalent view of lord-retainer relationships.[44] One exception is striking. In 858, during a crisis in the reign of Charles the Bald, Archbishop Hincmar of Rheims and other West Frankish bishops sent a letter to Louis the German, who had invaded his brother's kingdom. The 'Quierzy letter' is a complex moral and political tract, admonishing Louis while not openly defying him. The commonplace clerical moralizing that Louis should keep the day of death before his eyes

---

41   *Pseudo-Cyprianus: De XII abusivis saeculi*, ed. S. Hellman (Leipzig, 1909), pp. 43–5. H. H. H. Anton, 'Pseudo-Cyprian, De duodecim abusivis saeculi und sein Einfluß auf den Kontinent, inbesondere auf die karolingischen Fürstenspiegel', in Heinz Löwe (ed.), *Die Iren und Europa im früheren Mittelalter* (Stuttgart, 1982), pp. 2: 568–617 at p. 573 argues that in the original text the *dominus* is intended to refer to an abbot.

42   Hincmar of Rheims, *Ad Carolum III imperatorum ut Ludovici Balbi sobrini sui filiis regibus idoneos educatores et consiliarios constituat*, c. 5, PL 125, col. 992: *et non solum regi, sed et omni qui in dominationis est potestate.* Cf. Hincmar, *De ordine palatii*, ed. T. Gross and R. Schieffer, *MGH Fontes iuris Germanici antiqui* (Hanover, 1980), c. III (= c. 10), p. 50; Hincmar, *Ad episcopos regni admonitio altera: Pro Carolomanno rege apud Sparnacum facta*, c. 8, *PL* 125, col. 1012. Sedulius Scottus, *Liber de rectoribus christianis* (in *Sedulius Scottus*, ed. S. Hellman (Munich, 1906), pp. 1–91), c. 2 also uses extracts from this chapter, referring specifically to royal behaviour.

43   *Pseudo-Cyprianus*, pp. 43–4: *Tria ergo necessaria hos qui dominantur habere oportet, terrorem scilicet, et ordinationem, et amorem; nisi enim ametur dominus pariter et metuatur, ordinatio illius constare minime poterit per beneficia ergo et affabilitatem procuret ut diligatur, et per iustas vindictas, non propriae iniuriae, sed legis Dei, studeat ut metuatur.*

44   *Decretum Vermeriense* c. 9, *MGH Capitularia* I, no. 16, p. 41 discusses the case of someone who follows his lord, *cui fidem mentiri non poterit* to another province and whose wife refuses to follow him. *Capitulare Carisiacense 877*, c. 10, *MGH Capitularia* II, no. 281, p. 358: Charles the Bald envisages that some of his *fideles* may want to enter monasteries after his death, *Dei et nostro amore compunctus.*

suddenly includes the vivid picture of the king: 'when your soul will have passed away from the body ... and will pass away nude and forsaken, without the help of wife and sons and without the comfort and *comitatus* of advisors and *vassi*.'[45]

Carolingian literature and the lord

The Quierzy letter provides a rare glimpse of the expected emotions of a royal lord. Frankish narrative sources and literary texts have little more to offer. The numerous Carolingian historical works provide a few references to familiar themes of lordship. Men are seen avenging their lords,[46] and the affection felt toward a former lord is described.[47] Occasionally men are condemned for their betrayal of their lords,[48] and lords are also sometimes seen coming to the aid of their own men.[49] Such themes are not, however, developed into exemplary stories, unlike the *Anglo-Saxon Chronicle*'s

---

45 Council of Quierzy 858, c. 4, ed. Wilfried Hartmann, *MGH Concilia* III, p. 410: *quando anima vestra de corpore exiet ... et sine adiutorio uxoris ac filiorum et sine solatio et comitatu drudorum atque vassorum nuda et desolata exibit.*

46 See e.g., Regino of Prüm, *Chronicon*, ed. F. Kurze, *MGH SRG* (Hanover, 1890), s.a. 818, p. 73. Cf. Alcuin, *MGH Epistolae* IV, no. 231, p. 376 (on Torhtmund).

47 Einhard, *Vita Karoli Magni*, ed. O. Holder-Egger, *MGH SRG* (Hanover, 1911) [hereafter *VK*] c. 2, p. 5: Carloman in his monastic retirement was troubled by *nobiles* who wanted to greet their former lord; *VK*, preface, pp. 11–12: Einhard is writing in memory of Charlemagne, his *dominus et nutritor*, with whom he dwelt in *amicitia* in court.

48 See e.g., *Annales Fuldenses*, ed. F. Kurze, *MGH SRG* (Hanover, 1891) [hereafter *AF*] s.a. 863, 869, pp. 56–7, 67–8 (Count Gundachar); *Annales Bertiniani*, ed. G. Waitz, *MGH SRG* (Hanover, 1883) [hereafter *AB*], s.a. 874, pp. 125–6 (Salomon). *AB* s.a. 864, p. 74 reports, without particular disapproval, that Abbot Hubert of St Maurice was slain by his own men. *AF* s.a. 886, p. 105 claims that *Heimrih comes a suis desertus et ab hostibus circumdatus occiditur*, but *Annales Vedastini*, ed. B. von Simson, *MGH SRG* (Hanover, 1909), Abbo and Regino do not refer to any 'desertion'.

49 Nithard, *Nithardi Historiarum libri IIII*, 3–4, ed. E. Müller, *MGH SRG* (Hanover, 1907), pp. 33–4 (Charles the Bald comes to the rescue of his *fidelis* Adalgar); Regino s.a. 884, pp. 121–2 (Carloman protects the *satelles* who had fatally wounded him by accident). Charles the Bald also instituted memorial prayers for some of his *fideles* from the late 860s, a Merovingian tradition that Carolingian rulers had abandoned after 786. See E. Ewig, 'Remarques sur la stipulation de la prière dans les chartes de Charles le Chauve', in R. Lejeune and J. Deckers (eds), *Clio et son regard: Mélanges d'histoire, d'histoire de l'art et d'archéologie offerts à Jacques Stiennon, à l'occasion de ses vingt-cinq ans d'enseignement à l'Université de Liège* (Liège, 1982), pp. 221–33.

treatment of the Cynewulf episode.[50] Frankish 'historical' poetry, despite extensive descriptions of both lay nobles and warfare, mentions lordship only in passing. Ermoldus Nigellus' long poem *In honorem Hludovicii Pii*, for example, has only two fleeting references to the emotional bonds of lords and followers.[51] Abbo of St Germain-des-Prés in *Bella Parisiacae urbis* gives a detailed account of warfare against the Vikings in the 880s. Abbo shows the military retinues of lords fighting bravely for them,[52] but rarely stresses the affective nature of this relationship. When Robert Faretratus, the count of Chartres, is killed by Danes, his nephew Adalaelmus encourages 'the count's people' to avenge his death only in terms of kinship: 'Come on, brave men, take your arms and shields, / and let us rapidly hasten to avenge my uncle.'[53]

Indeed some Carolingian poems which might be expected to show the particular emotions of lordship decline to do so. Epitaphs of noble laymen do not stress the particular grief of their followers; all are invited to weep for them.[54] Angelbert's lament on the battle of Fontenoy complains of the treachery of Lothar's *duces*,[55] but he focuses on the evils of civil war and the breaking of Christian and kinship ties, not on a betrayed or valiantly

---

50   *ASC* A, E s.a. 755, *Two of the Saxon Chronicles Parallel*, ed. C. Plummer (Oxford, 1892), pp. 46–51: King Cynewulf of Wessex and his retainers are killed by the *ætheling* Cyneheard and his followers, who are themselves then killed in revenge. On this story see S. D. White, 'Kinship and lordship in early medieval England: the story of Sigeberht, Cynewulf and Cyneheard', *Viator* 20 (1989), pp. 1–18; D. G. Scragg, '*Wifcyþþe* and the morality of the Cynewulf and Cyneheard episode in the Anglo-Saxon Chronicle', in J. Roberts, J. L. Nelson and M. Godden (eds), *Alfred the Wise: Studies in Honour of Janet Bateley on the Occasion of her Sixty-fifth Birthday* (Cambridge, 1997), pp. 179–85.

51   *In honorem* v 528–9: William of Toulouse refrains from killing Zado from *regis amorque timorque*; v 1718–19: the *puer* of Coslus kills his slayer, *domini praevinctus amore*.

52   Abbo I 68–73 (Ebolus is wounded, but Frederick, his young *miles* is killed); II 28–30 (Odo's men come to his help); II 189–94 (the *senior* Segebertus and *iunior* Segevertus die together).

53   Abbo I 452–5: *Unde nepos ejus nimium tristans Adalaelmus / Consulis intererat populo, cui talia dixit: / 'Eia, viri fortes, clipeos sumatis et arma, / Ulciscique meum raptim properemus avunclum'*. Abbo then refers to Adalaelmus' revenge, not that of Robert's men (v 456–9).

54   See e.g., *MGH Poet.* I, pp. 109–10 (epitaph of Eggihard); Paulinus's lament on Eric of Friuli, *MGH Poet.* I, pp. 131–3. Cf. the *planctus* on Charlemagne's death (Godman, *Poetry*, pp. 206–11). *VK* 19, p. 24 describes Charlemagne's tears for the death of Pope Hadrian; there is no mention of him crying over nobles killed in battle. This contrasts with later works, such as the *Chanson de Roland*, where Charlemagne shows extreme grief for his slain warriors.

55   Angelbert, *Versus de bella quae fuit acta Fontaneto*, stanza 5, Godman, *Poetry*, pp. 262–5.

defeated lord. The *Carmen de Ludovico II imperatore*, which does show a betrayed king, casts Louis II not as a secular lord, but as a Christ-like martyr.[56]

Waltharius is the one Carolingian Latin poem that deals with 'Germanic' heroes, but its attitude toward lords remains ambivalent.[57] As Graus points out, fidelity to a lord is not automatically seen as overriding other relationships.[58] Certainly, Walter, the poem's hero, and his friend Hagan are hardly model retainers. Raised as a hostage at Attila's court and treated as his son,[59] Walter calls Attila his *dominus*, but nevertheless abandons and robs him.[60] Hagan's relationship with his original lord, the Frankish king Gunther, is more emotional. The poem refers to him fleeing to his lord,[61] and during the final fight, he pales at the sight of his lord's blood.[62] Gunther's role as lord, however, seems precarious: he has to make several long appeals to his men to fight during his unsuccessful attack on Walter.[63] Hagan initially refuses to fight Walter;[64] when he eventually agrees to help Gunther, he stresses Gunther's kingship more than an emotional tie.[65] Gunther may be an inadequate king, but this alone does not explain Hagan's failure to treat him as a 'dear lord'.[66]

---

56 *MGH Poet.* III, pp. 404–5.
57 I am not convinced by the view of several scholars that *Waltharius* is a parody: see F. B. Parkes, 'Irony in *Waltharius*', *MLN* 89 (1974), pp. 459–65; A. K. Bate, 'Introduction and Notes', in A. K. Bate (ed.), *Waltharius of Gaeraldus* (Reading, 1978), pp. 1–12, 52–67 and, in most detail, D. M. Kratz, *Mocking Epic: Waltharius, Alexandreis and the Problem of Christian Heroism* (Madrid, 1980), chapter 2. In particular, the argument that the presumed monastic author was satirizing a 'Germanic warrior-ethos' (Kratz, *Mocking Epic*, pp. 39–59; Parkes, 'Irony', pp. 459–60) ignores the parallels with Carolingian war poetry written by other religious authors, such as Sedulius Scottus, Ermoldus Nigellus and Abbo. The morality of *Waltharius*, taken at face value, is firmly within the mainstream of Carolingian thought.
58 Graus, 'Über die sogenannte germanische Treue', pp. 80–2.
59 *Waltharius* v 97–8.
60 *Waltharius* v 149–50.
61 *Waltharius* v 120.
62 *Waltharius* v 1366. After the fight, however, Hagan shows no particular concern for his wounded lord.
63 *Waltharius* v 941–53, v 1064–88.
64 *Waltharius* v 617–37. However, Hagan's anger when Gunther calls him a coward is seen ambiguously (v 632–3): *Tunc heros magnam iuste conceperat iram, / si tamen in dominum licitum est irascier ulli.*
64 *Waltharius* v 1098–1114.
66 Irving, 'Heroic role models' suggests the possibility of retainers becoming role-models for kings within epic poems. He comments (pp. 357–8) on the *Poem of the Cid*: 'the poem makes us feel that Alfonso [King of Castile] is wished into being a good king at last . . . What a king should be is projected so hard and firm against the vacant space that it at last becomes real.'

Only two Carolingian narrative texts do include substantial comments on loyal service to a lord. Nithard's history shows a keen interest in the conduct of noble laymen like himself, who had to make significant political choices as to which of the competing Frankish kings they would support in the early 840s.[67] He depicts such decisions in strong emotional and moral language. Nithard comments how in late 840, some of Charles the Bald's supporters abandoned him for Lothar, breaking their word *more servorum.*[68] In the next section he claims that others (including implicitly himself) 'chose to die nobly rather than betray and abandon their king.'[69] The same contrast is made in Walahfrid Strabo's panegyric on Ruadbern, who helped secure the release of Louis the Pious and Judith in 834. Walahfrid repeatedly praises his bravery and especially his loyalty to his *domini*. Such behaviour merits earthly fame and heavenly reward:

> Just as the man aware
> of his treachery wastes away, his breast racked by its poison,
> so, or rather much more, may those who have kept in their hearts
> an allegiance to their lords that has proved invincible
> in all disasters discover every balmy joy.[70]

The political ideology of lordship

Walahfrid's poem confirms that a learned Latin culture did not preclude Carolingian authors from celebrating lordship and loyalty. An explanation for the discrepancy between discussions of lordship must be sought elsewhere, in the different political cultures of Francia and Anglo-Saxon England. Many studies of Carolingian historical texts have discussed their ideological role,[71] and there has also been debate on the aims of Alfredian

---

67 On Nithard, see J. L. Nelson, 'Public *Histories* and private history in the work of Nithard', *Speculum* 60 (1985), pp. 251–93; S. Airlie, 'The world, the text and the Carolingian: royal, aristocratic and masculine identities in Nithard's *Histories*', in Wormald and Nelson (eds), *Lay Intellectuals*, pp. 51–76.

68 Nithard, 2–3, p. 16.

69 Nithard 2–4, p. 16: *elegerunt potius nobiliter mori quam regem proditum derelinquere.*

70 Walahfrid Strabo, 'Ex quo fama' v 89–93, Godman, *Poetry*, pp. 220–1:

> *Quantum sibi conscius ille*
> *Perfidiae confusa globis per pectora tabet,*
> *Tantum, vel potius multo magis, omnia secum*
> *Laetitiae fomenta habeant, qui fida reservant*
> *Corda suis dominis casusque invicta per omnes.*

71 For Carolingian texts see e.g., Hen and Innes (eds), *The Uses of the Past*; R. McKitterick, *History and Memory in the Carolingian World* (Cambridge, 2004).

texts, such as the first recension of the *Anglo-Saxon Chronicle*.[72] More recently, studies of Old English literary texts have focused on the ideological and political work these do.[73]

There has been particular interest in the political purpose of *The Battle of Maldon*. John Niles has argued, somewhat unconvincingly, that the poem is intended to justify Aethelred's policy of buying off the Danes.[74] Besides possible attempts to influence military strategy, John Hill has argued for the poet's creation of the idea of 'transcendental loyalty.'[75] Many previous commentators have stressed the role of the poem in creating or recreating an ideal of heroic behaviour and loyalty.[76] Edward Irving describes a move in the poem toward 'a world and a style where the individual merges his identity with that of his leader and the ancient heroes.'[77]

Hill identifies a similar phenomenon:

> the poem reflects a late development in the Anglo-Saxon heroic code: essentially a Christian transvaluation of retainer loyalty from a secular to a transcendental plane – one that produces the awesome spectacle of nearly immediate, suicidal loyalty to one's lord, plotted linearly as an ongoing set of redefined identifications with the dead lord rather than as a simultaneous experience of suffering and death.[78]

72 The view of R. H. C. Davis, 'Alfred the Great: propaganda and truth', *History* 56 (1971), pp. 169–82 that the *Chronicle* is 'propaganda' is rejected by Simon Keynes, but his own comments on the purpose of the annals (S. Keynes, 'A tale of two kings: Alfred the Great and Æthelred the Unready', *TRHS*, 5th series, 36 (1986), pp. 195–217 at p. 198): 'they project a view of the common history of the English peoples and the emergence of Alfred as their natural leader' suggests a different form of propaganda.

73 See e.g., J. D. Niles, 'Locating Beowulf in literary history', *Exemplaria* 5 (1993), pp. 79–109; J. Thormann, 'The *Anglo-Saxon Chronicle* poems and the making of the English nation', in A. J. Frantzen and J. D. Niles (eds), *Anglo-Saxonism and the Construction of Social Identity* (Gainesville, 1997), pp. 60–85; P. R. Richardson, 'Making thanes: literature, rhetoric and state formation in Anglo-Saxon England', *Philological Quarterly* 78 (1999), pp. 215–32.

74 Niles, 'Maldon and mythopoesis'. If so, the poem has to be considered a political failure, since Niles comments (p. 100) that modern students still delight in Byrhtnoth's refusal to pay tribute. Keynes, 'Two kings', p. 204 more accurately claims 'there is no mistaking what the poet considered to be the more honourable response.'

75 J. M. Hill, 'Transcendental loyalty in *The Battle of Maldon*', *Mediaevalia* 17 (1994), pp. 67–88; Hill, *Anglo-Saxon Warrior Ethic*, chapter 5.

76 See e.g., Robinson, 'God, death'; Frank, 'Ideal'; George Clark, '*The Battle of Maldon*: a heroic poem', *Speculum* 43 (1968), pp. 52–71.

77 Irving, 'Heroic style', p. 466.

78 Hill, 'Transcendental loyalty', p. 68.

Where Hill goes beyond previous commentators is in seeing the poem, along with parts of the *Anglo-Saxon Chronicle* (the Cynewulf and Cyneheard story and the *Chronicle* poems), as part of a politically inspired attempt by ninth- and tenth-century West Saxon rulers and their supporters to reshape and appropriate heroic values.[79] In contrast to *Beowulf* these later texts remove the option of a free warrior life; the focus of heroism becomes the retainer.[80] The standpoint of these poems is predetermined, avoiding the complex contingent views of behaviour in *Beowulf*.[81] There is a particular emphasis on triumphal lordship, the (West Saxon) king as sacrosanct and sacrificial loyalty by retainers.

A politically motivated appropriation of heroic values in also visible in Carolingian texts from the late eighth century onward, but focusing on a different social configuration. Frankish historiography shows a concerted attempt to glorify Carolingian rulers together with the Franks as a *gens* and the lay and clerical magnates.[82] Similar patterns are seen in much of the poetry of the period, including the rhythmical verse on Pippin's defeat of the Avars, the works of Ermoldus Nigellus and Sedulius Scottus, and the *Ludwigslied*.[83] In the mythology of the Franks as a warrior people,[84] the heroic deeds of magnates and the Carolingians as a line of rulers chosen by God, there is little room for a specific role for loyal retainers.

This particular ideological pattern was established from the start of the Carolingian dynasty. An obvious reason is the family's role as usurpers. While Alfred's laws could treat kingship as a form of lordship, Carolingian rulers and their supporters consistently stressed the difference between kings and magnates, even while emphasizing their co-operation.[85] Demanding absolute loyalty to a royal lord was also problematic, given the

---

79 Hill, *Anglo-Saxon Warrior Ethic*, p. 2.

80 Hill, *Anglo-Saxon Warrior Ethic*, p. 129.

81 Hill, *Anglo-Saxon Warrior Ethic*, pp. 131, 135–42.

82 R. McKitterick, 'Political ideology in Carolingian historiography', in Hen and Innes (eds), *The Uses of the Past*, pp. 162–74 at pp. 167–9.

83 The verse on the Avar victory (*Omnes gentes qui fecisti*) is in Godman, *Poetry*, pp. 186–91. See also *Carmen de conversione Saxonum*, ed. and trans. Susan A. Rabe, *Faith, Art, and Politics at Saint-Riquier: the Symbolic Vision of Angilbert* (Philadelphia, 1995), pp. 62–6.

84 See in particular *In honorem* v 368–79, 1406–11.

85 Abels, *Alfred*, p. 249; J. L. Nelson, 'The Lord's anointed and the people's choice: Carolingian royal ritual', in D. Cannadine and S. Price (eds), *Rituals of Royalty: Power and Ceremonial in Traditional Societies* (Cambridge: 1987), pp. 137–80; R. Stone, 'Kings are different: Carolingian mirrors for princes and lay morality', in F. Lachaud and L. Scordia (eds), *Le Prince au miroir de la littérature politique de l'Antiquité aux Lumières* (Rouen, 2007), pp. 69–86.

concerted attempt to depict the Merovingians as unworthy, 'do-nothing' kings, whose behaviour justified Pippin III's usurpation.[86] Moreover, ties to lords other than the ruler were potentially a threat, unless carefully controlled. Around twenty years before the *Anglo-Saxon Chronicle* made the Cynewulf and Cyneheard episode into an exemplary display of retainership, a very different attitude to a rebel prince's followers was seen in West Francia. There is no praise for the men who supported Charles the Bald's son Carloman in his repeated rebellions. Instead, Carloman's 'satellites' were described as 'sons of Belial', excommunicated and finally forced to take other lords. Those who did not were punished with the loss of their allodial land.[87]

Ninth- and tenth-century West Saxon kings faced a somewhat different challenge. There were fewer challenges to their dynastic legitimacy, but they were faced with more substantial military threats. Glorifying lordship as an eternal, emotional bond could potentially form part of a campaign to mobilize armies and rally military support. Such an emphasis may have been particularly important because the Viking take-over of Anglo-Saxon kingdoms meant far greater possibilities for English nobles to collaborate with them than Frankish magnates had. A moral imperative to spurn such changes of allegiance was a potentially valuable tool.

Similarly, the two Frankish texts which glorify retainers, Nithard's histories and the poem on Ruadbern, were both written at times of great vulnerability for particular rulers, when such changes of side were commonplace. Otherwise, the use of the lord-man relationship by Carolingian rulers and the authors supporting them can best be described as parasitic. They were keen to exploit lordship, both as a metaphor for obedience and as a practical means of social control, but they saw little need to reinforce this wider ideology of lordship. However dear some Frankish lords may have been, lordship as an ideal was not noticeably dear to Carolingian rulers.[88]

---

86   Similarly, treachery is not such a prominent theme in Carolingian texts as in Anglo-Saxon ones (on which see H. Magennis, 'Treatment of treachery and betrayal in Anglo-Saxon texts', *English Studies* 76 (1995), pp. 11–19.

87   *AB* s.a. 870, 871, pp. 115–16; *Capitulare Cariacense 873* c. 4, *MGH Capitularia* II, no. 278, pp. 344–5.

88   There is an interesting parallel here to the pattern of the Church''s attitude to lordship as discussed by Green, *Carolingian Lord* . Green sees the Church as first adopting the Germanic secular vocabulary of lordship and then appropriating it for its own ends by discouraging non-religious use.

9

Making a difference in tenth-century politics: King Athelstan's sisters and Frankish queenship*

Simon MacLean

'THE HOLY LAWS of kinship have purposed to take root among monarchs for this reason: that their tranquil spirit may bring the peace which peoples long for.' Thus in the year 507 Theoderic, king of the Ostrogoths, wrote to Clovis, king of the Franks.[1] His appeal to the ideals of peace between kin was designed to avert hostilities between the Franks and the Visigoths, and drew meaning from the web of marital ties which bound together the royal dynasties of the early sixth-century West. Theoderic himself sat at the centre of this web: he was married to Clovis's sister, and his daughter was married to Alaric, king of the Visigoths.[2] The present article is concerned with a much later period of European history, but the Ostrogothic ruler's words nevertheless serve to introduce us to one of its central themes, namely the significance of marital alliances between dynasties.

Unfortunately the tenth-century West, our present concern, had no Cassiodorus (the recorder of the king's letter) to methodically enlighten the intricacies of its politics, but Theoderic's sentiments were doubtless not unlike those that crossed the minds of the Anglo-Saxon and Frankish elite families who engineered an equally striking series of

---

* My title is plundered from J. L. Nelson, 'Making a difference in eighth-century politics: the daughters of Desiderius', in A. Murray (ed.), *After Rome's Fall: Narrators and Sources of Early Medieval History. Essays Presented to Walter Goffart* (Toronto, 1998), pp. 171–90. I am indebted to Charles Insley, Pauline Stafford and Alex Woolf for valuable comments on drafts of this article; to Ludger Körntgen for sending me copies of his work; to a seminar audience at Kalamazoo for their questions; and above all to Jinty Nelson for her encouragement and guidance over the last ten years.
1 *Cassiodori Senatoris Variae*, ed. T. Mommsen, *MGH AA* XII (Berlin, 1894), III.4, p. 80; trans. S. J. B. Barnish, *The* Variae *of Magnus Aurelius Cassiodorus Senator: Being Documents of the Kingdom of the Ostrogoths in Italy* (Liverpool, 1992), p. 48.
2 For context see I. Wood, *The Merovingian Kingdoms 450–751* (London and New York, 1994), pp. 164–75.

marital relationships among themselves just over 400 years later. In the early years of the tenth century several Anglo-Saxon royal women, all daughters of King Edward the Elder of Wessex (899–924) and sisters (or half-sisters) of his son King Athelstan (924–39), were despatched across the Channel as brides for Frankish and Saxon rulers and aristocrats. This article addresses the fate of some of these women through an analysis of their political identities. In particular, it is concerned with the ways by which they sought to exercise power in kingdoms where they were outsiders.

The sequence began in c.919 with the marriage of Eadgifu to the Carolingian king of West Francia, Charles the Straightforward (also known as 'the Simple').[3] In the years thereafter, the new queen's sisters (and half-sisters) made a habit of marrying members of continental dynasties. In 926 Eadhild married Hugh the Great, 'duke of the Franks', an extremely powerful magnate whose father, King Robert I (922–3), had fought a bloody civil war against Charles. Then in 929–30 Edith was married to the future emperor Otto I, son of Henry I of East Francia; and at the same time or slightly later Edgiva wedded Louis, the brother of King Rudolf II of Burgundy.[4] By the early 930s, then, four of Athelstan's half-sisters were married into four of the great dynasties of tenth-century Europe; a fifth, meanwhile, became the wife of Sihtric, Viking leader in Northumbria. The political careers of these women are shadowy. Only Edith, hitched to the rising star of the Saxon Ottonian dynasty, left anything approaching a significant

---

3   I refer to Charles as Straightforward following B. Schneidmüller, 'Die "Einfältigkeit" Karls III von Westfrankreich als frühmittelalterliche Herrschertugend. Überlegungen zu den cognomen *simplex*', *Schweizerische Zeitschrift für Geschichte* 28 (1978), pp. 62–6.

4   Edgiva is an alternative spelling of Eadgifu (they had different mothers). The identity of her husband was convincingly demonstrated by E. Hlawitschka, 'Die verwandtschaftlichen Verbindungen zwischen dem hochburgundischen und dem niederburgundischen Königshaus: Zugleich ein Beitrag zur Geschichte Burgunds in der 1. Hälfte des 10. Jahrhunderts', in W. Schlögl and P. Herde (eds), *Grundwissenschaften und Geschichte: Festschrift für Peter Acht* (Lassleben: Kallmünz, 1976), pp. 28–57, at pp. 50–7. Some historians continue to identify him as Louis of Aquitaine, Louis of Provence or Conrad of Burgundy: V. Ortenberg, 'Aux périphéries du monde carolingien: liens dynastiques et nouvelles fidélités dans le royaume Anglo-Saxon', in R. Le Jan (ed.), *La Royauté et les élites dans l'Europe carolingienne (début IXe siècle aux environs de 920)* (Lille, 1998), pp. 505–17 at pp. 507–8; S. Sharp, 'The West Saxon tradition of dynastic marriage with specific reference to Edward the Elder', in N. J. Higham and D. H. Hill (eds), *Edward the Elder, 899–924* (London, 2001), pp. 79–88 at pp. 83–5.

impression on the contemporary sources.[5] Yet collectively the presence of these sisters on the Continent is very striking; indeed, this pattern of amorous activity arguably marks the high point in cross-Channel royal links in the early Middle Ages as a whole.[6]

To understand just how much of a high point, we need to appreciate the exceptional nature in our period of these interdynastic marriages. Despite the criss-crossing dynastic connections which helped articulate politics in the age of Theoderic, Clovis and Alaric, in the context of more recent Frankish history the phenomenon of outsider queens was emphatically a novelty.[7] In the pantheon of early medieval dynasties, the ninth-century Carolingians were singular in the insularity of their marital strategies.[8] Charlemagne (768–814), so his biographer Einhard tells us, 'never wanted to give any of [his daughters] away to anyone, whether it be to a Frankish noble or to a foreigner.'[9] Einhard added that this was 'strange to report', but it would seem that the emperor's desire to restrict claims to inheritance must go a long way to explaining his

5   For references and discussion see K. Schmid, 'Neue Quellen zum Verständnis des Adels im 10. Jahrhundert', in *Zeitshrift für die Geschichte des Oberrheins* 69 (1960), pp. 185–232, esp. pp. 186–202; K. Leyser, 'The Ottonians and Wessex', in K. Leyser, *Communications and Power in Medieval Europe: I. The Carolingian and Ottonian Centuries*, ed. T. Reuter (London and Rio Grande, 1994), pp. 73–104 at pp. 75–81, 85–93; W. Glocker, *Die Verwandten der Ottonen und ihre Bedeutung in der Politik* (Cologne, 1989), pp. 18–27; W. Georgi, 'Bischof Keonwald von Worcester und die Heirat Ottos I. mit Egitha im Jahre 929', in *Historisches Jahrbuch* 115 (1995), pp. 1–40; K. Görich, 'Mathilde – Edgith – Adelheid: Ottonische Königinnen als Fürsprecherinnen', in B. Schneidmüller and S. Weinfurter (eds), *Ottonische Neuanfänge* (Mainz, 2001), pp. 251–91; L. Körntgen, 'Starke Frauen: Edgith – Adelheid – Theophanu', in M. Puhle (ed.), *Otto der Große: Magdeburg und Europa* (Mainz, 2001), vol. 1, pp. 119–32 at pp. 120–2.

6   For a useful (but imperfect) table of cross-channel marriages see Sharp, 'West Saxon Tradition', pp. 83–5.

7   On outsider queens in Late Antiquity see J. L. Nelson, 'Gendering courts in the Early Medieval West', in L. Brubaker and J. M. H. Smith (eds), *Gender in the Early Medieval World: East and West, 300–900* (Cambridge, 2004), pp. 185–97. Charles was not absolutely the first Frankish ruler of the age to take a foreign wife: that distinction seems to belong to Louis of Provence for his marriage to Anna, daughter of the Byzantine emperor Leo VI. See Hlawitschka, 'Die verwandtschaftlichen Verbindungen', pp. 36–43.

8   P. Stafford, *Queens, Concubines and Dowagers: the King's Wife in the Early Middle Ages* (London, 1983), pp. 47–8.

9   Einhard, *Vita Karoli*, ed. O. Holder-Egger, *MGH SRG* (Hanover, 1911), c. 19, p. 25; translation from P. E. Dutton, *Charlemagne's Courtier: the Complete Einhard* (Peterborough, Ont., 1998), p. 29.

motives.[10] His reluctance also reflected the Franks' deep sense of superiority over their neighbours. Pope Stephen III pandered to this sentiment when he attempted (in pursuit of his own agendas) to dissuade Charlemagne and his brother from the idea of a marriage alliance with the Lombards in 770: 'You are not at liberty to mix with the blood of another race. None of your forebears . . . took a wife from another kingdom or a foreign race . . . Take note, I beseech you, of how many and how great have been those powerful men who have fallen away from God's commandments by marrying into another people . . .'[11] Bitter experience may also have inspired the emperor's marital protectionism, for (having ignored the pope's pleading) Charlemagne well knew that the course of diplomatic love did not always run smooth. Attempts in the 780s and 790s to betroth his daughter to the young Byzantine emperor Constantine VI and his son to a daughter of King Offa of Mercia both collapsed amid recriminations and worsening relationships.[12]

Thereafter, Charlemagne and his successors kept a firm grip on the marriages of their family members. Occasional Carolingian princesses were despatched to seal alliances through marriage, such as Charles the Bald's daughter Judith who married Æthelwulf king of Wessex in 856.[13] However, this was a highly unusual case. In the case of royal sons in the ninth century there were to be no exceptions. This was spelled out explicitly in the *Ordinatio Imperii* of 817 which stated that, unlike their aristocratic followers, none of Louis the Pious's heirs 'should presume to take a wife of foreign nationality . . . in order to avoid discord and take away opportunities for harm.'[14] Instead, young Carolingian males were to marry only members of

10 Sexual motivations are also a possibility: see J. L. Nelson, 'Women at the court of Charlemagne: a case of monstrous regiment?', in J. L. Nelson, *The Frankish World, 750–900* (London and Rio Grande, 1996), pp. 223–42 at pp. 237–40.

11 *Codex Carolinus*, ed. W. Gundlach, *MGH Epistolae* III (Berlin, 1892), no. 45, pp. 560–3; translation from P. D. King, *Charlemagne: Translated Sources* (Kendal, 1987), p. 271.

12 The Empress Irene is also thought to have proposed a marriage between herself and Charlemagne: on these cases see J. L. Nelson, 'Carolingian contacts', in M. Brown and C. Farr (eds), *Mercia: An Anglo-Saxon Kingdom in Europe* (London and New York, 2001), pp. 126–43; J. Herrin, *Women in Purple: Rulers of Medieval Byzantium* (London, 2001), pp. 116–18, 121–9, 130–1; J. Story, *Carolingian Connections: Anglo-Saxon England and Carolingian Francia c. 750–870* (Aldershot, 2003).

13 P. Stafford, 'Charles the Bald, Judith and England', in M. T. Gibson and J. L. Nelson (eds), *Charles the Bald: Court and Kingdom*, 2nd edn (Aldershot, 1990), pp. 139–53; J. L. Nelson, *Charles the Bald* (London, 1992), p. 182.

14 *Ordinatio Imperii, MGH Capitularia* I, ed. A. Boretius (Hanover, 1893), no. 136, c. 13, pp. 270–3; trans. P. E. Dutton, *Carolingian Civilization: A Reader*, 2nd edn (Peterborough, Ont., 2004), p. 202.

the Frankish aristocracy, in order to seal political alliances within the empire.[15] Ninth-century Francia thus witnessed almost no interdynastic marriages. This norm later reasserted itself in the second half of the tenth century. After the 940s, high-profile political links between England and the Continent seem to have declined, a trend reflected in the fact that there were no more cross-Channel royal marriages until 1002, when the English ruler Æthelred II married Emma of Normandy.[16]

Against this background, the unions arranged for Athelstan's sisters stand out conspicuously. These marriages raise a whole host of questions. What do they reveal about the relative status of the various European dynasties in power at the time?[17] How do they inform our understanding of directions of political influence (usually assumed to be south-north) in the period? How deep were the underlying currents of cross-Channel contact on which they rested? How did these people communicate with each other? What was the character of the tenth century's multicultural courts? How did Athelstan's Frankish connections fit in with his patronage of political factions from Brittany and Norway? Other such issues are not hard to identify. However, this article cannot address them all. Rather, our spotlight will lie specifically on the positions of these English women themselves. Previous scholarship has noted their significance, but has tended to describe them as simple avatars of their male relatives' political agendas.[18] There is certainly some truth in this model: after all, the twelfth-century historian

---

15 In general on Carolingian marriages see S. Hellmann, 'Die Heiraten der Karolinger', in S. Hellmann, *Ausgewählte Abhandlungen zur Historiographie und Geistesgeschichte des Mittelalters*, ed. H. Beumann (Darmstadt, 1961), pp. 293–391; and in a wider context Stafford, *Queens, Concubines and Dowagers*, pp. 32–59.

16 The definitive history of cross-Channel political relationships in the tenth century remains to be written, though see V. Ortenberg, *The English Church and the Continent in the Tenth and Eleventh Centuries: Cultural, Spiritual, and Artistic Exchange* (Oxford, 1992). On Æthelred and Emma see P. Stafford, *Queen Emma and Queen Edith: Queenship and Women's Power in Eleventh-Century England* (Oxford, 1997); on the preceding period see Story, *Carolingian Connections*.

17 Leyser, 'Ottonians and Wessex', pp. 77–9 argues that the Ottonians needed some of the royal prestige of Edith's family at this early stage of their dynastic career.

18 S. Sharp, 'England, Europe and the Celtic world: King Athelstan's foreign policy', in *Bulletin of the John Rylands University Library of Manchester* 79 (1997), pp. 197–220, esp. pp. 206–9; Ortenberg, 'Aux périphéries'. A more nuanced reading of interdynastic marriages in the period is provided by J. Ehlers, 'Carolingiens, Robertiens, Ottoniens: politique familiale de relations franco-allemandes', in M. Parisse and X. Barral I Altet (eds), *Le Roi de France et son royaume autour de l'an mil* (Paris, 1992), pp. 39–45. Above all, see the highly interesting insights of Leyser, 'Ottonians and Wessex'; Hlawitschka, 'Die verwandtschaftlichen Verbindungen'; and J. L. Nelson, DNB 'Eadgifu'.

William of Malmesbury, here probably relying on a contemporary source, regarded the desire of foreign princes for his sisters' hands as evidence of Athelstan's greatness.[19] However, one of its weaknesses is that it casts the sisters in rather passive roles. The political centrality of royal women in this period, illuminated brightly in the work of historians such as Janet Nelson and Pauline Stafford, means that this implication of passivity should not pass unexamined.

In studying Eadgifu and her sisters, we cannot lose sight of the fact that they were rootless outsiders in the kingdoms and principalities they married into. This is not merely a curiosity. Rather, it takes us to the heart of their political identities. The women who became Carolingian queens before Eadgifu were, as we have seen, Frankish aristocrats chosen at least in part for the political resources they brought with them to the marriage. They gave their husbands access to political networks, family ties and lands in areas of the empire where they needed to build influence. At the same time, her position as bridge between the royal court and the regional aristocracy from which she emerged was one of the crucial and enduring bases of a ninth-century queen's own power.[20] However, when the queen in question came from outside the realm, of necessity this bridging role could not sustain her position in the same way. It is therefore the aim of this article to ask how queenship worked in such unusual circumstances. This aspect of the topic has not been fully explored. Much has been published on tenth-century Frankish queenship, but by and large the approach adopted

---

19 William of Malmesbury, *Gesta regum Anglorum*, ed. and trans. R. A. B. Mynors, completed by R. M. Thomson and M. Winterbottom (Oxford, 1998–9), vol. 1, c. 135, p. 216. On the utility of William's information for the reign of Athelstan see M. Wood, 'The making of King Athelstan's empire: an English Charlemagne?', in P. Wormald, D. Bullough and R. Collins (eds), *Ideal and Reality in Frankish and Anglo-Saxon Society* (Oxford, 1983), pp. 250–72 at pp. 265–6 and William of Malmesbury, *Gesta*, vol. 2, pp. 116–18. These argue against the sceptical arguments of M. Lapidge, 'Some Latin poems as evidence for the reign of Athelstan', *ASE* 9 (1981), pp. 61–98, at pp. 62–71.

20 The bibliography on early medieval queenship is now vast. See the vital contributions and further references collected in J. L. Nelson, *Politics and Ritual in Early Medieval Europe* (London, 1985); Nelson, *The Frankish World*; J. L. Nelson, *Rulers and Ruling Families in Early Medieval Europe: Alfred, Charles the Bald, and Others* (Aldershot: 1999); Stafford, *Queens, Concubines and Dowagers*; Stafford, *Queen Emma and Queen Edith*. The 'bridging' role of Carolingian queens is highlighted in S. MacLean, 'Queenship, nunneries and royal widowhood in Carolingian Europe', *Past and Present* 178 (2003), pp. 3–38.

has involved compiling fragments of evidence from across the period. Although useful, this serves to emphasize the common features of queenly power rather than highlighting individual peculiarities.[21] By directing attention to the outsider status of Athelstan's sisters, I hope to map out some of the contours of queens' power in tenth-century Francia, identifying differences between them as well as similarities.

The political era through which these women lived was defined by a generational change in the main European ruling dynasties in the middle years of the 930s. East of the Rhine, the Saxon king Henry was succeeded by his son Otto in 936; a year later Rudolf II of Burgundy also died, to be replaced by his young son Conrad III the Peaceable. The possible roles of Edith and Edgiva in these events have been superbly picked out from the sparse evidence by Karl Leyser and Eduard Hlawitschka.[22] Our attention, however, will be concentrated further west, on the career of Eadgifu in the kingdom of West Francia. Here, political change was also the order of the day. After the deposition and imprisonment of her husband Charles the Straightforward in 923, Eadgifu sent their infant son Louis across the sea to Wessex, where he was brought up at the court of his uncle Athelstan. She herself also went back to England, probably at the same time as her son, though possibly not until Charles's death in 929.[23] Eadgifu and Louis remained in exile until 936, when news arrived of the death of King Raoul (923–36), a non-Carolingian whose power base lay in Burgundy. The West Frankish magnates asked Athelstan to return his nephew, now aged 15 or 16, to be their king: he landed on the beach at Boulogne that summer and began to rule as Louis IV. History remembers him as Louis d'Outremer ('from across the sea').

Given his youth and the circumstances of his succession, it is hardly surprising that Louis was far from being master of all he surveyed. Although

---

21 I am thinking here principally of J. Verdon, 'Les Femmes et la politique en France au Xe siècle', in J. Schneider et al. (eds), *Économies et sociétés au moyen âge: Mélanges offerts à Edouard Perroy* (Paris 1973), pp. 108–19 which nonetheless remains very useful. More nuanced insights are provided by R. Le Jan, 'D'une cour à l'autre: les voyages des reines de France au Xe siècle', in R. Le Jan, *Femmes, pouvoir et société dans le haute moyen âge* (Paris, 2001), pp. 39–52; and, in the same volume, R. Le Jan, 'La Reine Gerberge, entre carolingiens et ottoniens', pp. 30–8.

22 Leyser, 'Ottonians and Wessex', pp. 75–93; Hlawitschka, 'Die verwandtschaftlichen Verbindungen', pp. 50–7.

23 Nelson, 'Eadgifu'.

it would provide useful context, space precludes meaningful discussion of the events of his reign.[24] Its Leitmotif, however, was conflict between on the one hand a group of extremely powerful aristocrats, led at various times by some combination of Hugh the Great (count of Tours and 'duke of the Franks'), Count Herbert II of Vermandois, William Longsword (leader of the Northmen based at Rouen) and Arnulf, count of Flanders; and on the other a ruler who had lost control of almost all the major estates on which his predecessors had depended. After some initial success in these struggles, bolstered by his marriage in 939 to Gerberga, sister of Otto I and widow of duke Giselbert of Lotharingia, Louis's fortunes declined further in the 940s and reached a nadir in 945–6 with his imprisonment at the hands of first William Longsword and then Hugh the Great. Only at the very end of the decade did he start to assert his power with consistent effectiveness. Yet this purple patch was cut short when, at the age of 33 in 954, he met his unfortunate death in an archetypally Carolingian hunting accident. The materials available for studying the first half of the tenth century are unenviable: much depends on gleanings from Louis's 53 known charters and the only major contemporary West Frankish narrative source, the *Annals* of Flodoard of Rheims.[25] We will use this material to address three main questions: How did Eadgifu's family ties interact with the politics of her son's reign? How was she integrated into a political landscape of which she was not by birth or background a part? And how might the unusual experience of Eadgifu and other outsider-queens have influenced the concept and practice of queenship in Francia?

24 P. Lauer, *Le Règne de Louis IV d'Outre-Mer* (Paris, 1900) remains a very useful, if narrow, narrative; as does C. Brühl, 'Ludwig IV. "der überseeische" (936–54)', in J. Ehlers, H. Müller and B. Schneidmüller (eds), *Die französischen Könige des Mittelalters: Von Odo bis Karl VIII. (888–1498)* (Munich, 1996), pp. 47–59. For broader context see R. McKitterick, *The Frankish Kingdoms Under the Carolingians 751–987* (London, 1983), pp. 305–40; O. Guillot, 'Formes, fondements et limites de l'organisation en France au Xe siècle', *Settimane* 38 (1991), pp. 57–124, esp. pp. 88–105; J. Dunbabin, 'West Francia: the Kingdom', in T. Reuter (ed.), *NCMH III 900–1024* (Cambridge 1999), pp. 372–97; J. Dunbabin, *France in the Making 843–1180*, 2nd edn (Oxford, 2000), pp. 44–123.
25 P. Lauer, *Recueil des actes de Louis IV, roi de France (936–954)* (Paris, 1914); Flodoard, *Annales*, ed. P. Lauer, *Les annales de Flodoard* (Paris, 1906); English translations are taken from or based on the extremely useful translation by S. Fanning and B. S. Bachrach, *The Annals of Flodoard of Reims, 919–966* (Peterborough, Ont., 2004). On Flodoard see above all M. Sot, *Un historien et son église au Xe siècle: Flodoard de Reims* (Paris, 1993).

The Anglo-Saxon sisterly network

Our first task is to ask what it meant for Eadgifu that so many of her sisters were married to the continental big hitters of the day. If, as an outsider, she lacked the access to political networks within Francia that others acquired during their youth, then did her natal family identity in fact have any bearing on her career? The evidence suggests that there was relatively substantial contact between the court in Wessex and its representatives on the Continent. For example, Nelson has plausibly argued that if Eadgifu remained in Francia until her husband's death, she may well have had a hand in arranging the marriage in 926 between her sister Eadhild and Hugh the Great.[26] Whether or not the dethroned queen's hand rested silently on the tiller in these negotiations, it must also be noted that the ambassadors who travelled to Wessex on Hugh's behalf to set up this union were members of the comital dynasty of Flanders.[27] This highlights another important family link, for Arnulf of Flanders was the grandson of King Alfred of Wessex (871–99). This tie was clearly still active in the 920s and 930s, and it features prominently as the conduit for communication between Francia and Athelstan in the reign of Louis IV.[28] It was Arnulf who organized Louis's landfall on the Continent in 936, at the key Flemish port of Boulogne.[29] He had also seen to the burial of Athelstan's brother at the Flemish comital monastery of St-Bertin after he was apparently drowned at

---

26 Nelson, 'Eadgifu'.
27 William of Malmesbury, *Gesta*, vol. 1, c. 135, p. 218. See also Æthelweard, *Chronicon*, ed. A. Campbell (London, 1962), p. 2. On other aspects of the mission see L. H. Loomis, 'The holy relics of Charlemagne and King Athelstan: the lances of Longinus and St Mauricius', in *Speculum* 25 (1950), pp. 437–56; K. Leyser, 'The tenth century in Byzantine-Western relationships', in his *Medieval Germany and its Neighbours 900–1250* (London, 1982), pp. 103–37 at pp. 116–17.
28 The key discussion of the Flanders-Wessex connection in this period is P. Grierson, 'The relations between England and Flanders before the Norman conquest', *TRHS* 4th series, 23 (1941), pp. 71–112. See also J. L. Nelson, 'Alfred's Carolingian contemporaries', in T. Reuter (ed.), *Alfred the Great* (Aldershot, 2003), pp. 293–310; H. Tanner, *Families, Friends and Allies: Boulogne and Politics in Northern France and England c. 879–1160* (Leiden, 2004).
29 Folcuin, *Gesta Abbatum Sithiensium*, ed. O. Holder-Egger, *MGH SS* XIII (Hanover, 1881), c. 102, p. 626; Grierson, 'Relations', p. 88. See also Flodoard, *Annales*, s.a. 936, p. 63; Flodoard, *Historia Remensis Ecclesiae*, ed. M. Stratmann (Hanover, 1998), IV.26, p. 417. On the possible use of an English *ordo* for Louis's royal inauguration see J. L. Nelson, 'The second English *Ordo*', in Nelson, *Politics and Ritual*, pp. 361–74 at pp. 368–9.

sea.[30] Arnulf's contacts with Athelstan were ongoing: when he captured the family of his nemesis Erluin of Ponthieu in 939, he sent them as hostages to England.[31] Louis IV's attempts to utilize this Anglo-Flemish family connection were conspicuous in the early years of his reign. We meet him twice in close congress with Arnulf. In 937 he issued a royal diploma at St-Bertin, and in 938 we meet the king and the count trying to improve cross-Channel communications by renovating a port at or near Quentovic.[32] The Flemish branch of this family network was also attached to Wessex by an underlying material basis. Arnulf had claims to lands in Wiltshire and the Isle of Wight which his grandfather King Alfred had bequeathed to his mother Ælfthryth. These included rights at Chippenham and Wellow, key royal estates where Athelstan held major assemblies in the earlier 930s, at which Louis and Eadgifu may well have been present.[33]

In the most spectacular instance of direct intervention by any early English king in West Francia, it can be argued that both the sisterly network and the Flemish connection played significant roles. In 939, Athelstan sent a fleet to Arnulf to help Louis in his struggle against the rebellious magnates. In the end it was no help at all: Flodoard tells us, without further explanation, that the fleet turned aside and attacked 'the places of the Morini touching the sea' instead, after which Arnulf seems to have joined the ranks of the young king's enemies.[34] Historians have been at a loss to explain this turn of events. Freeman suggested the fleet attacked Arnulf because Athelstan realized he was about to betray Louis, while Grierson

30 Folcuin, *Gesta*, c. 107, p. 629; S. Irvine (ed.), *The Anglo-Saxon Chronicle: A Collaborative Edition*, Vol. 7, *Ms E* (Cambridge, 2004), p. 55; D. Whitelock (ed.), *English Historical Documents*, vol. 1 (New York, 1968), no. 26, pp. 317–18.

31 Flodoard, *Annales*, s.a. 939, p. 72.

32 Lauer, *Recueil des actes de Louis IV*, no. 6; Flodoard, *Annales*, s.a. 938, pp. 69–70; Grierson, 'Relations', pp. 79, 89.

33 The will is translated and the properties mapped by S. Keynes and M. Lapidge, *Alfred the Great: Asser's Life of Alfred and Other Contemporary Sources* (Harmondsworth: 1983), pp. 173–8. Grierson, 'Relations', p. 85 suggests that Ælfthryth gave these away before she died: however, there is no evidence before *Domesday Book* that Chippenham and Wellow had returned to the fisc, so this assumption seems to rest purely on the mistaken belief that women could not control and bequeath land. Either way, Arnulf would have retained a claim to the land. On Athelstan's assemblies see P. H. Sawyer, *Anglo-Saxon Charters* (London: Royal Historical Society, 1968) (revised on-line edition by S. Kelly and S. Miller, accessed at www.trin.cam.ac.uk/chartwww/eSawyer.99/eSawyer2.html), nos. 405, 422, 423; F. M. Stenton, *Anglo-Saxon England*, 3rd edn (Oxford, 1971), pp. 349–51. Neither Eadgifu nor Louis appears in the witness lists of Anglo-Saxon royal charters (which does not prove they were not present).

34 Flodoard, *Annales*, s.a. 939, p. 73.

interpreted the raid as the cause of the count's defection. Steenstrup, meanwhile, hypothesized that the fleet had diverted to attack Danish settlers in Flanders.[35] None of these explanations is particularly compelling. A closer reading of the text in the context of relations between Athelstan and Arnulf suggests an alternative. The term 'Morini' was not Flodoard's usual term for the people of Flanders, but its use reflects his familiarity with the nuances of classical terminology. We must therefore take seriously the possibility that he consciously used it in its ancient sense to refer to the people of western Flanders, and intended to identify an area distinct from Flanders proper.[36] To the west of Flanders lay Ponthieu, with whose count Erluin Arnulf was in a state of open war at exactly this time. He thus had a motive to turn the ships sent by his cousin to his own ends, and his close ties to Wessex gave him the opportunity. Athelstan himself had interests in this zone, in the shape of close political ties with a community of monks based at Montreuil on the frontier between Ponthieu and Flanders: these links had proved important in orchestrating his intervention in Breton affairs in 936–7.[37] Arnulf had seized Montreuil from Erluin shortly before the arrival of the English ships with the help, according to Flodoard, of an insider, and sent the count's family into exile in Wessex. The convergence of Arnulf's and Athelstan's interests at Montreuil thus gives some support to the hypothesis that Arnulf was able to turn the fleet against his own local rival. This diversion of the force from its original purpose could also explain why Arnulf and Louis became enemies at this point.

Despite the failure of the fleet to fulfil its mission, the very fact that it was despatched at all is worth stressing: this is unique evidence for direct intervention by an English king in Frankish affairs in the period. Athelstan's charters from 939 may help to illuminate the matter more clearly. It is well known that royal charters were sometimes granted in anticipation of military campaigns in order to pave the way for the movement and provision of armies: Athelstan's own diplomas can be used in this way to pick out the progress of his armies into the north.[38] It is interesting in this context that in one of the king's charters from 939 we meet another of the king's sisters, Eadburh, a nun at Nunnaminster best known for her posthumous saintly

---

35 Grierson, 'Relations', p. 89 discusses this range of explanations.
36 See Fanning and Bachrach, *Annals of Flodoard*, p. 74, n. 102.
37 C. Brett, 'A Breton pilgrim in England in the reign of King Æthelstan', in G. Jondorf and D. N. Dumville (eds), *France and the British Isles in the Middle Ages and Renaissance* (Woodbridge, 1991), pp. 43–70, esp. pp. 49–50.
38 On Athelstan's forays into the north see Stenton, *Anglo-Saxon England*, p. 342; on the methodology, see C. R. Bowlus, *Franks, Moravians and Magyars: The Struggle for the Middle Danube 788–907* (Philadelphia, 1995), esp. pp. 30–2.

career, in which she is granted extensive properties (17 hides) in full possession at Droxford.[39] This is a very rare example of a privilege for a royal woman, and is susceptible to various interpretations.[40] However, given its date and the identity of the recipient, it is tempting to associate it with the naval expedition of 939. Droxford is southeast of Winchester, only a few miles from the Hampshire coast, and the properties granted are specifically designated as being on the river. We know that monastic institutions routinely had ships under their control; and this grant is one of a flurry of charters from the same period granted to recipients in various areas of Wessex.[41] It is thus possible that we are seeing here evidence of the preparations for Athelstan's naval intervention on behalf of Louis IV. The profile of Eadburh in this suggests that the sisterly network of which Eadgifu was part had been activated.[42] Moreover, the fact that Arnulf of Flanders claimed land on the nearby Isle of Wight indicates that he could well have been involved in the preparation of this campaign as well as in its execution.[43]

There are also signs that the sisters' relationships with each other could play a significant part in continental politics without referring back to Wessex. Hlawitschka and Leyser have identified various political exchanges

---

39 Sawyer, *Anglo-Saxon Charters*, no. 446; on her cult see S. Ridyard, *The Royal Saints of Anglo-Saxon England: a Study of West Saxon and East Anglian Cults* (Cambridge, 1988), pp. 18–19, 258–308; A. Thacker, 'Dynastic monasteries and family cults. Edward the Elder's sainted kindred', in Higham and Hill (eds), *Edward the Elder*, pp. 248–63, at pp. 259–60.

40 M. Bailey, 'Ælfwynn, Second Lady of the Mercians', in Higham and Hill (eds), *Edward the Elder*, pp. 112–27 at pp. 124–5 provides a table of grants to English royal women in this period.

41 On monastic ships see for example S. Kelly, 'Trading privileges from eighth-century England', in *EME* 1 (1992), pp. 3–28. Other relevant grants include Sawyer, *Anglo-Saxon Charters*, nos. 445, 447, 449; cf. 392.

42 Droxford seems not to have become part of the formal monastic estate, hinting that it may have been a special grant made personally to Eadburh: M. A. Meyer, 'Patronage of the West Saxon royal nunneries in Late Anglo-Saxon England', *Revue Bénédictine* 91 (1981), pp. 332–58 at pp. 347–8.

43 For Arnulf's claims on the Isle of Wight see above, n. 33. Another instance of cross-Channel contact came in 946, when King Edmund intervened to persuade Hugh the Great to release Louis from captivity: Flodoard, *Annales*, s.a. 946, p. 101. This embassy may coincide with the entry of the name Eadgifu in the *Liber memorialis* of Pfäffers alongside those of English envoys: it is not, however, clear whether this refers to Louis's mother or Edmund's: see S. Keynes, 'King Athelstan's books', in M. Lapidge and H. Gneuss (eds), *Learning and Literature in Anglo-Saxon England: Studies Presented to Peter Clemoes* (Cambridge, 1985), pp. 143–201 at pp. 198–201. Another context for the grant to Eadburh is offered by D. Dumville, *Wessex and England from Alfred to Edgar* (Woodbridge, 1992), pp. 177–8.

whose courses may have been smoothed by the bond between Edith in Saxony and Edgiva in Burgundy. For example, when Rudolf II of Burgundy sent prestigious relics to the Ottonian court late in his reign, the gift was conspicuously made jointly to both Otto and his queen.[44] I would like to contribute a further reconstruction which suggests that the English sister-hood may also have enabled Eadgifu to play an influential diplomatic role at the end of the 930s. One of Louis's charters places him at Breisach, at the bend of the Upper Rhine, in August 938.[45] This has puzzled historians, who have sought to redate it to 939, when we know (thanks to Flodoard) that the king passed through nearby Alsace.[46] However, this redating is arbitrary and doesn't fit well with Flodoard's annal for 939.[47] Breisach was situated in the frontier zone between Alsace, East Francia and the kingdom of Burgundy.[48] A plausible context for Louis's presence in this area in 938 is provided by the death of Rudolf II in the previous year. The king's demise, and the fact that his heir Conrad was a child, inevitably upset the balance of power in the area as rulers of neighbouring realms sought to take advantage of the minority. Even before the end of 937 Hugh of Provence turned up mob-handed, took Rudolf's widow as his wife and engineered another marriage between his own son and the late king's daughter. In the following year Otto intervened and took Conrad to Saxony to be educated at his court.[49] In these circumstances it would be surprising if Louis had not also sought to stake a claim, and this would explain his

---

44 Hlawitschka, 'Die verwandtschaftlichen Verbindungen', pp. 56–7; Leyser, 'Otton-ians and Wessex', p. 92. For another example note Arnulf's role as mediator between Louis IV and Otto I in the year 938, which must have rested partly on the English royal blood he shared with all parties: Flodoard, *Annales*, s.a. 939, pp. 71–2.

45 Lauer, *Recueil des actes de Louis IV*, no. 8.

46 T. Zotz, 'Das Elsaß: ein Teil des Zwischenreiches?' in H.-W. Herrmann and R. Schneider (eds), *Lotharingia: Eine europäische Kernlandschaft um das Jahr 1000* (Saarbrücken, 1995), pp. 49–70, at p. 67.

47 Flodoard, *Annales*, s.a. 939, p. 73 says that Louis went to Alsace, but Lauer, *Recueil des actes de Louis IV*, no. 11 shows that he was back at Laon by 2 August: in view of this, the charter's being issued in 938 on a trip unmentioned by Flodoard seems more likely than its being issued on the journey he does mention in 939.

48 It may also have been seen as a symbolic venue for the launching of claims to power in the middle kingdom: G. Althoff, 'Breisach: ein Refugium für Rebellen im frühen Mittelalter?', in H. Nuber, K. Schmid, H. Steuer and T. Zotz (eds), *Archäologie und Geschichte des ersten Jahrtausends in Südwestdeutschland* (Sigmaringen, 1990), pp. 457–72.

49 C. B. Bouchard, 'Burgundy and Provence, 879–1032', in Reuter (ed.), *NCMH III*, pp. 328–45 at pp. 341–2.

presence in southern Alsace and the Breisgau in August 938.[50] The people calling the shots in Burgundy in Conrad's absence must have been Rudolf's brother Louis and his wife Edgiva. At this time, then, Louis IV clearly had a window of opportunity to pitch for influence in an area where his aunt was one of the key power-brokers. Did he take advantage successfully? There is evidence that the answer is yes: it is suggestive that in the early 940s we find Louis in control of properties in areas which can only be explained as the result of a territorial concession by the rulers of Burgundy.[51] The most plausible context for this achievement is the period at the end of the 930s when Conrad's absence placed Edgiva in a particular position of power. In any case, at least as much as his Carolingian blood it was the family connections of his mother Eadgifu which legitimized any claims Louis had in the kingdom of Burgundy.

These snippets of evidence suggest that the network of Anglo-Saxon royal sisters at times played a significant role in continental politics during the later 930s. These women's membership of the royal house of Wessex, their kinship with the Flemish counts, and their relationships with each other constituted a political resource which was useful not only to the women themselves but also to the kings in their lives. Their natal family identity remained important to the sisters, and its part in Frankish politics (which had to be deliberately activated) shows that their role was anything but passive.

Kinship ties could be critical to political alliances and strategies, and this was explicitly recognized by contemporaries. When under siege in 946, for example, Archbishop Hugh of Rheims appealed for help in his hour of need to his relatives by marriage, described by Flodoard as 'some *principes* who seemed to be his friends.'[52] However, family relationships could not be relied on as an exclusive source of political stability. They did not map straightforwardly onto the contours of political relationships. Hugh the Great and Louis IV remained almost constantly at loggerheads, despite the fact that the latter's mother was the sister of the former's wife: nor did

---

50 For the properties and connections of the Burgundian rulers in these areas see G. Althoff, *Amicitiae und Pacta: Bündnis, Einung, Politik und Gebetsgedenken im Beginnenden 10. Jahrhundert* (Hanover, 1992), pp. 226–8; T. Schieffer and H. E. Mayer (eds), *Die Urkunden der burgundischen Rudolfinger. MGH Regum Burgundiae e stirpe Rudolfina diplomata et acta* (Munich, 1977), p. 10.
51 Schieffer and Mayer (eds), *Die Urkunden*, p. 14; Lauer, *Le Règne de Louis IV*, p. 51; Lauer, *Recueil des actes de Louis IV*, no. 12.
52 Flodoard, *Annales*, s.a. 946, p. 102; Fanning and Bachrach, *Annals*, p. 44.

things improve between them as a consequence of the fact that by 939 they were both married to sisters of Otto I. By the same token, multiple marriage connections did not automatically create peace between Louis and Otto. Indeed, by the middle of the tenth century almost all the leading families of Europe were related to each other in one way or another: in any given political context, an alliance suggested by one set of family relationships would therefore almost inevitably lead to conflict with another set of relatives. Marriage represented an opportunity for political alliance rather than the alliance itself.[53] Moreover, family members could die unexpectedly, as did Eadhild in 937 and Athelstan in 939, and the effects were unpredictable.[54] Family networks were thus a potential source of power, but by their very nature they were contingent, impermanent and fragile: an unstable foundation on which to build lasting political security and power. The power of women like Eadgifu had to be reinforced by being anchored to an underlying material base. As an outsider Eadgifu had to be socialized into the West Frankish kingdom, and her power naturalized in its political landscape. To understand how this was done, we will now turn to an examination of the lands she held.

Queens' lands

The material weakness of Louis IV's position upon his return to Francia in summer 936 is patent. The main estates on which Carolingian power in the region historically rested had long since passed from the dynasty's control, a fact illustrated by the contrast between the paucity of charters Louis issued dealing with Francia proper and the great number he dispensed for recipients in peripheral parts of his realm (Burgundy, Aquitaine and the Spanish March). Indeed, such was his desperation by 938 that he had to resort to handing out the treasure of the church of Laon to secure support.[55] The masters of political patronage and leadership in the heartlands of the kingdom were now Hugh the Great and Herbert of Vermandois, not the

---

53 R. E. Barton, *Lordship in the County of Maine, c. 890–1160* (Woodbridge, 2004), pp. 82–5, 93.

54 If Arnulf's shift in loyalties in 939 was not connected to the fate of the English fleet, it could have been a consequence of Athelstan's subsequent death: see above at n. 37.

55 Flodoard, *Annales*, s.a. 938, p. 71.

king.[56] Louis himself openly acknowledged this situation in 936 when Hugh, who had led the magnates requesting Louis's return from England, was referred to in royal charters by the exalted titles 'duke of the Franks' and 'second to the king.' But Hugh's sinister loyalty was a capricious commodity, hardly surprising since he was the son of a rival king killed in battle by Louis's father.[57] All Louis could really rely on at the beginning were his possession of the imposing fortress of Laon, the palace of Compiègne, and the allegiance of the Archbishop of Rheims. Accordingly, the early years of his reign were dominated by continuous military struggles to recapture key estates and fortresses from the powerful supermagnates so that he might establish a basis for effective rule.

Eadgifu's role in this struggle has passed largely unobserved. This is perhaps not surprising, for she appears in no charters of Louis (nor had she in those of her husband). However, when she arrived at the start of 937, presumably from England, Flodoard tells us that: 'King Louis withdrew himself from the management of the *princeps* Hugh [the Great] and received his mother [Eadgifu] at Laon.'[58] This phrase clearly suggests that Louis's rejection of the incredibly powerful Hugh was made possible because he thought his mother could somehow underwrite his authority instead. But how? The roots she put down in the late 910s, when she had been queen for only a matter of months at a particularly difficult time for her husband, could not have been deep. Since then she had been absent from Francia for between seven and fifteen years and could have held no land.

What she did have, however, was a series of claims to land. In this context, Flodoard's account of the first phase of Louis's campaigning in 938 is significant. These campaigns were directed principally against strongholds

56 On Hugh and Herbert see M. Bur, *La Formation du comté de Champagne, v.950–v.1150* (Nancy, 1977), pp. 87–97; K. F. Werner, 'Westfranken-Frankreich unter den spät-karolingern und frühen Kapetingern (888–1060)', in K. F. Werner, *Vom Frankenreich zur Entfaltung Deutschlands und Frankreichs* (Sigmaringen, 1984), pp. 225–77, esp. pp. 233–41; Y. Sassier, *Hugues Capet* (Paris, 1987), pp. 89–138; Guillot, 'Formes', pp. 80–105; H. Schwager, *Graf Heribert II. von Soissons, Omois, Meaux, Madrie sowie Vermandois (900/06–43) und die Francia (Nord-Frankreich) in der 1. Hälfte des 10. Jahrhunderts* (Kallmünz, 1994); Y. Sassier, 'Thibaud le Tricheur et Hugues le Grand', in O. Guillot and R. Favreau (eds), *Pays de Loire et Aquitaine de Robert le Fort aux Capétiens* (Poitiers, 1997), pp. 145–57.

57 G. Koziol, 'A Father, his son, memory, and hope: the joint diploma of Lothar and Louis V (Pentecost Monday, 979) and the limits of performativity', in J. Martschukat and S. Patzold (eds), *Geschichtswissenschaft und 'Performative Turn': Ritual, Inszenierung und Performanz vom Mittelalter bis zur Neuzeit* (Cologne, Weimar and Vienna, 2003), pp. 83–103 emphasizes the need to take account of such personal motivations.

58 Flodoard, *Annales*, s.a. 937, p. 65; Fanning and Bachrach, *Annals*, p. 19.

and estates controlled by Herbert of Vermandois, and sought to establish the king in the area around and between his three main power-centres, Laon, Compiègne and Reims. Among the very first on his list of strategic targets was Tusey on the Meuse 'which Louis's father had given to [Eadgifu] as a dower along with other *villae*.'[59] No charters survive giving details of Eadgifu's dower. However, Flodoard immediately goes on to relate the capture of the estate of Corbeny, near Laon. He identifies this as an estate which the church of Rheims had claims upon, betraying here his own agenda. But we know from earlier charters that Corbeny had a further significance: it was one of the two key estates which made up the dower of Frederun, Charles the Straightforward's second wife (who died in 917).[60] It is likely that this estate was subsequently given to his Anglo-Saxon bride, and that this was one of the other *villae* alluded to by Flodoard. So, the fact that two of the first three fortresses Louis attacked can be definitely associated with the queen suggests that his top priority in the early months of his reign was to establish his position by reconquering properties to which his mother held a dormant claim.[61]

From scattered references we can infer the identity of some of the other lands and *honores* that Eadgifu acquired in this early period of her son's reign. After she absconded with Count Herbert the Elder (a son of Herbert of Vermandois) in 951, Flodoard tells us that Louis took away from her the nunnery of St-Mary in Laon, and in the same breath strongly implies that she was simultaneously divested of the estate of Attigny.[62] Although Flodoard doesn't say so explicitly, it also seems likely that she held Ponthion: he reports that after the confiscations of St-Mary and Attigny, among Louis's first acts was to reconquer this estate from Herbert's men, supported by his wife Gerberga.[63] Both Attigny and Ponthion, moreover, had

---

59 Flodoard, *Annales*, s.a. 938, p. 69; Fanning and Bachrach, *Annals*, p. 30; Flodoard, *Historia*, IV.26, p. 418.

60 P. Lauer (ed.), *Recueil des actes de Charles III le Simple* (Paris, 1940), no. 56.

61 Louis's attempt to turn the clock back in this way is also reflected in his charters of this period, which reveal a systematic and ostentatious invocation of the styles of rulership employed by his father: see especially Lauer, *Recueil des actes de Louis IV*, no. 4 (issued at Compiègne on Christmas Day 936); and B. Schneidmüller, *Karolingische Tradition und frühes französischen Königtum: Untersuchungen zur Herrschaftslegitimation der westfränkische-französichen Monarchie im 10. Jahrhundert* (Wiesbaden, 1979), pp. 147–56.

62 Flodoard, *Annales*, s.a. 951, p. 132. Brühl, 'Ludwig IV.', p. 50 suggests that Louis did not hold Attigny before 951, but this is an over-literal reading of Flodoard's account.

63 Flodoard, *Annales*, s.a. 952, p. 134. On the significance of Gerberga's presence see below. Ponthion was also the other half of Frederun's dower.

been given as a pension to Charles the Straightforward by his captors in 928: this can only have strengthened Eadgifu's claim on them.[64] So too did the fact that dowers (if she held any of these estates as part of a dower) were intended to be held by one woman for one lifetime.[65]

These estates clearly had a material significance. For a start, they consti-tuted a significant proportion of all the properties Louis controlled which, in comparison to those belonging to Hugh and Herbert, were nugatory.[66] Moreover, places like Compiègne, Corbeny and Laon were physically asso-ciated with each other by their locations along and around the Aisne valley, and may have formed part of a linked estate hierarchy.[67] We may even catch a glimpse of one queenly estate functioning as a practical power-centre: control of Ponthion presumably underwrote Louis's ability to gather mili-tary support in the Perthois in 941 at a time when Laon was threatened by his enemies.[68]

More importantly, all of Eadgifu's holdings had extremely high-profile royal identities. Corbeny was associated with Reims, one of the centres of Carolingian dynastic legitimacy.[69] Tusey had hosted major political negotia-tions in the reign of Charles the Bald.[70] Both Ponthion and Attigny were sites of major Carolingian royal palaces. St-Mary in Laon was remembered in a charter of Charles the Straightforward as one of the nodal points of Carolingian dynastic history and legitimacy, along with Prüm, Aachen and Compiègne.[71] Properties like these were pregnant with meaning and could advertise something about the status of their holders.[72] Palaces in particular

---

64 Flodoard, *Annales*, s.a. 928, p. 43; cf. Flodoard, *Historia*, IV.22, p. 414; Richer, *Histo-riae*, ed. by H. Hoffmann (Hanover, 2000), I.55, p. 89. On Richer see J. Glenn, *Politics and History in the Tenth Century: the Work and World of Richer of Reims* (Cambridge, 2004).

65 F. Bougard, L. Feller and R. Le Jan (eds), *Dots et douaires dans le haut moyen âge* (Rome, 2002). Lauer, *Recueil des actes de Charles III*, no. 91 records a lifetime grant of Ponthion to Frederun's brother Bovo, bishop of Chalons-sur-Marne; however, this was before Charles's marriage to Eadgifu.

66 On the lands controlled by the various parties see Lauer, *Le Règne de Louis IV*, pp. 3–9; Schwager, *Graf Heribert II.*, pp. 46–66; Brühl, 'Ludwig IV.' p. 50.

67 I am grateful to Chris Loveluck for this suggestion: see C. Loveluck, 'Rural settle-ment hierarchy in the age of Charlemagne: an archaeological perspective', in J. Story (ed.), *Charlemagne: Empire and Society* (Manchester, 2005), pp. 230–58, at pp. 239, 251. Both Corbeny and Laon were fortified in this period.

68 Flodoard, *Annales*, s.a. 941, p. 82. Conversely, in 940 Louis's enemies used Attigny as the venue for a meeting with Otto: Flodoard, *Annales*, s.a. 940, p. 77.

69 See below, n. 78.

70 Nelson, *Charles the Bald*, p. 216.

71 Lauer, *Recueil des actes de Charles III*, no. 91.

72 Cf. Barton, *Lordship*, p. 198.

were potent focal points for political memory and dynastic identity.[73] In this context it is interesting to note that most of these estates also had a specifically queenly identity. Ponthion was the other half (in addition to Corbeny) of Frederun's dower; and St-Mary in Laon had also been controlled by a series of earlier royal women, including Charles the Bald's sister Hildegarde and his wife Ermentrude.[74] It is also striking that almost exactly the same group of properties later came under the control of Louis's wife Gerberga. Gerberga, the sister of Otto I, married Louis in 939 after the death of her first husband Duke Giselbert of Lotharingia: like Eadgifu, then, she was an outsider. The sources suggest, however, that she did not begin to eclipse the influence of her mother-in-law until the end of the 940s, when Louis's power was stabilized thanks to Otto's intervention.[75] This growth of influence is probably what caused Eadgifu to abscond from Louis's side against his wishes in 951 by marrying his enemy Count Herbert III the Elder.[76] After her departure, Louis with Gerberga at his side proceeded to take by force many of the estates which had hitherto been held by his mother, and the younger queen assumed their control.[77]

Eadgifu and Gerberga may not have controlled all of these properties in turn as dowers. After all, two charters of King Lothar, Louis's son, reveal

73   S. Airlie, 'The palace of memory: the Carolingian court as political centre', in S. Rees-Jones, R. Marks and A. Minnis (eds), *Courts and Regions in Medieval Europe* (Woodbridge, 2000), pp. 1–20.

74   Lauer, *Recueil des actes de Charles III*, no. 56 for the dower which, interestingly, was promulgated at Attigny: is this where the couple were married? On the previous proprietors of St-Mary see R. Le Jan, 'Douaires et pouvoirs des reines en France et en Germanie (VIe–Xe siècle)', in Le Jan, *Femmes et Pouvoir*, pp. 68–88 at p. 87 with n. 143. Louis the Pious sent the Empress Judith to St-Mary in Laon as rebels advanced on them in 830: Astronomer, *Vita Hludowici imperatoris*, ed. E. Tremp, *MGH SRG* (Hanover, 1995), c. 44, pp. 456–9.

75   For evidence of Gerberga's growing influence see Flodoard, *Annales*, s.a. 946, p. 101; Lauer, *Recueil des actes de Louis IV*, nos. 32–3, 38; Le Jan, 'La Reine Gerberge', p. 35. I will discuss her career in more detail elsewhere.

76   Flodoard, *Annales*, s.a. 951, p. 132. She ended her life and was buried at the Herbertine stronghold of Soissons: her epitaph is printed by J. Mabillon, *Vetera Analecta* (Paris, 1723), pp. 377–8. This relationship between Gerberga and Eadgifu is paralleled by evidence for tension at Otto's court between Edith and her mother-in-law: Leyser, 'Ottonians and Wessex', pp. 86–90.

77   Flodoard, *Annales*, s.a. 951, p. 132 for St-Mary and Attigny; s.a. 952, p. 134 for Ponthion. (The fact that Gerberga is specifically said to have been present suggests that she took control of the estate.) Lauer, *Recueil des actes de Louis IV*, no. 47 states that Corbeny was held by Louis; but the fact that the charter was issued expressly in Gerberga's presence suggests that she had a queenly stake in the estate. Cf. Le Jan, 'La Reine Gerberge', p. 35.

that his father had confirmed Frederun's grant of Corbeny to the church of St-Remi at Rheims shortly before his death.[78] Nevertheless, the fact that Gerberga's presence at and consent to this confirmation were highlighted in the charters suggests that the estate was considered to be closely associated with the queen in some particular way. Moreover, queenly estates like Corbeny and Ponthion remained important as focal points of dynastic commemoration. Frederun's gift of her dower estates Corbeny to St-Remi and Ponthion to the church of St-Corneille at Compiègne (which she had re-founded) had been made in return for annual commemoration of her death. These grants were posthumously endorsed by her husband.[79] Simultaneously, Charles ordered the monks of St-Remi to commemorate, alongside Frederun's demise, his own consecration (28 January, the anniversary of Charlemagne's death).[80] Association with elements of Frederun's dower therefore inserted her queenly successors into a series of relationships with the two principal centres of Carolingian legitimacy in the kingdom: Reims and Compiègne. Rheims was considered the traditional anointing place of the Frankish rulers, and Louis IV's consecration by Archbishop Artold confirms that he saw himself continuing this tradition. Compiègne, built by his great-grandfather Charles the Bald, was also very important to Louis, who used the palace for his most explicit statements of dynastic heritage.[81] These resonances were not lost on contemporaries like Flodoard, who refers to Compiègne as a 'customary royal residence'.[82] Association with these places plugged the queens into a network of commemoration arrangements whose dynastic orientation and political function is clear. These arrangements mattered: competitive commemoration was a central arena of dynastic conflict in the early tenth century, not a peripheral flourish.[83] We know that Louis and his women respected the commemoration arrangements focused on these estates: charter evidence shows they regarded

---

78 L. Halphen and F. Lot (eds), *Recueil des actes de Lothaire et de Louis V, rois de France (954–987)* (Paris, 1907), nos. 3, 4.

79 Lauer, *Recueil des actes de Charles III*, nos. 87, 91.

80 Lauer, *Recueil des actes de Charles III*, no. 88; cf. nos. 90 and 95.

81 Particularly Lauer, *Recueil des actes de Louis IV*, no. 4; on Charles and Compiègne see Schneidmüller, *Karolingische Tradition*, pp. 101–5.

82 Flodoard, *Annales*, s.a. 945, p. 96: *regalis sedis oppidum* (Fanning and Bachrach, *Annals*, p. 41).

83 Charles the Straightforward's ostentatious advertising of his Carolingian identity in this way is well known: Schneidmüller, *Karolingische Tradition*, pp. 121–38. Cf. Robert's counter-attempt to establish commemoration of his family at St-Denis as a foundation of his short reign in 923: J. Dufour (ed.), *Recueil des actes de Robert Ier et de Raoul, Rois de France (922–936)* (Paris, 1978), Robert no. 1.

themselves as holding these estates from the churches at Reims and Compiègne.[84]

All of this lends weight to the suggestion that the women in his life were seen by Louis IV to be a central support in his struggle for power and land in Francia. For him, the pursuit of claims to queenly lands that could be legitimized by reference to his mother and then his wife was a crucial political strategy. Their queenly associations justified his use of force to conquer lands that had long since slipped from his family's grasp. One wonders whether Louis's reliance on his mother early in his reign also reflects his upbringing at the court of Athelstan, a powerful ruler who does not seem to have been married, but whose court was populated by several formidable women.[85] It is also interesting that while previous Carolingian queens sometimes controlled elements of their dowers in sequence, these tended to be monastic institutions. The successive possession of queenly estates is a phenomenon perhaps better attested in Anglo-Saxon politics, and this model may also have inspired his thinking.[86]

English queens and Frankish queenship

How, in conclusion, does all this affect our appreciation of Frankish queenship – that is, of the way that queens' position in this period was conceptualized and enacted? Here we return to our starting point, namely the fact that Eadgifu and her sisters were outsiders. The distinctiveness of their origins leads us to wonder whether their queenship may also have been articulated in a distinctive way. The roles that Eadgifu (and Gerberga) played in acquiring these properties suggests that their possession was crucial not only to the king's position, but also to the queen's: making good their claims to these lands helped them legitimize their power as queens in West Francia. Not only did the women possess dormant claims to estates, there are also hints that they actually participated in their conquest.[87] This

---

84 I deduce this from Halphen and Lot, *Recueil des actes de Lothaire*, no. 3 (= Lauer, *Recueil des actes de Louis IV*, no. 47), which demonstrates that Louis recognized Corbeny's dependency on St-Remi.

85 On whom see P. Stafford, 'The King's wife in Wessex 800–1066', *Past and Present*, 91 (1981), pp. 3–27 at p. 25; Bailey, 'Ælfwynn', p. 122.

86 The dichotomy is not, however, cut and dried: see Le Jan, 'Douaires et pouvoirs', p. 87; Stafford, *Queen Emma and Queen Edith*, pp. 123–43; P. Stafford, 'Cherchez la femme: queens, queens' lands and nunneries: missing links in the foundation of Reading Abbey', *History* 85 (2000), pp. 4–27. On Anglo-Saxon queenship in general see Stafford, 'King's wife in Wessex'.

87 Flodoard, *Annales*, s.a. 952, p. 134.

suggests a pronounced emphasis in this period on a link between queen-ship as an idea or an office and the control of lands that had a queenly identity. Queenly status could be asserted through ceremonies such as consecration, through public appearances with the king, through the pro-duction of heirs, and so on. As an outsider, a woman like Eadgifu had to clutch at all these straws: her claims to land and authority rested exclusively on her queenly status, unsupplemented by access to wider resources and networks within the kingdom. This distinguished her from almost all of her predecessors since at least the reign of Charlemagne, and explains the significance for her of gaining control of particular estates: queenly status could rub off from land which had a queenly identity. The length of time that had elapsed since the deposition of Charles the Straightforward in 923 meant that Eadgifu's personal claim on these lands was slender. More important was the fact that they had other royal associations, and in par-ticular that many of them had been controlled by earlier queens of West Francia, particularly Frederun. Eadgifu's status had to be advertised: control of lands with queenly identities was important to the way she became part of the kingdom's political landscape; to how she was socialized into its tradi-tions; and to how her authority was legitimized.

Two final pieces of evidence help reinforce the point. First, a fragment: Flodoard refers to Gerberga, acting *as* queen, defending the crucial Caro-lingian fortress of Laon against Herbert of Vermandois 'along with her *fideles* gathered from all her royal residences'.[88] This phrase suggests that contemporaries acknowledged the close association between queenly status and queenly lands which we have observed: Gerberga's status is here implic-itly understood to be intimately bound up with her actual authority and the material basis of her power. These residences, wherever they were, had become integrated into the role of queenship and become a 'natural' adjunct to the queen's position.[89]

Secondly, a contrast. Queen Emma, the wife of King Raoul (923–36) features in the pages of Flodoard's annals engaged in many of the same prominent activities we have encountered in the careers of Eadgifu and Gerberga. Over winter 927–8 she was left in charge of the royal fortress at Laon; in 931 we learn of her confiscation of the *castrum* of Avallon from Count Gislebert of Autun, causing him to defect from the king; and in 933 she took possession of the Herbertine stronghold at Château-Thierry after

---

88 Flodoard, *Annales*, s.a. 948, p. 112: *regina Gerberga cum fidelibus suis ex omnibus suis regiis sedibus.*
89 Although according to the thrust of my argument so far, this phrase cannot refer to Corbeny, Ponthion, etc., which Eadgifu probably still controlled.

a siege.[90] These similarities have fed into composite images of tenth-century queens as powerful and independent figures.[91] However, on closer inspection there are clear differences between Emma and Eadgifu. Emma was an insider playing an insider's game. She was the sister of Hugh the Great, which is why she was so important to Raoul, whose power base was in Burgundy: he was the outsider, not she. In fact, she used her queenly status to pursue the interests of her natal family as often as she did those of her husband. The ambiguity of her identity is hinted at by Flodoard when he tells us that she refused to accompany Raoul to Burgundy in 928, but instead remained at Laon.[92] Her reluctance here and her participation in the conquest of Château-Thierry both suggest that the direction of her efforts was less pro-Raoul than it was anti-Herbert: it is in exactly this period that Herbert was at loggerheads with her brother Hugh.[93] Similarly, the attack on Avallon represented the reactivation of an ongoing rivalry between the family of Emma and Hugh and that of Gislebert.[94] The superficial similarity of Emma's actions to those of Louis IV's women therefore masks a fundamental difference in their positions and the bases of their power. As an insider, Emma had available to her a wide range of resources and strategies, not all of which depended on the exercise of her queenly status; outsider queens, by contrast, were uniquely dependent on their royal identities.

We can see the experience of Eadgifu as an outsider queen reflected in the forms of power she exercised. She lacked the local clout to interfere in Frankish patronage networks, hence her absence from royal diplomas in contrast to the standing of almost all previous queens and queen mothers. Her family ties could be activated at times, but the material basis of her position could not – unlike Emma's – be linked to her natal family. This is why it had to be built on association with lands controlled by previous queens. These lands carried Carolingian identities and also specifically queenly identities: Louis went to such lengths to acquire them because they advertised the queen's status and underwrote her power. Possession also involved their holders in commemoration of royal predecessors, particularly Frederun and her husband. This commemoration suited Louis's political persona as it was expressed more generally: his reign was partly based

90 Flodoard, *Annales*, s.a. 927, 928, 931, 933, pp. 39–41, 48, 55–6.
91 Verdon, 'Les Femmes', p. 112.
92 Flodoard, *Annales*, s.a. 928, p. 40.
93 For a useful periodization of relations between Hugh and Herbert see Werner, 'Westfranken', p. 237.
94 B. Simson (ed.), *Annales Xantenses et Annales Vedastini, MGH SRG* (Hanover, 1909), s.a. 900, p. 82; Le Jan, 'D'une cour', p. 48.

on an attempt to erase memories of the non-Carolingians who had reigned since his father's deposition.[95] Yet it was surely Eadgifu, an Englishwoman, who was responsible for educating her Frankish son in the traditions of his dynasty and people; and she who inculcated in him the belief in the need for a restoration of the queen's position in the kingdom.

Early medieval queenship was not a fixed institution, but a shifting concept constructed from a smorgasbord of ideas, always in the process of redefinition and change. Queens' political behaviour did not passively reflect the fulfilment of an office: rather, the practice of queenship was part of a process of creation and re-creation. With this in mind, we may end by asking whether the peculiar circumstances of women like Eadgifu might not have had the function of crystallizing family commemoration as a key part of the west Frankish queen's role. Dynastic commemoration was idealized as the central function of Ottonian queens in the second half of the tenth century.[96] Karl Ferdinand Werner has traced the heritage of this ideal back to mid-tenth-century West Francia, convincingly identifying its expression more or less fully formed in the *Life of Clothild* which was probably written for Gerberga during the 950s.[97] Was it in fact the particular experience of queens as outsiders in the age of Athelstan, Otto I and Louis IV that of necessity led to this emphasis on dynastic commemoration as a central basis of queenly identity? For, in contrast to all their predecessors, they were forced to rely much more on the traditions and resources of the families into which they married than of those into which they had been born.

95 Schneidmüller, *Karolingische Tradition*, pp. 147–56.
96 See especially P. Corbet, *Les Saints ottoniens: Sainteté dynastique, sainteté royale et sainteté féminine autour de l'an mil* (Sigmaringen, 1986).
97 *Vita S. Chrotildis*, ed. B. Krusch, *MGH SRM* II (Hanover, 1888), pp. 341–8; K. F. Werner, 'Der Autor der *Vita Sanctae Chrothildis*: Ein Beitrag zur Idee der "Heiligen Königin" und der "römischen Reiches" im X. Jahrhundert', in *Mittellateinisches Jahrbuch* 24/25 (1989–90), pp. 517–51; P. Corbet, '*Pro anima sua:* La pastorale ottonienne du veuvage', in M. Parisse (ed.), *Veuves et veuvage dans le haut Moyen Âge* (Paris: Picard, 1993), pp. 233–53. M. Goullet, *Adsonis Dervensis Opera Hagiographica*, CCCM 198 (Turnhout, 2003), pp. xlix–l shows that Werner's identification of the author as Adso is probably mistaken, but his arguments for Gerberga as the recipient survive her deconstruction.

10

The Carolingian capture of Aachen in 978 and its historiographical footprint

Theo Riches

T HE DEDICATEE OF this volume has illuminated many a corner of the political, cultural and social history of early medieval Europe, in particular but not only that part ruled by the Carolingian dynasty in the ninth century. Janet Nelson's work of late has concentrated on the greatest of that family, Charlemagne, and what amounts to an attempt to explain his achievement: how this man created such a large and functional political community. The answer has been seen to lie in military success and that certainly goes a long way to explain the creation of Carolingian charisma.[1] But as Weber long ago realized, such charisma must be institutionalized for a polity to survive. This is the issue she unapologetically calls 'state formation' and the centrepiece of this state was, after the abeyance of Charlemagne's personal military activity, the new palace complex of Aachen. It was here that Carolingian aristocrats were co-opted into imperial politics. It was from here that the capitularies were sent to every corner of the biggest European empire since the fall of the Roman West. It was from here that the moral revolution discernible in countless Church tracts and sermons was led.[2]

The violent, though temporary, seizure in 978 of this symbol and centre by Charlemagne's descendant, the penultimate Carolingian king, Lothar of West Francia, is, ironically, a subject that Janet Nelson's work on Aachen brings into sharp focus. The outlines of the event are fairly clear. In the summer of 978, while Emperor Otto II and his wife Theophanu were

---

1 T. Reuter, 'Plunder and tribute in the Carolingian empire', *TRHS*, 5th series 35 (1985), pp. 75–94; *idem*, 'The end of Carolingian military expansion', in P. Godman and R. Collins (eds), *Charlemagne's Heir: New Perspectives on the Reign of Louis the Pious* (Oxford, 1990), pp. 391–405.

2 J. L. Nelson, 'Aachen as a place of power', in M. de Jong, F. Theuws and C. van Rhijn (eds), *Topographies of Power in the Early Middle Ages* (Leiden, 2001), pp. 217–41; *eadem*, 'Was Charlemagne's court a courtly society?', in C. Cubitt (ed.), *Court Culture in the Early Middle Ages: The Proceedings of the First Alcuin Conference*, Studies in the Early Middle Ages 3 (Turnhout, 2003), pp. 39–57.

staying at Aachen, Lothar launched a rapid attack on the palace.[3] The imperial couple barely escaped capture. That autumn, after Lothar retreated to West Francia, Otto summoned the princes of the Empire and assembled an army with which he invaded the French lands, devastating them up to Paris. Unable to take the city, he began the retreat to the Empire. While Otto's army camped on the eastern side of the river Aisne, the baggage train failed to make it across the river before nightfall and was caught by Lothar's pursuing forces at the cost of many lives. Nonetheless, Otto reached his territory safely and two years later peace was arranged between both monarchs with Lothar renouncing Lotharingia.

Given the inconclusive nature of the events, it is hardly surprising that modern historiography has divided according to national sympathies. Positivist studies devoted to establishing what actually happened tended to be somewhat promiscuous, assuming a source was accurate insofar as it presented new information and questioning accounts' reliability only when two contradicted each other or when one was perceived as veering into tall tales.[4] What Ferdinand Lot excoriated as 'le chauvinisme historique' crept into these studies, including his own, nonetheless.[5] Even in cases where such chauvinism was not obvious – and there were many where it was crystal clear[6] – the concentration of the debate on what the two kings intended in their respective campaigns implied a judgement as to their success or failure.[7]

---

3 Whether this was Lothar's original intention or he was acting on an opportunity that presented itself during a more widely aimed invasion of Lotharingia has been debated. See W. Kienast, *Deutschland und Frankreich in der Kaiserzeit (900–1270). Weltkaiser und Einzelkönige*, 2nd edn, vol. 1, Monographien zur Geschichte des Mittelalters 9.1 (Stuttgart, 1974), pp. 90–1; C. Brühl, *Deutschland–Frankreich: Die Geburt zweier Völker*, 2nd edn (Cologne, 1995), p. 565.

4 For example K. Uhlirz, *Jahrbücher des deutschen Reiches unter Otto II. und Otto III.*, vol. 1 (Leipzig, 1902), criticizes Richer's version of Lothar's motivations and campaign preparation, which conflicts with other accounts (pp. 105–6, nn. 6–7), but takes his story of Lothar's hesitation before attacking Aachen – mentioned nowhere else – on trust (p. 107, n. 10) and F. Lot, *Les Derniers Carolingiens* (Paris, 1891), pp. 104–6, dismisses the *Gesta episcoporum Cameracensium*'s account of Otto II's challenge to Lothar across the Aisne as a fable (see also Kienast, *Deutschland und Frankreich*, p. 95, n. 209).

5 Lot, *Les derniers*, p. 106, n. 3. These comments elicited a tart and telling, albeit defensive, reply from Uhlirz (an Austrian), *Jahrbücher*, p. 118, n. 41.

6 Giesebrecht, *Geschichte der deutschen Kaiserzeit*, 5th edn, vol. 1 (Leipzig, 1881), pp. 580–3, can stand for numerous examples here.

7 The tendency to favour one side over the other continues even to this day, although no longer necessarily along national lines: compare the accounts by Michel Parisse and Jean Dunbabin in their chapters on 'Lotharingia' and 'West Francia' respectively in T. Reuter (ed.), *NCMH* III (Cambridge, 1999), pp. 320 and 388.

Another theme, which has in fact emerged more strongly with the abeyance of at least explicitly nationalistic studies, is the formation of national feeling in the embryonic France and Germany, a theme sometimes dealt with under the more neutral guise of the formation of the idea of a transpersonal state.[8] In this debate, 978 is examined for whether it betrays an increasing feeling of separation between the two successor kingdoms of the Carolingian Empire.[9] With exceptions, the consensus seems to be that it does not.[10] The retelling of the *story* of 978, on the other hand, does offer more fertile ground for enquiry – Karl Ferdinand Werner in particular has highlighted the role of the *Historia francorum Senonensis* in propagating a legend of French victory over the Germans.[11]

This essay can be seen to follow in that path, with some change in emphasis. In order truly to understand the role of accounts of 978 in the building of national feeling, some assessment of their reception would be necessary. That would require not just an examination of the different versions over the decades and centuries but also widespread manuscript studies to assess where and when each version was copied and in what contexts. Such a task is too great for the scope of this article. Instead, I will here focus on what might loosely be called authorial creativity: I am interested in cases where we know that the author has adapted the story for his own ends rather than simply inheriting it from an older source for his

8   Kienast, *Deutschland und Frankreich*, p. 95, n. 205; J. Ehlers, 'Die *Historia Francorum Senonensis* und der Aufstieg des Hauses Capet', *Journal of Medieval History* 4 (1978), p. 17. Ironically, nineteenth-century historians were well aware of the anachronism of projecting national feelings onto the tenth century: Lot, *Les derniers*, p. 106, n. 3.

9   A. Cartellieri, *Die Weltstellung des Deutschen Reiches 911–1047* (Berlin and Munich, 1932), p. 178; Kienast, *Deutschland und Frankreich*, pp. 94–5.

10   The question revolves around whether the unity between Lothar and Hugh Capet in the face of Otto's attack, in clear distinction to what happened between their fathers in 940 and 946, is an indication of a common national feeling as it might plausibly have been in 1124 or 1214. This cohesion is better explained as being forced by the need to oppose the imposition by Otto of Charles of Lotharingia as French king, rather than as a defence of France against Germany: Kienast, *Deutschland und Frankreich*, pp. 94–5, but see W. Mohr, 'Die lothringische Frage unter Otto II. und Lothar', *Revue belge de philologie et d'histoire* 35 (1957), pp. 715–16, 723. For Charles's anti-kingship, see below, n. 20.

11   K-F. Werner, 'Das hochmittelalterliche Imperium im politischen Bewußtsein Frankreichs (10.–12. Jahrhundert)', *Historische Zeitschrift* 200 (1965), pp. 99–10 and, for the events of 987, *idem*, 'Die Legitimät der Kapetinger und die Entstehung des "Reditus regni Francorum ad stirpem Karoli"', *Die Welt als Geschichte* XII (1952), pp. 210–13. But see also Kienast, *Deutschland und Frankreich*, p. 96.

compilation.[12] Thus, like Werner, I am more interested in how 978 fits into the historical narratives of the central Middle Ages than into our own. Unlike Werner, I am less interested in tracing the influence of a given account in itself – I am not attempting *Begriffsgeschichte* – than in how the historians in the immediately succeeding years and centuries processed, reported on, used and forgot the dramatic sequence of attack and counter-attack in 978.

This therefore is a study in historiography and, some might say, memory. The latter term has been much used in recent years, its meanings extended perhaps beyond what is analytically useful.[13] For that reason I will largely eschew it here. The sources are so diverse in type, time and place that a single 'textual community' whose memory would allegedly be examined cannot be said to have existed anyway.[14] Instead, I will proceed by and large chronologically, from our first spare and ambiguous witnesses in contemporaneous annals to the early twelfth century when we can be sure that respective French and German identities have developed. What interests me here is how the story of 978 was told and retold while that process was underway. I will therefore take 1124 and the rallying of French magnates to the side of Louis VI against Henry V as a symbolic end-point.

Our surviving contemporaneous annal entries come, perhaps not surprisingly, from Paris and the western edge of the Empire. Both the Parisian annals – of St-Germain and St-Denis – record simply that Otto came to Paris.[15] As is annals' wont, they indulge themselves in no speculation about

---

12 This approach thereby excludes most re-uses of the *Historia francorum Senonensis*, such as that by Orderic Vitalis, since the Sens text seems to have been so popular largely because it provided a short description of a thinly recorded period: Werner, 'Die Legitimät', p. 210. It is rightly fashionable nowadays to emphasize the intelligence with which medieval authors worked, but it is, I think, unarguable that more authorial choice can be shown to have been exercised on accounts that have been changed or edited than on those copied verbatim even where the mere choice of what to copy did in itself have some significance.

13 Note nonetheless that the concept of 'memory', in the senses of both remembering and remembrance, is explicitly attested in contemporary sources, unlike other modern historiographical concepts like gift exchange or feudalism.

14 The notion of 'textual community', first introduced by Brian Stock in his *The Implications of Literacy: Written Language and Models of Interpretation in the Eleventh and Twelfth Centuries* (Princeton, 1983), works insofar as we can identify a shared manuscript or textual base, but already in that book (pp. 90–1) Stock had argued that the texts were not necessary and could become 'internalized'. It is questionable how useful the extended version of this concept is.

15 *Annales s. Germani minores*, G. Pertz (ed.), *MGH SS* IV (Hanover, 1841), p. 4; *Annales s. Dionysii*, G. Waitz (ed.), *MGH SS* XIII (Hanover, 1881), p. 720.

motive or causes. Their reports are just a record of a significant local event and nothing more.[16] The German annals, from Cologne and St-Gall respectively, are a little more interesting. The Cologne annals are as spare as those from Paris, but their description of the French as 'Carlenses' should be noted – the word recurs in connection with 978.[17] The monks of St-Gall were somewhat more expansive. The *Annales Sangallenses maiores* allege that Lothar was in dispute with Otto over the borders of the kingdom, seized Aachen and claimed all the land between the Moselle and the Rhine for himself. Otto led '30,000 horsemen' into 'Francia' and by ravaging it carried out a most splendid campaign.[18] What is striking about our first remotely detailed account of 978 is that it could have been written by any nationalist historian of the nineteenth century. According to the monk of St-Gall, this was a campaign about borders between the leaders of two polities. A charter from Marmoutiers-lès-Tours, meanwhile, gives precisely the opposite account, claiming that Lothar had attacked the Saxons and put the emperor to flight.[19] Both French and German sources therefore split along 'national' lines.

Omitting the two vituperative letters exchanged between Bishop Dietrich I of Metz and Charles of Lotharingia (953–991) datable to 984,[20] which are not historiographical works at all, our next witness is Richer of Reims, writing in the 990s. With him, we have the first example of an author trying to cast the events of 978 into a wider historical narrative, in other words the first example of a historian proper. His account is too long to summarize here, but a number of elements need to be pointed out. First, Richer relies heavily on classical antecedents for his account, in particular Sallust, but also Livy and Vergil. He is not afraid, in fact he is eager, to recast relatively recent events in classical mode. His lack of influence, heavy reliance on the classics (including his unusual ideas about *Gallia* and *Germania*) and unreliability have led to his being dismissed as unworthy of study by some

16   Compare the influential early eleventh-century annals of Liège and Lobbes, G. Pertz (ed.), *MGH SS* IV (Hanover, 1841), p. 17. They report the arrival of Lothar at the palace of Aachen in very similar terms. They, too, will not be considered further in this paper.

17   *Annales Colonienses*, G. Pertz (ed.), *MGH SS* I (Hanover, 1826), p. 98.

18   *Annales Sangallenses maiores*, ed. G. Pertz *MGH SS* I (Hanover, 1826), p. 80.

19   F. Lot, 'Geoffroi Grisegonelle dans l'épopée', *Romania* 19 (1890), p. 392.

20   It is from these letters that we discover Charles was set up as an anti-king; Gerbert of Aurillac, *Die Briefsammlung Gerberts von Reims*, ed. F. Weigle, *MGH Epistolae. D.K.* II (Weimar, 1966), Letter 31 (Dietrich to Charles), pp. 54–7; Letter 32 (Charles to Dietrich), pp. 57–60. Gerbert of Aurillac, the author of the letters, later apologized to Dietrich for the tone of Charles's message: Letter 33, pp. 60–1.

more traditional modern students of the period.[21] But what interests us here is not the question of his reliability but what his depiction tells us about his understanding of 978. Richer's classical echoes are grouped in particular ways: references to Sallust's *Catilinarian Conspiracy* and Hegesippus's *Bellum Iudaicum* in speeches put into the mouths of the protagonists and a classicization of the military history, in particular a single combat between a German and French soldier before the gates of Paris.[22] There is some debate as to the import of these references. Jason Glenn argues for a maximal view of their meaning, claiming that readers would have known the original contexts and interpreted accordingly.[23] Hoffmann, meanwhile, argues the opposite: that Richer's total ignorance, not to say incompetence, in applying the classical echoes renders his account 'hollow'.[24] There is no way to decide such a debate, since it depends entirely upon the skill we attribute to contemporary readers and to Richer himself. But it can be said that Hoffmann's observations about Richer's style do not lead to the conclusion he draws from them. Even assuming that Hoffmann has exposed Richer's poverty of literary talent in comparison to that of Livy or Sallust and demonstrated that the references to honour and glory placed into Otto II's mouth when he rallies his princes are platitudes, that hardly renders them insignificant. The fact remains that Richer sees such considerations as plausible behaviour for his protagonist. Indeed, Hoffmann's demonstration of just how distant Richer's text is from his classical models strengthens that conclusion.[25]

21 Brühl, *Deutschland – Frankreich*, p. 564, describes him as *der phantasievolle Schwätzer Richer* (see also pp. 145–6, esp. p. 146, nn. 366–8).

22 Richer of Reims, *Historiae*, H. Hoffmann (ed.), *MGH SS* XXXVIII (Hanover, 2000), III, c. 76, p. 211, nn. 1, 2, 5 and 7; see H. Hoffmann, 'Die Historien Richers von Saint-Remi', *DA* 54 (1998), pp. 485–8. The single combat would go on to a long afterlife in the family histories of the dukes of Brittany and the counts of Anjou. Modern historiography has already dealt with this subject, so it will be omitted here: see R. Merlet (ed.), *La Chronique de Nantes (570 environ – 1049)* (Paris, 1896); L. Halphen and R. Poupardin, *Chroniques des comtes d'Anjou et des seigneurs d'Amboise* (Paris, 1913); Lot, 'Geoffroi Grisegonelle', 377–93; J. Dunbabin, 'Discovering a past for the French aristocracy', in P. Magdalino (ed.), *The Perception of the Past in Twelfth-Century Europe* (London, 1992), pp. 11–14, and N. Wright, 'Epic and romance in the Chronicles of Anjou', *ANS* 26 (2004), pp. 177–89.

23 J. Glenn, *Politics and History in the Tenth Century: the Work and World of Richer of Reims* (Cambridge, 2004), pp. 119–23.

24 H. Hoffmann, 'Die Historien', 502–8, quote at p. 504.

25 Glenn's argument suffers from a similar weakness. Just because Richer could have expected his audience to know the context of the original quotes, it does not follow that he intended them to be interpreted that way. If someone were to describe himself as 'suffering the slings and arrows of his career', that does not necessarily mean he is considering suicide or intends the comment as a 'cry for help'.

Secondly, Richer attributes the contest over Lotharingia (or, as he calls it, 'Belgica') to rivalry between the two kings and their respective inherited claims to the duchy.[26] The contest is simultaneously personal and political, but it is the theme of insults received and avenged that dominates Richer's account. Lothar is said to be furious at Otto's proximity when the latter stays at Aachen and in his alleged speech to his followers, it is this 'insult' that he emphasizes: 'that the greater insult was not what [lands Otto] occupied, but that, occupying [them] he did not hesitate to approach his borders.'[27] Lothar's behaviour at Aachen is also telling – as well as allowing his army to loot the palace, he is said to turn a bronze eagle which Charlemagne placed on the roof eastward, just as the Germans had originally turned it westward to show that their armies could march into France whenever they wanted.[28] It is, in other words, simultaneously a calculated insult and a claim to territory. Regarding the other side, we are told of Otto's good treatment of churches and his anger at his army's destruction of the nunnery of St-Balthilde-de-Chelles, and the single combat takes place after the German warrior repeatedly insults the 'Gauls'.[29] The emphasis on honour and insult seems to me to dominate any other consideration of political favouritism, despite his well-established interest in promoting the idea of a greater West Francia in using archaic terms such as *Gallia*.[30] While much ink has flowed trying to identify Richer's sympathies, his subject is the *congressus Gallorum*, and it is the aristocratic competition fuelled by political ambition and personal honour that forms the central subject of his work.[31] Consequently, his account of 978 ultimately turns on the rivalry

---

26 Richer, *Historiae* III, c. 67, p. 206.
27 *nec majori injuriae esse quod tenuerit quam quia tenens ad fines suos accedere non formidaverit*: Richer, *Historiae* III, c. 68, p. 207. This is not convincing as a genuine motivation, since we know of two other recent occasions when Otto II was in Aachen and Lothar did nothing: in July 973 (*Regesta imperii* II.2, 626–31) and Easter 975 (*Regesta imperii* II.2, 680a).
28 Richer, *Historiae* III, c. 71, p. 208. Thietmar repeats the same story with a variation: see below.
29 Richer, *Historiae* III, c. 74, p. 210 and III, c. 76, p. 211.
30 Brühl, *Deutschland–Frankreich*, pp. 299–300; Hoffmann, 'Die Historien', pp. 466–74.
31 Hoffmann, 'Die Historien', p. 457, and for an accurate, if unhelpfully dismissive, characterization of Richer's interests, p. 504: *Wie immer bei Richer ist man der chronique scandaleuse näher als der Tragödie.* See also Glenn, *Politics and History*, p. 148 and for Richer's inclination toward Charles of Lotharingia and his 'sustained predisposition for the Carolingian line' in general, see pp. 118–26; quote at p. 126. See, in contrast, H-H. Kortüm, *Richer von Saint-Remi: Studien zu einem Geschichtsschreiber des 10. Jahrhunderts* (Stuttgart, 1985), p. 44, described as *ziemlich falsch* by Hoffmann, 'Die Historien', p. 476, n. 124.

between Lothar and Hugh Capet, and Lothar's motivation for reconciling with Otto II is to pre-empt Hugh and possibly create a front against him.[32] As a historian Richer is exceptional here, as in so many other ways, in concentrating on high political melodrama even at the expense of his wider 'national' sympathies. There is nothing exceptional, however, in his attributing motives of honour and shame to the protagonists of 978.

By the time we enter the eleventh century, we can see a shift in the treatment of the incident. This is when we get our first extended narratives from the Empire and their interest in 978 is sometimes trumped by, or filtered through, Otto II's subsequent disastrous adventure in Calabria and his death. Brun of Querfurt's account, in his *Life of Adalbert of Prague*, is a particularly good example of how this works. Brun is still interested in the politics of the state – the passage in question is explicitly about the *res publica*. But, as with Richer, the question has become personalized at the same time as it is integrated into a longer narrative. It becomes one in a list of disasters culminating in Calabria and Otto II's untimely death, all fruit of 'unfortunate' Otto's sins.[33] First there is the rebellion of the Liutizi and a disastrous war with the Poles in which Margrave Otto loses his life in flight; then, although the campaign against the 'Caroline Franks' initially goes well, gluttony and drunkenness allow the imperial army to be routed and slaughtered.[34] Just as Richer recasts Lothar's activity as part of the *congressus Gallorum* leading up to 987, so Calabria becomes the filter for Brun's interpretation. There is a difference between Brun's approach and that of Richer, of course. They are both personalized, but while the Frenchman's chronicle interprets the events of 978 in what might be called secular or classical terms of honour and political rivalry, the German hagiographer takes it as a divine punishment for sin, as befits his purpose. It is also quite clear, however, that what poisons the German recollection of 978 is not the loss of the baggage train *per se* – Brun makes a point of the initial German victory and calls those who are killed *victores* – but the significance this gains in the light of later events. This is a new interpretation to those offered by the contemporaneous annals, albeit one that incorporates their initial triumphalism.

32 Richer, *Historiae* III, c. 78, p. 212.
33 *peccato Ottonis . . . regnante Ottonis infortunio*, Brun of Querfurt, *Vita secunda sancti Adalberti*, ed. G. H. Pertz, *MGH SS* IV (Hanover, 1841), c. 10, p. 598.
34 *Alia hora congregatus est optimus populus, et exercitus grandis nimis valde congrediuntur cum Karolinis Francis; cedunt hostes non durantes virorum forcium impetum fortissimum. Set dum vino ventrique colla flectunt, regnante Ottonis infortunio, victores in turpem fugam desinunt.* Brun, *Vita*, c. 10, p. 598.

We see the same dynamic – an essentially positive event poisoned by later developments – in the *De episcopis Mettensibus* by Alpert of Metz.[35] Alpert ascribes Lothar's attack to a desire to take Lotharingia and to capture Otto unawares. He adds that after Lothar's capture of Aachen he proceeded to Metz, where Alpert is careful to note he failed to achieve anything. Nevertheless, Dietrich of Metz wrote a letter to Otto, appealing to his sense that such insolence should not be tolerated. Otto decided that he could not allow the Franks to become used to raiding the empire with impunity and summoned nobles from all over the empire, including Italy, to take part in the expedition. Alpert relates the story of the raid to Paris as if there were no resistance at all and does not even mention the destruction of the baggage train. Instead he inserts a story about a French holy man who prophesied that everyone who was involved in the consultation to campaign in France would die within seven years. The prophecy was fulfilled with the disaster in Calabria. It is especially interesting to look at this report in comparison with that of Brun of Querfurt and of Richer. Here, in this episcopal *gesta*, you have a combination of the honour-centred secular politics visible in Richer's treatment and the providential explanation favoured in Brun's hagiography. Furthermore, just as Brun reads Otto II's failure in such a way as to foreground the fate of Adalbero's patron, Otto III, so Alpert is always careful to keep Dietrich as the hero of his narrative. The prophecy element of the story would, however, have its own afterlife, being added, for example, to the account of 978 by the *Gesta episcoporum Cameracensium* in one manuscript.[36]

Thietmar of Merseburg's *Chronicon* records the events of 978 as an unqualified victory for Otto and the Empire. Lothar – referred to here as the *rex Karelingorum* – is given no motivation, but Otto's response is said to have put terror into the enemy so that they would not dare attack again and repaid 'whatever insult had previously been inflicted upon us'.[37] Some time later Lothar is said to acquire Otto's friendship after visiting and handing over gifts as recompense. At no point does Thietmar incorporate the story into any providential history and, in contrast with the accounts of Brun and Alpert, the circumstances of Otto II's subsequent death do

---

35   Alpert of Metz, *De Episcopis Mettensibus Libellus*, ed. G. H. Pertz, *MGH SS* IV (Hanover, 1841), pp. 697–8.

36   Brussels MS BR 5468 (971), f. 186v. This twelfth-century manuscript excerpted chapters I: 94–8 and I: 104 (on the Calabrian disaster) from the *Gesta* to create a sort of mini-*Vita* of Otto II.

37   *quicquid dedecoris prius intulere nostris*, Thietmar of Merseburg, *Chronicon*, ed. R. Holtzmann, *MGH SRG* (Berlin, 1935), III, c. 8(6), p. 52.

not impinge on his account. The one larger context is the story that Lothar turned the eagle on the roof of the palace of Aachen. However, Thietmar reverses Richer's story so that the eagle was turned to face west since it was traditional, claims Thietmar, that whichever king held the palace would turn the eagle to face his Kingdom. It may well be that Lothar did intend some significance to what happened with the eagle, but it is clear that this was not an established or well-known tradition and that the intended insult, while understood in outline, became garbled in detail.

In sharp contrast to Thietmar's triumphalism on the German side, the author of the *History of the Franks of Sens* rewrites the events of 978 into a total victory on the part of Lothar, who is said to want to 'renew' the submission of Lotharingia to his rule.[38] The author gets his dates badly wrong, placing the events in 959,[39] and claims that Lothar seized Aachen without resistance and returned without pursuit. Otto eventually got to Paris, where among many others a *nepos* of his was killed at the gate of the city, having claimed he would break his lance on the doors. But Lothar called together Hugh Capet and Duke Henry of Burgundy and charged, putting the imperial troops to flight and pursuing them until Soissons. So many were killed trying to cross the river Aisne that the corpses made the river break its banks. Yet Lothar continued to pursue them, killing a great multitude, until finally he returned to France 'with a great victory'. In an echo of Alpert's reasoning that Otto had to fight back to prevent the French attacking again, the Sens chronicler claims that after Lothar's victory no other Otto would come to France either in person or with his army. This account, however, faces the difficulty that Lotharingia continued to be part of the Empire. The author resolves the problem ingeniously, claiming that, going against the wishes of Hugh and Henry, Lothar met Otto in Rheims and gave Lotharingia to him *in beneficio*. His actions were said to sadden the hearts of the French princes. As Joachim Ehlers has pointed out, the older interpretation that the Sens chronicler was following on the tradition of Archbishop Seguin of Sens in being pro-Carolingian does not make sense of this passage, since the Robertines Hugh and Henry are both depicted as advising against the surrender of Lotharingia.[40] Ehlers plausibly argued instead that the Sens chronicler's notably anti-Capetian account of 987 has

38 *Historia francorum Senonensis*, ed. G. Waitz, *MGH SS* IX (Hanover, 1851), p. 367.

39 Confusion over precisely which siege of Paris featured a single combat is also observable in the French dynastic histories: see for example Merlet (ed.), *La Chronique de Nantes*, c. XXXIII, pp. 97–101.

40 Ehlers, 'Die *Historia*', p. 11, arguing against A. Fliche, 'Les Sources de l'historiographie Sénonaise au XIe siècle', *Bulletin de la société archéologique de Sens* 24 (1909), p. 59, and Werner, 'Die Legitimität', pp. 208–9.

to do with Hugh Capet's alliance with Rheims, Sens's rival as French coronation site, and that in fact he is mainly interested in the interests of the West Frankish kingdom irrespective of who leads it.[41]

The year 978 is dealt with much more extensively in the *Gesta episcoporum Cameracensium*, a history of the bishops of Cambrai-Arras composed, at least at this point in the narrative, in 1024–25.[42] The context within which the account is placed is one of long-standing problems with aristocrats from across the border in France, whether on local, regional or national scales. At a local level, the author spends much time on the troubles of Bishop Tetdo, a German in a francophone see, and in particular his conflicts with rebellious *milites*.[43] At the regional, we also get an account of the attempt by the rebels Reginar and Lambert to retake the inheritance of which they had been deprived by Brun of Cologne.[44] According to the Cambrai author, Otto II is in Aachen to rest after his successful suppression of Reginar and Lambert when Lothar attacks.[45] Perhaps giving in to hyperbole, the author claims that Lothar sought to deprive Otto of his 'empire'.[46] The author's description of Otto's subsequent behaviour is explicitly contrasted with the underhand tactics of Lothar. Otto sends a messenger to Lothar, openly swearing vengeance, promising to exact it openly and announcing that he would invade France on 1 October. As recorded elsewhere, the author tells us of a meeting between Otto and the German magnates, and here again it is the disgrace of what happened that rouses them to action. But a new element has been added – a loyalty to the Fatherland (*patria*), which is compared to a *familia* in which the magnates have been brought up. The behaviour of the German army is also contrasted with that of the French. While the latter pillaged and revelled, Otto is said to have spared churches and instead given them donations. This, and a celebration outside the walls of Paris, are the only hints of religious activity or interpretation in the account, and the latter is explicitly presented as a demonstration of power and glory. In addition, the German turning back at Paris is attributed not

41 Ehlers, 'Die *Historia*', p. 17.
42 *Gesta epsicoporum Cameracensium*, ed. L. Bethmann, *MGH SS* VII (Hanover, 1846), pp. 438–41. For the dating, see E. van Mingroot, 'Kritisch onderzoek omtrent de datering van de *Gesta episcoporum Cameracensium*', *Revue belge de philologie et d'histoire* 53 (1975), pp. 281–332.
43 *Gesta epp. Cam.* I, c. 93, pp. 438–9.
44 *Gesta epp. Cam.* I, cc. 95–6, pp. 439–40.
45 *Gesta epp. Cam.* I, cc. 97–8, pp. 440–1.
46 *Lotharius rex karlensium . . . illum* [i.e., Otto II] *volens privare imperio . . .*, *Gesta epp. Cam.* I, c. 97, p. 440. Alternatively, the author may have meant to write *regnum* in reference to Lothar's desire to retake Lotharingia.

to a successful defence of the city but to Otto deciding that his insulted honour had been appropriately avenged.[47]

The secular context, and in particular the concern with honour, continues to be seen in the Cambrai author's account of the disastrous loss of the baggage train. Lothar is said to have pursued the German army because of the shame of his defeat.[48] The destruction and the drowning of the baggage train is attributed to Providence swelling the waters of the river Aisne to keep the two armies apart and prevent bloodshed. But Otto challenges Lothar to arrange the passage of one of the two armies safely across the river so that the conflict can be decided in battle. The Cambrai author thereby continues his characterization of Otto being concerned with honour and openness. What happens next, however, complicates any simple equation of individual and collective honour. A West Frankish Count Godfrey, almost certainly Godfrey (or Geoffrey) Greymantle of Anjou,[49] makes a different proposition, arguing it would be better for the two kings to decide the issue in battle between themselves rather than spilling any extra blood. An East Frankish namesake of his, on the contrary, takes this as an opportunity to abuse his enemy: 'We have heard that you always hold your king in contempt but we did not believe it, but now you yourselves have demonstrated that it is in fact true. Our Emperor will never fight while we rest. He will never put himself in danger while we are safe. But we do not doubt that he would be victorious, if he met your king in single combat.'[50]

Quite apart from the injection of epic elements into this story, such as the royal challenge and the call and response between the two aristocrats, it is clear that the Cambrai author is using the 978 incident as an opportunity to characterize the two nations, or at least their aristocracies. One, the

---

47 *exhausta ultione, Gesta epp. Cam.* I, c. 98, p. 441.

48 *ex pudoris tamen conscientia, Gesta epp. Cam.* I, c. 98, p. 441.

49 At around the same time that the *Gesta* were being produced, the *Chronicon Vindocinense* was recording Geoffrey's participation in a campaign of Lothar's against Lotharingia, although the chronicler did not know the date and so placed it in 954 alongside Lothar's accession. Whether Geoffrey actually was heavily involved in the campaign is another question, but it is clear that by the 1020s it had become part of his remembered deeds: F. Lot, 'Geoffroi Grisegonelle dans l'épopée', *Romania* 19 (1890), p. 392.

50 *Semper, inquit, vestrum regem vobis vilem haberi audivimus non credentes; nunc autem, vobismetipsis fatentibus, credere fas est. Numquam nobis quiescentibus noster imperator pugnabit, numquam nobis sospitibus in prelio periclitabitur. Haud tamen eum fore victurum diffidimus, si vestro cum rege conferretur singulari certamine. Gesta epp. Cam.* I, c. 98, p. 441.

51 *Gesta epp. Cam.* I, c. 99, pp. 441–2.

West Frankish, is fractious and ill-disciplined. The other, the East Frankish, is honourable and loyal to its king. Indeed, an attack on Otto is equated with an attack on the collective honour of the aristocracy and their Fatherland. This interest in loyalty to one realm and one emperor and its equation with cohesion within the ruling class is explicable by what immediately follows the account of 978 in the text.[51] Bishop Tetdo of Cambrai is said to have been duped by a local aristocrat, Walter of Lens, into thinking that Lothar was about to attack Cambrai and that Walter had the influence within the French court to stop it. The Walter mentioned here is the father of a Walter, castellan of Cambrai, who was troubling Gerard I, the bishop at the time of the initial composition of the *Gesta* of Cambrai. In other words, at this point the author is dealing with the origins of current troubles and does so by emphasizing the chronic fractiousness of the French, thereby turning the account into an appeal for loyalty to the Emperor (then Otto II, later Henry II). It should be pointed out, however, that this does not mean a subsuming of Lotharingian identity into that of the Germans. On the contrary, Tetdo's failure is partly because he speaks only German, not French, and elsewhere in the *Gesta* the indiscipline of the 'Karlenses' is explicitly contrasted to the discipline of the Lotharingians.[52] In other words, if there is a cultural distinction at work here, it is two cultures distinguished along regnal, rather than linguistic or 'national', lines.[53]

This issue needs closer examination, in particular because the formulation 'karlenses', or a variant, recurs in connection with accounts of 978. We have already seen it in the *Annales Colonienses*, Brun's *Vita* of Adalbert and in Thietmar's *Chronicon*. The *Gesta episcoporum Cameracensium* uses it by far the most frequently. There the designation first appears in the text in reference to the destruction caused to the properties of the abbey of Lobbes during the troubles of the 860s. They are attributed to the *inquietudo karlensium*.[54] The next references are to the flight of the rebels Reginar and Lambert to Adalbert of Vermandois *in partes karlensium* in 976, the surprise attack of Lothar, *rex karlensium*, on Aachen in 978 with which we

---

52   *Gesta epp. Cam.* III, c. 2, p. 466.

53   'Regnal' is a term coined by S. Reynolds, *Kingdoms and Communities in Western Europe 900–1300*, 2nd edn (Oxford, 1997), pp. 253–4, to avoid the modern connotations of 'national'.

54   The phrase occurs in the rubric: *Aecclesiam Laubiensem ab inquietudine Karlensium liberavit.* The phrase *liberare* implies that *inquietudo* is derogatory. Note that the chapter itself gives the reasons for the damage to the properties and *famulantes* of Lobbes as *Excrescente denique discordia inter Karlenses et Lotharienses, Gesta epp. Cam.* I, c. 55.

are concerned here, and the latter's alleged attempt to take Lotharingia after Otto II's death in 983.[55] In Gerard I's lifetime, he makes a recalcitrant castellan swear to put aside 'karlensian' customs and do Gerard honour just as Lotharingian *milites* honour their lords and bishops.[56] The phrase is, on the other hand, no simple insult; its derogatory connotations are added as we can observe when the *Gesta* use it as a simple ethnic denominator. Robert the Pious is referred to as *rex karlensium* when he allies with Henry II and Richard of Normandy to besiege Baldwin IV of Flanders.[57] Most importantly, Gerard of Cambrai himself, the commissioner of his work, is a *karlensis*, probably on his mother's side.[58] Yet when Gerard insists on being consecrated at his metropolitan see of Reims, Henry is said to make a point of giving him a 'book containing the consecration [rites] of clerics and the ordination [rite] of a bishop, so that, once he had been consecrated according to this [book], he would not have been ordained irregularly by the undisciplined customs of the Karlensians'.[59] Thus while the phrase is clearly derived from the various King Charleses that had ruled the West, just as Lotharingia was derived from Lothar, and while it did not necessarily have any derogatory connotations, it did lend itself to such a use.[60] Such an interpretation would explain why it was popular in descriptions of 978.

55 *Gesta epp. Cam.* I, c. 96–7, pp. 440–1.
56 *Fidelitatem sicut tibi promisi adtendam, quamdiu tuus fuero et tua bona tenuero; et postpositis Karlensibus custumiis, talem honorem tibi observabo, qualem Lotharienses milites dominis suis et episcopis. Et si quid contra te peccavero et ex parte tui de satisfactione facienda monitus fuero, talem iustitiam tibi, nisi mihi indulseris, faciam qualem supradicti Lotharienses milites suis dominis et episcopis faciunt. Gesta epp. Cam.* III, c. 40, p. 481.
57 *Gesta epp. Cam.* I, c. 114, p. 452.
58 *Gesta epp. Cam.* III, c. 1, p. 465.
59 *imperator . . . largitus est ei librum consecrationes clericorum et ordinationem episcopi continentem, ut per hunc videlicet consecratus, haud fortasse quidem indisciplinatis moribus Karlensium inregulariter ordinaretur. Gesta epp. Cam.* III, c. 2, p. 466.
60 Two other early recurrences support this contention. Widukind uses a variant twice to refer unmistakably to the West Franks as a whole, both of which in contexts of conflict between West and East Francia: Widukind of Corvey, *Res Gestae Saxonicae*, G. Waitz and K. A. Kehr (eds), *MGH SRG* (Hanover, 1904), I, c. 29, p. 36 and III, c. 2, p. 88. See H. Backes, 'Dulce France – Suoze Karlinge', *Beiträge zur Geschichte der deutschen Sprache und Literatur* 90 (Tübingen, 1968), pp. 35–6. Notker the German uses the (presumably original) German word in discussing the transferral of Roman rule from the Lombards to the Franks, 'whom we now call *chárlinga*', and finally to the Saxons: Notker the German, *Boethius, 'De consolatione Philosophiae' Buch I/II*, ed. P. W. Tax, *Die Werke Notkers des Deutschen, Neue Ausgabe*, vol. 1 (Tübingen, 1986), p. 6. So here the new term marks the Franks' 'demotion' from the sequence of imperial nations in favour of the Saxons.

At about the same time that the *Gesta episcoporum Cameracensium* was being written, the monk Raoul Glaber was writing his *Five Books of History* on the other side of France, in Aquitaine. Glaber depicts Lothar as wanting to take back Lotharingia as part of an assertion of authority after his accession to the throne.[61] The purpose of the Aachen raid is said to be the capture of Otto. Glaber then gives an account of the tit-for-tat actions, attributes the death of 'many' of the German troops to accident and finishes the story by saying that, 'the two kings ended the war, but Lothar had not gained what he wanted'.[62] There is no particular reason for Glaber to be interested in Lothar's efforts and his disinterest comes across in his dispassionate depiction of events. Like Thietmar, Glaber places the events in a strictly secular framework. (Contrast his description of the drowning of the German troops as accidental, with the claim of the Cambrai author that the will of Providence was at work.) Unlike Thietmar, he attributes glory or victory to no one. He acknowledges the importance of secular values, praising Lothar for his physical prowess and intelligence. But ultimately his laconic noting of the futility of Lothar's ambitions betrays Glaber's primary interest as a historian of religious revival. In comparison to that, secular deeds, however impressive, are fleeting and futile. Similarly, the *Life of Bishop Wolfgang*, by Othlo of St-Emmeram, virtually ignores secular motivations, with only the briefest reference to Otto II having invaded *partes Francorum* on account of an *iniuria*. Instead Othlo concentrates on attributing a safe crossing of the Aisne by Wolfgang's followers to divine intervention on behalf of the bishop.[63] The event is entirely subordinated here to Othlo's hagiographic purpose. The wider context is clearly irrelevant to the author.

From the mid-eleventh century, chroniclers, while still recording the events of 978, seem to have lost interest. In the 1030s, the *Annales Hildesheimenes* report that Otto 'invaded and ravaged Gaul', although not why, and that Lothar then made peace.[64] The *Annales Altahenses maiores*, based on the contemporary, but now lost *Annals of Hersfeld*, give pride of place to the Lotharingian rebels Reginar and Lambert and mention the destruction of the baggage train but imply that Otto was not at Aachen when Lothar

61 Raoul Glaber, *Historiarum libri quinque*, ed. and tr. J. France (Oxford, 1989), I.iii, c. 7, p. 17.
62 *Dehinc vero uterque cessavit, Lothario minus explente quod cupiit.* Glaber, *Historiam* I.iii, c. 7, p. 17.
63 Othlo of St-Emmeram, *Vita s. Wolfkangi episcopi*, ed. G. Waitz, *MGH SS* IV (Hanover, 1841), c. 32, p. 539.
64 *Annales Hildesheimenses*, ed. G. Waitz, *MGH SRG* (Hanover, 1878), p. 23.

attacked.[65] Forty years later, Lampert of Hersfeld, partially working from the same source, stripped the account of its references to Reginar and Lambert.[66] Neither Hermann of Reichenau nor Adam of Bremen has much to say on the matter, with Adam confusing Charles of Lotharingia with a putative 'King Charles' whom Otto subjected along with Lothar as evidence of his 'energetic' rule.[67] Sigebert of Gembloux, meanwhile, bases his account largely on that of the *Gesta episcoporum Cameracensium*, repeating the list of cities attacked by Otto and mentioning the emperor's mercy toward churches.[68] The account is heavily abbreviated, though, making much less of Otto's honourable dealing (though the date of the invasion is given), omitting the challenges to single combat and merely saying that some of the baggage was 'lost'. Sigebert seems to have been working from a manuscript of the *Gesta* which already included the prophecy, since he includes the 'prediction' that the instigators of 'this evil' would die within seven years. Like the *Gesta* of Cambrai and the *Annales Altahenses maiores*, the entire account is in the context of Otto resting after having pacified the kingdom against the rebellion of Reginar and Lambert. When he comes to tell of the peace agreement between Otto and Lothar in 980, Sigebert explicitly says that Lothar renounced any claim to Lotharingia. In other words, Sigebert keeps those elements of the Cambrai account that fit the 978 events into a story of the management and stability of the Empire, but de-emphasizes the issues of aristocratic loyalty and discipline that were so important to the beleaguered Cambrai bishops.[69]

By the twelfth century, it is fairly clear that respective French and German identities had been formed. It is equally clear that, at least on the German side, these identities no longer helped determine the interpretation of 978. A case in point is Ekkehard of Aura's re-use of Sigebert's account in the third recension of his chronicle where he, however, makes sense of the prophecy by contradicting the traditional ascription of piety to Otto II and

65 *Annales Altahenses maiores*, ed. Edmund von Oefele, *MGH SRG* (Hanover, 1891), pp. 13–14.

66 *Lamperti Annales*, ed. O. Holder-Egger, *MGH SRG* XXXVIII (Hanover and Leipzig, 1894), p. 44.

67 Hermann of Reichenau, *Chronicon*, in R. Buchner (ed.), *Quellen des 9. und 11. Jahrhunderts zur Geschichte der Hamburgischen Kirche und des Reiches*, Ausgewählte Quellen zur deutschen Geschichte des Mittelalters 9 (Berlin, 1961), p. 648; Adam of Bremen, *Gesta Hammaburgensis ecclesiae pontificum*, *MGH SS* VII, II:21, p. 313: *Otto medianus succedens, per decem annos strenue gubernavit imperium.*

68 Sigebert of Gembloux, *Chronica*, ed. L. Bethmann, *MGH SS* VI (Hanover, 1844), p. 352.

69 On Sigebert's imperial ideology, see M. Chazan, 'La Nécessité de l'Empire de Sigebert de Gembloux à Jean de Saint-Victor', *Le Moyen Âge* 106 (2000), pp. 9–11.

claiming he had destroyed churches during his campaign.[70] Here the historiographical tradition of 978 was reversed to make a point about the consequences of the imperial abuse of the Church. In France, 978 was to have a longer legacy as an example of national resistance against the Germans.[71] Most strongly of all, however, garbled versions of the single combat before the gates of Paris would become a myth of the ducal families of Brittany and Anjou.[72]

Such questions lie outside the purview of this essay, which has sought to trace the retelling of the events of 978 in France and Germany until the clear separation of the two kingdoms' identities. We have seen most obviously that it is authorial intention which determines the interpretation of the conflict over Aachen, whether narrowly, with the anonymous Cambrai canon with his obsession about unruly aristocrats, or broadly, in the respective weights given to secular and religious drives in chronicle and hagiography. Less predictably, the accounts favoured each side from the start, interpreting them in terms of *Staatspolitik* and the honour of great men. Lastly, a couple of omissions ought to be pointed out. First, we know from the letters exchanged between Dietrich of Metz and Charles of Lotharingia that the Ottonian counter-attack was much more serious than simply a reaction to an embarrassing raid: it constituted an attempt to oust Lothar and replace him with Charles.[73] There is virtually none of this in the later record, with the exception of the local knowledge of Alpert's fragmentary *De episcopis Mettensibus*. It was the dramatic face-off between the two kings which captured the 'headlines'. This might have been because Charles was soon to be beaten to the throne not by a brother but by an entire other family, meaning that the specifics of the political machinations of the 970s became lost behind the memory of those of the 980s. Certainly, Adam of Bremen's confusion would imply that. But it might also be a symptom of the increasing autonomy of the two realms' respective polities and the resultant implausibility of an alliance between the Ottonians and the Carolingians to control the throne of France. The other absence is much reference to Aachen as a symbolic imperial capital: only Richer mentions Charlemagne in connection with Lothar's manipulation of the eagle on the palace roof. Charlemagne, therefore, may have created Aachen as a centre for his empire, but it was made central by his presence and the presence of his magnates. This paper started with an irony – that a piece

70 Ekkehard of Aura, *Chronicon*, ed. G. Waitz, *MGH SS* VI (Hanover, 1844), p. 191.
71 Kienast, *Deutschland und Frankreich*, p. 96, esp. nn. 211–12.
72 See above, n. 22.
73 See above, n. 20.

dedicated to Janet Nelson should devote itself to Aachen's violent seizure by Charlemagne's penultimate heir. But in investigating how the events were retold we have discovered that the place itself was less interesting to later generations than the people, their motives and their feelings of honour and shame. Theirs was a regnal loyalty to crown, dynasty and country. Royal and imperial charisma could not be institutionalized in a place but was renewed with every new king just as old diplomata would be repeatedly reconfirmed. Charlemagne himself, of course, did live on and his charisma continued to work down the ages.[74] But it was not because of Aachen – just as 978 was remembered for the personalities, battles and politics, so Charlemagne lived on as a warrior and royal role model. If, after 800, he thought to establish his legacy with Aachen then he failed, because his reputation, like those of later kings, was founded on stories rather than on stone.

74 Most notably in our period on Otto III; see M. Gabriele, 'Otto III, Charlemagne, and Pentecost AD 1000: a reconsideration using diplomatic evidence', in M. Frasetto (ed.), *The Year 1000: Religious and Social Response to the Turning of the First Millennium* (New York, 2002), pp. 111–32.

11

Absoluimus uos uice beati petri apostolorum principis: episcopal authority and the reconciliation of excommunicants in England and Francia c.900–c.1150*

Sarah Hamilton

Introduction

A CCORDING TO WILLIAM of Malmesbury's twelfth-century account, the brothers of a man who refused to accept his (accidental) killer's offer of compensation told Bishop Wulfstan of Worcester (1062–95), when he intervened, 'they would rather be excommunicated than fail to avenge their brother's killing.'[1] Wulfstan responded by publicly declaring them to be sons of the devil and the assembled crowd 'shouted that this was true'; God's vengeance followed immediately, with one of the contumacious brothers being struck down with madness, whereupon the others offered peace and begged for mercy, which the bishop granted after mass, restoring the sufferer to health, and peace to all. This account is well-known in the context of discussion of feud in eleventh-century England, but it also points to the significance of excommunication – the invocation of God's vengeance – for episcopal authority at this time.[2] While excommunication was always presented as a weapon of last resort, because it entailed, theoretically, exclusion from both the Church and society, in the next life as well as this, it was not intended to be permanent but rather to resolve a dispute, forcing the excommunicant to repent and acknowledge the bishop's authority. To that extent lifting the sentence of

* I would especially like to thank Julia Crick and Helen Gittos for their comments on a draft of this paper and also the participants in the kolloguium on 'Neue Normen und veränderte Praxis. Kirchliches und weltliches Recht am Ende des 9. und am Beginn des 10. Jahrhunderts' at the Historisches Kolleg, Munich in April 2005.
1 William of Malmesbury, *Vita Wulfstani*, II. c. 15, ed. M. Winterbottom and R. M. Thomson, *William of Malmesbury: Saints' Lives* (Oxford, 2002), pp. 90–1.
2 P. R. Hyams, 'Feud in medieval England', *The Haskins Society Journal* 3 (1991), pp. 1–21 at 2–4.

excommunication was almost as significant an act of power as imposing it. As tales such as this suggest, reconciliation therefore embodied important aspects of the bishop's ministry, his roles as both peacemaker and judge. Yet while scholars have investigated the law and rituals surrounding the imposition of excommunication, little attention has been paid to the reconciliation rites which marked its end and which are the focus of this essay.[3] Specific services for the reconciliation of excommunicants are first recorded in Francia in the early tenth, and in England only from the early eleventh century. Investigation of the textual history of these services is intended to help fill this lacuna in the historiography and to illuminate further episcopal ideology in this period.

The English rite

Bishop Wulfstan II is not described as following a formal reconciliation service, although, as we shall see, the earliest surviving English example of this service was copied at Worcester during his pontificate. Moreover, this service is not found in any of the late tenth- and eleventh-century Anglo-Saxon pontificals: the earliest example of an English rite recorded in a liturgical book is that recorded in a mid-twelfth-century English pontifical, London, British Library, MS Cotton Vespasian D.xv (hereinafter *V*), under the rubric, '[Thus] begins [the rite] for those who after excommunication come to reconciliation with the grief of penance'.[4] According to the rite, it pleases all the senate that those who have been excommunicated should come to be corrected, and seek forgiveness through a contrite heart.[5] The excommunicants should come with their *intercessores* to the gate of the cemetery, barefoot and clad in ashcloth, and stay there while their sup-

---

3 Significant works include: P. Hinschius, *Das Kirchenrecht der Katholiken und Protestanten in Deutschland: System des katholischen Kirchenrechts mit besonderer Rücksicht auf Deutschland*, 6 vols. (Berlin, 1869–97), Vol. 5: pp. 1–492, esp. pp. 1–85, 145–56; H. C. Lea, *Studies in Church History* (Philadelphia, 1869), 223–487; F. D. Logan, *Excommunication and the Secular Arm in Medieval England* (Toronto, 1968); E. Vodola, *Excommunication in the Middle Ages* (Berkeley, 1986); L. K. Little, *Benedictine Maledictions: Liturgical Cursing in Romanesque France* (Ithaca, NY and London, 1993); R. H. Helmholz, 'Excommunication in twelfth-century England', *Journal of Law and Religion* 11 (1995), pp. 235–53. For a brief account of the Frankish rites see R. E. Reynolds, 'Rites of separation and reconciliation in the early Middle Ages', *Settimane* 33 (1987), pp. 405–33.

4 London, British Library, MS Cotton Vespasian D. xv, ff. 57v (l.10) – f. 61r (l.9), transcribed in Table 11.1. My transcription varies slightly from that in *The Pontifical of Magdalen College*, ed. Henry A. Wilson, HBS 39 (London, 1910), pp. 237–8.

5 The rite is analysed further at pp. 218–23 below.

porters plead their cause with the bishop. The *intercessores* then send the excommunicants in twos or threes to prostrate themselves before the bishop in front of the gate, while he says the seven penitential psalms followed by the *Kyrie eleison*, the *Pater noster*, various versicles, and a prayer petitioning the Lord to absolve the faults and sins of his servants, or servant (like the prayers a singular reading is added above the line). Once this prayer sequence is finished, the excommunicants follow the bishop to the doors of the church, and while the choir sings psalm 50, *Miserere mei deus*, the bishop takes the excommunicants one by one and personally conducts them inside the building. The penitents then prostrate themselves on the floor while the bishop absolves them, reciting two prayers, *Absoluimus uos uice beati petri apostolorum principis*, and *Deus innocentiae restitutor*. After this the excommunicants then go out and, having dressed in their own clothes, return to the bishop to seek his blessing and receive communion. They finally leave the bishop's presence while the cantor sings the antiphon, *Dedit pater poenitenti.*

This particular rite was added, together with one for enclosing an anchorite, in a different, albeit similar, Romanesque hand to those which wrote the main part of the collection.[6] The collection taken as a whole is a high-quality, if small manuscript, written in a large clear script with twelve lines to a page; the main part (ff. 4r–18v, 20r–46r,48r–57v) was written with red initials and rubrics, but the two additional rites have green initials as well, and black rubrics highlighted through in green.[7] The ruling is the same throughout the collection. A clue as to the collection's provenance may be found on f. 22r (l.1) where in the rite for ordaining an abbot, the abbot's promise of obedience made to the see of Canterbury, *Dorobernensi*, has been erased and emended in a very similar script to read *Exoniensi*, Exeter. While *V* shares some rites with other twelfth-century pontificals attributed to Canterbury, this reconciliation rite is one of several in *V* which are not found among its contemporaries.[8] *V*'s origins thus remain uncertain, although Canterbury or Exeter (based on a Canterbury model) are both possibilities.

Although not found in other pontificals, this service also survives in two examples of the early eleventh-century episcopal collection of law and

---

6 Ff. 57v (l. 10)–65r (l.9). It follows a rite for consecrating a cemetery (ff. 48v–57v). This complex collection requires further study as the rites in the main part were each copied on a separate folio; for a brief description see *Pontifical of Magdalen College*, xxviii–xxix.

7 Approximately 190 × 130 mm. Green initials are also used in texts added on ff. 19r, 46r, 46v.

8 *Pontifical of Magdalen College*, pp. vii–xiii, xxix.

liturgy, usually, if anachronistically, known as the 'commonplace book' of Archbishop Wulfstan of Worcester (1002–16) and York (1002–23): Cambridge, Corpus Christi College, MS 265 (hereinafter *C*) and Oxford, Bodleian Library, MS Barlow 37 (hereinafter *D*).[9] *C* was compiled at Worcester in the third quarter of the eleventh century, while *D* was probably copied there a century later, around 1200.[10] In his 1980 study of Wulfstan's collection Hans Sauer established that, although it is not a direct copy, the contents of *D* are closely related to those of *C*, and, moreover, that these collections are the only two copies to include the text of liturgies for both the imposition of excommunication and the reconciliation of excommunicants, his 'Block X'.[11] Sauer later edited the text of Block X, including the reconciliation service, as it appeared in *C* and *D*, but he was seemingly not aware that the rite also occurred in *V*.[12]

Both *C* and *D* are Worcester manuscripts, and although *V*'s origins are unknown the alteration on f. 22r suggests it was at Exeter in the twelfth century. Although the earliest example of the rite, *C*, dates from the third quarter of the eleventh century, another copy of Wulfstan's collection, Cambridge, Corpus Christi College, MS 190, pp. 1–294 (hereinafter *O*), provides earlier evidence for its existence: *O* was copied at Worcester in the first half of the eleventh century, and was in use at Exeter by the mid-eleventh century.[13] *O* includes a table of contents which mention (c. xiv) *De his qui post excommunicationem cum luctu penitentiae ad reconciliationem*

---

9 P. Wormald, *The Making of English Law: King Alfred to the Twelfth Century*, I: *Legislation and its Limits* (Oxford, 1999), pp. 210–24. On Wulfstan's collection both M. Bateson, 'A Worcester cathedral book of ecclesiastical collections made *c*.1000 AD', *EHR* 10 (1895), pp. 712–31, and D. Bethurum, 'Archbishop Wulfstan's commonplace book', *Publications of the Modern Language Association of America* 57 (1942), pp. 916–29 remain fundamental.

10 On *C* see N. R. Ker, *Catalogue of Manuscripts Containing Anglo-Saxon*, 2nd edn (Oxford, 1990), no. 53, pp. 92–4; Helmut Gneuss, *Handlist of Anglo-Saxon Manuscripts: A List of Manuscripts and Manuscript Fragments Written or Owned in England up to 1100* (Tempe, Arizona, 2001), no. 73, p. 35. Wormald, *Making*, pp. 211–19. On *D* see H. Sauer, 'Zur Überlieferung und Anlage von Erzbischof Wulfstans "Handbuch"', *DA* 36 (1980), pp. 341–84 at 348–56.

11 Sauer, 'Zur Überlieferung', pp. 369–73.

12 H. Sauer, 'Die Exkommunikationsriten aus Wulfstans Handbuch und Liebermanns Gesetze', in C. Pollner, H. Rohlfing and F.-R. Hausmann (eds), *Bright is the Ring of Words: Festschrift für Horst Weinstock zum 65. Geburtstag*, Abhandlungen zur Sprache und Literatur 85 (Bonn, 1996), pp. 283–307.

13 Wormald, *Making*, pp. 220–4. For the view that the main text is copied in a Worcester script see D. Dumville, *English Caroline Script and its Monastic History*, Studies in Benedictinism (Woodbridge, 1993), pp. 52 (n. 228), 55.

veniunt.[14] The relevant quire is now missing but this list suggests that the rite for the reconciliation of excommunicants belonged to an early recension of Wulfstan's collection.[15] This chapter was part of a larger section on excommunication which began (c. xi) *De excommunicatis ex concilio Antioceno.* That particular canon survives in other copies of Wulfstan's collection, and states that an excommunicant must either be reconciled by his own bishop or, at least, give an account of himself to a synod.[16] Sauer suggests that *C, D* and *O* are among the core group of manuscripts of Wulfstan's collection. The evidence of the text now missing from *O,* taken with Patrick Wormald's suggestion that *C* represents a later, and more polished, version of Wulfstan's collection, locates the English reconciliation rite as in existence at early eleventh-century Worcester.[17] Furthermore, *O*'s presence at Exeter from the mid-eleventh century means that the reconciliation rite could have been added to *V* at Exeter, even if the core of the pontifical was copied at Canterbury. Without a more detailed investigation of the entire codex, an Exeter origin for the service in *V* remains a hypothesis, and as Wulfstanian homiletic material was copied at Canterbury as early as the mid-eleventh century, a Canterbury origin for the rite in *V* remains a possibility.[18]

Whatever the case, *V* casts new light on the textual history of the rite. There are various minor differences between the text as it appears in *C* and *D,* as Table 11.1 makes clear, the most notable of which is that in the earliest example of the rite, the late eleventh-century *C,* the episcopal mass and benediction at the end is followed by a prayer for the absolution of the

14 M. R. James, *A Descriptive Catalogue of the Manuscripts in the Library of Corpus Christi College, Cambridge,* 2 vols. (Cambridge, 1912), vol. 1, pp. 452–63, at p. 454. This capitulum belongs to a collection of canon law, sometimes known as the *Excerptiones (Ps.-) Ecgberhti,* found in various manuscripts of Wulfstan's 'handbook' including *O;* on the reasons for believing the attribution to Archbishop Ecgberht of York (732?–766) to be later than the eleventh century see *Wulfstan's Canon Law Collection,* ed. J. E. Cross and A. Hamer (Cambridge, 1999), pp. 3–5.
15 Sauer, 'Zur Überlieferung', p. 369.
16 Recension A, no. 78: *Wulfstan's Canon Law,* 99. This canon is found in *C,* pp. 32–3, among other copies of Wulfstan's collection.
17 P. Wormald, 'Archbishop Wulfstan and the holiness of society', in *idem, Legal Culture in the Early Medieval West: Law as Text, Image and Experience* (London, 1999), pp. 225–51 at 231–40; *idem, Making,* pp. 216–17.
18 H. Gneuss, 'Origin and provenance of Anglo-Saxon manuscripts: the case of Cotton Tiberius A.iii', P. R. Robinson and R. Zim (eds), *Of the Making of Books: Medieval Manuscripts, their Scribes and Readers: Essays Presented to M. B. Parkes* (Aldershot, 1997), pp. 13–48; D. Scragg, *Dating and Style in Old English Composite Homilies,* H. M. Chadwick memorial lectures 9 (Cambridge 1999).

penitents, *Absoluimus uos uice beati petri*, which is totally omitted from the early thirteenth-century *D*. In twelfth-century *V*, however, this prayer is used as the absolution prayer said by the bishop immediately upon the excommunicants' physical re-entry into the church and there is no final absolution prayer. The placing of this prayer at the end of the *C* rite, it could be argued, confused the rite's message: the contrite excommunicants have already been absolved, re-entered the Church both metaphorically and physically, taken communion and received the bishop's blessing, and returned, dressed in their own clothes, as full members of society; a second absolution prayer thus appears somewhat otiose, and risks undermining the earlier message of the rite, namely that they had been restored to Christian society. It thus seems possible that the rite as recorded in *D* represents an intermediate state between that in *C* and that in *V* – the *Absoluimus uos uice beati petri* prayer was first omitted from the conclusion of the rite as unnecessary, but later recognized to be a powerful prayer, claiming for the bishop the power, as St Peter's representative, to absolve the contrite sinner in the first person, and was thus moved earlier in the rite to the point of the initial episcopal absolution of the penitents.[19] Such a chronology is speculative, but the comparison in Table 11.1 between these three examples of the rite, recorded between the late eleventh and early thirteenth centuries, demonstrates that the text was not static; it changed across time, suggesting it was a live rite, which the clergy of Worcester and Canterbury and/or Exeter sought to improve upon; a similar pattern of continuous small but significant change has been identified in the rites for public penance in tenth-, eleventh- and twelfth-century northern France and the *Reich*, with similar conclusions. Such differences are unlikely to be merely a result of scribal whim, but rather represent clerical interest in improving the performance of an important rite for the bishop's authority.[20] The Frankish rite for the reconciliation of excommunicants went

---

19 This prayer is unique to the English liturgy, see p. 223 below. Frankish bishops preferred to petition God to absolve the excommunicant, suggesting greater importance was attached to episcopal office in England: S. Hamilton, 'Rites for public penance in later Anglo-Saxon England', in H. Gittos and M. B. Bedingfield (eds), *The Liturgy of the Late Anglo-Saxon Church*, HBS subsidia 5 (London, 2005), pp. 65–103 at p. 81.

20 S. Hamilton, *The Practice of Penance 900–1050*, Royal Historical Society Studies in History (Woodbridge, 2001), pp. 104–72; M. Mansfield, *The Humiliation of Sinners: Public Penance in Thirteenth-century France* (Ithaca, 1995), pp. 159–247. C. A. Jones has argued for 'purposeful' liturgical innovation in the central Middle Ages driven as much by increasing conceptual sophistication as pragmatism: 'The origins of the 'Sarum'chrism mass at eleventh-century Christ Church, Canterbury', *Mediaeval Studies* 67 (2005), pp. 219–35 at p. 220.

through an even more marked evolution, and examination of the Frankish evidence casts further light on the English material.

The Frankish rite

The earliest example of the Frankish rite for the reconciliation of excommunicants was recorded over a century earlier than the English rite, in Regino of Prüm's early tenth-century collection of canon law (see Table 11.2).[21] There it comes after what are among the earliest examples of liturgical formulae for the imposition of excommunication.[22] Regino gave no authority for these particular texts, nor have his modern editors been able to find a precedent for this or the various other liturgical rites in his collection.[23] It seems likely, however, that, because these services are presented as normative, they represent liturgical practice as it was within the archdiocese of Trier in the early tenth century, and that they have their origins in earlier traditions.[24]

Under the rubric 'How the bishop should reconcile or receive the excommunicant' (note the singular compared to the plural of the English rite), when someone who has been excommunicated or anathematized has requested to do penance and promised to make amends, the bishop who had excommunicated him ought to stand before the doors of the church, with twelve priests.[25] The bishop should establish whether he has already made amendment for his crimes, or, following both 'divine and human law', set out how they should be corrected. Then the bishop should ask, if he is penitent, whether he wishes to receive canonical penance for perpetrating *scelera* – that is, particularly offensive and public sins – and if he, now prostrate on the ground, seeks mercy, confesses his guilt, and implores penance, pledging caution in the future, then the bishop, taking him by

---

21   *Reginonis abbatis Prumiensis Libri duo de synodalibus causis et disciplinis ecclesiasticis*, ed. F. W. H. Wasserschleben, revised and abridged with German translation by W. Hartmann (Darmstadt, 2004), II. 418, p. 446.

22   Regino, *Libri duo*, II, 412–17, pp. 438–44. Little, *Benedictine Maledictions*, pp. 34–44; for a brief description of these rites, together with those for reconciliation, see Reynolds, 'Rites'.

23   W. Hartmann, 'Die *Capitula incerta* im Sendhandbuch Reginos von Prüm', in O. Münsch and T. Zotz (eds), *Scientia veritatis: Festschrift für Hubert Mordek zum 65. Geburtstag* (Ostfildern, 2004), pp. 207–26.

24   Hartmann, 'Die *Capitula*', p. 208; Hamilton, *Practice*, p. 36.

25   The excommunicant is male in the Latin, reflecting common liturgical usage, rather than any sense that the rite was restricted only to male offenders.

the right hand, should lead him into the church, and return him to Christian community and society. After this the bishop should enjoin on him a penance in accordance with his guilt, and send letters throughout the diocese and also to other bishops notifying everyone of the excommunicant's return to Christian society. No bishop should presume to excommunicate or reconcile anyone from another diocese, without the knowledge and consent of the bishop of that diocese.

This much more legalistic service, with its greater emphasis on the excommunicant's penance, mirrored Regino's prescription as to how the sentence of excommunication should be imposed.[26] After the excommunicant has been warned three times by his own priest, at mass, of his imminent excommunication, and has not repented, the bishop, surrounded by the apostolically significant number of twelve priests, should declare the malefactor to be excommunicated from the body of the church, cut off like a putrid limb, lest he infect the rest of the body. Consequently when he was reconciled he was physically taken into the cathedral, and his return to Christian *societas* extensively publicized.

Regino dedicated his collection to Hatto, archbishop of Mainz, which perhaps explains why his description of the reconciliation service was copied, word for word, by the compiler of the earliest recension of the Romano-German pontifical (hereinafter the *PRG*) assembled in St Alban's Mainz *c*.950 (see Table 11.2).[27] The Mainz monastic compiler, however, added a liturgy headed 'the absolution of the excommunicants' to the end of Regino's text about a single excommunicant. While some of the prayers added refer to multiple penitents, including the absolution prayer, others, such as *Praesta quaesumus*, refer to only a single penitent. The resulting text is consequently rather confused and would require careful attention to grammar if it was to be administered accurately.

Less than seventy years later Burchard, bishop of Worms, incorporated yet another version of Regino's text into book XI, *De excommunicatione*, of his *Decretum* (see Table 11.2).[28] Burchard used Regino's collection exten-

---

26   Regino, *Libri duo*, II, 413, pp. 442–4.
27   Regino, *Libri duo*, Prefatio, p. 20. *Le Pontifical romano-germanique du dixième siècle*, ed. C. Vogel and R. Elze, 3 vols., Studi e testi 226, 227, 269 (Vatican City, 1963–1972), vol. 1, pp. 317–21. The rite is recorded in both Monte Cassino, MS 451, and Rome, Biblioteca Vallicelliana, Codex D. 5, and thus in the earliest recension of the text; *Le Pontifical* vol. 1, p. xli. The *PRG*'s compilers used Regino elsewhere; on the general history of the Romano-german pontifical see C. Vogel, 'Le Pontifical romano-germanique du Xe siècle: nature, date et importance du document', *Cahiers de civilisation médiévale* 6 (1963), pp. 27–48; Hamilton, *Practice*, pp. 104–6, 128–35, 211–23.
28   Burchard, *Decretum*, XI.8, *PL* 140, 860–1.

sively, and began here with Regino's text, departing from it only once, when he described the bishop as prescribing how crimes should be corrected in accordance only with divine law, omitting Regino's reference to human law.[29] This omission was almost certainly deliberate: according to Greta Austin, Burchard had a 'vision of canon law . . . based on the authority of the Bible' in which 'secular law is subordinate to the law of God'.[30] But unlike the *PRG*'s compiler, Burchard was not content to merely add the absolution liturgy to Regino's prescriptive rubric, but rather inserted the prayers into Regino's text; nor was his liturgy very similar to that in the *PRG*. As is clear from Table 11.2, while the *PRG* service incorporated prayers taken from both the Gregorian and Gelasian traditions, Burchard's rite drew solely on the Gelasian sacramentary.[31] The Worms liturgy was also more consistent than that in the *PRG*; all the prayers, including that for absolution, refer only to a singular penitent.[32] These differences suggest the rite in Burchard's *Decretum* had independent origins to those of the rite in the *PRG*: in other words, over the course of the tenth and early eleventh centuries two different liturgies for the absolution of excommunicants were interpolated into Regino's text, one recorded in mid-tenth-century Mainz, one in early eleventh-century Worms. They suggest that there was across the tenth century an ongoing interest among some, at least, of the east Frankish episcopate in developing and refining a liturgy for the reconciliation of excommunicants. The evidence for the Frankish rite therefore provides further support for the hypothesis suggested by the English evidence, namely that these rites were subject to continuing adjustment: the

29 On Regino's circulation see Regino, *Libri duo*, ed. Hartmann, 7, and Hamilton, *Practice*, pp. 29–31. On Regino's influence on Burchard see H. Hoffmann and R. Pokorny, *Das Dekret des Bischofs Burchard von Worms: Textstufen-Frühe Verbreitung-Vorlagen*, *MGH* Hilfsmittel 12 (Munich, 1991), especially pp. 173–244.

30 G. Austin, 'Jurisprudence in the service of pastoral care: the *Decretum* of Burchard of Worms', *Speculum* 79 (2004), pp. 929–59, at 933 and 946.

31 On the Gregorian and Gelasian sacramentaries, and the mixed tradition, see C. Vogel, *Medieval Liturgy: an Introduction to the Sources*, revised and trans. W. G. Storey and N. K. Rasmussen with J. K. Brooks-Leonard (Washington DC, 1986), pp. 64–105; E. Palazzo, *A History of the Liturgical Book from the Beginning to the Thirteenth Century*, trans. M. Beaumont (Collegeville, Minnesota, 1998), pp. 42–55.

32 The text in London, British Library, Cotton Tiberius C.i (n. France, s. xi[2]), f. 112v confirms the general accuracy of the *PL* text, including the reference throughout to a single penitent, but departs from the *PL* in placing Regino's prescription that the bishop take the penitent by the hand before the prayers, rather than between them as in the *PL*; it also omits the responses to the *preces*, and includes some careless copying errors, e.g., omission of *excommunicatus* from the first sentence, suggesting this particular example of the rite was not routinely consulted.

reconciliation of excommunicants was a significant issue for Frankish and English bishops throughout this period.

Comparisons

A comparison of the Frankish and English texts in Tables 11.1 and 11.2 reveals them to be very different from each other: despite the broad similarity of process – the bishop meets the repentant excommunicant outside the church before reintroducing him into the church as a physical sign of his restoration to the Church community – they do not share any prayers with each other, and only one psalm, David's confession of his sins (Psalm 50), and two common versicles.[33] Although the earliest records of the Frankish rite precede those for the English rite by over a century, they were composed independently of each other. Moreover, the rubrics for both the English and Frankish rites are distinct from the surviving services for the episcopal reconciliation of penitents on Maundy Thursday; while different versions of two of the prayers in the English excommunicants' reconciliation service are found in the English penitential service, only two prayers and the final antiphon are common to the *PRG*'s rites for the reconciliation of excommunicants and penitents.[34] What, therefore, do the differences between the English and Frankish excommunicants' reconciliation services tell us about the ways in which their compilers conceived of both excommunication and episcopal authority?

The Frankish rite begins abruptly with the lone penitent excommunicant presenting himself before the bishop and twelve priests at the doors of the church, while the English rite describes a communal occasion: because it has pleased the *senatus* that those who have been excommunicated come to correction and seek the indulgence of forgiveness by yielding a contrite heart, the repentant excommunicants should present themselves with their *intercessores* at the gate of the cemetery before the bishop. The presence of other priests is not mentioned in the English rite, although it is clear from

---

33 Both versicles *Saluum fac seruum tuum domine* and *Mitte ei, Domine, auxilium de sancto* are, for example, used in the *PRG* rite for the reconciliation on penitents on Maundy Thursday: *PRG* xcix.229, vol. 2, p. 61.

34 E.g., *Absoluimus uos uice* and *Deus innocentiae restitutor* exist, in slightly different versions, in the penitential rite in *Pontificale Lanaletense (Bibliothèque de la Ville de Rouen, A. 27, Cat. 368): a Pontifical Formerly in Use at St Germans, Cornwall*, ed. G. H. Doble, HBS 74 (London, 1937), p. 80 and *The Benedictional of Archbishop Robert*, ed. H. A. Wilson, HBS 24 (London, 1903), p. 60. PRG XCIX.235, XCIX.240, XCIX.251; see also the shared *preces* in the PRG version of the rite set out in Table 11.2.

the references to the choir and the cantor singing the psalm and the final antiphon that this service was as formal and elaborate as the Frankish one and that the bishop would, indeed, have been surrounded by his clergy, if not, perhaps, twelve priests. But who comprised the *senatus*? Although '*senatus*' (and its derivatives) retained its antique meaning when used of the secular nobility of Rome and Constantinople throughout this period, from the ninth century it was used in both Francia and England to describe the king's advisers, drawn from both the clerical and secular elites.[35] The reference to the *senatus* may therefore refer to a mixed group of secular and ecclesiastical nobles: one obvious location for such an assembly was a council or synod. There are no references to the specific reconciliation of particular excommunicants at English councils held in the tenth and eleventh centuries, but there are for Frankish ones. Flodoard, for example, records how Count Erlebald of Châtresais was posthumously reconciled at the synod of Trosly in 921; he had been excommunicated the previous year by Archbishop Heriveus of Reims for taking possession of two castles claimed by the see of Rheims and for attacking its *familia*.[36] When the count ignored the sentence, the archbishop had successfully besieged and retaken one of the disputed castles, whereupon the count had gone to the court of the Frankish king, Charles the Simple. Soon afterwards Erlebald was killed on campaign in the king's service. The following year, Archbishop Heriveus, in the presence of the king, Charles the Simple, presided over a synod at Trosly which, at the request of the king, reconciled the dead count.[37] Excommunicants were denied funeral rites and commemoration and a plea for mercy may have been the grounds for the king's intervention on behalf of the count who had not sought forgiveness while he was alive.[38] Charter evidence suggests that Erlebald was close to the king from 915

---

35 J. F. Niermeyer and C. van de Kieft, *Mediae latinitatis lexicon minus*, 2 vols., 2nd edn (Leiden, 2002), vol. 2, p. 247 (Frankish context); a search of the *New Regesta Regum Anglorum* on-line, www.anglo-saxons.net/hwaet/?do=show&page=Charters, reveals a similar broad meaning in ninth- and tenth-century England: S210, S346, S361, S367, S556, S557, S1431a.

36 *Les Annales de Flodoard*, ed. P. Lauer (Paris, 1905), a. 920, a. 921, 2–3, 5; Flodoard Remensis, *Historia Remensis ecclesiae*, ed. M. Stratmann, *MGH SS* XXXVI (Hanover, 1998), IV, c. 16, pp. 408–9. On this incident see R. Parisot, *Le Royaume de Lorraine sous les Carolingiens (843–923)* (Paris, 1899), p. 642; G. Schmitz, 'Heriveus von Reims (900–922): Zur Geschichte des Erzbistums Reims am Beginn des 10. Jahrhunderts', *Francia* 4 (1978), pp. 59–105 especially pp. 68–9; M. Sot, *Un historien et son Église: Flodoard de Reims* (Paris, 1993), p. 241.

37 I. Schröder, *Die westfränkischen Synoden von 888 bis 987 und ihre Überlieferung*, MGH Hilfsmittel 3 (Munich, 1980), no. 35, pp. 208–12.

38 Schröder, *Die westfränkischen Synoden*, p. 211. Lea, *Studies*, pp. 251–5, 406–7.

onward, and as Heriveus ceased to act as royal archchancellor after 921, the death of Erlebald may even have led to a quarrel between the king and the archbishop of Rheims.[39] Excommunication and subsequent reconciliation, as the Wulfstan case also suggests, often had wider ramifications.

Flodoard's report also provides a possible context for the reference in the English rite to the role of the *intercessores* who present the repentant excommunicant's case to the bishop. In the *Annales* Flodoard describes the king as merely placing his request for Erlebald's absolution before the synod, while in the *Historia*, Flodoard reports Charles as interceding on Erlebald's behalf.[40] There is the only one other account in Flodoard of someone interceding on behalf of an excommunicant, when in 953 King Louis successfully intervened at the request of Count Ragenoldus to prevent the issuing of the sentence of excommunication which was to have been declared against him by the synod of Rheims.[41] On both occasions it was the king who intervened, and royal office of course placed him in a quasi-sacerdotal position. The question remains therefore as to whether the *intercessores* referred to in the English rite were members of the clerical or the lay nobility. Despite the growing literature on political intercession, focused on the role of both clergymen and noblemen as negotiators in the settlement of disputes, the conclusion of which was often signified by formal displays of submission, the vocabulary of the sources is less consistent than that used by modern commentators.[42] Thus the word *intercessor*

---

39 Parisot, *Le Royaume de Lorraine*, pp. 642, 649; see also Schmitz, 'Heriveus', p. 86.

40 *Sinodus apud Trosleium habita, cui praesedit Heriveus archiepiscopus presente quoque Karolo rege, cuius obtentu Erlebaldus ibi Castricensis absolvitur*, Annales, ed. Lauer, a. 921, p. 5. *Quem tamen postmodum in synodo, quam apud idem Trosleium idem domnus archiepiscopus cum diocesaneis suis habuit, intercedente rege et obnixe flagitante a vinculo excommunicationis absolvit, Historia*, ed. Stratmann, IV.16, p. 409.

41 *Annales*, ed. Lauer, a. 953, p. 136.

42 See especially G. Althoff, 'Vermittler', *Lexikon des Mittelalters* 8: pp. 1555–7; idem, 'Das Privileg der deditio: Formen gütlicher Konfliktbeendigung in der mittelalterlichen Adelsgesellschaft', in his *Spielregeln der Politik im Mittelalter: Kommunikation in Frieden und Fehde* (Darmstadt, 1997), pp. 99–125; idem, 'Satisfaction: peculiarities of the amicable settlement of conflicts in the Middle Ages', in B. Jussen (ed.), *Ordering Medieval Society: Perspectives on Intellectual and Practical Modes of Shaping Social Relations*, trans. P. Selwyn (Philadelphia, 2001), pp. 270–84; G. Koziol, *Begging, Pardon and Favor: Ritual and Political Order in Early Medieval France* (Ithaca, 1992), pp. 70–6; A. Gawlik, 'Zur Bedeutung von Intervention und Petition', in W. Schlögl and P. Herde (eds), *Grundwissenschaften und Geschichte: Festschrift für Peter Acht* (Kallmünz, 1976), pp. 73–7; and the essays in J.-M. Moeglin (ed.), *L'intercession du Moyen Âge à l'époque moderne autour d'une pratique sociale* (Geneva, 2004), especially that by H. Kamp, 'L'intercession dans les relations politiques du Moyen Âge classique', pp. 67–87.

was only rarely used outside a religious context in Francia and England in this period, where it commonly denotes the clergy who interceded with God on behalf of the laity.[43] These political negotiators were instead referred to as seeking, intervening, suggesting, and only rarely interceding. The *intercessores* who presented the excommunicants to the bishop at the gates of the cemetery thus may well have been clergymen, just as in the *PRG*'s rite for the reconciliation of public penitents on Maundy Thursday where the penitent's parish priest was required to present him to the bishop for reconciliation on Maundy Thursday.[44]

The locus of the English rite is also different from that of the Frankish rite; the repentant excommunicants, with their *intercessores*, meet the bishop at the gates of the cemetery and not at the doors of the church, as in the Frankish rite. The Greek word *coemeterium*, and its variant spellings, while used in early medieval texts, seems to have gained much wider currency in the eleventh and twelfth centuries.[45] An active interest in defining cemeteries as sacred spaces can be found in England only from the tenth century. While English legal and archaeological evidence suggests that concern with defining the boundaries of graveyards, placed around church buildings, began in the late ninth and tenth centuries, and the earliest Anglo-Saxon pontificals, dating from the late tenth century onward, include a rite for the consecration of cemeteries which is more elaborate than the earliest surviving example of the rite, recorded in the mid-tenth-century Frankish *PRG*.[46] As the English reconciliation rite required a bounded cemetery, representing a sacred space controlled by the bishop, such evidence suggests it is at least possible that it was composed as late as the tenth or eleventh century.

Further support for such a date comes from the cathedral close of Worcester, the home of the earliest record of the rite. In the central Middle

---

43 Niermeyer, *Lexicon*, I, 719. C. du Fresne, Dominus du Cange, *Glossarium mediae et infirmae Latinitatis*, rev. D. Carpenterius, G. A. L. Henschel and L. Favre (Paris, 1885), IV.1, 389–90; R. E. Latham (ed.), *Revised Medieval Latin Word-list from British and Irish Sources* (London, 1965), p. 255.

44 *PRG*, xcix.229, II. 61; Hamilton, *Practice*, pp. 119–20.

45 Niermeyer, *Lexicon*, I, 215; du Cange, *Glossarium*, II, 388; Latham, *Word-list*, 79. A search of the *Patrologia Latina* database confirms this chronology.

46 H. Gittos, 'Creating the sacred: Anglo-Saxon rites for consecrating cemeteries', in S. Lucy and A. Reynolds (eds), *Burial in Early Medieval England and Wales*, Society for medieval archaeology monograph 17 (London, 2002), pp. 195–208. Gittos argues the Anglo-Saxon rite was independent of that in the *PRG*, while Nicholas Orchard suggests it was dependent on the *PRG* in his edition of *The Sacramentary of Ratoldus* (Paris, Bibliothèque nationale de France, lat. 12052), HBS 116 (London, 2005), p. cxix, especially n. 196.

Ages the part of the cathedral close at Worcester designated the lay cemetery lay to the north between the church and town, and had two gates
offering access from the town into the close.[47] The origins of this part of
the cathedral precinct lie, Julia Barrow has suggested, in the 960s, when
Oswald's rebuilding of the cathedral church(es) led to the establishment,
for the first time, of a firm boundary between secular and ecclesiastical
space within the city.[48] The English rite could easily have been performed
in such a setting, with the bishop meeting the excommunicants, with their
intercessores, at the boundary between the cathedral community's jurisdiction and that of the town. While it is extremely tempting to make a direct
link between this geographical evidence and the text, the area of ecclesiastical jurisdiction which bordered the town was also described, and used, as
a cemetery at other English cathedrals in the central Middle Ages; the
wording of the English rite need not tie it to Worcester.[49]

The record of the rite is, however, very strongly associated with Archbishop Wulfstan I who, we know from his other writings, was anxious to
promote the practice of both public penance and excommunication in
England so as to purify and protect the nation. He had a vision of bishops
as guardians of the state, preaching God's law, forbidding and taking action
against sin.[50] Wulfstan's views about the role of bishops perhaps explain
why he included the English rite for the reconciliation of excommunicants
in his own collection, although it does not confirm that he was its author.
Christopher A. Jones's recent work has shown that Wulfstan was something
of a liturgical magpie, collecting both English and continental rites: while

47   N. Baker and R. Holt, *Urban Growth and the Medieval Church: Gloucester and Worcester*
     (Aldershot, 2004), 308 (map 12.1).
48   J. Barrow, 'The community at Worcester, 961–1100', in N. Brooks and C. Cubitt
     (eds), *St Oswald of Worcester: Life and Influence* (Leicester, 1996), pp. 84–99 at 90. Her
     suggestions also fit into the more recent analysis by Baker and Holt, *Urban growth*,
     pp. 136, 154–6.
49   E.g., Exeter: D. Lepine and N. Orme, *Death and Memory in Medieval Exeter*, Devon
     and Cornwall Record Society, new series 47 (Exeter, 2003), pp. 4, 17–24; for refer-
     ences to the bishop's gate in Exeter see *HMC Report on Manuscripts in Various Collec-
     tions* IV (Dublin, 1907), nos. 283, 287, pp. 49, 56. E.g., Winchester: D. Keene, *Survey
     of Medieval Winchester* (Oxford, 1988), pp. 108, 574, 579–80. I must thank Christo-
     pher Norton for pointing out to me that the cathedral close was often referred to
     as the cemetery in York documents.
50   J. Wilcox, 'The wolf on shepherds: Wulfstan, bishops and the context of the *Sermo
     lupi ad anglos*', in P. E. Szarmach (ed.), *Old English Prose: Basic Readings* (London,
     2000), pp. 395–418; S. Hamilton, 'Remedies for "great transgressions": penance and
     excommunication in late Anglo-Saxon England', in F. Tinti (ed.), *Pastoral Care in
     Late Anglo-Saxon England* (Woodbridge, 2005), pp. 83–105.

those for public penance in *O* owe much to the *PRG*, the text of the chrism mass in the same manuscript is found only in an English context.[51] It is perhaps worth adding here that the absolution prayer, *Absoluimus uos uice beati petri apostolorum* used in *C* and *V* is unique to the English liturgy; a version of it was also used in rites for the reconciliation of public penitents which survive in English manuscripts from the last quarter of the tenth century onward.[52] Wulfstan's own practice, and analysis of the text of the rite itself, thus combine to suggest that Wulfstan probably copied an existing English rite into his collection, although it remains possible that he composed or commissioned this rite.[53]

While the ultimate origins of both the English and Frankish rites remain murky, nevertheless as they now survive they depict two rather different concepts of judgement. The Frankish rite concentrates much more on the authority of the bishop, focusing on the excommunicant's submission to law, his confession and acceptance of his penance, yet the bishop refrains from claiming the powers to absolve in the first person, merely petitioning the Lord to do so. The English rite, however, includes a prayer in which the bishop claims the right to absolve in the first person, but elsewhere

51 See C. A. Jones, 'A liturgical miscellany in Cambridge, Corpus Christi College 190', *Traditio* 54 (1999), pp. 103–40; *idem*, 'Wulfstan's liturgical interests', in M. Townend (ed.), *Wulfstan, Archbishop of York: the Proceedings of the Second Alcuin Conference* (Leiden, 2004), pp. 325–52; *idem*, 'The chrism mass in later Anglo-Saxon England', in Gittos and Bedingfield (eds), *The Liturgy of the Late Anglo-Saxon Church*, pp. 105–42; *idem*, 'Origins of the "Sarum" chrism mass'.

52 A. Nocent, 'La Pénitence dans les ordines locaux transcrits dans le *De Antiquis Ecclesiae Ritibus* d'Edmond Martène', in G. Farnedi (ed.), *Paschale mysterium: Studium in memoria dell'abate Prof. Salvatore Marsili (1910–83)*, Studi Anselmiania 91/Analecta Liturgica 10 (Rome, 1986), pp. 115–38 at 119. S. Hamilton, 'Rites for public penance in later Anglo-Saxon England', in Gittos and Bedingfield (eds), *The Liturgy of the Late Anglo-Saxon Church*, pp. 65–103 at 80 and 93–103; in addition to the specific manuscripts listed there, it also appears in the rite for the reconciliation of penitents on Maundy Thursday *Sacramentary of Ratoldus*, ed. Orchard, no. 851, p. 193. It should be noted, however, that most of these versions of the prayer are shorter, ending at *indultor*; a longer version is found in both Ratoldus and the Canterbury Benedictional (British Library, MS Harley 2892) but it reflects the text in *C* rather than that in *V*.

53 Further support for the resilience of the English rite may be found in an eleventh-century German *PRG* manuscript at Sherbourne, then Salisbury, by s. xi³/⁴ (London, British Library, MS Cotton Tiberius c. i), which includes some of the excommunication formulae (ff. 195v–199r) but ends abruptly as the verso side of the folio on which the text continued was erased to make way for a text of Easter vespers (f. 199v), added in a twelfth-century hand; it seems probable that the original manuscript may have included a rite for reconciliation of excommunicants but that it was not needed at Salisbury.

hints at a rite which relies rather more on collective judgement of the sort depicted by William of Malmesbury in his tale of Wulfstan's judgement at Gloucester.[54] The emphasis in the rite is as much on the *intercessores* promoting his cause before the judges as on the excommunicant's penance. Such a change in emphasis may also explain why the Frankish rite is more (albeit not entirely in the case of the *PRG*) focused on the reconciliation of a single excommunicant, while the English rite's primary focus is on several.[55] This change in focus may, perhaps, point to the relative political fragility of Frankish bishops compared to their English counterparts, but we should also heed Janet Nelson's warning about the dangers of reading a specific political ideology into the normative platitudes of the coronation rites as perhaps having a more general application.[56] The textual history of the reconciliation rites presented here nevertheless reveals a living tradition: bishops invested time and parchment in improving a liturgy which symbolized their supreme authority, as the representative of St Peter, who had the power to bind and to loose.

Tables

Abbreviations used in the tables:

Gelasian   *Liber sacramentorum Romanae aeclesiae ordinis anni circuli: sacramentarium Gelasianum*, ed. L. C. Mohlberg, Rerum ecclesiasticarum documenta series maior fontes 4 (Rome, 1968)

Hadrianum   *Le Sacramentaire grégorien: ses principales formes d'après les plus anciens manuscrits*, ed. J. Deshusses, 4 vols., Spicilegium Friburgense 16, 24, and Subsidia 9, 11 (Fribourg, 1971, 1979, 1982)

PRG   *Le Pontifical romano-germanique du dixième siècle*, ed. C. Vogel and R. Elze, 3 vols., Studi e testi 226, 227, 269 (Vatican City, 1963–1972)

s.xii PR   *Le pontifical romain du XIIe siècle*, ed. M. Andrieu, Studi e testi 86 (Vatican City, 1938)

---

54 On the collective nature of early medieval justice see S. Reynolds, *Kingdoms and Communities in Western Europe 900–1100* (Oxford, 1984), pp. 23–36.

55 The *V* copyist, however, allowed for the possibility that the rite might be administered to a single penitent: see Table 11.1.

56 'The rites of the Conqueror', *Politics and Ritual in Early Medieval Europe* (London, 1986), pp. 375–401, esp. 383.

Table 11.1 The English rite for the reconciliation of excommunicants[a]

C Cambridge, Corpus Christi College, MS 265, pp. 213 (l. 23)–215 (l. 17)	V London, British Library, MS Vespasian D. xv, ff. 57v (l.10)–f. 61r (l. 9)	D Oxford, Bodleian Library, MS Barlow 37, ff. 41r (l.30)–41v (l. 20)
DE HIS QUI POST EXCOMMUNI-CATIONEM CUM LUCTU PENITENTIE AD RECONCILI-ATIONEM UENIUNT	Incipit de his qui post excommunicationem cum luctu paenitentiae ad reconciliationem ueniunt	De his qui post excommunicationem cum luctu penitentie ad reconciliationem ueniit.
Placuit uniuerso senatui ut hi qui excommunicati ad emendationem ueniunt et indulgentie ueniam petu/n\t, accorde conpuncto penitentie subdantur, et cum intercessoribus ad cimiterii portam perueniunt maneant illic discalciati laneisque induti, quousque eorum interuentores promoueant episcopum,	Placuit uniuerso senatui ut hi qui excommunicati ad emendationem ueniunt et indulgentiae ueniam petunt ac corde conpuncto penitentiae subdantur et cum intercessoribus ad portam cymiterii quandoque perueniunt maneant illic dicalciati laneisque induti quosque eorum interuentores promoueant episcopum quocumque	Placuit uniuerso senatui ut hii qui excommunicati ademendationem ueniunt et indulgencie ueniam petunt ac corde compuncto penitencie subduntur et cum intercessoribus ad portam cimiterii perueniunt maneant illic discalciati laneisque induti maneant ibi quosque eorum interuentores promoueant episcopum quocumque modo potuerint. Tardante autem episcopo bis aut ter uel sepius aliquem suos interuentores ad illum mittant flebiliter ueniant rogantes.

225

Table 11.1 *Continued*

C Cambridge, Corpus Christi College, MS 265, pp. 213 (l. 23)–215 (l. 17)	*V* London, British Library, MS Vespasian D. xv, ff. 57v (l.10)– f. 61r (l. 9)	*D* Oxford, Bodleian Library, MS Barlow 37, ff. 41r (l.30)–41v (l. 20)
qu/o\ecumque modo potuerint. Tardante autem episcopo, bis aut ter uel sepius suos interuentores ad illum mittant flebiliter ueniam rogant/es\	modo potuerint. Tardante autem episcopo bis aut ter uel sepius aliquando suos interuentores ad illum mittant flebiliter ueniam rogantes.	
Procedente ad ultimum episcopo ante portam se prosternant et super illos tunc dicat. uii.penitentiae psalmos cum precibus ceteris.	Procedente adultimum episcopo ante portam excommunicati se prosternant et super illos dicat episcopus vii penitentiales psalmos cum his precibus.	Procedente adultimum episcopo ante portam se prosternant et super illos tunc dicat episcopus vii penitentie psalmos cum precibus ceteris.
	Kyrie eleison Christe eleyson Kyrie.	

Table 11.1 *Continued*

C	V	D
Cambridge, Corpus Christi College, MS 265, pp. 213 (l. 23)–215 (l. 17)	London, British Library, MS Vespasian D. xv, ff. 57v (l.10)– f. 61r (l. 9)	Oxford, Bodleian Library, MS Barlow 37, ff. 41r (l.30)–41v (l. 20)
	Pater noster. Et ne nos. Peccauimus[b] cum p(at)ribus nostris. Domine non secundam peccata nostra. Domine ne memineris. Adiuua nos deus. Non nobis domine non nobis. Reminiscere miserationum tuarum domine. Saluum/os\ fac seruum/os\ tuum/os\. Non intres in iudicium cum seruis/o\ tuis/o\ domine.	

Table 11.1 *Continued*

C Cambridge, Corpus Christi College, MS 265, pp. 213 (l. 23)–215 (l. 17)	V London, British Library, MS Vespasian D. xv, ff. 57v (1.10)–f. 61r (l. 9)	D Oxford, Bodleian Library, MS Barlow 37, ff. 41r (1.30)–41v (l. 20)
	Mitte eis domine auxilium. Esto eis domine turris fortitudinem. Exurge. Absolue quaesumus domine tuorum/i\ delicta famulorum/i\ . . . . (Hadrianum no. 702)	
Hac expleta oratione sequantur episcopum ad ostium aecclesiae et singulos illos per manum tunc inducat, psalmum canens, Miserere mei, deus, prosternantur que in pauimento ecclesie.	Completa autem oratione sequantur episcopum ad hostium aecclesiae episcopo incipiente, Cor mundum crea in me deus, et choro praesequente psalmus Miserere mei deus, et ibi accepta disciplina singulas inducat episcopus in aecclesiam psalmus supradictum canens.	Hac expleta oratione sequantur episcopum ad ostium ecclesiae et singulos illos per manum tunc inducat psalmum canens, Miserere mei deus, prosternanturque in pauimento ecclesie.

228

Table 11.1 *Continued*

C Cambridge, Corpus Christi College, MS 265, pp. 213 (l. 23)–215 (l. 17)	*V* London, British Library, MS Vespasian D. xv, ff. 57v (l.10)– f. 61r (l. 9)	*D* Oxford, Bodleian Library, MS Barlow 37, ff. 41r (1.30)–41v (l. 20)
	Tunc prosternantur in pauimento aecclesiae et absoluat eos episcopus dicens.	
Et post hec absoluat eos uice sancti petri apostoli cui dixit dominus 'Quodcumque ligaueris super terram', et reliqua.	Absoluimus uos /te\ uice beati petri apostolorum principis cui dominus potestatem ligandi atque soluendi dedit et quantum ad uos/te\ pertinet accusatio et ad nos remissio sit uobis/ tibi\ deus omnipotens uita et salus et omnium peccatorum uestrorum/ tuorum\ pius indultor. Et qui uobis/tibi\	Et post hec absoluat eos uice sancti petri apostoli cui deus dixit, 'Quodcumque ligau(eris) super ter(ram) et cael(em)'.

229

Table 11.1 *Continued*

C Cambridge, Corpus Christi College, MS 265, pp. 213 (l. 23)–215 (l. 17)	V London, British Library, MS Vespasian D. xv, ff. 57v (1.10)– f. 61r (l. 9)	D Oxford, Bodleian Library, MS Barlow 37, ff. 41r (1.30)–41v (l. 20)
	compunctionem cordis dedit det ueniam omnium delictorum morumque emendationem et in bonis operibus perseuerantiam ut ad uitam perueniatis/at\ sempiternam prestante domino nostro iesu christo qui uiuit. Deus innocentiae restitutor et amator qui non uis mortem peccatoris set . . . [c]	

Table 11.1 *Continued*

C Cambridge, Corpus Christi College, MS 265, pp. 213 (l. 23)–215 (l. 17)	V London, British Library, MS Vespasian D. xv, ff. 57v (l.10)– f. 61r (l. 9)	D Oxford, Bodleian Library, MS Barlow 37, ff. 41r (l.30)–41v (l. 20)
His ita peractis progrediantur exterius et induant se uestimentis suis optimis et reuertentes ad episcopum pete/a\nt benedictionem dataque benedictione panem quoque accipiant benedictum edentes coram episcopo uel cum episcopo more penitentis filii substantia luxuriose deuorata, cui adgaudebat pater eius dicens Adducite uitulum saginatum et occidite et manducemus et epulemus, quia filius meus mortuus fuerat et reuixit.	His per actis egrediantur et induant se uestimentis suis et reuertentes ad episcopum petant benedictionem dataque benedictione panem quoque benedictum ab eo accipiant edentes coram episcopo uel cum eo more poenitentis filii substantia luxuriose deuorata cui ad gaudebat pater eius dicens: Adducite uitulum saginatum et occidete et manducemus et epulemus.	His peractis progrediantur exterius et induant se uestimentis suis optimis et reuertentes ad episcopum petant benedictionem panem quoque accipiant benedictum edentes coram episcopo uel cum episcopo more penitentis filii substantia luxuriose deuorata cui ad gaudebat pater eius dicens: Adducite uitulum saginatum et occidite et man(ducemus) et epu(lemus), quia filius meus mor(tuus) fu(erat) et re(uixit).

231

Table 11.1 *Continued*

C	V	D
Cambridge, Corpus Christi College, MS 265, pp. 213 (l. 23)–215 (l. 17)	London, British Library, MS Vespasian D. xv, ff. 57v (1.10)–f. 61r (1. 9)	Oxford, Bodleian Library, MS Barlow 37, ff. 41r (1.30)–41v (1. 20)
Hisque peractis incipiat cantor ANTIPHONAM: Dedit pater penitenti filio stolam primam pariter et anulum [manui] et calciamenta illi tribuens celebrauit magnum conuiuium. Habemus stolam primam in lauacrum et anulum fidei signaculum.	Quibus peractis incipit cantor An(tiphon): Dedit pater poenitenti. Gloria patri. Kyri eleison. Pater noster. Saluos fac et reliqua.	Hisque peractis incipiat cantor. Dedit pater penitenti filio. Gloria patri. Kiri eleison. Pater noster. Saluos fac. Et Israel.

Table 11.1 *Continued*

C Cambridge, Corpus Christi College, MS 265, pp. 213 (l. 23)–215 (l. 17)	*V* London, British Library, MS Vespasian D. xv, ff. 57v (l.10)–f. 61r (l. 9)	*D* Oxford, Bodleian Library, MS Barlow 37, ff. 41r (1.30)–41v (l. 20)
Hacque finita dicat presul: Saluum/os\ fac seruum/os\ tuum/os\ Mitte ei/os\ domine. Esto ei/os\ domine. D(ominu)s uobiscum. Et cum spiritu tuo. ABSOLUTIO PENITENTIUM. Absoluimus uos/te\ uice beati Petri, apostolorum principis, cui dominus potestatem ligandi atque soluendi dedit et quantum		

233

Table 11.1 *Continued*

C Cambridge, Corpus Christi College, MS 265, pp. 213 (l. 23)–215 (l. 17)	V London, British Library, MS Vespasian D. xv, ff. 57v (l.10)– f. 61r (l. 9)	D Oxford, Bodleian Library, MS Barlow 37, ff. 41r (l.30)–41v (l. 20)
ad uos/te\ pertinet accusatio et ad nos remissio sit deus omnipotens uobis/tibi\ uita et salus et omnibus peccatis uestris/tuis\ indultor /o\ Et qui uobis/tibi\ compunctionem cordis dedit det ueniam peccatorum, longeuamque uobis/tibi\ atque felicem uitam in hoc seculo		

234

Table 11.1 *Continued*

C	V	D
Cambridge, Corpus Christi College, MS 265, pp. 213 (l. 23)–215 (l. 17)	London, British Library, MS Vespasian D. xv, ff. 57v (l.10)– f. 61r (l. 9)	Oxford, Bodleian Library, MS Barlow 37, ff. 41r (l.30)–41v (l. 20)
largiatur et in futuro cum Christo et omnibus sanctis eius sine fine manentem per eundem saluatorem nostrum qui uiuit et regnat in saecula, Amen.		
Hisque peractis unusquisque redeat ad propria.	Et his ita gestis accepta benedictione episcopali reuertantur ad propria.	Et his ita rite gestis accepta benedictione episcopale disiungant se singuli remeantes cum pace ad propria.

a While all three rites have been edited by Hans Sauer and Henry Wilson (see nn. 4 and 11 above), I have checked their transcriptions against the manuscripts and amended them where necessary; the punctuation is also mine.

b 'D(omi)ne' is added in the margin in front of this line.

c A longer version of this prayer appears in the penitents' reconciliation rite in various late Anglo-Saxon service books: Hamilton, 'Rites for public penance', 100.

235

Table 11.2[a] The Frankish rite for the reconciliation of excommunicants

Regino, *Libri duo*, II, 418	Romano-German Pontifical XCI	Burchard of Worms, *Decretum*, XI, 8
Qualiter episcopus reconciliet vel recipiat excommunicatum.	Qualiter episcopus reconciliet vel recipiat excommunicatum.	Reconciliatio excommunicati.
Cum aliquis excommunicatus uel anathematizatus poenitentia ductus veniam postulat et emendationem promittit, episcopus, qui eum excommunicavit, ante ianuas ecclesiae venire debet, et XII presbyteri cum eo, qui eum hinc inde circumstare debent, ubi etiam adesse debent illi, quibus iniuria vel damnum illatum est, et ibi secundum leges divinas et humanas oportet damnum commissum emendari, aut, si iam emendatum est, eorum testimonio comprobari.	Cum aliquis excommunicatus vel anathematizatus, penitentia ductus, veniam postulat, et emendationem promittit, episcopus, qui eum excommunicavit, ante ianuas aecclesiae venire debet et XII presbiteri cum eo, qui eum hinc inde circumdare debent; ubi etiam adesse debent illi quibus iniuria vel damnum illatum est et ibi, secundum leges divinas et humanas, oportet damnum commissum emendari aut, si iam emendatum est, comprobari.	Cum aliquis excommunicatus, vel anathematizatus, poenitentia ductus veniam postulat, et emendationem promittit, episcopus qui eum excommunicavit, ante ianuas ecclesiae venire debet, et duodecim presbyteri cum eo, qui eum hinc inde circumstare debent. Ubi etiam adesse debent illi quibus iniuria vel damnum illatum est, et ibi secundum leges divinas oportet damnum commissum emendari, aut si iam emendatum est, eorum testimonio comprobari.
Deinde interroget episcopus, si poenitentiam, iuxta quod canones praecipiunt, pro perpetratis sceleribus suscipere velit, et si ille, terrae prostratus, veniam postulat, culpam confitetur, poenitentiam implorat, de futuris cautelam spondet, tunc episcopus, apprehensa manu eius dextra, eum in ecclesiam introducat, et ei communionem et societatem Christianam reddat.	Deinde interroget episcopus si penitentiam iuxta quod canones praecipiunt pro perpetratis sceleribus suscipere velit. Et, si ille in terram prostratus veniam postulat, culpam confitetur, paenitentiam implorat, de futuris cautelam spondet, tunc episcopus, apprehensa manu eius dextra, eum in aecclesiam introducat et ei communionem et societatem christianam reddat.	Deinde interroget episcopus, si poenitentiam juxta quod canones praecipiunt pro perpetratis sceleribus suscipere velit. Et si ille terrae prostratus veniam postulat, culpam confitetur poenitentiam implorat, de futuris cautelam spondet, tunc episcopus, septem psalmos decantet, cum istis precibus.

236

Table 11.2[a] *Continued*

Regino, *Libri duo*, II, 418	Romano-German Pontifical XCI	Burchard of Worms, *Decretum*, XI, 8
		Kirie eleison. Pater noster. Salvum fac servum tuum, Deus meus, sperantem in te. Mitte ei, domine, auxilium de sancto, Et de Sion tuere eum. Nihil proficiet inimicus in eo, Et filius iniquitatis non etc Esto ei, domine, turris fortitudinis, A facie inimici. Domine exaudi orationem meam, Et clamor meus ad te veniat. Dominus vobiscum, Et cum spiritu tuo. Oratio. Oremus. Praesta quaesumus, domine. . . . (Gelasian no. 357; *PRG* XCIX no. 235) Item alia. Maiestatem tuam quaesumus, domine, sancte pater . . . .(Gelasian no. 366; *PRG* XCIX no. 240))

237

Table 11.2ᵃ *Continued*

Regino, *Libri duo*, II, 418	Romano-German Pontifical XCI	Burchard of Worms, *Decretum*, XI, 8
		Tunc episcopus, apprehensa manu eius dextera, in ecclesiam eum introducat, et ei communionem et societatem Christianam reddat, et hanc orationem dicat: Deus misericors, deus clemens, qui secundum multitudinem miserationum tuarum. . . . (similar beginning to *PRG* XCIX.239; combination of Gelasian, nos. 364, 367)
Post haec secundum modum culpae poenitentiam ei iniungat, et literas per parochiam dirigat, ut omnes noverint, eum in societate Christiana receptum. Aliis etiam episcopis hoc notum faciat. Nullus autem episcopus alterius parrochianum excommunicare vel reconciliare praesumat, sine conscientia vel consensu proprii episcopi.	Post hoc secundum modum culpae poenitentiam ei iniungat et literas per parochiam dirigat, ut omnes noverint eum in societate christiana receptum. Aliis etiam episcopis hoc notum faciat. Nullus autem episcopus alterius parrochianum excommunicare vel reconciliare presumat sine conscientia vel consensu proprii episcopi.	Post haec secundum modum culpae poenitentiam ei iniungat, et litteras per parochiam dirigat, ut omnes noverint eum in societate Christiana receptum. Aliis etiam episcopis hoc notum faciat. Nullus autem episcopus alterius parochianum excommunicare vel reconciliare praesumat, sine conscientia vel consensu proprii episcopi.

Table 11.2ᵃ *Continued*

Regino, *Libri duo*, II, 418	Romano-German Pontifical XCI	Burchard of Worms, *Decretum*, XI, 8
	Absolutio excommunicatorum	
	Primitus dicat episcopus hos psalmos:	
	Domine ne in furore tuo II. totum. (Ps. 37)	
	Miserere mei Deus, usque, omnes iniquitates meas dele. (Ps 50, 1–11)	
	Deus in nomine tuo salvum. (Ps 53)	
	Benedic anima mea domino, usque, renovabitur ut aquilae iuventus tua. (Ps 102)	
	Sequitur Pater noster qui es in caelis.	
	Oratio. Preces.	
	Ego dixi: Domine miserere mei.	
	Exaudi me, domine, quoniam benigna est misericordia tua.	
	Salvum fac servum tuum, domine. (*PRG* XCIX.229)	
	Convertere, domine, usquequo.	
	Illustra, faciem tuam super servum tuum. (*PRG* XCIX.229)	
	Exaudiat te dominus in die tribulationis.	
	Mittat tibi domini auxilium de sancto. (*PRG* XCIX. 229)	
	Tribuat tibi dominus secundum cor tuum.	

Table 11.2ª *Continued*

Regino, *Libri duo*, II, 418	Romano-German Pontifical XCI	Burchard of Worms, *Decretum*, XI, 8
	Dominus custodiat introitum et exitum tuum.	
	Domine exaudi orationem. (*PRG* XCIX.229)	
	Ad te levavi oculos meos.	
	Sequitur oratio. Maiestatem tuam. (Only the incipit is given; possibly Gelasian nos 365 or 366; *PRG* XCIX.240?)	
	Deus inmensae clementiae et inestimabilis indulgentiae qui humanae fragilitatis lapsum . . .	
	Praesta, quaesumus, domine, huic famulo N. dignum paenitentiae fructum . . . (Gelasian no. 357; *PRG* XCIX.235)	
	Deus, qui peccantium animas . . . (Hadrianum no. 861)	
	Deus cui proprium . . . (Hadrianum no. 851)	
	Omnipotens sempiterne Deus, misericordiam tuam . . . (Hadrianum no. 720)	

Table 11.2[a] *Continued*

Regino, *Libri duo*, II, 418	Romano-German Pontifical XCI	Burchard of Worms, *Decretum*, XI, 8
	Omnipotens sempiterne Deus, humani generis benignissime conditor. . . . (Gelasian no. 358)	
	Absolutio pluralis.	
	Fratres ill. absolutionem et remissionem peccatorum vestrorum, per invocationem sacrati nominis Dei et per ministerium nostrum, percipere mereamini hic et in aeternum. Et. R. Amen. (s. xii PR, XXX A.25)	
	Deinde sequentur benedictiones.	
	Benedic, domine, hos penitentes . . .	
	Prostratos alleva . . .	
	Dele ab eis omnem peccati maculam. . . .	
	Quod ipise praestare	
	His aspergat eos aqua benedicta, addens odorem incensi.	
	Et postea dicat: Exurge qui dormis, exurge a mortuis et illuminabit te Christus.	
	(*PRG* XCIX.251)	

a The text is based on that in the editions mentioned in nn. 20, 26 and 27 above.

12

Fontenoy and after: pursuing enemies to death in France between the ninth and eleventh centuries[1]

John Gillingham

I N THIS ESSAY I shall consider the moral choices made by men at war when they decided either to kill their enemies or to spare them. I am less concerned with theoretical discussions of the sinfulness or otherwise of homicide in war as evidenced, for example, in Hrabanus Maurus (see below, pp. 254–5), and much more with questioning the narrative sources in an effort to discover what men actually did – or at least were said to have done. My focus will be on battles rather than sieges, partly for reasons of space, but partly also because sieges provided opportunities for negotiation, whereas battles occurred when negotiations had broken down. Thus although battles, in this period as in others, were rare events even during phases of almost constant warfare, it was probably during or immediately after battle that warriors were most likely to kill. In most studies of warfare in this period, campaigns against external enemies – Vikings, Magyars and Muslims – are prominent, entirely rightly given how prominent they are in the primary sources. But in this paper I am concerned only with the battles of the Carolingian civil wars and of subsequent struggles between Frankish/French princes – that is, between enemies who unquestionably shared a common culture.[2] The reason for leaving battles against external enemies out of consideration here is that I wish to focus on the problem of 'chivalry', using that word to mean a code of conduct that encouraged high-status warriors to avoid killing each other. The status-specific aspect of this warrior's code makes me prefer to call it 'chivalry'

---

1 For their help and advice I am much indebted to Paul Fouracre and Matthew Strickland.
2 Hence not with wars against Moravians and Danes, nor, until the later tenth century, those involving Normans and Bretons, even though it can be argued that 'to a surprising extent' they and the Franks 'shared a common political culture', T. Reuter, 'Plunder and tribute in the Carolingian empire', *TRHS* 5th series 35 (1985), pp. 75–94, at p. 91. A recent book of essays has advocated the use of the terms 'intracultural' and 'transcultural' wars: see in particular S. Morillo, 'A general typology of transcultural wars – the early Middle Ages and beyond', in H-H. Kortüm (ed.), *Transcultural Wars from the Middle Ages to the 21st Century* (Berlin, 2006), pp. 29–42.

rather than 'humanity' or 'forbearance', but whatever we choose to call it, for combatants it could be a matter of life or death.[3] Matthew Strickland, for example, writes:

> While by the eleventh or twelfth century, a knight could surrender to a fellow knight with a reasonable expectation that his life would be spared for ransom, the choice in earlier centuries for vanquished warriors was a stark one between flight or almost certain death.[4]

Most historians, including early medievalists, share the perception that in this sense warfare in the ninth and tenth centuries was less chivalrous than it became later.[5] Since in the 'age of chivalry' the reasonable expectation that a knight's life would be spared for ransom applied much more in intracultural than in transcultural wars, it follows that when considering earlier centuries we should focus on intracultual wars, with the consequence that we set aside precisely those wars which dominate the image of the period, wars between Franks and their external enemies.[6] If we do this, does the warfare of the period emerge less bloody than commonly believed? Have we fallen all too easily for the poetry of the (probably ninth-century) *Waltharius*, the 'Rhineland Chainsaw Massacre'?[7] Or was Richer of Reims

3   D. Crouch, *The Birth of the Nobility* (London, 2005), pp. 63–6 opts for 'forbearance'. For the point that '*la chevalerie*' encompassed '*la prouesse et le spectacle*' as well as restraint see D. Barthélemy, 'Les Origines de la chevalerie' (forthcoming). The term can, of course, be used very differently to denote elite violence 'ecclesiastically validated, consecrated in the service of God', as in J. L. Nelson, 'Carolingian violence and the ritualization of ninth-century warfare', in G. Halsall (ed.), *Violence and Society in the Early Medieval West* (Woodbridge, 1998), pp. 90–107, at 104.

4   M. Strickland, 'Killing or clemency? Ransom, chivalry and changing attitudes to defeated opponents in Britain and Northern France, 7th–12th centuries', in H-H. Kortüm (ed.), *Krieg im Mittelalter* (Berlin, 2001), pp. 93–122, 106. For a depiction of Count William of Auvergne rejecting Count Hugh's attempted surrender, preferring instead to run him through with a lance, see Abbon, *Le Siège de Paris par les Normands*, ed. H. Waquet (Paris, 1942), p. 108. I owe this reference to an episode in the early 890s to the kindness of Rachel Stone.

5   'It would be quite wrong to think of fighting in this period as a particularly chivalrous or magnanimous pursuit', K. Leyser, 'Early medieval warfare', in his *Communications and Power in Medieval Europe: The Carolingian and Ottonian Centuries*, ed. T. Reuter (London, 1994), pp. 20–50, at 41. See below, p. 247 for Guy Halsall's views.

6   When Michael Howard asserted that the twentieth century witnessed 'total war of a kind that had been barely seen in Europe since the Dark Ages', I imagine it was primarily transcultural wars that he had in mind. M. Howard, 'Constraints on warfare' in. M. Howard, G. J. Andreopoulos and M. R. Shulman (eds), *The Laws of War: Constraints on Warfare in the Western World* (New Haven and London, 1994), pp. 3, 8.

7   Discussed in J. L. Nelson, 'England and the Continent in the ninth century: IV, Bodies and Minds', *TRHS* 6th series 15 (2005), pp. 1–27, at 14–18, esp. n. 58 on the assumption of a cultural divide between the earlier Middle Ages and the twelfth century.

right when, in the late tenth century, he asserted that his countrymen were all too easily roused to engage in pitiless slaughter?[8] Given that, in Karl Leyser's words, 'war was a primary and perennial preoccupation of Carolingian and post-Carolingian society from the eighth to the early eleventh century', the absence from volumes two and three of the *New Cambridge Medieval History* of any discussion of warfare and of the codes of honour it may have entailed, is a matter of great regret.[9] My impression is that historians of early medieval politics have spent so much time and effort in trying to understand the negotiations and rituals by which armed conflict was avoided, that they have only rarely looked in as much detail as the – admittedly very meagre – sources allow at what happened when negotiations failed. Battles have been left to the specialist military histori-ans – who, by and large, have not been interested in the questions addressed in this paper. Hence it is at least possible, to put it no more strongly, that the bloodiness of early medieval intracultural conflicts has been exaggerated.

Within the broad category of intracultural wars a distinction potentially relevant here is that between a rebellion against a king and a war between 'regional magnates'. Taking up arms against someone whose followers regarded him as a king made a man vulnerable to a charge of *lèse-majesté*, and theoretically therefore more likely to die than in armed conflict between magnates of similar status.[10] But in the twelfth and thirteenth centuries – in stark contrast to circumstances in later centuries – the lives of knights tended to be spared whether they were engaged in rebellions or in other types of war. Hence I shall consider both types here. For the purposes of this discussion I define battle extremely loosely to mean little more than an engagement that has attracted the notice of one or more chroniclers, in particular, of course, when they had something to say about

8 *Omnium ergo Galliarum populi innata audatia plurimum efferuntur, calumniarum impa-tientes. Si incitantur cedibus exultant efferatique inclementius adoriuntur.* Richer, *Histoire de France*, ed. and trans. R. Latouche (Paris, 1930), p. 8.

9 Leyser, 'Early medieval warfare', p. 29. As noted by John France, 'Recent writing on medieval warfare: from the fall of Rome to *c.*1300', *Journal of Military History* 65 (2001), pp. 441–73, at 441.

10 According to Richer, because the defenders of Verdun in 985 were guilty of *lèse-majesté*, they feared for their lives. Nonetheless, and although King Lothar himself had been wounded in the attack, they were granted terms and made prisoner *sine aliqua ultionis injuria*. Six years later men who fought for Odo of Blois against King Hugh (Capet) at Melun were found not guilty of *lèse-majesté* on the grounds that they had been loyal to their lord. The man who betrayed Melun to Odo was hanged, as was his wife, in her case upside down and naked, Richer, *Histoire*, ii. pp. 138, 272–4 (III, c. 107, IV c. 78).

the fate of the losers. By this criterion I have taken account of twenty-eight engagements that took place in Gaul (West Francia) and the Rhineland between 841 and 1068, a few so obscure that they can be neither precisely dated nor located. The changing political structure is no doubt reflected in the fact that whereas kings took part in seven out of the thirteen battles that I have counted in the first half of this period, up to 955, they were directly involved in only two out of fifteen in the second half (in 994 and 1047).

The battle of Fontenoy (25 June 841, near Auxerre), about which Janet Nelson has written often and always illuminatingly, is by far the most famous of these battles, and by far the best recorded. Two of the combatants, Nithard and Angelbert, fighting on opposing sides, wrote about it, one in a remarkable prose history, the other in a remarkable poem. It figures not only in contemporary and near-contemporary accounts by the annalists of St Bertin, Fulda and Xanten, but also in two histories composed south of the Alps by Andreas of Bergamo and Agnellus of Ravenna. It attracted so much notice partly because much was at stake in a battle in which the brother kings, Louis the German and Charles the Bald, fought against their elder brother, the emperor Lothar, and their nephew, Pippin II of Aquitaine. Partly also because by common consent it was the bloodiest of battles, and in consequence came to be seen as a turning point in Frankish history. According to Agnellus of Ravenna, more than 40,000 fell on Lothar's and Pippin's side alone.[11] Andrew of Bergamo took the view that the heavy casualties among the Aquitanian nobility meant that in his day (i.e., c.860) the duchy was still vulnerable to the Northmen.[12] The dimensions of the disaster grew with time. Wace was reflecting widespread eleventh- and twelfth-century opinion when he wrote that 'the flower of France

---

11 Agnellus of Ravenna, *Liber Pontificalis Ecclesie Ravennatis*, ed. G. Waitz, *MGH SRL* (Hanover, 1878), p. 390. Cf. the dating clause of a Breton deed in name of Nominoe, *Factum est . . . vii kal. Febr. in illo anno quando pugnavit Hlotarius cum fratribus suis et ceciderunt multa milia in illo certamine. Cartulaire de Redon*, ed. A. de Courson, p. 359.

12 *Andreae Bergomatis Historia*, ed. G. Watiz, *MGH SRL* (Hanover, 1878), p. 226. The absence of any ninth-century Aquitanian narrative may explain why, as Janet Nelson noted, 'we cannot identify a single casualty for certain'. Nelson, 'Carolingian violence', p. 100. Nearly 200 years later Ademar of Chabannes named Pippin's brothers-in-law as casualties, *Ademari Cabannensis Chronicon*, ed. P. Bourgain, R. Landes and G. Pon (Turnhout, 1999), p. 134, but this may have been no more than his plausible guess. For his methods, J. Gillingham, 'Ademar of Chabannes and the history of Aquitaine in the reign of Charles the Bald', in M. Gibson and J. Nelson (eds), *Charles the Bald: Court and Kingdom* (Aldershot, 1990), pp. 41–51.

perished' in this battle, and that the loss of more than a hundred thousand fighting men opened the way for pagans to conquer the land.[13]

In the early 840s there were two other battles, both much less well recorded and less well remembered. The first was fought near Nördlingen on 13 May 841 when Louis the German slew Adalbert of Metz and an 'uncountable number of men'.[14] The second occurred on 14 June 844 somewhere in the Angoumois, when an army hurrying to reinforce Charles the Bald outside Toulouse was surprised and rapidly overwhelmed by troops loyal to Pippin II. Among the 'great many' fatalities that day were Counts Eckhard and Hrabanus as well as Charlemagne's son, Abbot Hugh of St Quentin, and two of his grandsons, Abbot Richbod of St Riquier and the historian Nithard.[15] These three battles of Christian Frank against Christian Frank must have been shocking. After several generations during which the Franks had become accustomed to seeing war as something that was fought against external enemies and which brought success, plunder and tribute, they now had to confront another of war's faces. According to Hincmar of Rheims, writing in the 870s, the Franks had seen nothing like Fontenoy since the battle of Vinchy in 717.[16] The evidence that what Janet Nelson has called 'the trauma of Fontenoy' aroused exceptionally painful feelings of guilt is strong. But was the result merely that churchmen hastened to construct rituals in order 'to make sense of, and legitimize, war, not against pagan outsiders, but of Christian Franks against Christian Franks'?[17] Or did it mean that from then on the combatants in intracultural wars tried harder to avoid killing each other?

If we are to believe Odo of Cluny, writing c.920, then there was at least one band of fighting men who very successfully avoided shedding blood. These were the followers of Gerald of Aurillac, who obeyed their commander's orders to use only the flat of their swords and the butts of

---

13 Wace, *The Roman de Rou*, trans. G. S. Burgess (St Helier, 2002), Appendix, lines 313–18.

14 *The Annals of Fulda*, trans. T. Reuter (Manchester, 1992), p. 19. This battle rates one sentence in the *Annals of St Bertin* and eight words in Nithard, though the latter had earlier noted that Adalbert had a mortal hatred for Louis: Nithard, *Histoire des fils de Louis le Pieux*, ed. Ph. Lauer (Paris, 1926), pp. 58, 66.

15 *The Annals of St Bertin*, trans. Janet L. Nelson (Manchester, 1991), pp. 58–9; *Annals of Fulda*, p. 22; Janet L. Nelson, *Charles the Bald* (London, 1992), pp. 6, 141.

16 Hincmar, *Instructio ad Ludovicum Balbum*, PL 125, cols. 985–6. If Cannstadt against the Alemans in 747 can be regarded as a civil-war battle, then Hincmar had overlooked what was evidently a very bloody affair. On the Alemans and the battle see P. Fouracre, *The Age of Charles Martel* (London, 2000), pp. 100–1, 105–7, 169. But since that was almost a hundred years before Fontenoy, the point would still hold.

17 Nelson, 'Carolingian violence', pp. 101, 103–4.

their spears.[18] Recent scholars have felt this was ridiculous, using phrases such 'a whiff of the absurd' and 'bizarre'.[19] All of this offends against common sense – especially perhaps against the common sense of historians of the early Middle Ages. After all, this was surely a way to lose battles – hence the Fulda annalist's report on Charles the Bald's defeat at Andernach in 876: it was as though his men had been fighting with blunted weapons.[20] Guy Halsall's study of warfare in the period 450–900, for example, offers an extremely vivid description of the 'final demise of an early medieval army', the 'hideous screams, pleas for mercy, crushed skulls, hacked limbs, ripped bodies and faces, gallons of blood and spilt brains and intestines', while explaining that this was 'not the result of innate blood lust', but rather the 'pent-up release of emotion' and 'the desire to make sure that a threat, once removed, is removed for good'. He points out, surely rightly, that when emotions were so whipped up, 'it would not have been easy to take prisoners' and hence that the attempt to 'surrender immediately after close fighting was a risky business'.[21] Historians tend to take it for granted that in battles people get killed. So they do, of course, but it is important to remember that it was commonly during the pursuit, the final phase of many but not all battles, that casualties were heaviest.[22] That this is what happened at Fontenoy is stated by the author of the Annals of St. Bertin (at this point probably Prudentius): 'there was a general slaughter of those fleeing (*palantium caedes passim agitabatur*)'.[23] The Fulda

18   *suis imperiosa voce praecepit, mucronibus gladiorum retroactis, hastas inantea dirigentes pugnarent, Vita S. Geraldi* I, c. 8, *PL* 133, col. 646.

19   S. Airlie, 'The anxiety of sanctity: St Gerald of Aurillac and his maker', *Journal of Ecclesiastical History* 43 (1992), pp. 372–95, 376, 387; J. Nelson, 'Monks, secular men and masculinity c.900', in D. M. Hadley (ed.), *Masculinity in Medieval Europe* (Harlow, 1999), pp. 121–42, esp. 126.

20   *Annals of Fulda*, pp. 81–2.

21   G. Halsall, *Warfare and Society in the Barbarian West 450–900* (London, 2003), p. 211. In support of this he cites incidents drawn from the First and Second World Wars as described in J. Keegan, *The Face of Battle* (London, 1976), pp. 47–9. Such parallels may be less applicable to periods when officers wore body armour and especially to periods when the practice of ransom meant that many high-status prisoners were worth more alive than dead.

22   That casualties were very high at Val-ès-Dunes (1048) is clear from the account by William of Jumièges, *The 'Gesta Normannorum ducum' of William of Jumièges, Orderic Vitalis and Robert of Torigni* (Oxford, 1992–5), vol. 2, pp. 120–2. When this was adapted by the former soldier William of Poitiers, he focused almost exclusively on the flight and pursuit, *The Gesta Guillelmi of William of Poitiers*, ed. R. H. C. Davis and M. Chibnall (Oxford, 1998), p. 10.

23   *Annales Bertiniani*, ed. F. Grat, J. Vielliard and S. Clémencet (Paris, 1965), p. 38; *Annals of St Bertin*, p. 50.

annalist made a similar point about the battle between Louis 'the Younger' and Charles the Bald at Andernach in 876. When Charles's army fled, 'Louis pursued them and dealt out considerable slaughter.'[24]

But although it was far from easy to take prisoners while a battle still hung in the balance, it was a good deal easier during the pursuit. The Fulda annalist's next sentence runs: 'Louis also took alive many of Charles's leading men, whom in his humanity (*propter suam humanitatem*) he ordered to be spared unharmed'. Hincmar's account of Andernach is almost entirely taken up with a description of the chaotic flight of Charles's troops, ending with 'and those whom their pursuers did not want to kill (*quos insequentes occidere noluerunt*) fled naked away'.[25] The narratives of later battles similarly indicate that it was during the pursuit that the victors could choose whether or not to kill. This is clearly implied by Richer's re-working of Flodoard's account of Helouin's defeat of a *chevauchée* by the men of Count Arnulf of Flanders in 939. 'Banners were unfurled and a fierce engagement ensued. Almost all the robbers were killed with the exception of those who fled from the violence of the struggle. Yet even these were hunted down by Helouin and pitilessly (*atrociter*) massacred.'[26] Thus when Orderic Vitalis famously noted how few of the knights engaged in the battle of Brémule (1119) were killed – only three, he said, out of about 900 – he focused on the pursuit: the victors, he wrote, were more concerned to capture than to kill the fugitives (*nec tantum occidere fugientes quam comprehendere satagebant*).[27] Flodoard's laconic account of an encounter between King Lothar and Duke William of Aquitaine in 955 tells essentially the same story. 'William turned in flight. The king's troops pursued, they killed many Aquitanians, and captured alive some of the nobler ones. William just managed to escape with a few of his men.'[28] Other battles too were little more than pursuits. When Pippin II ambushed the army marching to reinforce Charles in 844, 'in a short time and without casualties among his own men, he scattered it so completely that once the leaders had been killed, the rest who had

24 *Annals of Fulda*, p. 81.
25 *Annales Bertiniani*, p. 209; *Annals of St Bertin*, p. 197.
26 *Annales de Flodoard*, ed. Ph. Lauer (Paris, 1906), p. 74; Richer, *Histoire* II, c. 15. On Richer as a source for military matters, J. France, 'La Guerre dans la France féodale à la fin du IXe et au Xe siècle', *Revue Belge d'Histoire Militaire* 23 (1979), pp. 177–98, 179, 192–3.
27 *The Ecclesiastical History of Orderic Vitalis*, ed. M. Chibnall, 6 vols. (Oxford, 1969–80), vol. 6, p. 240.
28 *Annales de Flodoard*, 141. Richer, *Histoire* III, c. 4 (interestingly reversing Flodoard's ratio of those killed to captured).

started to flee even before battle was joined, with the exception of a very few who got away, were either taken prisoner or allowed to return home'. Among those taken prisoner were two bishops, Ebroin of Poitiers and Ragenar of Amiens, Abbot Lupus of Ferrières, two named counts, and four others nameworthy including the two sons of Count Eckhard, as well as 'a fair number of other nobles'.[29] This was an impressive haul.

The question then arises: if you tried to take alive men who struggled to escape, then how did you go about it? According to the twelfth-century *Gesta consulum Andegavensium*, at Pontlevoy (1016) Fulk Nerra's victorious Angevins, after slaughtering the foot on the field of battle, pursued the fugitives for as far as they could or dared, knocking down (*prosternentes*) all the *equites* whom they were able to reach. At the battle of Nouy (1044) the pursuers, with Geoffrey Martel himself at their head, powerfully knocking down those fleeing (*fortissime et fugante fugientes et prosternente*), caught knights, foot and horses, sparing many of them alive, killing a few.[30] Of course, it would be naïve to read these later accounts as though they were repositories of facts about long-ago battles. Nonetheless they may tell us something about a neglected subject, the management of a success-ful pursuit, and not just in the twelfth century.[31] According to the Fulda annalist's account of a campaign against the Moravians in 872, some Thuringian and Saxon counts who were trying to flee were allegedly clubbed to the ground by women.[32] Did fighting men choose to turn their weapons into clubs, using flat of sword and butt of spear? Perhaps the orders given *imperiosa voce* by Odo's Count Gerald were not quite so absurd after all. Much would depend upon the stage of a conflict at which they were given. According to Odo, both Gerald's enemies and his followers would have found the order ridiculous and entirely inappropri-ate, had Gerald and his men not discovered by experience that 'by fighting

29 *Annals of St Bertin*, pp. 58–9.
30 *Gesta consulum Andegavensium*, in *Chroniques des comtes d'Anjou*, eds L. Halphen and R. Poupardin (Paris 1913), pp. 52–3, 57–8. On Pontlevoy see B. S. Bachrach, *Fulk Nerra* (Berkeley, 1993), pp. 149–50. Cf. Jordan Fantosme's narrative of the attack on the defeated Flemings at the battle of Fornham in 1173: 'the knights in armour busied themselves with nothing more than knocking them down', *Jordan Fantosme's Chronicle*, ed. and trans. R. C. Johnston (Oxford, 1981), lines 1082–3.
31 Military historians generally speaking – as they do – tend to be interested in pursuits only when they affect the outcome of a battle, i.e. when they go wrong. But for dis-cussion of twelfth-century pursuits see M. Strickland, *War and Chivalry: The Conduct and Perception of War in England and Normandy, 1066–1217* (Cambridge, 1996), pp. 166–8.
32 *Annals of Fulda*, pp. 67–8.

in this new way' (*novo praeliandi genere*) they were always victorious.[33] Perhaps it was that when they fought in this way, they already were victorious.

One of the intriguing aspects of the contemporary and near-contemporary reports of Fontenoy is what none of them says: not one of them mentions any combatants being taken prisoner. The only person known to have been taken alive was Archbishop George of Ravenna. According to Prudentius, he had been sent by Pope Gregory to Lothar and his brothers to arrange a peace, but had been detained by Lothar and not allowed to go on to Louis and Charles. Although Agnellus of Ravenna took a far more cynical view of George's mission, it is plain that it was not as a fighting man that he was in Lothar's camp when captured.[34] This silence on the subject of captives is unusual. Most accounts of most ninth-, tenth- and eleventh-century battles contain references to men being captured as well as to men being killed. Apart from Fontenoy, the only battles about which we have more than a single sentence, in which there is no extant contemporary or near contemporary record of prisoners taken are Soissons (923), Bar (1037) and Val-ès-Dunes (1048).[35] About Soissons, the only contemporary source, Flodoard, explained that the victors decided not to pursue Charles and the Lotharingians because their own leader, King Robert, had been killed in the battle.[36] About the battle of Bar, little is known (to me at least), apart from the names of the leading nobles, headed by Odo II of Blois, killed there, so the 'fact' that no prisoners were taken may be more

---

33 *Ridiculum hoc hostibus foret nisi . . . Quod etiam suis valde videbatur ineptum ni experimento probassent, quod Geraldus . . . invincibilis semper esset. Cum ergo viderent quod novo praeliandi genere mista pietate triumpharet, irrisionem vertebant in admirationem. Vita S. Geraldi,* c. 8.

34 *Annals of St Bertin,* pp. 50–1; Agnellus, *Liber pontificalis,* pp. 389–90. Nelson, *Charles the Bald,* p. 119, vividly describes the reception the captured archbishop received in Charles's camp.

35 Whereas the taking and sometimes the release of prisoners is mentioned in battles in 844, 876, 922, 939 (at both Birten and Andernach), 955, 962, 1018, 1033, 1044, 1054, 1057, 1068. The cases of Conquereuil (992) and Pontlevoy (1016) are doubtful, although according to Glaber, Conan of Brittany was captured alive at the former, *Rodulfus Glaber Opera,* ed. J. France, N. Bulst and P. Reynolds (Oxford, 1989), II, c. 3, and later Angevin tradition related that two of Conan's sons together with many barons, knights and footsoldiers were taken prisoner, *Gesta consulum,* p. 49.

36 Flodoard, 13. For the political context of Soissons which 'of ninth- and tenth-century battles among the Franks, only Fontenoy exceeded in infamy', see G. Koziol, 'Is Robert I in Hell?' and 'Charles the Simple, Robert of Neustria and the *vexilla* of Saint-Denis', *EME* 14 (2006), pp. 233–67, and pp. 355–90, the quotation at p. 369, n. 36.

apparent than real.[37] As for Val-ès-Dunes, not only do both the contemporary William of Jumièges and the near-contemporary source William of Poitiers not mention any taking of prisoners, but the account by the later author Wace reflects the abiding local memory of it as a particularly savage affair. 'They all fled in great confusion . . . terrified to cross the Orne. Those who pursued them did not take pity on them; they tore them to pieces and routed them. They threw so many into the Orne and so many were killed and so many drowned that the mills of Borbeillon, it is said, were brought to a standstill.'[38]

In the light of all this, it is worth taking a closer look at the pursuit at Fontenoy. Nithard's treatment dealt with it in a manner very different from Prudentius's clear statement that there was a general slaughter of those fleeing and that a halt was called only after Louis and Charles, 'afire with generous feelings' ordered that the killing must stop 'so that the pursuit was not taken any further from the camp and in order to to uphold the standards of Christianity'.[39] In his first version of the battle, written (he tells us) on 18 October 841, Nithard did not mention the pursuit at all. Instead he ended the second of his two books of history at that point when Lothar's men turned in flight. And that was it. But not much later, probably in 842, Nithard felt impelled to add a third book, 'in case anyone', as he put it in the preface to this book, 'tricked by some means or other, should dare to give an inaccurate account of recent events'. At the same time he claimed that he had wanted to regard his work as complete when he ended Book II. There could, after all, be no more fitting conclusion to a work commissioned by Charles the Bald than a description of the way in which Charles and Louis had 'put the issue in the hands of God' and been rewarded with a God-given victory.[40] Yet he was persuaded, somewhat reluctantly, to continue the story.[41] The first sentence of book 3 plunges straight back into the events of 25 June:

---

37 *Glaber Opera* III, c. 38. Hugh of Flavigny, writing at least 50 years later, relied heavily on Glaber's account, but did add the names of a few more casualties, referring to it as *illud lacrimabile bellum, Chronicon, PL* 154, col. 258.

38 Wace, *Roman de Rou*, Part 3, lines 4147–56. See M. Bennett, 'Wace and Warfare', *ANS* 11 (1988/9), pp. 37–57. Cf. above, n. 22.

39 *Quin etiam longius a castris obtentu Christianitatis fugientes persequi desierunt, Annales Bertiniani*, p. 38.

40 Nithard, *Histoire* II, c. 10, pp. 76–80. On Nithard's silences and the interval between books 2 and 3 see the fundamental study by J. L. Nelson, 'Public histories and private history, *Speculum* 60 (1985), pp. 251–93, repr. in her *Politics and Ritual*, 195–237, esp. 204–11.

41 *Tertium libellum ut adderem acquievi*, Nithard, *Histoire*, p. 80.

The tough fighting over, Louis and Charles, still on the field of battle, began to discuss what ought be done about those who were in flight. Some voices, motivated by anger, pressed for a pursuit; others, and especially the kings, having pity on their brother and his people, and desiring with their customary charity that the defeated, since they had been crushed by the Judgement of God and by the blow they had suffered, should now repent their wickedness and greed, and with God's help from now on be of one mind with them in their quest for true justice, they [the kings] urged their followers to put everything in God's hands. The rest of the army gave their assent, and they halted the fighting and pillaging . . . The booty and the slaughter were both immense and amazing, but so too was the pity shown by the kings and by all the people.[42]

Nithard then went on to describe at some length the post-battle rituals that took place on the next day, a Sunday, the rituals of repentance and the burial of the dead of both sides.[43] Nithard's is a very peculiar battle narrative, with the division between his Books II and III coming in the middle of it. It is not surprising that Franz Pietzscker sensed that Nithard was covering something up. He argued that although Nithard mentioned 'pillaging' only at the end of the battle, it had in fact occurred earlier, after a first round of fighting, and had to be called off, not for the good moral reasons adduced by Nithard, but simply because the troops of Lothar's ally, Pippin of Aquitaine, arrived and had to be faced. By inserting a phase of plundering between two rounds of fighting, Pietzscker prolonged the overall length of the battle, and by then arguing back from Nithard's statement that the victors were back at their camp at Thury (7 kilometres away) at midday, he felt justified in saying that the fighting must have begun before 8 a.m. His conclusion was that Charles and Louis had launched an early-morning attack, breaking the terms of the truce they had agreed with Lothar on 23 June, according to which both sides would refrain from fighting until the second hour of the day on 25 June. Nithard's account was intended to conceal the treachery of the man who had commissioned the history.[44]

But Pietzscker can't be right. As Janet Nelson pointed out, none of the several sources favourable to Lothar laid a charge of treachery against Charles and Louis.[45] Ferocity and exhaustion could well have meant that a

---

42 Nithard, *Histoire* III, c. 1.
43 Nelson, 'Carolingian violence', pp. 100–1; On Nithard's claim that the bodies of the fallen of both sides were buried, see J. Gillingham, ' "Holding to the rules of war (*bellica iura tenentes*)": right conduct before, during and after battle in north-western Europe in the eleventh century', *ANS* 29 (2006/7), pp. 11–15, at p. 5.
44 F. Pietzscker, 'Die Schlacht bei Fontenoy', *ZRG, Germanistische Abteilung* 81 (1964), pp. 318–40, at p. 338.
45 Nelson, 'Public Histories', p. 207; Nelson, *Charles the Bald*, p. 118.

battle which began at 8 a.m. was all over by 10 a.m.[46] Pietzscker, I suggest, was right to suspect a cover-up, but looking at the wrong phase of the battle. It was the carnage that Nithard had wanted to avoid writing about. When Angelbert in his poem *The Battle of Fontenoy* wrote *fracta est lex Christianorum*, it was not in the first verse when he described the early-morning dawn on the day of battle, but in his third verse: 'There has been no worse massacre on the field of battle. Christian law is violated; blood flows in waves; and in hell the maw of Cerberus opens with glee'.[47] In Book II Nithard had said nothing about pursuit and slaughter. He mentioned hard fighting, but that was precisely what was expected from honourable warriors, indeed he highlighted his own 'not inconsiderable' part in the fighting.[48] Not until Book III did he mention the plunder and the carnage, and even here all he said about a pursuit was that it was called off. Whatever the other reasons that persuaded him to embark on a third book may have been, it looks as though he was now reluctantly aware that the scale of the slaughter of Christian by Christian could not be ignored. In the preface to Book III he did, after all, say that there were some things about our people (*quiddam ex genere nostro*) which he found painful to hear and even more painful to write about.[49] If we ask why this killing of fellow-Franks was so controversial, one answer might be that it was precisely during the pursuit that prisoners could be taken, but that in this case they were not.[50] And yet, by placing his wordy explanation of the purity of the victors' conduct at precisely this point in his narrative, he managed to give the impression that the pursuit was called off almost before it began. In the light of both the high mortality and Prudentius's account of the pursuit, it does indeed look as though

---

46 Even assuming that their camp was still at Thury, and had not been moved up to the hill near Lothar's camp, which according to Nithard, they occupied while waiting for eight o'clock.

47 Edited and translated in P. Godman, *Poetry of the Carolingian Renaissance* (London, 1985), pp. 262–5.

48 Nithard, *Histoire* II, c. 10, p. 78: *Strenue confligunt . . . quibus haud modicum supplementum Domino auxiliante prebui . . . strenue conflixit.*

49 *Nithard*, Histoire II, c. 10, p. 78.

50 This supports Janet Nelson's contention that in 841 Charles and Louis were determined not to repeat the 'tactical error' of 833/4, and now intended 'a battle to the death'. In a dynastic dispute 'killing was the only sure means of achieving' a decisive result: J. L. Nelson, 'The quest for peace in a time of war: the Carolingian Brüderkrieg, 840–843', in J. Fried (ed.), *Träger und Instrumentarien des Friedens im Hohen und Späten Mittelalter*, Vorträge und Forschungen 43 (Sigmaringen, 1996), pp. 87–114, at p. 107. At Tinchebrai (1106) and Lincoln (1141) men chose not to use such sure means. For Hastings in 1066 see below, p. 265.

Nithard was protesting too much.[51] Even when he accepted that he could no longer conceal the scale of the slaughter, it seems that he still thought that the pursuit could at least be glossed over. It was one thing to write, as Nithard finally did, that the slaughter was huge, quite another to make explicit, as Prudentius did, that the worst of it had happened when, as soldiers knew, it could have been avoided. On this subject Nithard, the warrior-aristocrat, felt more uneasy than the churchman, Prudentius.[52]

Thus it was Nithard – but not Prudentius – who acknowledged that sins (*aut ira aut odio aut vana gloria*) had been committed on 25 June, including that sin (anger) which he explicitly associated with the pursuit. According to him, the bishops at Fontenoy on 26 June declared that among the victorious soldiers only those ill-motivated individuals had been guilty of the sin of homicide. But which of those who took part in the pursuit could feel confident that they had not harboured anger or hatred or vainglory? To the Xanten annalist it appeared that 'in a great slaughter Christians had fought each other like madmen (*debachati sunt*)'.[53] Hence it is not altogether surprising that, again according to Nithard, a three-day fast was ordained not just for the remission of the sins of their dead brothers, but also 'because they knew that they themselves were not perfect, for they had sinned in many ways both wittingly and unwittingly'.[54] It is evident that, equally unsurprisingly, neither the bishops' judgement nor the three-day fast stifled debate about the morality of the slaughter at Fontenoy. When Hrabanus Maurus, at the request of Archbishop Otgar of Mainz, entered into the controversy concerning that *homicidium quod nuper in seditione et proelio principum nostrorum perpetratum est*, he was evidently familiar with, and had no time for, the opinions expressed by the complaisant bishops at Fontenoy. His discussion took the form of a rebuttal of those who argued that they were innocent of sin and had no need to do penance on the

---

51 See Nelson, 'Public Histories', pp. 204, 206, 217 for discussion of other silences and the contrast between the brevity of Nithard's account of the actual battle and his detailed presentation of the preliminaries, and – I would add – of what happened afterward.

52 'Nithard, here as elsewhere, lets us catch echoes of the world of oral dicourse in which Carolingian politics were enacted', J. L. Nelson, 'Ninth-century knighthood: the evidence of Nithard', in C. Harper-Bill, C. Holdsworth and J. L. Nelson (eds), *Studies in Medieval History presented to R. Allen Brown* (Woodbridge, 1989), pp. 255–66, rep. *The Frankish World*, pp. 75–87, 83–4.

53 *Annales Xantenses, MGH SRG*, ed. B. von Simson (Hanover, 1909), p. 11. cf *Dani intestino inter se proelio dimicantes, adeo tridui concertatione obstantissima bacchati sunt ut, Orico rege et ceteris cum eo interfectis regibus, pene omnis nobilitas interierit*, *Annales Bertiniani*, 70.

54 Nithard, *Histoire* III, c. 1, pp. 80–2.

grounds that they were following orders.[55] That was an argument which those who killed during a pursuit might well have found more relevant and more comforting than Halitgar of Cambrai's recent concession that killing in battle was no sin when it was to defend oneself and one's kin. Hrabanus and later writers on penance continued to insist that all killing in war, even on the orders of a legitimate ruler, involved sin.[56] This implies that many soldiers thought differently, but men such as Nithard were evidently deeply disturbed.

Did the anguished post-Fontenoy debate contribute to the rise of chivalry? Is it possible that when high-status prisoners were taken in the civil-war battles of 844 and 876, men were consciously drawing back from the standard set in 841? The treatment of prisoners of war in this period has never, so far as I know, been systematically studied.[57] In later centuries ransom was central. In his *L'arbre des batailles*, once thought of as the oldest textbook of international law, the fourteeenth-century author, Honoré Bonet, observed that, 'by written law, good custom and usage, and between Christians great and small, there exists the custom of commonly taking ransom one from another'. This he explicitly contrasted with what he perceived to be the situation in antiquity. 'Nowadays we have abandoned the ancient rules of making slaves of prisoners and of putting them to death.'[58] By the late eleventh century the taking of ransoms was seen as a major element in the profits of war. Orderic Vitalis, who lived in Normandy from 1085, observed of the French defending the Vexin against Norman attack in the 1090s that they 'did not wish the high honour of the French (*insignem Francorum laudem*) to be tarnished, and fought the enemy to the death for the defence of their country and the glory of their people (*pro defensione patriae et gloria gentis suae ad mortem*)'. To the death? A few sentences earlier he had observed that 'the needy French were encouraged to keep

55 In the chapter headed *De illis qui se excusant quasi insontes ab homicidio in proelio commisso iussu principum*, MGH, *Epistolae* V, pp. 463–4. Cf. K-G. Cram, *Iudicium Belli* (Münster, 1955), p. 38. Both Hrabanus and Otgar were sympathetic to Lothar's cause: R. Kottje, *Die Bussbücher Halitgards von Cambrai und des Hrabanus Maurus* (Berlin, 1980), pp. 240–4.

56 S. Hamilton, *The Practice of Penance 900–1050* (Woodbridge, 2001), pp. 190–6; D. S. Bachrach, *Religion and the Conduct of War c.300–c.1215* (Woodbridge, 2003), pp. 24–30, 60–2, 98–106, provides a summary account.

57 Hence the editor's comment, 'Untersuchungen liegen leider nicht vor' in R. Overmans (ed.), *In der Hand des Feindes* (Cologne, 1999), p. 3. But see Halsall, *Warfare and Society*, p. 213 and the recurrent suggestions in J. Dunbabin, *Captivity and Imprisonment in Medieval Europe 1000–1300* (Basingstoke, 2002).

58 'According to written law in ancient times a man could at will kill his prisoner', *The Tree of Battles of Honoré Bonet*, ed. G. W. Coopland (Liverpool, 1949), p. 152.

on fighting by the rich ransoms (*redemptionibus opimis*)' and a few sentences later that 'they put up a vigorous defence, but did not forget their fear of God and humanity (*timoris Dei et humanae societatis*). Thoughtfully and generously (*provide benigniterque*) they spared the bodies of the attackers and turned the ferocity of their anger against their enemies' costly chargers.'[59] Orderic's dual emphasis on the prowess, honour and glory as well as on the intention of sparing the lives of those who rode expensive horses nicely illustrates the status-specific nature of the two faces of chivalry.

But was there a ninth- or tenth-century custom of taking ransom? It is commonly said that in the early post-Roman centuries prisoners of war were enslaved if they could not pay ransoms, but – with one exception – the only instances of the supposed ransoming of prisoners (*redemptio captivorum*) that I have noticed so far relate to the work of saintly men in buying their release, as also in the decrees of the council of Ver (844).[60] But these are pious acts clearly different from what is conventionally understood by the term 'ransom' in modern discussions of medieval war. In these it is the captive himself or his family or lord who was responsible for raising the money. The one exception occurs in Gregory of Tours' narrative of the siege of Chastel-Marlhac during Theuderic's attack on the Auvergne in 532. When the besieged made a rash sortie, about fifty of them were captured and would have been killed by the Franks had their fellows not ransomed them there and then.[61] Undoubtedly those for whom raiding was a busi-

---

59 Orderic, *Ecclesiastical History*, v, pp. 216–19. The neat translation of *provide benigniterque* as 'out of chivalry' runs the risk of giving readers who do not read Latin the impression that a Latin word for the concept existed. Orderic believed that Viscount Hubert of Maine and those who supported him against William I in the war of St Suzanne (1083–85) had been able to enrich themselves honourably (*honorifice*) by capturing and ransoming wealthy English and Norman lords, *ibid.* iv, pp. 48–9. See M. Strickland, *War and Chivalry* (Cambridge, 1996), pp. 183–96.

60 According to Raymond Van Dam on the Merovingians, 'because their campaigns, whether within Gaul or against their neighbours, produced so much booty and so many captives who could be ransomed, the armies were virtually self-supporting', in P. Fouracre (ed.), *NCMH* I (Cambridge, 2005), p. 211. *MGH Concilia* III, ed. W. Hartmann (Hanover, 1984), pp. 42–3.

61 Gregory of Tours, *Historiarum Libri Decem*, ed. R. Buchner, *MGH SRM* I (Berlin, 1955), III c. 13: *Adquiverunt obsessi, ne hi interfecerentur, singulos treantes dare in redemptionem suam.* Evidently discouraged by this, the defenders of Chastel-Marlhac paid the Franks to call off the siege; in Gregory's words *ne captivi adducerentur, redemptione data, liberantur.* But here *redemptio* would appear to mean what later experts in the laws of war would call *appatis* or *raencons du pays*, translated by Maurice Keen as 'the tribute of the countryside', M. Keen, *The Laws of War in the Late Middle Ages* (London, 1965), pp. 82, 251–3. The people of Chastel-Marlhac bought their freedom in the sense that had they been captured and not ransomed, they would have been enslaved.

ness, in the ninth and tenth centuries most obviously the Vikings, were at times prepared to invest in keeping wealthy prisoners alive in order to make a profit greater than the gain made by despoiling them.[62] But rarely do we hear that the raiders themselves paid a ransom, though Widukind reports that in 938 Otto freed a Magyar chief in return for a 'great price'.[63] It is even harder to find any mention of ransoms in the sources relating to wars 'between Christians great and small'.

Could it be that ransoms were prevalent, yet authors preferred not to mention them? Is it possible that the desire of the victors to present the outcome of Fontenoy and other battles fought within the context of civil war as the just judgements of God meant that the notion of 'ransom', with its implications of combatants' greed, was studiously avoided by authors such as Prudentius and Nithard?[64] Yet Nithard made no effort to conceal the material gains made by the victors of Fontenoy in the shape of plunder (*ingens numerus praedae*). The custom of nobles carrying with them a high proportion of their movable wealth when they went to war ensured rich pickings here.[65] In the case of Andernach in 876 both Hincmar and the Fulda annalist positively revelled in the plunder taken on the battlefield from both dead and living.[66] Nor had Prudentius had any compunction about observing that before those taken prisoner in 844 were set free, they were despoiled as well as bound by solemn oaths (*spoliatos sacramentoque adstrictos*).[67] What was it they had sworn? To pay a ransom? Or something else, for example to take no further part in the war, or to try to persuade Charles the Bald to recognize the validity of Pippin II's claim to Aquitaine? Lupus of Ferrières, we know, was soon released but there is no evidence that he had to raise a ransom. On his return to his monastery he faced problems, and he described them in his letters, but none were explicitly

---

62 Strickland, 'Killing or Clemency', pp. 99–101. The practical difficulties facing such businessmen are vividly revealed by Thietmar of Merseburg's story of how his uncle Siegfried managed to escape from them in 994, Thietmar, *Chronicon*, ed. and trans. W. Trillmilch (Darmstadt, 1974), IV, cc. 24–5.

63 *pretio magno redimitur*, Widukind, *Rerum gestarum Saxonicarum*, ed. G. Waitz, *MGH SRG* (Hanover, 1882), II, c. 14, p. 44.

64 Matthew Strickland pointed out that Orderic, owing to his desire to present Henry I's soldiers as fighting a just war with right intent and in defence of their home, studiously avoided any mention of ransom in his explanation of why so few knights were killed in the battle of Brémule, although 'we know from many other references by Orderic himself that the ransoming of knightly captives was in practice widespread'. Strickland, 'Killing or Clemency', pp. 94, 100–1.

65 Leyser, 'Early Medieval Warfare', pp. 34–5.

66 *Annals of St Bertin*, p. 197; *Annals of Fulda*, p. 81.

67 *Annales Bertiniani*, p. 46.

ascribed to the pressure to raise a ransom.[68] Lupus's silence on this subject stands in contrast to Thietmar's account of the contributions made by his mother, by the king and by 'all the Christians of our region' to meet the ransom demanded by the Vikings in 994.[69]

Once again Odo's Life of Saint Gerald deserves to be taken a little more seriously. According to Odo, Gerald, *collecto militum agmine*, defeated a 'robber baron' named Arlald and captured both him and his castle. He then released him without demanding a hostage or any sort of oath. What Odo did not say is that Gerald did not demand a ransom from him either. Ransoming, this may imply, was not what conventional commanders did in the early tenth century; if they had, Odo would surely have added Gerald's renunciation of ransom to his hagiographical portrait. On the other hand Gerald did not allow Arlald to take any of his goods with him. He did this, according to Odo, piously explaining to Arlald that it was *pro compensatione praedae, quam exercere solitus es.*[70] If even saints justified despoiling those they defeated in war, it is hardly surprising to find victors everywhere doing the same. Flodoard reported that when Hugh 'the Black' encountered and defeated a 200-strong force of Hagano's men plundering the estates of Reims in 922, he killed only three of them; the rest he sent back home loaded down with ignominy, for he took from them their arms and horses.[71] In Hincmar's words, when Charles's men fled or died at Andernach, 'everything which those plunderers who were with the emperor had, and even they themselves, now became the plunder of someone else . . . It was a great blow against a people of plunderers (*in populo praedatore*)'.[72]

After an asembly at Frankfurt in January 877, the prisoners taken at Andernach, among them Charles's archchancellor Abbot Gauzlin, were allowed to return home.[73] Did they pay or promise to pay ransoms? If they did not, why else might they have been released? To give their support to Louis the Younger in the event of Charles the Bald dying? Perhaps to assist him in obtaining those territories which Charles had gained by the treaty of Meersen in 870? Although in the event Charles did not die until October 877, he had been at death's door at Christmas 876; the likely consequences

---

68 *Loup de Ferrières, Correspondance*, ed. L. Levillain (Paris, 1927), letters 35–40.
69 Thietmar, *Chronicon* IV, c. 23.
70 *Vita S. Geraldi* I, c. 40.
71 Flodoard, p. 9.
72 *Annales Bertiniani*, p. 209.
73 *Annals of Fulda*, p. 82. The others named were Bishop Ottulf of Troyes, and Counts Aledramn, Adalard, Bernard and Everwin, *Annals of St Bertin*, p. 197.

of his death must have been discussed at Frankfurt.[74] When Charles's son, Louis the Stammerer, died in April 879, Abbot Gauzlin led a group of magnates who invited Louis the Younger to take over West Francia. According to Hincmar, 'Abbot Gauzlin counted on the friendly relationships he had formed with King Louis and his wife and with the magnates of that country, when he had been taken east of the Rhine after being captured at the battle of Andernach'.[75] That is one way of putting it. Might it not also have been that Louis and his wife counted on Gauzlin and friends, in return for their freedom, supporting his cause in power struggles which were bound to come?[76] In the event Louis the Stammerer's position as his father's heir turned out to be too strong to be challenged by Louis the Younger in 877; not until 879 and 880 was the understanding reached in January 877 activated.

That agreements of this kind were sometimes made is clear from an early eleventh-century case. Duke Godfrey of Lower Lorraine led troops in support of Bishop Adalbold of Utrecht's expedition against Count Dietrich of Holland in 1018, an expedition ordered by Henry II. He was wounded and captured in the bloody battle at Vlaerdingen (the worst of the misfortunes that befell us in Henry's reign, according to Thietmar), and he was released on condition of promising to intercede with the emperor on his captor's behalf. He was required, in other words, to switch sides in the dispute between Count Dietrich on the one hand and the bishop of Utrecht and the merchants of Tiel on the other. According to the most vivid account of the battle and the negotiations which followed, Godfrey had to leave behind his fellow captives as a guarantee that he would keep his promise.[77]

The earliest clear-cut reference to Franks ransoming fellow Franks that I have noticed dates from the late 1020s. It occurs in the narrative of Hugh

---

74 All the more so in the light of the 'dogged determination' (Nelson, *Charles the Bald*, p. 246) with which, despite Andernach, Charles attempted to make inroads into Louis the Younger's territory, *Annnals of St Bertin*, p. 198.

75 *Annals of St Bertin*, pp. 216–17. K. F. Werner, 'Gauzlin von Saint-Denis und die westfränkische Reichsteilung von Amiens (880)', *DA* 35 (1979), pp. 395–462, refers to Gauzlin's imprisonment only in passing, 404 n. 36, 427 n. 103. Cf. S. MacLean, *Kingship and Politics in the Late Ninth Century* (Cambridge, 2003), p. 103, n. 116.

76 For the role of another of the prisoners of Andernach, Count Aledramn, and for Aledramn's brother Theoderic, MacLean, *Kingship and Politics*, pp. 103, 106–7, 125.

77 Thietmar, *Chronicon*, VIII, cc. 27–8; Alpert, *De diversitate temporum*, II, c. 21, *MGH SS* IV pp. 719–20. According to the *Gesta episcoporum Cameracensium*, III, c. 19, Godfey was too important a man to be safely kept prisoner; even so it was on condition of interceding for him that Count Dietrich released him, *MGH SS* VII, p. 471.

of Lusignan's dispute and settlement with Duke William of Aquitaine, that 'breathtakingly fortunate survival' in which actions were described 'in relation to a set of moral standards and acknowledged codes of behaviour', thereby revealing 'some startling glimpses of the attitudes and outlook of great laymen, virtually stripped of conventional religious sentiments'.[78] Hugh claimed that having captured 43 of the best horsemen of Thouars, he could have had peace and security for his lands and 40,000 solidi if he had wished to accept a ransom, *redemptionem*.[79] Thanks to the language of the *conventum*, making it clear that by the 1020s ransoming was taken for granted, we can be confident that Geoffrey Martel of Anjou was not doing anything revolutionary when he freed William count of Poitou in return for *multis pecuniis* three years after capturing him at battle of Montcouë (1033).[80] From now on references to ransoms become more and more common. By contrast the silences of ninth- and tenth-century sources are resounding ones. As Matthew Strickland observed, interaction with Vikings could have stimulated the practice of ransom within Francia, yet it apparently did not.[81] In the meantime, valuable prisoners of war could be used in other ways, for example for purposes of exchange as when Helouin recaptured Montreuil in 939 and spared the lives of some of Arnulf's men in order to exchange them for his wife.[82] Or as pieces on the chessboard of international or interregional diplomacy as suggested here for 876–7, and as they continued to be. For example, the King of France's men taken prisoner at the battle of Mortemer in 1054 were kept until a peace treaty was made between the king and Duke William, at which the former agreed that the latter could lawfully hold any gains he made at the expense of Geoffrey of Anjou.[83] No captor was ever obliged to accept a ransom, even

---

78 J. Martindale, 'Dispute, settlement and orality in the *Conventum inter Guillelmum Aquitanorum comitem et Hugonem Chiliarchum*: a Postscript to the edition of 1969', in J. Martindale, *Status, Authority and Regional Power: Aquitaine and France, 9th to 12th Centuries* (Aldershot, 1997), VIII, pp. 11–36, the quotations on pp. 1, 21, 29, 35. See also the discussion of the Conventum in D. Barthélemy, *L'an mil et la paix de Dieu* (Paris, 1999), pp. 329–54.

79 *Conventum inter Guillelmum Aquitanorum comitem et Hugonem Chiliarchum*, Martindale, *Status, Authority and Regional Power*, VIIb, p. 543, repr. with same pagination plus translation from *EHR* 84 (1969), pp. 528–53.

80 Glaber IV, c. 26. Writing a generation later, the Norman William, known as 'of Poitiers' because he attended the schools in Poitiers, criticized Geoffrey's treatment of the count of Poitou, *Gesta Guillelmi*, i. 15, p. 20.

81 Strickland, 'Killing or Clemency', p. 100.

82 Flodoard, *Annales*, p. 72 (cf. Richer, *Histoire* II, c. 14).

83 *Gesta Guillelmi*, p. 50. Cf. in same source William's assertion that Geoffrey Martel extorted an oath of alliance from the count of Poitou, p. 20.

though Guibert de Nogent, looking back from *c.*1115, implied that princes such as William of Normandy ought to have ransomed their captives, not kept them in prison for life.[84]

The earliest case known to me of a writer expressing surprise at the small number of battle casualties also dates from the second quarter of the eleventh century. Ralph Glaber's account of Nouy (1044), written very soon after the event, concluded with the observation that 'everyone was fearfully astonished to hear that over 1,700 men well-trained in war could be captured in battle without any blood being shed'. Glaber explained it in terms of the miraculous power of St Martin, whom the loser (Count Theobald of Blois) had offended and to whom Geoffrey Martel had prayed.[85] Glaber's reaction, of course, implies that generally speaking the battles with which he was familiar, whether from story or from personal experience, were much bloodier than this. Did Nouy mark the beginning of a shift? Given the fragmentary nature of the evidence, it is not easy to be confident one way or the other. It is worth noticing, however, that the ancestral history of the counts of Anjou composed by Fulk Rechin, count of Anjou (1068–1109) does, apparently unconsciously, enshrine a memory of precisely such a shift. In it Fulk touches upon the outcomes of seven battles fought by him and three predecessors. Of the earliest he said only that Geoffrey Grisegonelle defeated the count of Poitou *in prelio campestri* at Les Roches and pursued him as far as Mirebeau. Of the two pitched battles fought by his grandfather Fulk Nerra (Conquereuil in 992 and Pontlevoy in 1016), he said that there was great slaughter and made no mention of any prisoners. Of the three he claimed were won by his uncle Geoffrey Martel (Montcoüé in 1033, Nouy in 1044, and one undated and unlocated against Herbert count of Maine), he mentioned only the capture of prisoners and said nothing about any killing. And finally the same is true of his own battle against his brother Geoffrey at Brissac in 1068, where he noted that his

---

84 He had his father's fate in mind, though he exaggerated the length of the imprisonment, see *Self and Society in Medieval France: The Memoirs of Abbot Guibert de Nogent*, ed. and trans. J. F. Benton (New York, 1970), Appendix 1. The contention that 'ransom of captives was not a prominent part of western conventions in pre-Crusade Europe' – see Y. Friedman, *Encounter between Enemies: Captivity and Ransom in the Latin Kingdom of Jerusalem* (Leiden, 2002), pp. 60–72, 62 – is defensible only by pressing the word 'prominent' very hard. See M. Strickland, 'Rules of war or war without rules? – some reflections on conduct and the treatment of non-combatants in medieval transcultural wars', in Kortüm (ed.), *Transcultural Wars*, pp. 107–40, at 129–30.

85 Glaber V, c. 19.

brother was taken and a thousand of his supporters with him.[86] As Jane Martindale has pointed out, Fulk was very largely concerned with his ancestors' military deeds and their prowess. They were *probissimi comites*.[87] Irrespective of what happened in any of these seven battles, Fulk created an image of the right way for a noble count to win battles, with over time a shift away from killing and toward the taking of prisoners, in the last two of the series not just the capture of the enemy commander but also of a thousand of his followers.

If such a shift did occur, then expectations would have changed over time too. In consequence there would still have been battles which struck observers as less bloody than anticipated – hence the comments of twelfth-century writers such as Orderic on Brémule (see above p. 248) and the author of the *Historia Welforum* on the 'battle' in 1164 between the forces of Welf VII and Hugh of Tübingen. A section of the Welf army came to grips with the main Tübingen force and 'all fought most fiercely for two hours yet, except for one man, no one was killed. They were all so well protected by their armour that it was much easier to capture than kill them. But while some of our men fought hard, the rest took to flight and so handed the enemy an undeserved victory, bringing eternal shame on themselves and their descendants. When the enemy realized this, they took prisoner almost all those who had fought . . . and then set off in pursuit. They hauled them in like grazing sheep brought into the fold, taking in all 900 prisoners and an immense amount of booty'.[88]

---

86 At Conquereuil *periit idem Conanus et mille de equitibus suis*; at Pontlevoy *ubi multa fuit strages Gallorum et Andegavorum*; at Montcoué *ubi comitem Pictavensem apprehendit et aliud contra Cenomannenses ubi comitem eorum similiter cepit*; at Nouy *Teothbaldus captus est et usque ad mille de equitibus suis;* at Brissac, *fuit ipse captus et michi redditus et mille de civibus suis cum eo*, 'Fragmentum historiae Andegavensis', in Halphen and Poupardin, *Chroniques*, pp. 234–5, 237. Halphen's scepticism about the reality of the battle against the men of Maine is not relevant to the question of Fulk Rechin's presentation of the past. Fulk Nerra's gift to St Maurilius at *Angers pro penitentia tam magna straga christianorum quae acta est in planicie Conquareth* may well have helped to keep alive the memory of carnage at Conquereuil, *Cartulaire noir de la cathédrale d'Angers*, ed. C. Urseau (Angers, 1908), no. 27.

87 J. Martindale, 'Secular propaganda and aristocratic values: the autobiographies of Count Fulk le Réchin of Anjou and Count William of Poitou, Duke of Aquitaine', in D. Bates, J. Crick and S. Hamilton (eds), *Writing Medieval Biography: Essays in Honour of Frank Barlow* (Woodbridge, 2006), pp. 143–59, 146, 151. On Fulk's keen sense of the risks of battle, J. Gillingham, 'William the Bastard at War', in C. Harper-Bill et al. (eds), *Studies in Medieval History*, pp. 141–58, 147.

88 *Historia Welforum*, ed. E. König (Sigmaringen, 1978), p. 64. G. Althoff, 'Shranken der Gewalt: Wie gewalttätig was das "finstere Mittelalter"', in H. Brunner (ed.), *Der Krieg im Mittelalter und in der Frühen Neuzeit* (Wiesbaden, 1999), pp. 1–23, at pp. 11–12.

Also relevant to the notion of a shift are those passages in which eleventh-century authors presented the model ruler as someone who treated enemies, including rebels, mercifully, much as William of Poitiers presented William of Normandy. Some fifty years earlier Ademar of Chabannes had done the same. Describing William of Aquitaine's dispute with the count of La Marche in the late 990s, Ademar claimed that, having captured the count, 'William did not wish to kill his enemy, but out of mercy preferred to release him unharmed and on oath. He always acted in this merciful fashion, in that he prevented those whom he could take alive from being harmed, instead ordering them to depart rescued from death and safe from bodily mutilation.'[89] By implication, of course, other rulers were not like this.[90] Although there was nothing new about the representation of good rulers as merciful, the particular emphasis on the merciful treatment of high-status enemies may be. And if in eleventh-century intracultural wars princes really did begin to treat fellow aristocrats with greater compassion – as seems to be the case – then why might this have happened?

On this I still find the arguments put forward by Matthew Strickland the most persuasive: endemic local and regional war went hand in hand with the proliferation of castles leading to more frequent negotiation between enemies and a greater awareness of the mutual advantage to be gained by refraining from killing.[91] Some scholars have linked this with the Peace and Truce of God. But the only way, in my view, that these movements could have made a difference is 'by clearly reiterating the principle that the conduct of war between Christians ought to be fundamentally different from the conduct of war between Christians and non-Christians'.[92] Basic to chivalrous compassion, however, was a fundamental difference between the treatment of one class of Christian and another, between men of low and high status. Once the enslavement of prisoners was no longer

---

89 *Ademari Chronicon*, pp. 11–12.

90 Rather they were like those nobles, among them Fulk Nerra, who in another anecdote advised William to wreak stern vengeance (*graviter vindicare iniuriam suam*), allowing Ademar to present the 'good duke' as choosing to go down the way of peace and reason (*omnia pacifice et cum ratione sicut eum decebat finivit et disposuit*). In Ademar's last recension this became *regali more cum pietate et providentia rationis causam pacificavit, Ademari Chronicon*. pp. 14, 177.

91 M. Strickland, 'Slaughter, slavery or ransom? The impact of the Conquest on conduct in warfare', in C. Hicks (ed.), *England in the Eleventh Century: Proceedings of the 1990 Harlaxton Symposium* (Stamford, 1992), pp. 41–59, at 58–9. Proliferation of castles, particularly with stone walls, also made the detention of knightly prisoners easier and cheaper: Dunbabin, *Captivity and Imprisonment*, pp. 32–9.

92 R. C. Stacey, 'The age of chivalry', in Howard (ed.), *Laws of War*, pp. 27–39, at pp. 29–30.

on the menu of choices in north-western Europe, then ordinary soldiers may have been even more likely to be killed in battle than they had been before.[93] The code of chivalry was almost entirely the creation of the secular aristocracy.

Changes in the technology of war were important. Both Orderic and the author of the *Historia Welforum* drew attention to the high quality of body armour worn by the combatants in those engagements that struck them as remarkably bloodless. Timothy Reuter associated 'armies where not only the leaders but all the followers were fully armed' with the observation that 'there were few engagements in post-Frankish Europe with really heavy casualties between 950 and 1050'.[94] Armour, of course, was not determinative. Well-armed men in England in 1265 chose to kill at the battle of Evesham, whereas only a year earlier in the battle of Lewes similarly armed men had chosen not to kill.[95] Ultimately it was what men chose to do that counted. Even so, the fact that a higher proportion of warriors had better armour gave their enemies more time to choose, particularly – it may be – in the case of heavily armoured knights lying stunned on the ground after having been unhorsed.[96]

In addition we might consider the possibility that a widespread convention of ransoming is easier to operate in a relatively highly monetized society'.[97] Numismatic evidence suggests that 'over the 9th century . . . the volume of coinage in general circulation had shrunk', reflecting a shortage of silver which lasted 'until the discovery of new ores in the Harz mountains'.[98] Then sharp increases in production from the Rammelsberg and other silver mines meant that 'the last years of the tenth century and the

93 On the other hand ordinary civilians, including women and children, were much better off once they were no longer the target of slave raids.

94 T. Reuter, 'Carolingian and Ottonian warfare', in M. Keen (ed.), *Medieval Warfare: A History* (Oxford, 1999), pp. 13–35, at 35. On the diminishing cost, and hence wider availability, of arms and armour in the eleventh century see J. Gillingham, 'Thegns and knights in eleventh-century England: who was then the gentleman?', *TRHS* 6th series. 5 (1995), pp. 129–53, reprinted in J. Gillingham, *The English in the Twelfth Century* (Woodbridge, 2000), pp. 163–85.

95 D. A. Carpenter, *The Battles of Lewes and Evesham 1264/65* (Keele, 1987).

96 Barthélemy, 'Les origines'. Cf. G. Duby, *Le Dimanche de Bouvines* (Paris, 1973), p. 26.

97 As suggested in J. Gillingham, 'Conquering the barbarians: war and chivalry in Britain and Ireland', *Haskins Society Journal* 4 (1992), 67–84, at 79, repr. in Gillingham, *The English in the Twelfth Century*, pp. 41–58, at 53. I am grateful to Jonathan Jarrett for sceptical discussion of this point.

98 M. Blackburn, 'Money and coinage', in R. McKitterick (ed.), *NCMH* II (Cambridge, 1995), p. 557.

first half of the eleventh were in many ways the most significant period for the early growth of the use of coin in western Europe.'[99] In these same decades princely and seigneurial mints proliferated.[100] But ransoms could, of course, still be paid in bullion or treasure rather than in coin, and the most spectacular profit made by way of ransom came not in the shape of coin but of a great city, Theobald's cession of Tours to Geoffrey Martel in return for his freedom in 1044. It was the greatest gain made by an eleventh-century Frenchman in a single military campaign until Duke William of Normandy made himself king of England in 1066. At Hastings, of course, William – or rather, in Orderic's terms, almighty God – ended the battle with a pursuit and systematic slaughter.[101] But Hastings was not a re-run of Fontenoy. Fontenoy was intracultural, a battle between brothers and kinsmen. Hastings by contrast was a battle in which the victorious French looked upon their enemies as Anglo-Danish barbarians who could be killed because they stood outside the 'charmed circle' of those who lived by chivalric values. The replacement of the Anglo-Danish by a French elite after the Norman Conquest meant that henceforward England too, but not as yet the rest of Britain and Ireland, was brought within that charmed circle.[102]

99   P. Spufford, *Money and its Use in Medieval Europe* (Cambridge, 1988), pp. 74–7, 99–105.
100   A. Blanchet and A. Dieudonné, *Manuel de numismatique française*, 4 vols. (Paris 1912–36), vol. 4, pp. 20, 73, 98, 122, 183, 289, 303–4, 311, 370–2.
101   'For on that Saturday as Norman fury became uncontrollable, he [almighty God] massacred many thousands of the English', *Orderic*, ii, p. 176.
102   Gillingham, 'Conquering the Barbarians', pp. 82–3 and J. Gillingham, '1066 and the introduction of chivalry into England', in G. Garnett and J. Hudson (eds), *Law and Government in Medieval England and Normandy* (Cambridge, 1994), pp. 31–55, at 39–40, 53, repr. in Gillingham, *The English in the Twelfth Century*, pp. 209–31, at 215–16, 227–8. I have borrowed the phrase 'the charmed circle' from R. R. Davies, *Domination and Conquest* (Cambridge, 1990), p. 51.

13

The death of Burgheard son of Ælfgar and its context

Stephen Baxter

I
N THE SPRING of 1061, Burgheard son of Earl Ælfgar of Mercia died
returning from a journey to Rome, and his body was taken for burial
in the basilica of the abbey of Saint-Rémi, Reims. Shortly afterward,
his grieving parents gave the abbey an estate in Staffordshire, together with
a beautifully illustrated gospel book, for the sake of their son's soul. The
evidence for this, like the event itself, is unusual, and unusually arresting.
It comprises a thirteenth-century cartulary copy of the charter recording
Ælfgar's grant of land to Saint-Rémi; a transcription of a Latin epitaph
carved on Burgheard's tombstone; a description of the gospel book's sump-
tuously decorated cover, and a transcription of five lines of Latin verse
inscribed upon it. The most recent study of this material established that,
although its cover has been lost, the gospel book is almost certainly an
extant manuscript, now Reims, Bibliothèque Municipale Carnegie, MS 9.[1]
The present paper examines two questions which illuminate this matter
further: can Burgheard be identified in Domesday Book? and why did
Burgheard go to Rome? In doing so, it addresses some of the methodologi-

---

1   W. M. Hinkle, 'The Gift of an Anglo-Saxon gospel book to the Abbey of Saint-Rémi,
    Reims', *Journal of the British Archaeological Association*, 3rd series 33 (1970), pp. 21–35.
    Throughout this paper, Anglo-Saxon charters are cited by the number assigned to
    them in P. H. Sawyer, *Anglo-Saxon Charters: An Annotated List and Bibliography*, Royal
    Historical Society Guides and Handbooks 8 (London, 1968), rev. edn, ed. S. E. Kelly,
    currently available online at www.trin.cam.ac.uk/chartwww, abbreviated as S; *Domes-
    day Book* is cited by folio and column number from *Great Domesday Book: Library
    Edition*, ed. A. Williams and R. W. H. Erskine, Alecto Historical Editions (London,
    1986–92), abbreviated as 'GDB', by folio number from *Little Domesday: Library Edition*,
    ed. A. Williams, Alecto Historical Editions (London, 2000), abbreviated as 'LDB',
    and by the numbering system used in *Domesday Book*, ed. J. Morris *et al.*, Phillimore,
    34 vols. (Chichester, 1974–86). I would like to thank Laura Ashe, Jacqueline Glomski,
    Susan Kelly, Simon Keynes, and Richard Sharpe for their advice and help in the
    preparation of this paper.

cal problems which have arisen in connection with recent work on Anglo-Saxon prosopography, in which Janet Nelson has played a leading role.[2]

The material relating to Burgheard's death

Burgheard's family played a prominent role in English politics between the early 990s and early 1070s. His great-grandfather, Leofwine, was an ealdorman in the south-west Midlands under Æthelred 'the Unready' and Cnut between 994 and about 1023; his grandfather, Leofric, was earl of Mercia, between the late 1020s and 1057; his father, Ælfgar, was earl of East Anglia in 1051–2 and 1053–7, and earl of Mercia between 1057 and his death in about 1062; his brothers Eadwine and Morcar were earls of Mercia and Northumbria respectively in 1066, remaining in office in the immediate aftermath of the Conquest before falling from power in 1071. In addition, Burgheard's sister, Ealdgyth, was married to Gruffudd ap Llewelyn, king of Wales, who was killed in 1063, and then to Harold Godwineson, king of England until his death at Hastings on 14 October 1066.[3] Given the political importance of this family, it is disappointing that Burgheard fails to make any impact on the charter evidence prior to his death; however, by comparison with that of most of his peers, his death is unusually well documented.

The key text is Earl Ælfgar's charter.[4] Two copies of this are known: one is preserved in a thirteenth-century cartulary of the Benedictine abbey of Saint-Rémi, Reims (I shall refer to this as 'C');[5] the other is printed by Sir

2 *The Prosopography of Anglo-Saxon England*, currently online at www.pase.ac.uk/ (hereafter *PASE* 2005). The first phase of the project, concerned with the period up to 1042, was published in May 2005, and was directed by Janet Nelson, Simon Keynes and Harold Short, and researched by Alex Burghart, David Pelteret and Francesca Tinti. The second phase of the project, which is concerned with the period from 1042 to *c.*1100, will be published in 2009, with the author joining the team of co-directors for this stage of the project. For background, see the homepage of the website itself, together with J. L. Nelson and F. Tinti, 'The aims and objectives of the prosopography of Anglo-Saxon England: 1066 and All That?', in D. Geuenich and I. Runde (eds), *Name und Gesellschaft im Frühmittelalter: Personennamen als Indikatoren für sprachliche ethnische, soziale und kulturelle Gruppenzugehörigkeiten ihrer Träger* (Hildesheim, 2006), pp. 241–58.

3 This family is the principal focus of S. Baxter, *The Earls of Mercia: Lordship and Power in Late Anglo-Saxon England* (Oxford, 2007).

4 S 1237.

5 Reims, Archives Départementales de la Marne, Annexe de Reims, Cartulaire B de Saint Rémi (56 H 1029 (formerly H 1411)), fol. 143r–143v; printed in *Archives Administratives de la Ville de Reims*, ed. P. Varin, Collection de documents inédits sur l'histoire de France, 5 vols. (Paris, 1839–48), vol. 1, pp. 207–8.

William Dugdale in his *Monasticon Anglicanum* (I shall refer to this as 'D').[6] The text of the latter is said to have been taken *ex ipso autographo apud Sanctum Remigium Rhemis,* but this cannot be taken at face value; Dugdale is not known to have visited Reims, his intermediate source is unknown, and the text he provides is seriously flawed.[7] The edition printed below is therefore based on 'C'.

> *In nomine Domini nostri Iesu Christi, summe et indiuidue Trinitatis. Notum sit cunctis cultoribus Christi, Algarum quemdam Anglorum comitem ingenuum, consentiente Edwardo Dei gratia rege Anglorum, Sancto Remigio Remensis ecclesie quandam uillam pro anima sui filii scilicet nomine Burchardi, dedisse, que Lappeleia cum suis appenditiis anglico uocitatur sermone, cujus etiam puerili corpori Roma quidem redeunti^a in prescripte poliandro ecclesie^b diuina predestinatio sepulturam ordinauit, quatenus pro eo ibi sancte seruientes ecclesie deum^c semper remuneratorem omnium bonorum fideliter precarentur precibus assiduis. Et hoc ergo tali pacto publice affirmari decreuit ut si forte quis sancte uiolator ecclesie, mortifera diabolo instigante cupiditate imbutus, ab eo unquam illam auferre uoluerit, cum Dathan et Abiron quos terra uiuentes deglutiuit, detestabilem sustinens condempnationem perpetualiter anathema sit. Quicumque uero ad augendum predictum stipendium custodiendumque studuerit, simul cum sancto Remigio, ubi cum Christo gloriatur, hilarem benedictionem consequatur in coelis; quod largiatur misericordia Saluatoris qui uiuit. Et hoc quidem, ut certius crederetur, idoneis stabiliuit sub testibus, quorum nempe nomina ordinatim conscribuntur. Inprimis enim Edwardus Dei gratia rex Anglorum testis fuit ueridicus, nec non Edgith regina, ex cujus prosapia originem duxerat; et Stigandus archipresul, simul et Aldredus, et Heremanus episcopus, et Leuricus episcopus, et Alwoldus episcopus, et Leuuinus episcopus et Willelmus episcopus, et Walterus episcopus, et Gyso presul. Preterea Haroldus dux, Tostinus, Gyrd et Lewinus, Waltef similiter cum multis prepotentibus principibus. Hoc scriptum in duabus cartis habetur diuisum; quarum unam anglica lingua scriptam idem comes Algarus secum retinuit, aliam uero latine dictatam sancto Remigio deuotus transmisit.*

a) *redeunti* C] *uenienti* D
b) *ecclesie* C] *basilice* D
c) *deum* D] *dum* C, possibly for *dnm*

6 R. Dodsworth and W. Dugdale, *Monasticon Anglicanum,* 3 vols. (London, 1655–73), vol. 1, p. 1022 (reprinted in W. Dugdale, *Monasticon Anglicanum,* ed. J. Caley, H. Ellis and B. Bandinel, 6 vols. in 8 (London, 1817–30), vol. 4, p. 1042 (no. 1)). Dugdale's text was translated by C. G. O. Bridgeman, 'Staffordshire pre-Conquest charters', in *Collections for a History of Staffordshire,* William Salt Archaeological Society (1916), pp. 69–137, at pp. 126–9.
7 Numerous bad readings point not so much to a faulty exemplar as to inaccurate reproduction of its readings, more likely to be uncorrected errors by the typesetter than textual blunders in any manuscript. Compare the following: *quemdam Anglorum comitem ingenuum* C] *quondam Anglorum comitem ingenium* D; *nomine Burchardi* C] *nomine Burobardi* D; *puerili corpori* C] *putrili corpori* D; *poliandro* C] *polianeso* D; *et hoc ergo* C] *de hoc ergo* D; *sustinens* C] *sustineat* D; *in coelis* C] *ecclesiis* D; *Haroldus dux* C] *Harotens dux* D; *aliam uero latine* C] *aliam uoce latine* D.

Translation:

In the name of our Lord Jesus Christ, [and] of the highest and indivisible Trinity. Let it be known to all worshippers of Christ that Ælfgar, a certain noble earl of the English, has given, with the consent of Edward by grace of God king of the English, to the church of Saint Remigius, Reims, a certain vill which is called in the English language Lapley, together with its appurtenances, for the sake of the soul of his son Burgheard, for whose youthful body, when returning from Rome, divine predestination ordained a place of burial in the cemetery of the aforesaid church, in order that the servants of the holy church there would faithfully intercede for him to God, always the rewarder of all good men, with unremitting prayer. And therefore he decided that this be affirmed publicly in such a way that if perchance some violator of the holy church, imbued with deadly greed at the instigation of the devil, should ever wish to steal this from Him, he will be forever excommunicated, enduring detestable condemnation with Dathan and Abiram, whom the earth swallowed up alive. However, whoever might devote himself to augmenting or protecting the aforesaid gift, let him obtain glad blessing in heaven together with St Remigius where he is exalted with Christ: may the mercy of the Saviour, who lives, grant this. And this indeed, in order that it be more surely believed, he [Ælfgar] has established before qualified witnesses whose names are clearly written in order. Namely, in the first place, Edward, by grace of God king of the English, was a truthful witness; and also Queen Edith, from whose family he [Ælfgar?] originated, Archbishop Stigand, and also Ealdred, and Bishop Hereman, and Bishop Leofric, and Bishop Ælfwold, Bishop Leofwine and Bishop William, and Bishop Walter, and Bishop Giso. In addition, Earl Harold, Tostig, Gyrth and Leofwine and Waltheof, together with many other very powerful nobles. This text is divided into two charters, of which the one written in the English language the same Earl Ælfgar retained for himself, the other written in Latin, the devoted man transmitted to Saint Remigius.

Although it is anomalous in certain respects, there is no reason to doubt the essential veracity of this charter: it probably represents an attempt by a continental scribe who was unfamiliar with Anglo-Saxon diplomatic to translate or paraphrase a document originally drawn up in Old English. Some of the formulae suggest that its draftsman was not English.[8] Others

---

8 For example, an English scribe would not have styled Ælfgar *comes Anglorum ingenuus*. Old English *eorl* was invariably translated *dux*, not *comes*, in Latin texts in England before the Norman Conquest: C. P. Lewis, 'The early earls of Norman England', *ANS* 13 (1991), pp. 207–23, at p. 215. An English scribe would have been more likely to style Ælfgar *dux Merciorum*, as Earl Leofric was sometimes styled, not *comes Anglorum*. See S 1392, 1395, 1396; and *The Bayeux Tapestry*, ed. D. M. Wilson (London, 1985), plate 2, where Harold is styled *dux Anglorum* – an exception which proves the rule. According to *Regesta Regum Anglorum*, a searchable edition of the corpus of Anglo-Saxon royal diplomas 670–1066 compiled by Dr Sean Miller (currently at www. anglo-saxons.net), the adjective *ingenuus* is not used to describe the donor, beneficiary or witness in any pre-Conquest royal diploma.

are rare in Anglo-Saxon charters.[9] It is also problematic that Edith's subscription is followed by the phrase *ex cujus prosapia originem duxerat,* for she
and Ælfgar are not otherwise known to have been related.[10] However, such
anomalies need not necessarily arouse suspicion, for they are readily explicable as a function of the way the charter was produced. The last sentence
of the charter is certainly plausible: non-royal charters were often drawn
up in duplicate or triplicate in late Anglo-Saxon England, usually in the
form of a chirograph, so that the beneficiary, grantor and (if deemed necessary) a third party could each retain a copy; and since the beneficiary
was in this case a French religious house, it is not impossible that the document was originally drawn up in English and Latin, just as the charter states.
An alternative possibility is that Ælfgar's charter was issued in the form of
a chirograph comprising two (or three) versions of the Old English text,
and that one of these was subsequently translated into Latin.[11] Either way,
it is possible that a representative of the community at Reims visited England
in order to take possession of the charter and the property it conveyed,
and was involved in the drafting of the Latin text. This hypothesis would
explain some of its idiosyncrasies. Whatever the case, there remain good
reasons for regarding this as an essentially authentic document, albeit one
produced in unusual circumstances. There are not many extant charters
issued in the names of late Anglo-Saxon earls, but a handful of those that
survive were issued in the names of Ælfgar and his father Leofric.[12] Our
witness list contains plausible Latin renderings of Old English names, and
its subscriptions are consistent with a date range of 1060 x 1063.[13] That

---

9 For example, the *notum sit . . . didisse* construction is almost never used in the dis-
   positive section of authentic pre-Conquest charters (this may have been an attempt
   to render a formula beginning *her swutelað* in the Old English). Dr Susan Kelly (pers.
   comm.) informs me that the structure of anathema and blessing are both unusual
   in an English context. The formula *testis fuit veridicus* does not occur in any pre-
   Conquest royal diploma.

10 Though it may just be relevant that Edith's brother, Harold, married Burgheard's
   sister, Ealdgyth, within about five years of Burgheard's death: Baxter, *Earls of Mercia,*
   pp. 299–300.

11 J. Mabillon, *De Re Diplomatica Libri VI,* 2 vols. (Paris, 1681–1704), vol. 1, pp. 6–7, first
   drew out the interest of the manner in which S 1237 describes the form in which
   is was issued.

12 Of these, S 1232 and 1478 are the most reliable. However, there are others which
   are either dubious or spurious in their extant form, but which may partly have been
   based on authentic charters or memoranda: S 1226, 1223, 1238, 1398 and 1479.

13 The formal dating limits are *c.*1060, when Archbishop Ealdred of York, Bishop
   Walter of Hereford and Bishop Giso of Wells were elected to these positions, and

Ælfgar granted the estate in question is certain, for Domesday Book demonstrates that St Remigius held three hides at Lapley in 1066, and that this grant was subsequently augmented.[14]

Two further texts, which were composed at about the same time, confirm that Burgheard died during the course of a journey to Rome and was buried in the cathedral there. One of these is a Latin epitaph known to have been carved on Burgheard's tombstone. The tombstone itself is thought to have been lost in the Revolution.[15] However, both the location of Burgheard's burial and the text of his epitaph are known. Dom Guillaume Marlot OSB (1596–1667), a monk of Saint-Rémi, observed that Burgheard's tomb could be seen in the south choir of the church;[16] and the eighteenth-century *Ordinaire du sacristain de l'abbaye de Saint-Remy de Reims* records that it lay in front of a great gilded candelabra on the epistle side of the choir.[17] Marlot also transcribed and printed the epitaph:

*c.*1062/3 when Ælfgar died, but there are strong grounds for thinking it was issued in 1061, probably in or after June: see below, pp. 278–80. Hinkle, 'Gift', p. 30 observed that the subscription of Bishop Ælfwold of Sherborne is problematic since William of Malmesbury implies that he died in 1058, but it is demonstrable that Ælfwold was alive in the early 1060s: see S. Keynes, 'Giso, Bishop of Wells (1061–88)', *ANS* 19 (1997), pp. 203–71, at p. 208, n. 34.

14 The entry for Lapley is GDB 222d (Northamptonshire 16:1). The next entry establishes that St Remigius Reims held one hide at Lapley Marston in Staffordshire in 1086, which had been held by a certain Godwine 'with sake and soke' *TRE*; the Godwine in question may have been Ælfgar's uncle, for whom see Baxter, *Earls of Mercia*, p. 298. Elsewhere we learn that Earl Ælfgar granted two further estates in Staffordshire to St Remigius, and that St Remigius held one hide at Silvington in Overs Hundred in Shropshire *TRE*: GDB 247c (Staffordshire 5:1–2), 252b (Shropshire 3a:1, with note).

15 Hinkle, 'Gift', p. 31 n. 3.

16 Dom Guilelmi Marlot, *Metropolis Remensis Historia*, 2 vols. (1666–1679), vol. 1, p. 340: *in choro ecclesiæ ad dextrum.*

17 Reims, Bibliothèque Municipale Carnegie, MS 339 (N. fonds), fol. 64r–64v: *devant le pied du candelabre . . . entrant au choeur . . . est le comte Burchard, anglais.* See also P. Chastelain, 'Histoire abrégée de l'église de Saint-Remy de Reims', Reims, Bibliothèque Municipale Carnegie, MS 1828 (N. fonds), p. 49: *On vois encore dans le choeur la tombe de Burchard jeune comte anglais, qui mourut en france, l'an mil soixante, en faisant le voyage de Rome et dont le corps fut apporté a Saint Remi, comme il paroit par son epîtaphe. Il est dans un petit caveau sous les stales du choeur du cote de l'épître.* See also P. Tarbé, *Les Sépultures de l'Église Saint-Remi de Reims* (Reims, 1842), p. 45; and A. Lacatte-Joltrois, *Essais Historiques sur L'Église de Saint Remi de Reims* (Reims, 1843), p. 165. It is a nice coincidence that Burgheard was buried close to an individual who has been the focus of much of Janet Nelson's teaching and research, for Hincmar of Reims was buried in the nave of the same church: Tarbé, *Les Sépultures*, pp. 43–4; Lacatte-Joltrois, *Essais*, pp. 168–72.

Anglica quem genuit, hunc tellus Gallica condit;
Clara stirpe cluit, Anglica quem genuit.
Proh dolor exul obit, dum Romam pusio tendit,
Dum te Petre petit, proh dolor exul obit.
Se petiit revehi Remis sub limine laeti
Aulae Remigii, se petiit reuehi.
Dulcis ephebe tuis, heu primi gratia floris,
Heu lugende nimis dulcis ephebe tuis.
Altera lux aderat, qua taurus sole flagrabat;
Dum pubeda meat, altera lux aderat.
Quem tegit hoc taphium Burchardi nomen adeptum,
Grande decus procerum, quem tegit hoc taphium.
Lector habes titulum, pete Petrum pandere regnum,
Anglus adibat eum, lector habes titulum.[18]

Translation:
Whom English (soil) gave birth to, French soil hides;
he is famous for his distinguished lineage, whom English (soil) gave birth to.
Alas, he dies an exile, while still a youth he makes his way toward Rome;
while he seeks you Peter, alas, he dies an exile.
He begged to have himself brought to Reims on the threshold of death;
to the church of Remigius he begged to have himself brought.
Young man, dear to your family, alas in the grace of youthful prime,
Alas, too much to be mourned, young man, dear to your family.
The other light arrived, when Taurus was bright with the sun
While the young man is on the road, the other light arrived.
He whom this tombstone covers was given the name of Burgheard,
A great glory of noblemen, he whom this tombstone covers.
O reader, you see this inscription, entreat Peter to open the kingdom;
An Englishman visited him, O reader, you see this inscription.

Marlot also recorded that Earl Ælfgar gave to Saint-Rémi a gospel book with richly decorated covers, sheathed in gold, and that one of the covers bore an *inscriptio* in its borders. Marlot transcribed the text of this in his unpublished history of St-Rémi,[19] and the following decade published a slightly revised text in the first volume of his *Historia*.[20] These texts are collated below (with two suggested emendations given in italics):

18 Marlot, *Metropolis Remensis Historia*, vol. 1, p. 340. The text is also printed by C. Poussin, *Monographie de l'Abbaye et de l'Église Saint-Remi de Reims* (Reims, 1857), p. 268. Hinkle, 'Gift', p. 31, n. 3 prints the first three couplets erroneously. For the church in which Burgheard was buried, see J.-P. Ravaux, 'L'église Saint-Remi de Reims au XIe siècle', *Bulletin Archéologique du Comité des Travaux Historique et Scientifique*, n.s. 8 (1972), pp. 51–98.
19 Dom G. Marlot, *Mémoires pour l'histoire de l'abbaie de St-Remy de Reims* (1658), Bibliothèque Nationale, Collection de Champagne, no. 27, fol. 293v; printed by Hinkle, 'Gifts', p. 31, n. 4.
20 Marlot, *Metropolis Remensis Historia*, vol. 1, p. 340. This version of the text is reprinted by Poussin, *Monographie de St-Remi*, p. 268, n. 1, and (with French translation) by Lacatte-Joltrois, *Essais Historiques*, p. 165.

Hic codex veniae lapsis, legatio vitae,
Te pii[21] Burchardi[22] memorare magne Remigi,
Postulat, ut coelis, tecum ceu commanet aruis
Algar[23] dux anglus[24] simul, et consors lateralis,
Algiua[25] Pontificum summo dant munus amicum.

Translation:
This book of forgiveness for the fallen, an embassy of life, begs you, great Remigius, to be mindful of pious Burgheard so that he may remain with you, in heaven just as on earth. An English earl, Ælfgar, with his wife at his side, Ælfgifu, gives a friendly gift to the foremost of bishops.

This gospel book and its covers were evidently magnificent objects. Marlot described the book as being *couvert de lames d'or*;[26] and in the eighteenth century, Dom Pierre Chastelain (1709–1782) described it as being *couvert d'or et de pierreries*.[27] In addition, an inventory of the abbey's treasure drawn up in 1549 begins with a description of a gospel book, which is almost certainly identical to that given to the abbey by Earl Ælfgar:

Premier ung livre d'evangille servant aux gros doubles ayans deux fermeaux d'argent dore l'un des coste couvert d'une platyne d'or, et aux bordures d'argent dore. A l'autre ung cruxifiement notre dame et saint Jehan et ung dieu le pere. Et quatre petitz anges d'argent dore sur icellui avec quelques piereries. Excepte huit places que les pierres sont perdues. Et l'aultre coste couvert de velour rouge ayant cinq gros cloux d'argent dore.[28]

---

21 Marlot, *Mémoires*: *pie*. Marlot, *Historia*, seems to have conjectured *vobis* instead of *te pie*. Richard Sharpe (pers. comm.) suggests the emendation *pii*, observing that '*vobis* cannot be right, since the next line uses *tecum*; but *pie* is both ill-placed for agreement with *Remigi* and implausible since he is also given the adjective *magne*'.

22 Marlot, *Mémoires*: *Buchardi*.

23 Marlot, *Historia*: *Alegar*.

24 Marlot, *Historia*: *anilis*. Marlot's editorial conjecture to maintain the internal rhyme between the caesura and line-end otherwise deployed throughout the text (*ueniae/uitae*, *Burchardi/Remigi*, etc.); but this is implausible since the author is unlikely to have wanted to attribute Earl Ælfgar the characteristics of an old woman.

25 Marlot, *Memoires*: *Algrea*; Marlot, *Historia*: *Alegiea*. Neither is plausible as Latin rendering of Old English *Ælfgifu*.

26 Marlot, *Mémoires*, fol. 293v.

27 Chastelain, 'Histoire abrégée de l'église de Saint-Remy de Reims', p. 49: *Le pere de ce comte nomme algar ou allegar fit present a l'église de Saint Remi a l'occasion de l'inhumation du corps de son fils, d'un livre des evangiles couvert d'or et de pierreries que l'on conserve depuis ce temps et autour duquel sont gravés cinq vers Latins qui en font memoire.*

28 Reims, Archives Départementales de la Marne, Annexe de Reims, 56 H 907 (formerly H 1289), 'Inventaire des reliques', fol. 154v. Translation: 'First, a Gospel book for the greater festivals, with two gold clasps, one of the sides covered with a gold plate, and edged with silver-gilt. On the one side a crucifixion scene with Our Lady

Unfortunately, the cover of the gospel book has been lost.[29] However, to gain an impression of what it may have looked like, one can contemplate the magnificent front cover of New York, Pierpont Morgan Library, MS 708, which is one of the gospel books known to have been owned by a contemporary of Earl Ælfgar: Countess Judith of Flanders, wife of Earl Tostig.[30] As Hinkle observed, this book cover and that described in the Reims inventory appear to have been very similar: the former consists of a wooden board sheathed in gold and an engraved silver-gilt frame, gems mounted in gold filigree, and separately mounted silver figures representing Christ in majesty in one register and the Crucifixion in another. To judge from the Reims inventory, the only significant difference between this and the cover of Ælfgar's gospel book is that the former has two angels whereas the latter had four.[31] Happily, whoever took the treasure in which Ælfgar's gospel book was bound apparently decided to leave the gospel book itself behind, and it remains in Reims to this day.[32]

and Saint John, and a God the Father. And four little silver-gilt angels on it with settings of precious stones. Except that in eight places the stones are lost. And the other side covered with red velvet, and with five large silver-gilt studs.' Hinkle, 'Gift', pp. 24–6, prints this section of the inventory and shows that it almost certainly describes Ælfgar's gospel book, observing that nine parchment folios were added to the beginning of the gospel book in the seventeenth century which contained readings for the principal feast days celebrated at Saint-Rémi – presumably the 'gros doubles' referred to in this text.

29 Its rich decoration is presumed to have been lost in the Revolution, but the original oak boards survived until the twentieth century, for they were described by H. Loriquet, *Catalogue général des manuscrits des bibliothèques publique de France, Tome XXXVIII: Reims* (Paris, 1904), p. 15: *De la reliure couverte de velours rouge ornée sur le plat initial d'une plaque de métal précieux ou d'une planche d'émail, et sur le plat final d'un encadrement et de clous d'orfèvrerie, il ne reste que les deux ais de chêne disloqués.* These boards appear not to have been kept after the manuscript was rebound in 1950: Hinkle, 'Gift', p. 26, n. 2.

30 For illustrations and discussion of Pierpont Morgan Library, MS 708, and its cover, see P. Needham, *Twelve Centuries of Bookbinding 400–1600* (New York and London, 1979), plate 8 (p. xxi), and pp. 33–5; H. Swarzenski, *Monuments of Romanesque Art: the Art of Church Treasures in North-Western Europe*, 2nd edn (London, 1974), plate 64; H. M. Nixon and M. M. Foot, *The History of Decorated Bookbinding in England* (Oxford, 1992), plate 3 and pp. 19–20; T. H. Ohlgren, *Anglo-Saxon Textual Illustration: Photographs of Sixteen Manuscripts with Descriptions and Index* (Kalamazoo, Michigan, 1992), plates 12.1–12.9. See further P. McGurk and J. Rosenthal, 'The Anglo-Saxon gospelbooks of Judith, Countess of Flanders: their text, make-up and function', *ASE* 24 (1991), pp. 201–308.

31 Hinkle, 'Gift', pp. 32–5 and plate 9.

32 Reims, Bibliothèque Municipale Carnegie, MS 9.

Burgheard in Domesday Book

Attention may now be turned to the question of whether or not Burgheard can be identified in Domesday Book. Curiously, this matter has never been addressed before.[33] What follows is an attempt to address it using an approach which *PASE* aims to facilitate.

The identification of pre-Conquest landholders in Domesday Book is notoriously problematic.[34] Very often, the best that one can do is simply to balance probabilities by addressing a series of diagnostic questions. How common is the name? Were the persons identified using by-names or titles? To whom were they connected through bonds of lordship? Did the estates in question pass to one or several 'successors' between 1066 and 1086? Were these estates geographically concentrated? Were they similar in size? Anyone familiar with Domesday prosopography will know that it can be an extremely laborious task to gather the data needed to address such questions. *PASE*, however, will enable users to assemble all of the Domesday data relating to a particular name instantaneously, presenting search results in the form of tables and maps which have been specifically designed to facilitate prosopographical judgement. By way of illustration, the entries relating to persons named Burgheard in Domesday Book are set out in the Appendix to this volume in the format currently under development for *PASE*.

Several factors combine to suggest that the majority of these entries relate to a single individual.

1. Burgheard was not a common name. According to the *PASE* database, it occurs in just twelve documents which relate to at most five individuals, all of whom lived before the year 900.[35] This makes it unlikely that the Domesday entries relate to several different individuals.

2. The size of Burgheard's estates. The largest estate attributed to Burgheard was Mendlesham in Suffolk: this was assessed at seven carucates

33 For example, the question seems not to have been addressed by P. A. Clarke, *The English Nobility under Edward the Confessor* (Oxford, 1994); M. Bailey, 'Introduction', in *Little Domesday Book, Suffolk: Introduction, Translation and Indexes*, ed. A. Williams and G. Martin (London, 2000), pp. 9–30; or by A. Wareham, *Lords and Communities in Early Medieval East Anglia* (Woodbridge, 2005).

34 For an important discussion of the problems addressed below, see C. P. Lewis, 'Joining the dots: a methodology for identifying the English in Domesday Book', in K. S. B. Keats-Rohan (ed.), *Family Trees and the Roots of Politics: The Prosopography of Britain and France from the Tenth to the Twelfth Century* (Woodbridge, 1997), pp. 69–87.

35 *PASE* 2005, s.n. 'Burgheard 1–5'; the name also occurs in the Durham *Liber Vitae*, fol. 44r.

and forty-two acres and was attributed a value of £25. This was a sub-stantial estate by any standards in eleventh-century England. Estates of this size were generally held only by individuals who were sufficiently wealthy to hold land in several locations. None of the other estates attributed to Burgheard were anything like as large as Mendlesham, but the two estates in Buckinghamshire were of sufficient size to qualify a man for the rank of thegn, and all of the remaining estates were fairly substantial: they were all worth more than any of the holdings held by people commended to Burgheard.

3.   The geographic proximity of the estates. With the exception of two outliers in Buckinghamshire, all of the estates attributed to Burgheard lay in three adjacent shires, and seven of them lay in Suffolk.

4.   Burgheard's successors. The majority of Burgheard's estates were held by one individual in 1086. This is significant. One of the ways in which King William distributed land after 1066 was to assign all or most of the estates which had been held by a particular Englishman in 1066 to just one of his followers: according to the legitimating propaganda of the Conqueror's regime, the Englishman in question was defined as the tenant-in-chief's *antecessor*.[36] It follows that if several of the estates attributed to a given English name in 1066 passed to the same tenant-in-chief in 1086, it is likely that those estates were held by the same individual before the Conquest. This logic establishes a strong connec-tion between Burgheard of Shenley in Buckinghamshire, Burgheard of Fundenhall in Norfolk, and Burgheard of north-east Suffolk, for all of these estates were held by Hugh d'Avranches, earl of Chester, in 1086.

5.   Lordship patterns. It is known that modest pre-Conquest landholders tended to commend themselves either to men of national stature, or to men who held substantial estates in their own shire or locality.[37] Burgheard of Mendlesham was clearly a substantial local landholder,

---

36   G. Garnett, 'Coronation and propaganda: implications of the Norman claim to the throne of England in 1066', *TRHS* 5th series 36 (1986), pp. 91–116.

37   For patterns in commendatory lord-seeking, see R. Abels, 'An Introduction to the Bedfordshire Domesday', in A. Williams and G. H. Martin (eds), *The Bedfordshire Domesday* (London, 1991), pp. 1–53; R. Abels 'An Introduction to the Hertfordshire Domesday', *ibid.*, pp. 1–36; Clarke, *English Nobility*, p. 105; A. Williams, 'Little Domesday and the English: the Hundred of Colneis in Suffolk', in E. Hallam and D. Bates (eds), *Domesday Book* (Stroud, 2001), pp. 103–20; Baxter, *Earls of Mercia*, pp. 211–12, 293–4.

and it is therefore probable that he was identical with the man of that name who attracted numerous commended men with modest holdings near Mendelsham and elsewhere in Suffolk. This establishes a connection between Burgheard of Mendlesham and the *antecessor* of Earl Hugh.

Each of these points is in itself suggestive; taken together, they tip the balance of probability strongly in favour of the proposition that all but the last two of the entries in the table relate to the same individual.

Was Burgheard of Mendlesham and of Shenley identical with the son of Earl Ælfgar? A potentially serious objection to this hypothesis is that Burgheard son of Ælfgar died in 1061, five years before Domesday's notional cut-off date. However, this does not preclude the possibility that Burgheard of Mendlesham was the earl's son, for Domesday Book attributes estates to several members of the English nobility who died long before 1066: men such as earls Godwine, Siward, Ralph, Leofric and Ælfgar.[38] Indeed, the fact that Domesday attributes numerous estates to Earl Ælfgar strengthens the case for thinking that it also lists those of his son Burgheard. Further considerations point in the same direction. Ælfgar held the earldom of East Anglia between 1051 and 1057, and was therefore in a position to acquire property in the eastern counties. Ælfgar also held land in all of the shires where Burgheard held land; and his wife Ælfgifu was a substantial landholder in Suffolk. It is also relevant that a large proportion of the estates held by Burgheard's brothers, earls Eadwine and Morcar, were held by King William and Earl Hugh in 1086.[39] Taken together, these points amount to a powerful case for thinking that Burgheard of Mendlesham was indeed Ælfgar's son. If so, he held a total of eleven estates assessed at eleven hides, eighteen carucates and 102 acres which were assigned an aggregate value of £50 *TRE*; and therefore belonged to an elite group of secular landholders in England whose estates were worth more than £40.[40]

---

38 For the problem as to why Domesday attributes estates to earls who died (or were exiled) before 1066, see S. Baxter and J. Blair, 'Land tenure and royal patronage in the early English Kingdom: a model and a case study', *ANS* 28 (2006), pp. 19–46 at pp. 24–5; and Baxter, *Earls of Mercia*, pp. 135–8.

39 For the estates of the house of Leofwine, and their holders in 1086, see Baxter, *Earls of Mercia*, pp. 125–51, 290–1, 315.

40 His name should be added to the list of pre-Conquest landholders with estates worth £40 compiled by Clarke, *English Nobility*, pp. 32–3.

The date and context of Burgheard's journey to Rome

It has been suggested that Burgheard was one of several Englishmen who went to Rome on various missions in the spring of 1061.[41] This suggestion can be strengthened. The question as to why Burgheard may have gone has never been addressed, but a plausible case can be made for thinking that Burgheard was sent to escort and support Bishop Wulfwig of Dorchester, for his business in Rome was of special interest to Burgheard's family and their political calculations.

Several sources reveal the presence of English churchmen and noblemen in Rome in 1061. The 'D' text of the *Anglo-Saxon Chronicle* records that Archbishop Cynesige of York died on 22 December 1060, and that his successor Ealdred went to Rome to receive his pallium from Pope Nicholas II the following year.[42] John of Worcester adds that Ealdred was accompanied by Tostig, earl of Northumbria; and that two newly appointed bishops, Giso of Wells and Walter of Hereford, were consecrated by the pope.[43] The *Vita Edwardi* supplies more detail. It records that Tostig was accompanied by his wife Judith and his younger brother Gyrth; that they travelled to Rome through Saxony and the upper reaches of the Rhine; and that they were received honourably by Pope Nicholas and invited to attend a synod of Rome. Giso and Walter were duly ordained by the pope, but Ealdred fared less well: he was rebuked for holding two bishoprics, contrary to canon law, and was both denied the pallium and deposed from episcopal rank. Realizing that this would make his stay in Rome more protracted than he had anticipated, Tostig sent Judith back to England, escorted by many of his own men. The pope remained implacable in the negotiations that followed, and Ealdred was eventually compelled to leave Rome together with Giso, Walter, Tostig and what remained of the latter's entourage. However, on the first day of their journey, the party was attacked by bandits and was forced to return to Rome. Tostig was spared capture by a kinsman of King Edward named Gospatric, who confused the bandits by posing as the earl. Hearing of these misfortunes, and perhaps fearing Tostig's wrath, the pope eventually decided to reinstate Ealdred as bishop and to give him the

---

41   E. A. Freeman, *The History of the Norman Conquest of England: Its Causes and Its Results*, 3rd edn, 6 vols. (Oxford, 1870–79), vol. 2, pp. 462, 466, 679–80; Hinkle, 'Gift', pp. 27–31.

42   *The Anglo-Saxon Chronicle: A Revised Translation*, ed. D. Whitelock, D. C. Douglas and S. I. Tucker (London, 1961), [hereafter *ASC*] MS D *s.a.* 1060, 1061 (p. 135).

43   *The Chronicle of John of Worcester*, ed. R. R. Darlington and P. McGurk, 3 vols. (Oxford, 1995–), *s.a.* 1061 (vol. 2, pp. 586–8).

pallium. The party then returned to England, apparently without further incident.[44]

Further details relating to these events can be gleaned from other sources. A text which purports to be the 'autobiography' of Bishop Giso records that he was consecrated by Pope Nicholas on Easter day (15 April) 1061, and that he was back in England between 17 and 23 June that year.[45] Wells Cathedral Library preserves, in its original form, a privilege of Pope Nicholas to Bishop Giso, dated 25 April 1061, confirming him in the rights of his see.[46] A second privilege was issued by Pope Nicholas on 3 May 1061 in favour of Bishop Wulfwig of Dorchester, confirming him in possession of all things pertaining to his see.[47] Peter Damian's *Desceptatio Synodalis* records that a Tuscan nobleman, Gerard, count of Galeria, was excommunicated for leading the attack on the English party outside Rome, and for stealing about £1,000 worth of silver from them.[48] William of Malmesbury records that Ealdred received the pallium only after agreeing to leave Worcester, and that papal legates were then despatched to England, *inter alia* to ordain a suitable candidate for that see.[49] Finally, the anonymous author of a twelfth-century chronicle of the archbishops of York remarked that Ealdred was given a letter of privilege from Pope Nicholas; but unfortunately, the author only transcribed the first sentence of this privilege.[50]

Since Burgheard is not mentioned in any of these sources, Freeman's suggestion that he formed part of this English contingent has been called

---

44   *Vita Ædwardi Regis qui apud Westmonasterium requiescit*, ed. and trans. F. Barlow, *The Life of King Edward Who Rests at Westminster*, 2nd edn (Oxford, 1992), I, c. 5 (pp. 52–6).

45   Keynes, 'Giso, Bishop of Wells', p. 267.

46   *Councils and Synods, with other Documents relating to the English Church, 871–1204*, ed. D. Whitelock, M. Brett and C. N. L. Brooke, 2 vols. (Oxford, 1981), no. 77 (pp. 548–50). For discussion, see Keynes, 'Giso', pp. 228, 255.

47   *Councils and Synods*, ed. Whitelock *et al.*, no. 78 (pp. 550–2), trans. *English Historical Documents*, ed. Douglas and Greenway, vol. 2, no. 75 (pp. 641–2).

48   Peter Damian, *Desceptatio Synodalis*, ed. L. de Heinemann, *MGH, Libelli de Lite Imperatorum et Pontificum Saeculis XI et XII Conscripti* (Hanover, 1891), I, pp. 76–94 at p. 91; *Two of the Saxon Chronicles Parallel*, ed. J. Earle and C. Plummer, 2 vols. (Oxford, 1892–9), vol. 2, p. 250.

49   William of Malmesbury, *Vita Wulfstani*, ed. and trans. M. Winterbottom and R. M. Thompson, *William of Malmesbury: Saints' Lives* (Oxford, 2002), c. 10 (pp. 40–2); William of Malmesbury, *Gesta Pontificum Anglorum*, ed. and trans. M. Winterbottom (Oxford, 2007), III, c. 115 (pp. 380–2).

50   *Chronica Pontificum Ecclesiæ Eboracensis*, in *The Historians of the Church of York and its Archbishops*, ed. J. Raine, Rolls Series 71, 3 vols. (London, 1879–1894), vol. 2, pp. 346–7.

into question.[51] There are, however, excellent reasons for thinking that he did. Ælfgar's charter is datable by its witness list to the period between Ealdred's appointment to the archbishopric in 1061 and c.1062 when Ælfgar died; and, as Hinkle observed, the charter is also subscribed by five of the men who are known to have been in Rome in 1061: bishops Ealdred, Giso and Walter, and earls Tostig and Gyrth.[52] To this can be added one further, clinching, piece of evidence. Burgheard's epitaph contains the line: *Altera lux aderat, qua taurus sole flagrabat* ('the other light arrived, when Taurus was bright with the sun'). The 'other light' is surely the celestial light of the afterlife; and if so, the clear implication is that Burgheard died during the month of Taurus – that is, between mid-April and mid-May.[53] This corresponds very neatly with the dates when the English contingent is known to have been in Rome. Ælfgar's charter says that Burgheard died *Roma redeunti* – on his way back from Rome.[54] This presumably happened a few days after 3 May, when Wulfwig's privilege was issued.[55]

What was Burgheard doing in Rome? One possibility is that he was sent there by the king. It would have been logical for the king to send the son of the earl of Mercia to escort a party which included the bishops of three Midland sees (Dorchester, Worcester and Hereford). In this connection, it may be significant that Burgheard of Shenley is styled *huscarle regis Edwardi* in Domesday Book, for the king's housecarls were often employed as messengers and bodyguards.[56] Here it may also be relevant that the inscription on the cover of Ælfgar's gospel book contains a play on the words *legatio*

---

51 Freeman, *Norman Conquest*, vol. 2, pp. 462, 466, 679–80; Barlow (*Vita Edwardi*, p. 52, n. 128), considers the evidence for this 'very doubtful'.

52 Hinkle, 'Gift', pp. 29–30.

53 According to early medieval calculations, the Sun entered Taurus on 17 April every year: see, for example, A. Borst, *Die Karolingische Kalenderreform, MGH*, Schriften 46 (Hanover, 1998), p. 267. For discussion, see D. Juste, 'Neither observation nor astronomical tables: an alternative way of computing the planetary longitudes in the early Western Middle Ages', in C. Burnett et al. (eds), *Studies in the History of the Exact Sciences in Honour of David Pingree* (Brill, 2004), pp. 181–222, esp. pp. 182–7. I am grateful to Sophie Page and David Juste for these references.

54 A possible objection here is that the line in the epitaph which says *dum Romam pusio tendit, dum te Petre petit* could be read as implying that Burgheard died on his way to Rome, though an alternative reading might be that he died at some stage during a journey to and from Rome. Given this ambiguity, the more definite evidence supplied by the charter is to be preferred.

55 Varin, *Archives Administratives de la Ville de Reims*, p. 207 n asserts that Burgheard died at Aosta in Piedmont. I have been unable to find corroborating evidence for this.

56 GDB 146d (Buckinghamshire 13:2); N. Hooper, 'The housecarls of England in the eleventh century', *ANS* 7 (1985), pp. 161–76.

vitae: perhaps the author intended to convey the idea that the gospel book would serve as an embassy for Burgheard's life, just as he had been an ambassador by profession when he died?

However this may be, there are also strong grounds for thinking that Burgheard was sent by Earl Ælfgar to escort Bishop Wulfwig of Dorchester to Rome, for Wulfwig's privilege demonstrates that the business he conducted there had an important bearing upon the interests of the earl and his family. Before turning to the text of this document, it is necessary to sketch some elements of the political background which help place it in context.

Four points must be registered here. In the first place, it is demonstrable that the archbishops of York and bishops of Dorchester competed with one another for control of the former see of Lyndsey throughout much of the late Anglo-Saxon and early Norman periods.[57] Second, the earls of Mercia and the earls of Northumbria also vied with one another for control of Lincolnshire and other shires in the east Midlands in the late Anglo-Saxon period.[58] Third, and partly for these reasons, Earl Leofric of Mercia and Bishop Wulfwig reached an agreement concerning the endowment of St Mary's Stow in Lincolnshire, at some stage between October 1053 and March 1055. The text of this agreement is complex, and contains hints of tension between the bishop and the community at Stow, who were to be the principal beneficiaries of the proposed grant; but it remains clear that it served to cement an alliance between a bishop and an earl who were both determined to exercise jurisdiction in Lincolnshire, and to resist the southward-looking ambitions of the earl of Northumbria and the archbishop of York.[59]

Fourth, however, the political circumstances which had made this alliance desirable and possible in the early 1050s began to look very different by the late 1050s. When the Stow agreement was made, Leofric and his son Ælfgar were earls of Mercia and East Anglia respectively, and so between them controlled a nearly contiguous block of territory between Cheshire in the northwest and Essex in the southeast. Lincolnshire lay between their two commands. It therefore made sense for Leofric to augment Stow's endowment, for this would serve as a tangible expression of his family's

57 P. H. Sawyer, *Anglo-Saxon Lincolnshire* (Lincoln, 1998), pp. 149–54.

58 D. Whitelock, 'The dealings of the kings of England with Northumbria in the tenth and eleventh centuries', in P. Clemoes (ed.), *The Anglo-Saxons: Studies in some Aspects of their History and Culture presented to Bruce Dickens* (London, 1959), pp. 70–88, at pp. 81–8.

59 S 1478. I am grateful to Susan Kelly for sending me a copy of her edition, translation and discussion of this document in advance of publication.

power and influence in that shire. However, the balance of power between King Edward's earls changed dramatically shortly after the Stow agreement was made. Four earls died between 1055 and 1057, and the sons of Earl Godwine were the principal beneficiaries of the redistribution of power that followed: Tostig succeeded to the earldom of Northumbria when Siward died in 1055; Harold succeeded to Herefordshire and Gloucestershire, which appear to have been controlled by Odda and Ralph until they died in 1056 and 1057 respectively; Leofwine succeeded to Ralph's command in the east Midlands after 1057; and although Ælfgar succeeded to the earldom of Mercia when Leofric died in 1057, he was compelled to cede control of East Anglia to Gyrth. These appointments had a profound impact on the balance of power within the kingdom as a whole. They also shattered Ælfgar's family's plans to build up a power base in Lincolnshire. Ælfgar perhaps protested too vigorously, for he was exiled and compelled to force his way back into power in 1055 and again in 1058.[60] Either way, he was powerless to prevent Tostig and his brothers from building up a power base in the east Midlands, and in Lincolnshire in particular.[61]

It thus emerges that Earl Ælfgar and Bishop Wulfwig had grounds for feeling insecure about their interests in Lincolnshire in the late 1050s and early 1060s. Their concerns were doubtless compounded by the appointment of Bishop Ealdred of Worcester to the archbishopric of York, for Ealdred was an ambitious prelate who was determined to retain power and influence south of the Humber, as was clearly signalled by his refusal to renounce the see of Worcester.[62] All this is sufficient to explain why Wulfwig went to Rome in the spring of 1061: his objective was to seek papal support for his jurisdictional rights in Lincolnshire. The text of the privilege he received on 3 May 1061 demonstrates this, and proves that he was successful. The relevant passage of the document reads as follows:

---

60 *ASC* MS CDE *s.a.* 1055–1058; Baxter, *Earls of Mercia*, pp. 45–7, 64–71.
61 Domesday Book reveals that Tostig held more land than any other earl in Bedfordshire, Buckinghamshire and Nottinghamshire. Before he was forced into exile in October 1065, Tostig probably also held the extensive estates in Lincolnshire attributed to earls Eadwine and Morcar in Domesday Book. Tostig is addressed in writs pertaining to Northamptonshire and Nottinghamshire (S 1110, 1160); he had the third penny in Nottingham (GDB 280a (Nottinghamshire B:2)); and the *Vita Edwardi* (ed. Barlow, p. 76) implies that Lincoln lay within his earldom in 1065.
62 For Ealdred's career, see M. K. Lawson and V. King, DNB, 'Ealdred (d. 1069). Ealdred's determination to maintain a foothold in the Midlands is demonstrated by his reluctance to relinquish the see of Worcester, and by the fact that he retained control of several Worcester episcopal vills until he died: *Vita Wulfstani*, ed. and trans. Winterbottom and Thompson, pp. 42–50, 60–4.

Igitur quia petisti a nobis, karissime fili, cum Edwardi regis legatis atque litteris nostri vide-licet amici, ut per nostri privilegii paginam tue ecclesie tibique necnon successoribus tuis omnia perpetualiter confirmaremus, que prefate ecclesie iuste et legaliter competunt, sugges-tioni tue gratanter annuentes per huius nostre constitucionis decretum et apostolice sedis liberale edictum concedimus et confirmamus tibi sicut supra legitur, tuisque successoribus ibidem canonice promovendis inperpetuum, queque prefate ecclesie pertinent, tam que in presentiarum possidet vel possedit, et maxime parrochiam Lindisi ecclesiamque Stou cum Newerca et appendiciis quas iniuste Aluricus archiepiscopus Eboracensis invasit, uti per legatorum nostrorum dicta et per antecessorum testimonia et scripta agnovimus, quamque in futuro quocumque modo divinis et humanis legibus adquirere poterit, scilicet prenominata ecclesia cum omnibus rebus et possessionibus suis ac pertinenciis mobilibus et inmobilibus, seseque moventibus, castris scilicet, cassis, uillis, territoriis, ecclesiis cum primitiis et decima-tionibus, cum omnibus quoque que pia devotio fidelium sacris contulit sibi uel contulerit oblationibus pro salute vivorum quamque etiam mortuorum.

Translation:

Since therefore you, dearest son, have asked us to confirm by the writing of our official document of privilege, with the messengers of King Edward and with our own friendly letters, we on our part, gladly consenting, do now grant this charter of our own free will and as a grant freely made by the apostolic see. And we confirm that there should pertain to you and your successors to be subsequently canonically appointed in your place, all those things which the aforesaid church of Dorchester has possessed and now possesses: and especially the diocese of Lindsey and the churches of Stow with Newark and its appurtenances which, as we have heard from our legates and have learnt from the written testimony of our predecessors, Ælfric, archbishop of York, wrongfully seized. And we confirm to the aforesaid church [of Dorchester] whatever it may in future by divine and human law be able to acquire; and all its property and possessions both moveable and unmoveable; and all its buildings, vills and lands; and its churches with their revenues and tithes; and all holy things which the pious devotion of the faithful has conferred or will confer in gifts for the salvation of the living or the dead.[63]

This proves that Wulfwig was determined that the diocese of Lindsey should remain within his jurisdiction, and demonstrates that he was anxious to protect the terms of his agreement with Leofric and Godiva with respect to the endowment of Stow. It also helps to explain why: Ælfric 'Puttoc' had been archbishop of York between 1023 and 1051, so it would appear that Stow had been the source of some tension between Dorchester and York shortly before Wulfwig was appointed to his bishopric in 1053. Newark was a large and valuable estate in east Nottinghamshire, close to the Lincoln-shire boundary. Domesday Book reveals that it was held by Ælfgar's mother, Lady Godiva, in 1066; and three charters preserved in the Eynsham archive reveal that it was the most valuable of the estates assigned by her for the

---

63 *Councils and Synods*, ed. Whitelock *et al.*, p. 551; *English Historical Documents*, ed. Douglas, vol. 2. no. 75 (pp. 641–2).

endowment of Stow.[64] It thus emerges that Wulfwig's purpose in going to Rome was closely related to the interests of Burgheard's family. So if, as seems likely, Burgheard was indeed among the *legati Edwardi regis* who went to Rome in the spring of 1061, it would seem likely that he also went with his father's blessing.

Conclusion

The prosopography of late Anglo-Saxon England is not for those who seek comfort in historical certainty: the nature of the evidence dictates that it is more often than not a matter of managing doubt and balancing probability. Frequently, the best that one can do is simply to assemble the available evidence as accurately as possible before trying to identify patterns and connections within it. This paper has assembled all of the material relating to Burgheard, son of Earl Ælfgar, and has defended the essential authenticity of Ælfgar's charter in favour of Saint-Rémi, Reims. It also argues that most of the estates attributed to men named Burgheard in Domesday Book were held by the same individual; that he was identical with the son of Earl Ælfgar; that he was one of several Englishmen who went to Rome on various missions in the spring of 1061; that his family had made previously arrangements for the endowment of St Mary's Stow Lincolnshire, partly in order to secure a politically valuable foothold in that part of the east Midlands; that this foothold was undermined by changing political circumstances (above all, the growing power of the sons of Godwine) in the late 1050s and early 1060s; and that Burgheard's purpose in going to Rome was partly to help Bishop Wulfwig of Dorchester obtain papal protection for Stow's endowment, and thus for his family's interests in Lincolnshire. Since some of these suggestions are necessarily speculative, it may be as well to conclude with one more definite proposition. There is much potential for prosopographical research to illuminate some of the darker corners of Edward the Confessor's England, and thus deepen understanding of English politics on the eve of the Norman Conquest.

---

64 GDB 283d (Nottinghamshire 6:1); S 1233; *Regesta Regum Anglo-Normannorum: The Acta of William I (1066–1087)*, ed. D. Bates (Oxford, 1998), nos. 276–7.

14

The representation of queens and queenship in Anglo-Norman royal charters

David Bates

T HE SUBJECTS OF queens and queenship have figured prominently among Janet Nelson's publications. She has analysed both
the women and the contexts within which they acted across a
broad chronological range and in different kingdoms.[1] *Genre* and conse-
quential variations in representation in different types of source have also
been a major theme of her work.[2] Also, with a large literature now in existence showing how profoundly eleventh- and early twelfth-century England
and Normandy belonged to the Frankish world to whose illumination she
has contributed so much, and to which this volume is dedicated, the role
of queens and the representation of queenship in the extraordinary circumstances which followed the conquest of England in 1066 are a fit
subject to offer as a tribute.

Important work has been published in recent years on the histories of
English queens and queenship in the eleventh and early twelfth centuries.
Pauline Stafford's book on Queens Emma and Edith is of fundamental
importance for the eleventh century. And in many places this essay's debt
to Lois Huneycutt's work on Edith-Matilda, Henry I's first wife (henceforth
referred to as Matilda II to distinguish her from William the Conqueror's
wife Matilda, who is henceforth Matilda I) will be obvious. She too has
worked on Matilda's writs and writ-charters and has grasped just how
remarkable Matilda II's queenship was. Her conclusions therefore have
much in common with what is argued here; note especially her statement
that 'when Matilda of Scotland was the queen of England, the queen was

1 The subjects of queens and queenship appear in many of Janet Nelson's publications.
  See in particular for general issues, J. L. Nelson, 'Medieval queenship', in L. E.
  Mitchell (ed.), *Women in Medieval Western European Culture* (New York and London,
  1999), pp. 179–207; and 'Early medieval rites of queen-making and the shaping of
  medieval queenship', in A. Duggan (ed.), *Queens and Queenship in Medieval Europe*
  (Woodbridge, 1997), pp. 301–16.
2 Janet L. Nelson, 'Gender and *genre* in women historians of the early Middle Ages',
  in J-P. Genet (ed.), *L'Historiographie médiévale en Europe* (Paris, 1991), pp. 149–63.

an integral part of the institution of monarchy'.[3] Additionally, both she and Heather Tanner have identified the period of Matilda I's and Matilda II's queenship (1068–1118) as a distinct and very remarkable episode in the history of English queenship.[4]

For all this, the subject of the representation of queenship in charters across the period from 1066 to 1135 does merit special treatment. First, it bridges the chronological gap between the reigns of the three queens who were the central subjects of Pauline Stafford's and Lois Huneycutt's books. Secondly, the specific focus on representation in the manuscripts of original charters and in the texts of charters provides sufficient evidence to say something new about the scripts, norms and special contingencies which defined queenly activity and agency in this period. Thirdly, it deepens knowledge of the gendered and, in this specific case, largely collaborative, role of women and men.[5] And, fourthly, although the essay is primarily a study of medieval queenship, it also allows me to revisit after twenty-five years, within the conceptual framework of the histories of women, queenship and life-cycle, the subject of the arrangements which the Norman kings made to rule over their cross-Channel realm. This in turn demonstrates just how remarkable in western European terms these arrangements were; while fundamentally a variant within the matrix of structures and ideas deeply embedded in the world of the Frankish West, they were also a creative, albeit short-lived, response to novel circumstances.[6]

Matilda and Adeliza of Louvain, the two queens of Henry I, are the first English queens whose seals survive.[7] The possibility that Matilda I used a

---

3   See especially P. Stafford, *Queen Emma and Queen Edith: Queenship and Women's Power in Eleventh-century England* (Oxford, 1997); L. L. Huneycutt, *Matilda of Scotland. A Study in Medieval Queenship* (Woodbridge, 2003); L. Wertheimer, 'Adeliza of Louvain and Anglo-Norman Queenship', *Haskins Society Journal* 7 (1995), pp. 101–15. For Lois Huneycutt on Matilda's queenship, see her *Matilda*, 78–9, 92–3.

4   L. L. Huneycutt, '*Alianora Regina Anglorum*: Eleanor of Aquitaine and her Anglo-Norman predecessors as Queens of England', in B. Wheeler and J. C. Parsons (eds), *Eleanor of Aquitaine: Lord and Lady* (London, 2002), pp. 115–32; H. J. Tanner, 'Queenship: office, custom or *ad hoc*?: the case of Queen Matilda III of England (1135–1152)', in Wheeler and Parsons (eds), pp. 135–58.

5   For this approach, see P. Stafford, 'Writing the biographies of eleventh-century queens', in D. Bates, J. Crick and S. M. Hamilton (eds), *Writing Medieval Biography: Essays in Honour of Frank Barlow* (Woodbridge, 2006), pp. 99–111.

6   For my earlier treatment, D. Bates, 'The origins of the justiciarship', *ANS* 4 (1982), pp. 1–12, 167–71.

7   Durham, Dean and Chapter Muniments, 1.3.Ebor.13 and 1.2. Spec.23*; British Library, Add. Charters, nos. 19,573 and 19,574; *Reading Abbey Cartularies*, ed. B. R. Kemp, 2 vols., Camden Society, 4th series, 31–2 (1986–7), vol. 1, no. 370 (for a specimen of Adeliza's seal in a private collection).

seal cannot, however, be ruled out. The survival of a copy of a writ in her name, for example, makes it very likely that she had one, but its appearance can only be a subject of speculation.[8] The two surviving specimens of Matilda II's seal are attached to Durham documents. Already well described elsewhere, they display images which are both obviously royal and obviously feminine. In her right hand, for example, she holds a sceptre surmounted by a dove; and in her left, an orb surmounted by a cross. Her place in a queenly succession is also spelled out by the legend, deduced from the two damaged seals to have been + *SIGILLUM MATHILDIS SECUNDAE DEI GRACIA REGINAE ANGLIE.*[9] The point that she was the second Matilda was clearly one with a wide currency, since it also appears in her attestation to an original diploma for the abbey of Cluny, seemingly written by a scribe supplied by the beneficiary, and in the inscription on her tomb in Westminster Abbey.[10] This emphasis on queenly succession and, with it, the implicit assumption that queenship was seen as a continuing, indeed institutionalized, part of royal rule is also made by the three surviving specimens, all appended to documents dating to after King Henry's death, of Adeliza's seal, which closely resembles Matilda II's seal in many details. The appearance of the word *SECUNDA* in the legend is presumably there to distinguish her as Henry's second queen, but, taken together with other aspects of the seal, it also suggests something close to a slavish copying of her predecessor's seal. It is unlikely that this copying was arbitrary. Taken together, the two queens' seals demonstrate that, while there was unquestionably a gendered feminine side to queenship, it was considered to be an office, an adjunct to kingship.

Only four documents survive which were formally issued in the name of Matilda I.[11] On the other hand, she attests sixty-one of the royal diplomas which survive from the period between 1066 and her death in 1083.[12] On originals, her cross is usually placed in close proximity to her husband's.[13]

8   *Regesta Regum Anglo-Normannorum: The Acta of William I (1066–1087)*, ed. D. Bates (Oxford, 1998), no. 289.

9   Matilda's seals have been much discussed. See in particular, G. Zarnecki *et al.* (eds), *English Romanesque Art, 1066–1200* (London, 1984), p. 305; S. M. Johns, *Noblewomen, Aristocracy and Power in the Twelfth-century Anglo-Norman Realm* (Manchester and New York, 2003), pp. 125–6, 203.

10 J. Tardif, *Archives de l'Empire: monuments historiques* (Paris, 1866), p. 199 (*Regesta Regum Anglo-Normannorum* II, *1100–1135*, ed. C. Johnson and H. A. Cronne (Oxford, 1956), no. 646); *Liber monasterii de Hyda*, ed. E. Edwards, Rolls Series (London, 1866), p. 312.

11 *Regesta*, ed. Bates, nos. 58, 193, 229, 289.

12 *Regesta*, ed. Bates, pp. 9, 43, 93, for these figures.

13 *Regesta*, ed. Bates, pp. 93–4.

Although there are only eighteen surviving English (as opposed to Norman and French) documents in diploma form from William I's reign, it is very striking, given that she spent a lot of time acting on William's behalf in Normandy, that Matilda attests all the major surviving English diplomas of the period between 1066 and 1083;[14] these include the two texts of the Primacy Agreement between Canterbury and York, which she and her husband are the only members of the laity to attest, and the great diplomas for Saint-Martin-le-Grand, Wells, Exeter and Bury St Edmunds, as well as the diploma partly in Anglo-Saxon form for Saint-Denis. In all cases her *signum* is placed second after her husband's, and on two originals, those for Exeter and Saint-Denis, Matilda appears respectively in a single line with William above three columns of *signa* and with William and their second son Richard in a trinity of *signa* separated from the rest; the Saint-Denis diploma is also remarkable because it is written throughout in the plural as a joint grant by king and queen.[15] In the case of a diploma for Worcester cathedral, it is possible that confirmation was deliberately delayed until Matilda was available.[16] There are also occasions in Norman diplomas where Matilda is portrayed with her husband and some of her sons in agreeing collectively to a particular gift, as in an original diploma for Saint-Ouen of Rouen (*concessu domini mei Willelmi Anglorum regis et Mathildis regine, coniugis eius, filiorumque eorum Rotberti atque Willelmi*).[17] And when William and Matilda's foster-son, Simon, count of Amiens, Valois and the Vexin, returned Gisors to Rouen cathedral at a ceremony before the high altar of the cathedral, he did so in the presence of Matilda, 'the most noble and glorious queen' (*nobilissima et gloriosissima regina*) accompanied by several nobles. In this case, however, her role is qualified in relation to the gendered male authority of William's and Matilda's eldest son and designated heir in Normandy, Robert, since the diploma concludes with two *signa*, seemingly written by a different scribe, of which the first is Robert's and the second of Robert de Beaumont, one of the nobles.[18]

Matilda is on occasion portrayed in diplomas as acting in partnership with William. Thus, a plea involving the collegiate church of Saint-Léonard of Bellême is said to have been heard 'at the palace in the presence of the king and queen of the English' (*in palatio et in presentia regis et regine Anglorum*), with the two of them jointly ordering the court to make a judgement

---

14 For the evidence for Matilda's role in cross-Channel government, Bates, 'Origins of the justiciarship', pp. 6–7.

15 *Regesta*, ed. Bates, nos. 39, 67, 68, 138, 181, 254, 286.

16 *Regesta*, ed. Bates, no. 345.

17 *Regesta*, ed. Bates, no. 246.

18 *Regesta*, ed. Bates, no. 229. For Robert's status in Normandy, *ibid.*, pp. 94–6.

(*his auditis rex et regina iusserunt*).[19] Similarly, a memorandum describing a dispute involving the abbey of Jumièges says that a plaintiff brought her plea before William and Matilda at Bonneville-sur-Touques (*perveniens ad Willelmum ducem, iam factum regem, et ad Matildam uxorem eius in uillam qui dicitur Bona uilla*) and William and Matilda together are portrayed as being able to make the judgement (*qui illi facerent rectum de suis clamoribus*).[20] The most intriguing evidence for the representation of Matilda I's queenship is a *notitia* from the abbey of Marmoutier which describes how the monks reacted to the usurpation of customs at Héauville in the north of the Cotentin by sending a monk to seek out the king in England to complain. William, angered (*iratus*) – it is not clear whether this was because of the usurpation or because the monks had troubled him unnecessarily by sending someone to England – ordered the monk back to Normandy so that Matilda could do justice to the suit. Matilda is said to have obeyed her husband's orders (*regi obediens*) and restored the usurped customs in the company of two bishops and several others at Cherbourg on 27 December 1080.[21]

The use of the verb 'to obey' in this account, alongside the use of the verb 'to order' in a unique document in which William both notifies and orders Matilda to carry out various other acts in favour of Marmoutier (*Mando etiam tibi . . .*) is undeniable evidence of the dominant role of kingship within the relationship of king and queen.[22] Yet the picture deriving from Matilda's known central place in the government of Normandy during William's absences before 1072 and the unique representation of her queenship in diplomas both English and Continental point to her elevation above the aristocracy in a role which defies easy description. While the adjective 'vice-regal' is a commonplace among historians of the Anglo-Norman realm to describe her role, that term's possible connotations of deputy make it seem unsatisfactory. The term 'regency' also has its problems in this context. Sharing in rule, at the same time having an authority associated with kingship and subordinate to it, comes closest to the mark.[23] Although it is a mid-twelfth-century voice, the writer of the *Abingdon Chronicle* in his description of Matilda, who 'was then at Windsor and was doing justice concerning pressing matters, in the place of the king who was in

19 *Regesta*, ed. Bates, no. 29(I).
20 *Regesta*, ed. Bates, no. 162. This document is also discussed with similar themes in mind by Elisabeth van Houts, 'Gender and authority of oral witnesses in Europe (800–1300)', *TRHS*, 6th. series, 9 (1999), pp. 201–20, at 201–2.
21 *Regesta*, ed. Bates, no. 200.
22 *Regesta*, ed. Bates, no. 202.
23 For an excellent discussion, Stafford, *Queen Emma and Queen Edith*, pp. 185–91.

Normandy' (*per hos dies Wildesore constitutam, querimonia de illata sibi mouere-tur, que regis uice Normannie degentis iusticiam rerum ingruentium impendebat*), arguably portrays how contemporaries must have seen the situation.[24] It fits well with the well-known evidence from Domesday Book for Matilda's activi-ties as a judge.[25]

The charters of the abbey of La Trinité of Caen, the abbey which Matilda had founded before 1066, supply plentiful evidence of personal agency. To use the great confirmation charter of 1082 as a quarry, we can cite from a multitude of examples: statements such as the one that 'Matilda has pur-chased from Richard son of Herluin the lands he held at Tassilly and Monbouin on the basis that Richard will hold the lands from the abbey during his life-time'.[26] The document is full of instances of Matilda's inter-ventions to increase the nunnery's holdings by purchases and through negotiations with the aristocratic families of the region.[27] Yet the example I have used, like almost every other transaction in the diploma, refers to her husband's agreement (*annuente domino meo rege*). With the single excep-tion of a plea heard before William, all the charters of La Trinité are written in the plural; the great confirmation of 1082, for example, presents the foundation as a joint enterprise (*pro salute animarum nostrarum coedificaui-mus, ibique sanctas ac religiosas feminas secundum institutionem sancti Benedicti, sub abbatissa Domino seruituras, in perpetuum constituimus*). And in a case where a unique charter survival does show Matilda acting alone in 1075 to oversee the grant of the castle of Le Homme to La Trinité, the subsequent confirmation in the 1082 charter inserts William into the transaction.[28] If kingly confirmation becomes the umbrella to approve and sanction a great deal of queenly activity, the confirmation charter does not apparently sup-press the latter to any great extent in favour of the former; it is indeed clear that both queenly and kingly activity mattered to the authors of the docu-ments and that, in their minds, both needed to be recorded. In general, this and other La Trinité charters accord to Matilda an identity which is more than queenly; whereas elsewhere she is almost invariably entitled simply *regina*, at La Trinité her kindred were identified, and she is also

24 *Historia Ecclesie Abbendonensis: The History of the Church of Abingdon*, vol. 2, ed. and trans. J. Hudson (Oxford, 2002), pp. 14–15.

25 E.g. *Domesday Book, seu Liber Censualis Willelmi primi regis Anglie*, ed. A. Farley, 2 vols. (London, 1783), 1, fos. 48v, 238v.

26 *Les Actes de Guillaume le Conquérant et de la reine Mathilde pour les abbayes caennaises*, ed. L. Musset (Caen, 1967), no. 8 (*Regesta*, ed. Bates, no. 59).

27 For Matilda's contribution to La Trinité, L. Musset, 'La Reine Mathilde et la fonda-tion de la Trinité de Caen (Abbaye-aux-Dames)', *Mémoires de l'académie nationale des sciences et belles-lettres et arts de Caen*, n.s. 21 (1984), pp. 191–210.

28 *Actes pour les abbayes caennaises*, no. 21 (*Regesta*, ed. Bates, no. 58).

styled 'the daughter of Count Baldwin of Flanders' and, on two occasions, also as the kinswoman of Henry I, king of the Franks.[29] Matilda's one surviving English diploma, recording a grant to the abbey of Malmesbury, also places her action within the framework of William's kingship.[30]

The surviving original diplomas attested by Henry and Matilda II and by Henry and Adeliza represent queenship in almost exactly the same way as in the time of Matilda I. The *laudatio*-type clauses of eleventh-century Norman diplomas scarcely appear in the charters of this period, but the consistent placing of the queens' *signa* adjacent to the king's continues, a point made by both Lois Huneycutt and Laura Wertheimer.[31] Thus, an original charter for Norwich cathedral of 1107 × 1116, unquestionably written by a scribe supplied by the beneficiary, has Matilda's cross directly below the king's in the first column of *signa*.[32] In like manner, a surviving original diploma for Totnes priory has a first line of *signa*, of whom the first is *Signum Regis* and the second *Signum Regine*, and a narrative of a *concordia* between William, abbot of Fécamp, and Philip de Briouze, dated 13 January 1103 at Salisbury, has Henry and Matilda as the sole *signa* followed by a large number of *testes*.[33] Two diplomas for Cluny, both seemingly written by scribes supplied by the beneficiary, illustrate exactly the same pattern, with one for Lenton priory written in a way which suggests that the *signa* of king and queen, which are placed on the left-hand side of the parchment below the text, and those of the donors, William Peverel, his wife and his son, were written next to the royal *signa* before the other *signa* were added; the second, recording gifts in London to Saint-Martin-des-Champs again has Henry and Matilda as the first two *signa*.[34] And finally, from several other examples, the original diploma confirming the establishment of the see of Ely has three columns of *signa*, the first three of which in the left-hand column are Henry, Matilda and their daughter Matilda;

29 *Actes pour les abbayes caennaises*, nos. 9, 12 (*Regesta*, ed. Bates, nos. 60, 62).

30 *Regesta*, ed. Bates, no. 193.

31 Wertheimer, 'Adeliza', pp. 103–4.

32 *The Charters of Norwich Cathedral Priory*, vol. 1, ed. Barbara Dodwell, Pipe Roll Society 78 (London, 1974), no. 9 (*Regesta* II, ed. Johnson and Cronne, no. 1158).

33 H. R. Watkin, *The History of Totnes Priory and Medieval Town*, 3 vols. (Torquay, 1914–17), vol. 2, plate ii (*Regesta* II, ed. Johnson and Cronne, no. 735a); Archives départementales de la Seine-Maritime, 7H 57 (*Regesta* II, ed. Johnson and Cronne, no. 626). The badly damaged original of this second document has never been printed: see *The Cartae Antiquae Rolls 11–20*, ed. J. C. Davies, Pipe Roll Society 71 (London, 1960, for 1957), pp. 149–51, no. 544.

34 *Facsimiles of Early Charters from Northamptonshire Collections*, ed. F. M. Stenton, Northamptonshire Record Society 4 (Lincoln and London, 1930), plate LXIII (*Regesta* II, ed. Johnson and Cronne, no. 920); Archives Nationales, K21, 1[4] (*Regesta* II, ed. Johnson and Cronne, no. 646).

this example is of course a continuation of the elevation of the royal family above the aristocracy observable in William I's diplomas, with, in this instance, additional special reasons for the inclusion of the daughter, since Matilda is described as 'the betrothed wife of the king of the Romans' (*sponsa regis Romanorum*).[35]

There are also several particularly telling examples of a similar representation in cartulary copies. The 1101 diploma for Bath abbey, for example, which has features reminiscent of an Anglo-Saxon diploma, both singles Matilda out for special mention in precedence to the aristocracy (*Presente Mathilde regina, et uiris illustribus, et principibus totius Anglie, ecclesiasticis et secularibus*) and places her *signum* first above the archbishop of Canterbury.[36] A Norwich diploma, dating from the same time as the Bath document, also gives Matilda special prominence (*presente regina M. filia Regis Scotie et uiris illustribus totius Anglie ecclesiasticis et secularibus*) and places her and Henry above all other *signa*, along with Henry's brother Robert Curthose; a description of the lost original of this diploma shows that it may well have had the three attestations of Henry, Matilda and Robert prominently placed across the width of the parchment above three columns of *signa*.[37] Then there is a diploma of Bishop Gundulf for his church of Rochester, copied into the contemporary *Textus Roffensis*, where Henry and Archbishop Anselm form a first pair of *signa* and Matilda and Gundulf a second, with Matilda identified as Anselm's spiritual daughter, after which there are four lines of *signa* arranged in three columns.[38] Almost all surviving diplomas in which Matilda appears among the *signa* conform to the patterns described in this and the previous paragraph: the two exceptions may very convincingly be regarded as ones which really do prove a rule, since in a notice for Saint-Etienne of Caen, preserved in the early twelfth-century sections of the abbey's cartulary, Matilda is placed third behind the only rank of individual who would be expected to precede a queen, namely

35 British Library, Harleian Charter 43, C.111 (*Regesta* II, ed. Johnson and Cronne, no. 919); Marjorie Chibnall, *The Empress Matilda* (Oxford, 1991), p. 16.

36 *Two Chartularies of the Priory of St Peter at Bath*, ed. W. Hunt, Somerset Record Society 7 (1893), pp. 43–5, no. 40 (*Regesta* II, ed. Johnson and Cronne, no. 544).

37 *Charters of Norwich Cathedral Priory*, no. 3 (*Regesta* II, ed. Johnson and Cronne, no. 548). For the possible lost original, F. B. Blomefield, *An Essay towards a Topographical History of the County of Norfolk*, 5 vols. (Fersfield, 1739), vol. 4, p. 37 note. I owe this reference to Richard Sharpe. For Robert in English charters in 1101, see also, D. Bates, 'A neglected English charter of Robert Curthose, Duke of Normandy', *Bulletin of the Institute of Historical Research* 49 (1986), pp. 122–4.

38 *Textus Roffensis*, ed. P. H. Sawyer, 2 vols., Early English Manuscripts in Facsimile, vols. 7 and 11 (Copenhagen, 1957–62), fos. 219v–20r (*Regesta* II, ed. Johnson and Cronne, no. 636).

her brother Edgar, king of Scots, while the fact that she is placed fourth on a later copy on a *Cartae Antiquae Roll* must surely be the result of the practice of the scribe of the *Roll*, rather than of the appearance of the original he was copying.[39] The practice of queenly pre-eminence was also transferred to writ-charters, since, without exception, Matilda is always the first of the *testes* in all documents which survive.[40]

Personal agency is every bit as evident in the career of Matilda II as in that of Matilda I. She too was closely associated in the exercise of royal government and was, like her predecessor, a patron of several religious houses.[41] But, as we shall see, since the writs and writ-charters which become more widely used after 1100 can be more revealing of process than diplomas, they can allow narratives to be constructed of a kind which are less often possible for the first Matilda.[42] Especially important is the existence of several pairs of writs and writ-charters in which Matilda and Henry confirm the same grant. A straightforward example, which replicates the type of partnership evident in the case of William I and Matilda I, is Matilda II's famous writ-charter concerning Lewknor (Oxon.), which possibly involved a consultation of Domesday Book, and which refers to 'my lord's court and mine meeting in the (royal) treasury at Winchester (*in curia domini mei et mea, apud Wintoniam in thesauro*).[43] And, among other examples, there are references to 'the firm peace of the King and my own' (*firmam pacem regis et meam habeant*) in one of her writ-charters for Waltham and an identical phrase in a notification for the cathedral church of Worcester.[44] As with Matilda I, the notion that the political relationship of Matilda

---

39 Archives départementales du Calvados, Cartulaire de Saint-Etienne de Caen, fos. 21v–22r (*Regesta* II, ed. Johnson and Cronne, no. 601); *The Cartae Antiquae Rolls 1–10*, ed. L. Landon, Pipe Roll Society 55 (London, 1939), no. 30 (*Regesta* II, ed. Johnson and Cronne, no. 599). It should be noted that the scribe of the cartulary of Saint-Etienne of Caen consistently omits crosses and the word *signum*, replacing it with a narrative (*Illorum uero qui hanc cartam firmauerunt ista sunt nomina*) in this case.

40 *Regesta* II, ed. Johnson and Cronne, nos. 534, 538, 550, 554, 602, 607, 613, 634, 661, 667, 668, 693, 700, 702, 706, 722, 742, 756, 765, 769, 822, 843, 862, 863, 1120, 1134, 1152, 1160, 1163, 1164, 1177.

41 For her religious patronage, Huneycutt, *Matilda*, pp. 103–24; Judith A. Green, *Henry I* (Cambridge, 2006), pp. 279–80.

42 For a list of Matilda II's *acta*, Huneycutt, *Matilda*, pp. 151–60.

43 *Historia Ecclesie Abbendonensis*, II, pp. 170–1 (*Regesta* II., ed. Johnson and Cronne, no. 1000).

44 *The Early Charters of the Augustinian Canons of Waltham Abbey, Essex, 1062–1230*, ed. Rosalind Ransford (Woodbridge, 1989), no. 15 (*Regesta* II, ed. Johnson and Cronne, no. 1090); *The Cartulary of Worcester Cathedral Priory, Register I*, ed. R. R. Darlington, Pipe Roll Society 76 (London, 1968), no. 40.

II and Henry I should be defined in terms of partnership was the view of contemporary commentators. Thus, for example, the mid-twelfth-century Abingdon chronicler told the story of how an outlaw had sought mercy from the king in Normandy and the queen in England, while Gregory of Ely described her competence as not dissimilar to the king's (*Regno rex aberat; sceptrum regina regebat/Sed non dissimilis regi probitate Mathildis*).[45]

If, however, the partnership of king and queen in the exercise of royal authority is every bit as evident in the case of Matilda II and Henry as it was with Matilda I and William the Conqueror, so too is the language of gendered male superiority, since Matilda's *acta* frequently describe Henry as *dominus*.[46] A good example of the mixture of kingly/queenly partnership and kingly superiority in action is provided by two pairs of writs of Matilda and Henry for Worcester cathedral priory. For the present purpose they have the advantage of having almost identical texts, with adjustments being made only in relation to whether kingly or queenly authority was being represented.[47] The king's authority stands alone (e.g., *in manu mea sunt et habent firmam pacem meam* and *nec eas reddat nisi per me concedo et confirmo illam donationem*), whereas the queen's is represented as an extension of the king's (*in manu regis sunt et mea et habent firmam pacem regis et meam, nec eas reddat nisi per regem aut per me, concedo et confirmo ex parte domini mei regis et mea*). In addition, a passage in a letter of the canons of Wolverhampton to Pope Eugenius III, dating from 1148×1153, supplies a statement of how the couple's charters were respectively viewed to the effect that 'King Henry with Queen Matilda had given their assent to this grant, and he had confirmed it by his charter and the impression of his seal' (*huicque donationi rex Henricus cum Matilde regina assensum prebuit, et eam carta sua et sigilli impressione firmauit*).[48] Although indicating that it was ultimately the king's charter that mattered, this letter shows that while the queen's role might be subordinate, mention of it was necessary because it added substance.

Matilda's two surviving original writ-charters present two different versions of how queenly agency was expressed and of how it was distinct from, yet integrated into, the king's. One, by which she notifies Bishop Rannulf of Durham and the sheriffs and barons of Northumberland that she has

---

45 P. A. Thompson and E. Stevens, 'Gregory of Ely's verse Life and Miracles of St Æthelthryth', *Analecta Bollandiana* 106 (1988), p. 377; cited in Huneycutt, *Matilda*, p. 92. I am grateful to Sophia Fisher for a discussion of this passage.

46 There are a multitude of examples. To cite in full the phrase from every text would make for a very long footnote. Note, for example, *Regesta* II, ed. Johnson and Cronne, nos. 902, 1000.

47 *Cartulary of Worcester Cathedral Priory*, nos. 39, 40, 261, 262.

48 *Cartulary of Worcester Cathedral Priory*, no. 267, describing *ibid.*, nos. 39 and 40.

granted the church of Carham to Durham has as its single witness Matilda's chamberlain Aldwin, emphasizing an origin for the document outside the curial group of administrators who worked with the king. But the place of issue was a major centre of royal power, Windsor, and the document's production was undertaken by a member of the royal chancery, the royal scribe who wrote numerous royal writs and writ-charters, as well as the *Pipe Roll* of 1131.[49] It is interesting, given the number of pairs of kingly and queenly writs and writ-charters which do survive, that there is no confirmation by Henry of Matilda's writ-charter, a *lacuna* which is surprising in an archive so well preserved as Durham's, but possibly explicable because Henry judged Durham's claim to be a tendentious one and that he therefore should not add his confirmation to his wife's.[50]

The second of Matilda's writ-charters was almost certainly written by a Durham scribe.[51] It confirmed to the church of Durham one and a half hides in Epping (Essex) and a half hide in Nazeing (Essex) which her canon Bruning had held on the day he died. This time there is a Henry confirmation which survives as an original, although as in the case of Matilda's writ-charter, the scribe cannot be identified.[52] There are so many textual similarities that dependence can be assumed, and the fact that both were issued at Westminster suggests that their composition was almost contemporaneous, but since Henry's writ mentions Matilda's, hers was presumably already in existence (*omnia que predicta regina eis per breue suum dedit*) when the king's confirmation was drawn up. Of the two, however, Henry's is fundamentally the formulaic record of a standard royal writ-charter, while Matilda's is much more a narrative of a negotiation than a simple confirmation of the outcome of one, since, unlike Henry's, it includes a statement that the lands are to be held of Durham during his lifetime by her canon Adam. The verbs used in the pronouncements of the two documents emphasize Matilda's agency in giving (*Sciatis me concessisse et dedisse*) and

---

49 Durham, Dean and Chapter Muniments, 1.2. Spec.23* (*New Palaeographical Society Facsimiles* I, plate 71(a); *Regesta* II, ed. Johnson and Cronne, no. 1143). For the scribe, T. A. M. Bishop, *Scriptores Regis* (Oxford, 1961), plate XIII(a). I am grateful to Tessa Webber and Michael Gullick for their advice on the script of these two Durham documents and to Bill Aird for advice on the content of the Carham writ.

50 W. M. Aird, *St Cuthbert and the Normans: The Church of Durham, 1071–1153* (Woodbridge, 1998), p. 21.

51 Durham, Dean and Chapter Muniments, 1.3.Ebor.13 (*New Palaeographical Society Facsimiles*, I, plate 71(b)); *Waltham Charters*, no. 11. The scribe cannot be identified, but various features of the hand make it likely that it was written by a Durham scribe.

52 Printed, *Regesta* II, ed. Johnson and Cronne, no. XCVI (no. 1109).

Henry's in conceding and confirming (*Sciatis me concessisse et dono meo confirmasse illud donum quod Mathildis regina Anglorum dedit*). Matilda's document is witnessed by her brother Earl David and her chamberlain Aldwin, as well as her and Henry's son William, a group drawn primarily from her kin and her entourage, while Henry's is witnessed by Matilda alone.

In other cases where there is both a Matilda and a Henry document dealing with the same transaction, the pattern whereby Matilda's supplies more narrative is a common one, but not a universal one. Her grant to the canons of Waltham of her mills in Waltham in exchange for the church of Holy Trinity, Aldgate, includes a clause about the canons of Holy Trinity being allowed to repair their church and those of Waltham to develop the mills in the future, reasonable stipulations presumably designed to prevent subsequent squabbles, which are not present in Henry's document. In this case there is also the same clarity about Matilda as the donor and agent as in the Durham pair of documents discussed above.[53] Three writ-charters for the cathedral church of York, dealing with Matilda's grant of Laughton as a prebend, in contrast, exhibit only small differences of phrasing and the two documents in Matilda's name do not contain additional narrative. There is, however, a significant evolutionary narrative across the series of documents; Matilda's first writ is a short one issued at York addressed to the barons of the honour of Blyth. Her second one, like Henry's confirmation of her grant, was issued at Lillebonne, but is addressed to the sheriff of Nottinghamshire as well as to the barons of Blyth, and made it clear that the monks of Blyth should not interfere in the prebend.[54] There is an interesting pattern to the witnessing in that Henry's was witnessed by William d'Aubigny, but said to have been executed through the agency of John de Sées (*per Iohannem de Sagio*) who had witnessed both Matilda's earlier writs at York and Lillebonne; as also had Matilda's chaplain Bernard, the future Bishop of St David's. It is clear that it was Matilda who had arranged the local transaction, and possible that the three documents illustrate a chain of communication either deemed desirable to achieve Henry's confirmation, or made unusually explicit because the property granted was in dispute.[55]

53 *Waltham Charters*, nos. 6 and 8 (*Regesta* II, ed. Johnson and Cronne, nos. 908, 909).
54 *The Historians of the Church of York and its Archbishops*, ed. J. Raine, 3 vols., Rolls Series (London, 1879–94), vol. 3, pp. 30–1 (*Regesta* II, ed. Johnson and Cronne, nos. 720, 808, 809).
55 On Laughton, see Huneycutt, *Matilda*, pp. 84–5.

The pattern is significantly different in the case of the series of documents dealing with the grant of the island of Andersey to the abbey of Abingdon during Matilda's confinement before the birth of the future Empress Matilda. Matilda's first writ, addressed to the sheriff of Berkshire, is a very short text telling him to allow the abbey to have lead from the houses on Andersey for the construction of the abbey. The witnesses are local figures and the place of issue is Sutton Courtenay within a few miles of the abbey, and the likely place of Matilda's confinement.[56] Matilda's second writ records a more generous grant of houses and of all the buildings on Andersey. It records that Henry had granted all this to Matilda at her intercession and is witnessed by a national figure, the royal chancellor Roger, the future bishop of Salisbury, and by one of Matilda's doctors, Grimbald. It is, however, Henry's confirmation which in this instance contains the most detail, a reversal of the pattern observable in most other cases which presumably occurred because the property was ultimately Henry's, rather than Matilda's, to grant – the Conqueror had spent time at Andersey for blood-lettings and rest-cures – and because Matilda's role was the Esther/queenly one of intercessor with a powerful husband, rather than donor. It was drawn up at Windsor and presumably therefore after the successful delivery of the child. This time the witness-list was drawn entirely from the king's world, with Matilda as the first witness and Roger the chancellor the second, followed by several notable royal servants.[57] There are other examples of Matilda's activity in the role of intercessor in writ-charters for the abbey of Westminster and for the nuns of Malling in Kent; the second of these is also notable as the one document among the entire collection surveyed in this essay to mention love on the part of either wife or husband (*hoc concedo et confirmo pro amore et deprecatione uxoris mee Mahaldis regine*).[58]

There are occasional instances in which a pair of documents exist where there is little or no difference between the queen's and the king's writs, as

56 For Matilda's confinement, Chibnall, *The Empress Matilda*, p. 9, note 10.

57 *Historia Ecclesie Abbendonensis*, II, pp. 72–7 (*Regesta* II, ed. Johnson and Cronne, nos. 550, 565, 567).

58 J. Armitage Robinson, *Gilbert Crispin, Abbot of Westminster* (Cambridge, 1911), p. 144 (*Regesta* II, no. 668); *Calendar of Charter Rolls*, v, 56–7 (*Regesta* II, ed. Johnson and Cronne, no. 634). On Matilda's intercessions, L. L. Huneycutt, 'Intercession and the high-medieval queen: the Esther Topos', in J. Carpenter and S-B. MacLean (eds), *Power of the Weak: Studies on Medieval Women* (Urbana IL, 1995), pp. 147–77; Huneycutt, *Matilda*, pp. 82–5.

in the case of Matilda's grant of Nettleham to Lincoln cathedral.[59] However, as we have seen, the more normal pattern is for queenly action to be recorded in the first instance without reference to the king's precedence, in most cases with it being integrated subsequently into the framework of kingly power. In general, Matilda did the local work, but the confirmation by her and her husband usually took place at a gathering of the court, or at the least at a major royal centre. A letter of Walter, dean of Waltham, arguably sums up the process very well when it says that a church 'had been given to them by Queen Matilda in an exchange and conceded to them by the lord King Henry'.[60] As with Matilda I, there are indications of a distinctive queenly and personal identity in the case of Matilda II, but, as with her predecessor, they appear very clearly to be secondary to representation as the king's partner. References in the writs and writ-charters issued in her name to her kin are, for example, relatively few. Her brother, the future King David, witnesses only two other documents beyond the Durham one on which her seal survives.[61] *Pro anima* clauses, where they occur, usually refer to her husband and their children; perhaps surprisingly, given her status as heir to the Old English royal house which was so frequently mentioned in the literary sources, only three documents written in Matilda's name explicitly ask for prayers for the souls of her ancestors and one of these, a grant to the abbey of St Alban's, requests prayers only for the soul of her father, King Malcolm III.[62] In contrast, members of Matilda's household are prominent as witnesses to her writs and writ-charters, indicating clearly that, as with Matilda I, the two factors of witness by those with responsibilities relating to the grant being made and of her position as the king's partner were ultimately central to the normal representation of queenship.[63]

Henry I's second queen, Adeliza of Louvain, is represented in diplomas in exactly the same way as with the two Matildas. Her *signum* is always in

---

59   *The Registrum Antiquissimum of the Cathedral Church of Lincoln*, ed. C. W. Foster and K. Major, 10 vols., Lincoln Record Society (1931–68), 1, nos. 15, 16, 61, 62 (*Regesta II*, ed. Johnson and Cronne, nos. 534, 535, 536, 743).

60   *The Cartulary of Holy Trinity Aldgate*, ed. Gerald Hodgett, London Record Society (1971), p. 224.

61   *Regesta II*, ed. Johnson and Cronne, nos. 818a, 1108, 1180.

62   For the *pro anima* clauses, *Waltham Charters*, no. 11; *The Coucher Book of Selby*, ed. J. T. Fowler, 2 vols. (Durham, 1891–93), 1, p. 25; W. S. Gibson, *The History of the Monastery founded at Tynemouth, in the Diocese of Durham*, 2 vols. (London, 1846–47), vol. 2, Appendix, no. 19. References to Matilda's descent from the line of English kings are conveniently collected in H. M. Thomas, *The English and the Normans: Ethnic Hostility, Assimilation and Identity 1066–c.1220* (Oxford, 2003), p. 144.

63   For Matilda's household, Huneycutt, *Matilda*, pp. 99–101.

close proximity to the king's on surviving originals and she is always placed second on later copies. On an original notice dating from 1121 for the abbey of Le Bec, the *signa* and their crosses are placed in a single line across the width of the parchment, with Henry's first and Adeliza's second.[64] And on a large diploma for the abbey of Savigny, Henry's *signum* is a continuation of the text and Adeliza's is placed directly below his.[65] Very similar arrangements exist on two originals for Saint-Martin d'Ecajeul and one for Saint-Pierre-sur-Dives.[66] No English original survives, but later copies from Merton priory, Exeter cathedral, Reading abbey, Kenilworth priory and Great Malvern priory all indicate that her *signum* was placed second after the king's.[67] And in the one surviving writ-charter to which she is a witness, her name is once more placed first as Matilda II's always was.[68] She is, however, the author of only a single writ-charter, which deals with the affairs of the queen's dower of Waltham Abbey and does no more than confirm conditions that had existed in the time of Matilda II.[69] Laura Wertheimer has very capably pointed out the contrast between Adeliza and her predecessor. The status of the queen remains the same, but the level of agency evident in charters declines almost to nothing. Her itinerary becomes Anglo-Norman in a way that Matilda II's was not, demonstrating that she was much more regularly with the king; her relative youth and the unfulfilled hope that she would produce a male heir to replace the drowned William are the obvious explanations of this.[70] The evidence stands in illuminating counter-point to that for Matilda I and Matilda II, yet at the same time it shows the enduring status of the queen as a unique personage alongside the king.

The overriding impression from the diplomas, writs and writ-charters discussed in this essay is of Anglo-Norman queenship as a significant office and a carefully choreographed one. It has its roots in the Carolingian world and evolved in direct ideological succession from the liturgical

---

64 Archives départementales de l'Eure, H28 (*Regesta* II, ed. Johnson and Cronne, no. 1303).

65 Archives Nationales, K22, no. 7.4 (*Regesta* II, ed. Johnson and Cronne, no. 1588).

66 Archives départementales du Calvados, 2D 11, no. 1 and H7031. For the second, R. N. Sauvage, 'Les diplômes de Henri I, roi d'Angleterre et duc de Normandie, pour l'abbaye de Saint-Pierre-sur-Dive', *Société de l'Histoire de Normandie, Mélanges* 12 (1933), pp. 115–39, at p. 139.

67 *Regesta* II, ed. Johnson and Cronne, nos. 1301, 1391, 1427, 1428, 1489.

68 *Regesta* II, ed. Johnson and Cronne, no. 1467.

69 *Waltham Charters*, no. 16.

70 Wertheimer, 'Adeliza', pp. 103–4. See also, Green, *Henry I*, pp. 169–70.

consecrations of queens which began in the eighth century and the subsequent entrenchment of these ideas into the framework of royal rule in the ninth. It was an expression of ideas which represented queens as partners with kings in rule, one which had been applied in many varying ways in the centuries which followed.[71] It flowed into post-Conquest England through the dual channels of pre-Conquest queenship in which, as Pauline Stafford has shown, partnership – albeit one frequently qualified by complex and dramatic events and circumstances – was the stated norm, and Normandy, where the ducal charters show the duke's wife consistently prominent alongside the duke.[72] But, for all that there were these continuities, as both Pauline Stafford and Laura Gathagan have recognized, 1066 – or more specifically the *Laudes* sung at the time of Matilda I's coronation at Whitsun 1068 – was a turning-point, because 'what is thus most striking about the revisions made for William and Matilda is the equality (in the representation of king and queen)'.[73]

The sheer intensity of reference to queenly activity in the times of Matilda I and Matilda II is truly remarkable. And, taking the broader perspective, it is the acts of judgement and the associated long-term institutional role which make the roles of these two queens remarkable in the history of the medieval West. If Janet Nelson's remark that 'even rarer, but still more significant, are queenly acts of judgement . . .', proceeding to cite only Charlemagne's wife Fastrada and Matilda I, does under-estimate somewhat the number of instances in which queens did justice, the basic point still holds.[74] And it is important to recognize too that Matilda I and Matilda II lived at a time when such female involvement in rule was controversial: witness, for example, the views of Bonizo of Sutri, writing in *c.*1090 and, subsequently, Gratian.[75] I am not certain that Matilda I and Matilda II did ultimately transcend gender; they did, however, make queenship truly an office and pushed its potential close to the limits acceptable to contempo-

---

71 Nelson, 'Early Medieval Rites of Queen-Making', *passim.*
72 Stafford, *Queen Emma and Queen Edith*, pp. 162–92 and pp. 193–206.
73 Stafford, *Queen Emma and Queen Edith.*, pp. 183–4, with the quotation at p. 184; Laura L. Gathagan, 'The trappings of power: the coronation of Mathilda of Flanders', *Haskins Society Journal* 13 (1999), pp. 21–39.
74 Nelson, 'Queenship' p. 200. For further examples, van Houts, 'Gender and Authority', pp. 217–19; Tanner, 'Matilda III', pp. 141–2.
75 See the references cited in van Houts, 'Gender and Authority', p. 218, note 65. On the Empress Matilda's well-nigh unique activities as a judge within the Empire, see now, A. Fossel, *Die Königin im mittelalterlichen Reich: Herrschaftsausübung, Herrschaftsrechte, Handlungsspielraüme* (Stuttgart, 2000), pp. 106–7, 159–61. I am grateful to Johanna Hodge's University of Cambridge MPhil dissertation for this reference.

raries, acknowledging always that the ultimate determinant of their role was the masculine authority of the king. That Robert Curthose left the tragically short-lived Sibyl of Conversano in charge in Normandy in 1101 only highlights still further the strength of the idea.[76]

The life-cycle implications and emotional content of marriages which combined the necessity of child-bearing with lengthy separation for political ends can ultimately only be a subject for speculation. Matilda I and William the Conqueror were universally reported to have been a devoted couple. They were also a very well-established one by 1066, the last of their nine known children – the future Henry I – being born in the last months of 1068, and the pressures to produce male heirs having long since passed. Matilda II is a more complex case. Born in 1080, she was arguably still capable of bearing children at the time of her death in 1118. Yet only two, and possibly three, offspring, the future Empress Matilda, the ill-fated William, and a boy named Richard, who died young, are known, and all were born in the very first years of the marriage. The pattern after Henry had gained control over Normandy in 1106, whereby the couple met mostly at great courts in England when Henry was in his kingdom, was certainly not one to rule out further children, but as far as we know none was conceived.[77] Her succession to the role performed by Matilda I is usually connected to her known intelligence, her awareness of her descent from the Old English royal house, and her feelings for, and largely second-hand memory of, her mother St Margaret.[78] A further factor must be that she grew up in the south of England in circles connected closely to her husband's right-hand man, Roger, the future Bishop of Salisbury.[79] She was remarkably well trained to take on her predecessor's role and, in all probability, temperamentally and personally committed to performing it. With Adeliza of Louvain, the situation was very different, since child-bearing was crucial. We see as a result a reversion to a situation in which the queen remained pre-eminent in status, but institutionally much less prominent than her two predecessors.

76 *The Gesta Normannorum Ducum of William of Jumièges, Orderic Vitalis, and Robert of Torigni*, ed. and trans. E. M. C. van Houts, 2 vols. (Oxford, 1992–95), vol. 2, pp. 222–3.

77 On the subject of Matilda and children, see Huneycutt, *Matilda*, pp. 77–8; Green, *Henry I*, p. 58, with references. Note William of Malmesbury's speculations that she ceased to desire children.

78 For Matilda and her mother, see especially, Huneycutt, *Matilda* pp. 2–4, 9–16.

79 Stephen Marritt, 'Coincidences of names: Anglo-Scottish connections and Anglo-Saxon society in the late eleventh-century West Country', *Scottish Historical Review* 83 (2004), pp. 150–70, at pp. 163–5.

The debates about the relationship of Normandy and England during the Anglo-Norman period have gone quiet in recent times.[80] This essay is nonetheless a small additional contribution to them. What is ultimately striking is the pragmatic and highly effective extension of the deeply embedded and conventional ideas of queenship into an overarching structure of cross-Channel rule. For all this, the enhancement of queenly status during the period from 1068 to 1118 was arguably always going to be a temporary expedient because, in the last resort, it depended on a view of royal rule apparently shared by William the Conqueror and his youngest son and on the dutiful character and high abilities of the two Matildas. Matilda I's defiance of her husband in support of their eldest son notwithstanding, there is nothing of the court intrigue and sexual tension associated with many of the queens of the Frankish world; Jezebel was most certainly not a queenly model much in evidence at the Anglo-Norman court, but the position's potentialities and the complexities of the institution of marriage always meant that the disruptive queen and the dysfunctional marriage would be as good as certain to reappear.

Anglo-Norman diplomas, writs and writ-charters passed through significant changes between 1066 and 1135 and, as we have seen, the surviving evidence for the activities of the three queens who are the subject of this essay are qualitatively and quantitatively somewhat different. However, when like is compared with like – that is, diploma with diploma – and the significance of difference is correctly assessed – namely, when the many references to Matilda I's activities in diplomas and *pancartes* are treated as equivalent to the similar number of references to Matilda II's activities in the writs and writ-charters which came to be more extensively used in both Normandy and England after 1100 – this essay also affirms Janet Nelson's wise words that 'changes in diplomatic practice are difficult to calibrate with political change'.[81] As a result, my argument is yet another demonstration of the wrong-headedness of the old argument that the growth of bureaucracy and the supposedly 'public' character of royal rule meant that 'from the mid-eleventh century to the close of the medieval era, queens . . . were excluded from public life', because bureaucracy unquestionably grew in the period I have discussed while two out of the three

---

80 For a recent survey, D. Bates, 'Introduction: la Normandie et l'Angleterre de 900 à 1204', in P. Bouet and V. Gazeau (eds), *La Normandie et l'Angleterre au Moyen Age* (Caen, 2003), pp. 9–20.

81 Nelson, 'Medieval queenship', p. 201.

reigning queens were quite extraordinarily prominent and active.[82] The queenship of Matilda I and Matilda II supplies an interesting illustration of the role's possibilities. Yet, the apparent turning point of 1068 was not a long-term change in the history of queenship, but the inauguration of an episode which lasted for half a century. Taken together with Adeliza's reduced role and, for whatever reasons, her failure to bear children for Henry, this essay ultimately underlines two more themes which have been central to Janet Nelson's work on queenship, namely its institutional frailty and the centrality of the queen's responsibility to bear children to ensure dynastic stability.

82 The classic essay is J. McNamara and S. Wemple, 'The power of women through the family in medieval Europe, 500–1100', in M. Erler and M. Kowaleski (eds), *Women and Power in the Middle Ages* (Athens, GA, and London, 1988), pp. 83–101, with the quotation at p. 97. See further Nelson, 'Medieval queenship', pp. 201–2.

15

Franks and Bretons: the impact of political climate and historiographical tradition on writing their ninth-century history

Wendy Davies

C HAPTER TWO OF the key volume of La Borderie's *Histoire de Bretagne*, published in 1898, is devoted to the 'deliverance' of Brittany during the period 826–46.[1] Deliverance was brought from the 'yoke' of the Franks and the deliverer was Nominoë, a Breton who had been set in charge of the region by the emperor Louis about 831, in the wake of Carolingian military expeditions and conquest. La Borderie goes on to write of the liberation of Brittany, of the formation of the Breton monarchy, of recognition of Breton royalty by the Franks, and of the creation of the Breton nation: 'Les vieux saints [du sixième siècle] avaient fondé le peuple breton: Nominoë l'a constitué en nation, assurant... son indépendance, la persistance et le développement de son génie et de son caractère national'.[2] In the next generation, he continues, Nominoë's son Erispoë defeated the Carolingian Charles the Bald and extended Brittany to include the Breton March (that is, the Frankish frontier zone), before adding the rest of Neustria to the independent Breton realm.[3] Under the following ruler Salomon, Erispoë's cousin, the Breton monarchy reached its 'apogee', according to La Borderie; Salomon's all-encompassing power affected peace as it did war; counts and bishops attended his court; his artistic tastes and wonderful palaces were celebrated.[4] Catastrophes followed, however, and the unity of the realm was shaken, particularly at the hands of the Vikings, whose violent attacks by massed cruel hordes

---

1 A. Le Moyne de la Borderie, *Histoire de Bretagne*, 6 vols. (Rennes/Paris, 1896–1914), vol. 2, pp. 27–51; La Borderie died in 1901 and the three final volumes were completed by B. Pocquet.

2 La Borderie, *Histoire de Bretagne*, vol. 2, p. 66. 'The saints [of the sixth century] had founded the Breton people; it was Nominoë who turned them into a nation, assuring their independence, their tenacity and the development of their spirit and national character.'

3 La Borderie, *Histoire de Bretagne*, vol. 2, pp. 70–83.

4 La Borderie, *Histoire de Bretagne*, vol. 2, pp. 84–122.

brought blood, destruction, pillage and ruin – 'ce fléau terrible'.[5] The Bretons mounted valiant resistance, with Gurwant, one of two successors of Salomon (who died in 874), worthy of the name Roland or even Achilles; indeed, worth even more, for while those two heroes were the stuff of legend Gurwant was 'a hero of authentic history'.[6] Troubles followed, particularly those occasioned by the attacks of more Viking hordes; despite the glorious victory of King Alain the Great at Questembert in 888, Viking attacks became Viking 'inundation', a situation condoned by the treacherous Franks, who confirmed the Vikings in possession of Brittany.[7] 'Resurrection' finally came, with the triumphant return of the ruler Alain Barbetorte in the 930s and with his victory in the 'supreme struggle'.[8] In all this the Franks were the implacable enemies of the Bretons, would-be subjugators of the people and of other peoples too; their political leaders were committed to military suppression and domination; their religious leaders were infused with 'anti-Breton passion'.[9] So hated were they, the Bretons could not stomach the idea of marriage between the eldest son of Charles the Bald and Erispoë's daughter: that would mix the blood of the great Liberator with that of the oppressors.[10]

If we come forward a century, much of this interpretation of Franco-Breton relations in the ninth century has gone, whether we read Breton, or French, or other historians. Indeed, it is common to refer to La Borderie as anachronistic, wrong and nationalistic: 'patriotique, romantique et parfois passionnée', as Noel-Yves Tonnerre puts it.[11] The work of Breton scholars, such as J.-P. Brunterc'h, Hubert Guillotel, Tonnerre himself, or Bernard Merdrignac, suggests by contrast that although we may reasonably see the reign of Erispoë in the mid-ninth century as the period of the formation of the Breton state and of the establishment of its historic frontiers, his father Nominoë's revolt had been 'nothing whatsoever to do with any scheme of emancipation for Brittany'; Guillotel goes as far as to say that anyone who sees Nominoë as the creator of the Breton nation will fail to

5　'This terrible scourge.' La Borderie, *Histoire de Bretagne*, vol. 2, pp. 318–30, 356.
6　La Borderie, *Histoire de Bretagne*, vol. 2, p. 323.
7　La Borderie, *Histoire de Bretagne*, vol. 2, pp. 347–80.
8　La Borderie, *Histoire de Bretagne*, vol. 2, pp. 384–98.
9　La Borderie, *Histoire de Bretagne*, vol. 2, p. 57.
10　La Borderie, *Histoire de Bretagne*, vol. 2, p. 81.
11　'Patriotic, romantic and sometimes impassioned.' N.-Y. Tonnerre, *Naissance de la Bretagne: géographie historique et structures sociales de la Bretagne méridionale (Nantais et Vannetais) de la fin du VIIIe à la fin du XIIe siècle* (Angers, 1994), p. 76, n. 2. Cf. N.-Y. Tonnerre, 'Introduction: douze siècles d'historiographie bretonne', in N.-Y. Tonnerre (ed.), *Chroniqueurs et historiens de la Bretagne du moyen âge au milieu du XXe siècle* (Rennes, 2001), pp. 9–20, at p. 16, on the fact that the work has 'aged a lot'.

understand ninth-century Breton history.[12] The Breton state is now seen to have been much more obviously interpenetrated with Carolingian influence, an influence which had its ultimate consequences in the late twelfth century; the 'survival of the [Breton] kingdom was only possible because its chiefs had become integrated into the Frankish model'.[13] The Carolingians are now allowed competence in strategic planning and they occasion respect; aristocratic families of the whole of north-west France have been the subject of much detailed research – Breton and Frankish aristocracies are seen to have had shared interests, with a good deal of opportunistic intercourse between them; royal abbeys were established by the Carolingians to deal with local 'turbulence' in Brittany; the effects of 'royal vassality' are demonstrated by the multiplication of small administrative districts; and the Viking menace has dwindled to small-scale, intermittent disruption, with Viking alliance sought by rulers of all kinds.[14] (Neil Price has noted how the 1987 exhibition in Caen only allowed the Vikings a 'fleeting role' in Brittany.[15]) The shape-changing Breton March is alternatively held by the Carolingian nobility, integrated into the Seine/Loire Carolingian kingdom, dismembered, re-established, handed over to the Breton ruler Erispoë, assigned to his cousin Salomon, and extended farther east into Neustria, before it (or some of it) is finally handed over to the Loire Vikings in 921.[16] Meanwhile, the 'original' Breton March was absorbed, once and for all, into the duchy (later region) of Brittany; and the Breton 'nation' has effectively disappeared as a subject for historical discussion.[17]

12 B. Merdrignac, in P.-R. Giot, Ph. Guigon, B. Merdrignac, *Les premiers Bretons d'Armorique* (Rennes, 2003), pp. 140, 143; H. Guillotel in A. Chédeville and H. Guillotel, *La Bretagne des saints et des rois: Ve–Xe siècle* (Rennes, 1984), p. 229.

13 Merdrignac, *Premiers Bretons*, p. 147; Guillotel, *La Bretagne*, pp. 249–94; Tonnerre, *Naissance*, p. 1; Tonnerre, 'Introduction', p. 10, n. 3.

14 Guillotel, *La Bretagne*, pp. 201–46, 297–321; J.-P. Brunterc'h, 'Le duché du Maine et la marche de Bretagne', in H. Atsma (ed.), *La Neustrie: les pays au nord de la Loire de 650 à 850. Colloque historique international*, 2 vols (Sigmaringen, 1989), vol. 1, pp. 29–127 (p. 80 for 'vassality').

15 N. S. Price, 'The Vikings in Brittany', *Saga Book of the Viking Society* 22 (1989), pp. 327–440, at p. 327.

16 Guillotel, *La Bretagne*, pp. 363–91, and as cited above, nn. 13, 14; Brunterc'h, 'Le duché du Maine', pp. 54–74; Tonnerre, *Naissance*, pp. 77–9; Merdrignac, *Premiers Bretons*, pp. 122–47.

17 Although I am focusing on Breton historiography in this paper, it is worth noting that the recent English historiography also reflects these attitudes and, if anything, states them even more extremely. The Breton nation does not feature in Janet Nelson's treatment of the reign of Charles the Bald; Charles is lord over the Breton ruler as over other kings; Salomon's regalia become 'royal gear'; J. L. Nelson, *Charles the Bald* (Harlow, 1992), pp. 123, 242–3, 208–9. Cf. the influential treatment of J. M. H. Smith, *Province and Empire: Brittany and the Carolingians* (Cambridge, 1992),

Although we are accustomed to expect changes in historical interpretation over the passage of time, such a stark reversal is very striking. How can we explain such changes in approach, particularly given the fact that historians of the late nineteenth and of the late twentieth centuries were essentially using the same source material? The answers are partly obvious and partly not. In what follows, I shall explore both the roots of the historical interpretation and the stimuli for change, by considering the long historiographical tradition, attitudes to textual sources, and the changing political environment.

The historiographical tradition

Let me begin with the historiographical tradition. La Borderie was not the first to utter the nationalist sentiments of the late nineteenth century, for he wrote within an already existing interpretative framework.[18] He was well aware that he worked within this tradition: in the preface to volume three of his work, he explicitly paid tribute to his early modern predecessors, saying that he was going to add something more to their research, because he was going to treat the whole of Breton society.[19] That there is plenty of background is perfectly clear, because La Borderie quotes from earlier historians, often at length, as he also engages critically with earlier work: volume two has an appendix of nearly 100 pages of textual criticism and critical assessment.[20] That apart, his work is suffused with references to Breton histories of the preceding 400 years, from frequent citations of the nineteenth-century periodical literature (and even the occasional reference to English works), and of La Villemarqué's mid-nineteenth-century collections of Breton songs, back through Lobineau (d. 1727), Le Grand (d. 1640), and d'Argentré (d. 1589), to Pierre Le Baud (d. 1505).[21] His admiration for the work of Dom Lobineau is demonstrated by the fact that he delivered the dedicatory speech at the erection of a monument to

---

especially pp. 88, 111–15, 192: 'their power [Erispoë's and Salomon's] . . . now had the trappings of Carolingian regality' (p. 113).

18 Cf. Giot's cameo of the tradition, in Giot, Guigon, Merdrignac, *Premiers Bretons*, pp. 13–17.

19 La Borderie, *Histoire de Bretagne*, vol. 3, pp. i–ii.

20 La Borderie, *Histoire de Bretagne*, vol. 2, pp. 441–534; note *ibid.* his sustained refutation of the work of the Abbé Gallet (d.1725), pp. 446–51, 459–63: 'c'est archi-grotesque'.

21 La Borderie, *Histoire de Bretagne*, vol. 2, pp. 55, 353, 505; 497, 513; 67; 74, 459, 458, 377, for example.

Lobineau in the 1880s; a picture of this monument, with books representing the latter's *Histoire de Bretagne* and his *Vies des Saints de Bretagne* in front of it, forms the frontispiece of the commemorative publication.[22] Of all of them, however, it is the late fifteenth-century work of Le Baud that is most frequently selected and cited: using Le Baud's accounts of Pope Leo's authorization of a golden crown for Nominoë, of the death of Nominoë, of the Vikings' flight before Erispoë, of the latter's murder by Salomon, and of Salomon's council, La Borderie then quotes from him substantially for late ninth- and early tenth-century events, particularly in the context of attack by the Vikings ('les Normands').[23] 'Les pirates de Norwèghe, avecques innumerable assemblée de nefs nageans par la mer Océanne, degastèrent toute Bretaigne, ne nul n'y avoit qui resister leur pût, quar lors, par la division des seigneurs et occasion du peuple, estoient les forces des Bretons trop grandement affeblies et tellement que, parce qu'ilz avoient perdue toute esperance de ressources et pour fuir aux crudelitez et inhumanitez d'iceulx Normans, les comtes, vicomtes, barons et autres nobles, et le clergié s'espandirent tous par France, par Bourgongne et par Acquitaine. Mais les pouvres Bretons cultivans la terre demourèrent soubz la puissance des Normans.'[24]

22 A. de la Borderie, *Inauguration du monument élevé à la mémoire de Dom Lobineau* (Nantes, 1886); his speech includes a survey of historians preceding Lobineau, *ibid.*, pp. 35–40. See also P. Kershaw, ' "Time's abuse and the negligence of men": changing attitudes to the inscriptions of early medieval Brittany', in W. Davies et al., *The Inscriptions of Early Medieval Brittany* (Oakville CT and Aberystwyth, 2000), pp. 6–22, at pp. 18–19, for discussion and reproduction of the picture.
23 La Borderie, *Histoire de Bretagne*, vol. 2, pp. 55, 63, 79, 82, 114, and frequently within pp. 322–77.
24 La Borderie, *Histoire de Bretagne*, vol. 2, p. 356. 'The Norwegian pirates, with a vast fleet of boats travelling via the Atlantic coast, devastated the whole of Brittany; no one could resist them, for Breton forces were weakened and divided, because they had lost all hope of supplies; fleeing from the cruelty and inhumanity of these Normans, the counts, viscounts, barons and other nobles, and clergy, all dispersed throughout France, Burgundy and Aquitaine. But the poor Bretons cultivating the land remained under the power of the Normans.' (This is, in fact, Le Baud's considerably embellished rendering of the text of the Chronicle of Nantes, for which see below, p. 312 and n. 46; Le Baud, *Cronicques*, vol. 3, p. 144.) La Borderie was working from an unpublished edition of the work, 'Compillation des cronicques et ystoires des Bretons' (which he called 'Histoire de Bretagne'), BN ms. fr. 8266, now published as P. Le Baud, *Cronicques et ystoires des Bretons*, ed. C. de la Lande de Calan, 4 vols. (Rennes, 1907–22), the first, 1480, version of his work (this published version runs to 1305 only); P. Le Baud, *Histoire de Bretagne*, ed. C. d'Hozier (Paris, 1638) is an edition of his 1505 revision and amplification of the 1480 work, 'Le Livre des chroniques des roys, ducs et princes royaulx de Bretaigne armoricane aultrement nommée la moindre Bretaigne', BL Harl. MS 4371.

Although they drew on extant earlier histories, the work of Le Baud and his contemporaries in the late fifteenth and early sixteenth centuries established a clear and distinctive view of the place of Brittany in European history.[25] This was in many ways the beginning of the tradition of which La Borderie is the best known example. However, although La Borderie cites and quotes him frequently, it was not so much the quality of Le Baud's attitude to the French that infused La Borderie's History but that of the renowned Breton jurist Bertrand d'Argentré, a century later.[26] The first edition of d'Argentré's *Histoire de Bretagne* was published in 1588.[27] Here we find the Carolingian period interrupting a long (though not unbroken) succession of Breton kings. For d'Argentré, Nominoë was the man who recovered Breton liberty from the Emperor Louis's 'oppression'; he was the ultimate warrior hero, 'bruslant et ruinant le pays', paying back the French for everything Charlemagne and Louis the Pious had done to Brittany, and chasing them far to the east of the March, incorporating Anjou into 'Nova Britannia'. The treacherous Frankish king even unfairly manipulated his own counts, but Brittany was again a polity, Nominoë restoring its freedom, recovering the crown, and becoming sovereign and absolute king.[28] Erispoë continued his father's tradition, a valiant warrior who defeated Charles the Bald and ruled in Anjou, Maine, and Touraine.[29] Salomon, on the other hand, was renaissance man: 'homme fort conscientieux, religieux, affectionné à l'Église, homme droict, de vie civile, courtois et iuste en ses actions'. Salomon's murder signalled the end of the kingdom; this was the vengeance of God brought down by his crime in killing Erispoë, despite his religious inclination.[30] Meanwhile, the Vikings arrived in very large numbers, pillaging and ravaging, causing devastation and ruin with their cruel butchery, until Charles the Simple was forced to concede Neustria (later called Normandy) to the Viking Rollo and offer him the

25 Cf. the comments of Michael Jones, in P. Galliou and M. Jones, *The Bretons* (Oxford, 1991), p. 231; and the elegant paper by J. Kerhervé, 'Aux origines d'un sentiment national: les chroniqueurs bretons de la fin du moyen âge', *Bulletin de la société archéologique du Finistère* 108 (1980), pp. 165–206, giving biographical detail of the seven writers he considered at pp. 202–6. See below, pp. 315–16.
26 Although La Borderie took issue with d'Argentré on the legend of Conan, *Histoire de Bretagne*, vol. 2, pp. 458–9.
27 B. d'Argentré, *Histoire de Bretagne* (Paris, 1588; 3rd edn, 1618). The third edition is used here; grateful thanks are due to Bill McCann for the loan of it.
28 D'Argentré, *Histoire de Bretagne*, pp. 163–70.
29 D'Argentré, *Histoire de Bretagne*, pp. 179–82.
30 'A really conscientious man, religious, attached to the church, upright, refined, courteous and just in his actions', d'Argentré, *Histoire de Bretagne*, pp. 183–92.

homage of Brittany.[31] God finally relented in the 930s, with the Breton leader Alain returning from exile as 'sovereign' duke, ejecting the Vikings at last.[32]

The Breton historical tradition continued to be developed in the eighteenth century, and the Maurist Dom Guy Alexis Lobineau published his History in 1707. He notes the counts and dukes of the Breton nation in the sixth century and comments that the leaders of the time had the quality of kings even when their title was that of count; he emphasizes that the Bretons were independent.[33] Bowing their heads under the yoke of France in the early ninth century, the Bretons were too weak and divided, with no one capable of restoring its ancient liberty to the nation until the emergence of Morvan; after that, under their leader Nominoë, the Breton nation initially committed to remain loyal to Charles the Bald but the latter made threats (which did not frighten Nominoë), and Charles ran away after his defeat at Ballon.[34] Although Charles wanted to keep the peace between the two nations, Nominoë was now thinking of being crowned king, and was consecrated shortly after at Dol.[35] After Erispoë's military successes in Anjou and Maine, Salomon was 'not at all scared of the French', but preferred to assure his nation of the advantages of peace; after further treaties, Salomon's royalty was acknowledged – for Salomon had rights by birth to the crown of Brittany – and he was ultimately murdered while occupied with repairing damage caused by the Vikings, whose pillaging and ravaging was recurrent from the 840s.[36] After many vicissitudes, the victories of Alain Barbetorte finally restored their liberty to the Bretons.[37]

Lobineau's successor as historian, Dom Hyacinthe Morice, published a collection of documents before his narrative history.[38] The characteristic approach was sustained, for Morice's prefaces to the documents emphasize the kingship and independence of early medieval Breton leaders, as also the adoption of the title 'duke' from the late ninth century.[39] In

31 D'Argentré, *Histoire de Bretagne*, pp. 165–6, 181, 193–6, 199–201.

32 D'Argentré, *Histoire de Bretagne*, p. 203.

33 G. A. Lobineau, *Histoire de Bretagne*, 2 vols. (Paris, 1707), vol. 1, pp. 14, 9, cf. p. 49.

34 Lobineau, *Histoire de Bretagne*, vol. 1, pp. 29, 35, 40–1.

35 Lobineau, *Histoire de Bretagne*, vol. 1, pp. 43, 47.

36 Lobineau, *Histoire de Bretagne*, vol. 1, pp. 61, 65, 63, 66; Vikings: pp. 38, 42, 52, 62, 78, 79, for example.

37 Lobineau, *Histoire de Bretagne*, vol. 1, pp. 80–1.

38 H. Morice, *Mémoires pour servir de preuves à l'histoire ecclésiastique et civile de Bretagne*, 3 vols. (Paris, 1742–46).

39 Morice, *Mémoires pour servir de preuves*, vol. 1, pp. ii–iii, vol. 3, col. 1.

fact, an interest in the distinctive quality of the ducal title which had been established in the early Middle Ages was sustained by these historians across several hundred years, and has a special significance, as we shall see below.

Attitudes to textual sources

If the tradition was long-standing, what about source material? In theory new sources could have become available, thereby accounting for changes in interpretation. In fact, the written texts used in the fifteenth and sixteenth centuries are remarkably similar to those used in the late twentieth. Redon and other charters, papal and other letters, capitularies and conciliar decisions, Breton and Frankish annals, hagiographical tracts and other narrative sources, inscriptions on stone.[40] Indeed, the entire historiographical tradition is characterized by respect for text and by a concern to deal with inconsistencies. D'Argentré and Lobineau, like La Borderie, devote many pages to textual criticism, and quote at length in Latin from early medieval texts; La Borderie was especially concerned to master every detail.[41] The courtly perspective of much ninth- and tenth-century material is thereby reflected in their works, as are the statements of devastation, desertion and loss of political control that accompany accounts of the impact of the Vikings. Pre-twentieth-century approaches are often a very direct reflection of the perspective of the texts used, although d'Argentré, for example, certainly discusses the distinctive approaches and contradictions of different chronicles.[42]

What distinguishes more recent approaches are their attitudes to some of these texts and in particular to the medieval narratives, such as the Chronicle of Nantes, the work of Dudo of Saint-Quentin, and the Chronicle

40 See the 'Orientation bibliographique' in Chédeville and Guillotel, *La Bretagne des saints et des rois*, pp. 196–200, for a very useful list of most of the currently available primary sources. For inscriptions, see Davies et al., *Inscriptions of Early Medieval Brittany*; the use of inscriptions did not come into the historiography in any substantial way until the seventeenth century; Lobineau's work on them was important: see Kershaw, '"Time's abuse"', p. 13.

41 For textual criticism, see for example d'Argentré, *Histoire de Bretagne*, pp. 178, 187–90, 198, and La Borderie's appendix cited above, n. 20; cf. M. Denis, 'Arthur de La Borderie (1827–1901) ou "l'histoire, science patriotique"', in Tonnerre (ed.), *Chroniqueurs* (Rennes, 2001), pp. 143–55, at p. 145. Le Baud quotes from text too, but in French translation, and he has a tendency to embellish the text with words of his own (see above, p. 308).

42 D'Argentré, *Histoire de Bretagne*, pp. 186–7, for example.

of Saint-Brieuc. The historians of the fifteenth and sixteenth centuries drew heavily on these works, quoting at length from them, as did La Borderie, who drew in particular on Le Baud's citations.[43] La Borderie again and again introduces these quotations with a comment that Le Baud has faithfully preserved for us chronicles that are now lost.[44] As for the earlier works: Dudo's celebration of the early dukes of Normandy is an eleventh-century history, controversial for its suggestions that Brittany was handed over to the Vikings/Normans in the early tenth century and that Breton rulers voluntarily submitted to William Longsword in the 930s; it has been much criticized but is currently the subject of re-assessment.[45] The Chronicle of Nantes is a medieval history of uncertain date, reconstructed by its modern editor from late medieval citations, including those of Le Baud; it is notable for its treatment of the elevation of Nominoë to the kingship of Brittany (*de regno Britanniae renovando*).[46] The Chronicle of Saint-Brieuc, which repeats much of the Chronicle of Nantes, is a long and rambling history of Brittany, by an anonymous author (*un fougueux patriote breton*), put together between 1389 and 1416;[47] Léon Fleuriot called it a chaotic work and it is a puzzling read, running backward and forward

---

43 Although not from Dudo, whom he despatched in some scornful pages, La Borderie, *Histoire de Bretagne*, vol. 2, pp. 496–504; cf. pp. 378–83.

44 La Borderie, *Histoire de Bretagne*, vol. 2, pp. 63, 334, 351, for example.

45 Dudo, Dean of Saint-Quentin, *De moribus et actis primorum Normanniae ducum*, ed. J. Lair (Caen, 1865), especially pp. 168–85. See Guillotel, *La Bretagne*, pp. 399–400; F. Neveux, 'La Fondation de la Normandie et les Bretons (911–933)', in C. Laurent, B. Merdrignac, D. Pichot (eds), *Mondes de l'Ouest et villes du monde* (Rennes, 1998), pp. 297–309. A new edition is in preparation.

46 *La Chronique de Nantes (570 environ–1049)*, ed. R. Merlet (Paris, 1896), pp. 32–9 especially, although it implies subjection to the Franks in the later tenth century, in that Conan, Count of Rennes, 'held (*tenebat*) the greater part of Brittany from Count Theobald of Blois', *Chronique de Nantes*, p. 113. Merlet dated the text to 1050–59, although Guillotel has suggested that it may be as late as the early thirteenth century; see H. Guillotel, 'Genèse de l'"Indiculus de episcoporum depositione"', in Laurent et al., *Mondes de l'Ouest*, pp. 129–38, at pp. 134–8.

47 'An enthusiastic Breton patriot'; Kerhervé, 'Aux origines d'un sentiment national', pp. 205–6. Partly published in *Chronicon Briocense*, ed. G. Le Duc and C. Sterckx (Paris/Rennes, 1972); some other parts are available in the collections of volume two of Lobineau and volume one of Morice, but much remains unpublished. J.-C. Cassard, 'Les Chroniqueurs et historiens bretons face à la guerre de Succession', in Tonnerre, *Chroniqueurs et historiens*, pp. 57–75, at p. 59, dates it to *c.*1407. Michael Jones has in press a detailed study of *Chronicon Briocense* which will considerably extend the analysis currently available: M. Jones (ed.), *Le Premier Inventaire du trésor des chartes des ducs de Bretagne (1395): Hervé Le Grant et les origines du Chronicon Briocense* (Bannalec, 2007).

through stories of Conan Meriadec, Arthur, Merlin, early (pre-ninth-century) Breton kings, and later ducal history;[48] it is violently anti-English (*Natio saxonica est pessima et crudelissima natio . . . natio peior quam vipera*) and treats the Franks as 'oppressors'.[49]

These medieval histories directly reproduce some earlier texts, such as charters and letters, but their narrative frameworks tend to embellish and glorify the rulers of the ninth century – more than ninth-century texts do – and embellish the devastation caused by the Vikings. In particular, the treatment of Nominoë's request that the Pope confirm his kingship, which is found in the Chronicle of Nantes and Le Baud's work, is an elaboration of the embassy to the Pope detailed in the ninth-century *Gesta Sanctorum Rotonensium*:[50] where the ninth-century *Gesta* asks the Pope for relics and for advice on deposition of bishops, the later works go further to ask about the kingship, although the Pope replied that the title of duke over the people of Brittany was appropriate, albeit a duke with a golden coronet (*circulum*); Le Baud adds that his reply was influenced by letters from the king of France.[51] The Chronicle of Saint-Brieuc, Le Baud and d'Argentré all include details of the long line of pre-Carolingian Breton kings, running from King Conan in the late fourth century.[52] Since the eighteenth century there has been growing criticism of these earliest of histories, since they drew the list of early kings from the inventive twelfth-century history of Geoffrey of Monmouth and the complex of stories known as the 'matter of Britain'.[53] La Borderie himself played a significant part in these critical assessments, classifying Dudo as 'fabulous' (because of the story of the cession of Brittany to the Rouen (i.e. Seine) Vikings in 911 and *c*.930–31);[54]

---

48 *Chronicon Briocense*, p. 9; pp. 56, 64, 86, 120, 126, 136, for example.
49 *Chronicon Briocense*, pp. 94, 216. 'The Saxon nation is the worst and cruellest of nations . . . a nation worse than a viper.'
50 *The Monks of Redon: Gesta Sanctorum Rotonensium and Vita Conuuoionis*, ed. and trans. C. Brett (Woodbridge, 1989), ii.10, pp. 174–83.
51 *La Chronique de Nantes*, pp. 34–6; Le Baud, *Cronicques et ystoires*, vol. 3, pp. 100–4. Cf. the revised version of Le Baud, *Histoire de Bretagne*, p. 107, which omits the point about letters from the king of France.
52 *Chronicon Briocense*, e.g. pp. 46–56, 86–90; Le Baud, *Cronicques et ystoires*, vol. 2; d'Argentré, *Histoire de Bretagne*, pp. 110–60.
53 Guillotel, 'Genèse de l'"Indiculus de episcoporum depositione"', p. 136. Perhaps not entirely attributable to Geoffrey, given Gwenael Le Duc's case for the existence of a Breton tradition of the activity of a *dux* (not king) called Conan in the late Roman period, at least by 1012, 'L'Historia Britannica avant Geoffroy de Monmouth', *Annales de Bretagne* 79 (1972), pp. 819–35, at pp. 825–8.
54 See Dudo, *De moribus et actis*, pp. 168–9, 182–3 (cc. 28, 38); also confirmed in 933 according to Flodoard. Modern interpretation sees the land ceded as comprising

he also dismissed d'Argentré's use of the tale of the fourth-century King Conan and the pre-Carolingian Breton kings.[55] He was not the first, though, because he drew on Lobineau's dismissal of Conan – the story was 'incompatible' with contemporary sources – and of the Norman traditions about the early tenth century.[56] In all this it is particularly interesting that La Borderie rejected some of d'Argentré's texts while perpetuating some of his judgments and attitudes.

The eighteenth-century historians searched for sources – Lobineau is especially explicit about his approach to sources and both his volume two of '*preuves*', and then Morice's work, are invaluable in collecting and presenting the unadorned relevant texts.[57] In fact, La Borderie himself paid tribute to the Maurists for establishing the rules of sound criticism: 'no more stories! the truth! the entire truth! nothing but the truth!', a response reflected in Lobineau's epitaph.[58] However, one of the things that makes for difference between sixteenth- or eighteenth- and late twentieth-century interpretations is a changing attitude to text.[59] We are no longer so concerned to find absolute truth; we are as interested in perspective as in fact; and nowadays we acknowledge that we can learn quite a lot from forgeries. Crudely, one might also say, we are now not only more critical but more sceptical, more inclined to doubt, more inclined to look for hidden meaning; we look for the points concealed beneath the words, rather than the points made by the words. To take an example, the *Annals of Saint-Bertin*

---

essentially those parts of Brittany that lay east of its mid-ninth-century border (in effect the acquisitions of Salomon in Neustria and any lands to the east subsequently settled by Bretons), though William Longsword issued a coin proclaiming his title 'Dux Bri(tonum)'; Lobineau, *Histoire de Bretagne*, vol. 1, p. 79; Guillotel, *La Bretagne*, pp. 391–402; Neveux, 'La fondation de la Normandie'. Meanwhile, however, the county of Nantes had been ceded to the Loire Vikings in 921 (confirmed in 927); Price, 'Vikings', pp. 361–2; Guillotel, *La Bretagne*, pp. 377–9, 390–1.

55 La Borderie, *Histoire de Bretagne*, vol. 2, pp. 380–3, 441–63.
56 Lobineau, *Histoire de Bretagne*, vol. 1, pp. 66–7; cf. p. 79: it is 'absolutely false' to suggest that the Viking Rollo was given Brittany in 911; cf. Lobineau's hatchet-job on this matter in his volume two, col. 76–9.
57 Lobineau, *Histoire de Bretagne*, vol. 1, Preface (unpaginated), and vol. 2; Morice, *Mémoires pour servir de preuves*; their importance is indicated by the fact that both collections are still used by scholars to access otherwise unpublished texts.
58 La Borderie, *Inauguration du monument*, pp. 39–40; 'Il aima uniquement la vérité. Le premier, dans les obscurités des annales bretonnes, il porta la lumière de la critique', *ibid.*, pp. 69–70.
59 Cf. the comments of Kerhervé, 'Aux origines d'un sentiment national', p. 201; Cassard, 'Les Chroniqueurs et historiens bretons', p. 75; Denis, 'Arthur de La Borderie', pp. 147–8.

record that in 852 Salomon became the *fidelis* of Charles the Bald and was given a third of Brittany (*tertiaque parte Britanniae donatur*). Whereas La Borderie, citing this entry, comments that Salomon 'shamefully' acquired the protection of the Frankish king and acquired a vast principality (comprising Rennes and most of the North of the peninsula) from Erispoë, Hubert Guillotel, in an ingenious reconstruction of border politics, sees the Frankish king pro-actively ensuring the loyalty of Salomon and giving him the former Breton March (which had only recently been incorporated into the Breton kingdom).[60] More extremely, Guillotel sees nothing retrievable from the tales of the deeds of Alain the Great after his possible victory at Questembert, not even the date of his death, where La Borderie, following Le Baud and the Chronicle of Nantes, has pages on the victory, the restoration of the royal title, and Alain's well-earned epithet.[61]

The political environment

The most obvious explanation for changing interpretations is the changing contemporary political environment. Pierre Le Baud and fellow historians of the fifteenth and early sixteenth centuries wrote at a time when the dukes of Brittany had established sophisticated instruments of government and public procedures of elaborate display – coronations and burials were performed with royal ceremony in 'royal' clothes. Although owing homage to the king of France, the fifteenth-century dukes insisted on a distinctive form of homage that preserved their dignity and some sense of independence. This was a time when the state of Brittany in some real sense formed; so much so that Hervé Martin could ask in 1982: was this a revival of the Breton kingdom of Nominoë and Salomon?[62] It was certainly a time when regular taxation was established in the duchy and a professional central accounting office, when the duchy's chancery took its shape, as did the military machine, when the dukes built magnificent residences, when court life was expansive and representations were loaded with royal symbolism,

60 *The Annals of St-Bertin. Ninth-century Histories*, Vol. I, trans. J. L. Nelson (Manchester, 1991), p. 74; La Borderie, *Histoire de Bretagne*, vol. 2, p. 75; Chédeville and Guillotel, *La Bretagne des saints et des rois*, pp. 285–7.
61 Chédeville and Guillotel, *La Bretagne des saints et des rois*, p. 368; La Borderie, *Histoire de Bretagne*, vol. 2, pp. 331–46.
62 J.-P. Leguay and H. Martin, *Fastes et malheurs de la Bretagne ducale 1213–1532* (Rennes, 1982), p. 9.

and when the three Breton Estates of clergy, nobles and *bourgeois* began to meet annually.[63] Those who wrote history were often ducal servants, some of them with chancery affiliation, and they had access to ducal records as well as to the stories of British/Breton heroes that constituted the 'matter of Britain'.[64] Their histories spelled out the nature of the (distinctive) Breton polity and the shape of ducal privilege, with its emphasis on ducal 'regalities' or sovereign rights – 'un duc roi en son duché';[65] while conceding a relationship with the king of France, they insisted on the intrinsically sovereign status of the Breton polity. They emphasized what it meant to be Breton, stressing the Breton's love of the land: *la gent britannicque . . . elle est simple, ignorante de fraudes, humble, laborieuse, bien subiecte, patiente si elle n'est exaspérée et esmeuë, saine de chair, joyeuse en face, preuse en force, loyale envers ses seigneurs et ne cognoist les vices inhumains*;[66] Le Baud cited the Chronicle of Saint-Brieuc on the fertility of the land and rivers full of fish, the beautiful woods and forests, the birds and the beasts, a land good for labourers, hunters, hawkers, mariners.[67] Another historian of this period set the Bretons – disfigured, broken and wounded, not saying much but doing a lot – beside the French, in fine embroidered clothes, with forked beards, dancing and singing.[68] Altogether, these writers provided, in the words of Michael Jones, 'a coherent Breton ideology'.[69] The historians were very much a part of the prevailing political climate.

By the time d'Argentré was writing a hundred years later, Breton quasi-independence had been overtaken by the marriage of Duchess Anne to two French kings and by a more solid political union. Leading a practical life as a lawyer, d'Argentré reformed the 'Customs' of Brittany; he remains, for many Bretons, 'the greatest Breton jurist of modern times'. A man of

---

63 Leguay and Martin, *Fastes et malheurs*, pp. 162–93; J. Kerhervé, *L'État breton aux 14e et 15e siècles: les ducs, l'argent et les hommes*, 2 vols. (Paris, 1987), and for detail of financial organization; see vol. 1, fig. 1, p. 5, for representation in a Book of Hours of Duke Pierre II in royal clothes, with crown.

64 Cf. Kerhervé, 'Aux origines d'un sentiment national', pp. 170–2.

65 'A duke who was king in his duchy'; cf. *Chronicon Briocense*, e.g. p. 82: *Hodie tamen non vocatur Rex imo Dux. Veruntamen utitur omnibus iuribus et libertatibus regalibus in ducatu suo tamquam Rex.*

66 'The Breton people are simple, ignorant of fraud, humble, hard-working, good subjects, patient unless unreasonably pressured, sound in body, of cheerful expression, strong and valiant, loyal to their lords and unaware of unnatural vices'; Le Baud, *Histoire de Bretagne*, p. 19.

67 Le Baud, *Histoire de Bretagne*, pp. 36, 41.

68 Kerhervé, 'Aux origines d'un sentiment national', pp. 197–8.

69 Galliou and Jones, *The Bretons*, pp. 230–3; cf. Leguay and Martin, *Fastes et malheurs*, p. 168; Kerhervé, 'Aux origines d'un sentiment national', pp. 186–200.

the active political life, his *Histoire* was written for, and formally presented to, the Breton États in Rennes (despite the union, the États continued to meet until 1789).[70] Hostility to the French runs through the *Histoire* (which had to be revised before publication) – Louis XI was *un roi terrible*. D'Argentré stressed the early origin of the duchy and its line of kings, which had been established long before that of the Franks. Like Le Baud, whose great-nephew he was, he continued the concern with the nature of the homage done by the Breton duke, insisting still that it was homage preserving the ancient customs of Brittany, not straightforward obedience, insisting also on the *royal* pomp of the dukes.[71] The vision of an independent Breton polity was thereby sustained, as of the Breton nation, in his clearly articulated concept of nationality: the *nation breton* (*sic*) ever present.[72]

Lobineau's history was something of a political act in itself: encouraged by the Breton États, at that time objecting – on the grounds of the long history of the duchy – to new impositions by the French crown, it was determined that a new history was essential to demonstrate the duchy's antiquity; the initial success of the enterprise was marked in November 1707 by proclaiming Lobineau historiographer of Brittany and awarding him a pension of 300 *livres*.[73] However, in the interests of truth, Lobineau denied the long line of pre-Carolingian kings and thereby the greater antiquity of the Breton kingship. This excited local politics because the leading Breton noble house of Rohan traced its ancestry back to Conan: Lobineau therefore had to make some changes between his first and the published version, but he refused to reinstate King Conan and the line of early kings (although he frequently attributes the 'quality of king' to the early rulers, and he referred to the Breton nation in the early post-Roman centuries, and he cited Nominoë's letter as authority that the Bretons were established in north-west France long before the Franks).[74] Such was the anger of the Rohans, who argued that Lobineau was controlled by his (French) Maurist superiors, that the pension was revoked and the third

70 A. Croix, *L'âge d'or de la Bretagne 1532–1675* (Rennes, 1993), pp. 41–4, 454; cf. M. Planiol, *Histoire des institutions de la Bretagne*, 2nd edn, 5 vols. (Mayenne, 1981–84), vol. 5, pp. 371–2, on d'Argentré's 'doctrine des statuts', a kind of principle of subsidiarity.

71 Cf. J. Kerhervé, 'Écriture et récriture de l'histoire dans l'*Histoire de Bretaigne* de Bertrand d'Argentré: L'exemple du Livre XII', in Tonnerre (ed.), *Chroniqueurs et historiens*, pp. 77–109.

72 D'Argentré, *Histoire de Bretagne*, p. 164; cf. pp. 126, 169.

73 J. Quéniart, 'Les Mauristes et l'historiographie bretonne', in Tonnerre (ed.), *Chroniqueurs et historiens*, pp. 111–23, at pp. 116–17.

74 Lobineau, *Histoire de Bretagne*, vol. 1, pp. 9, 14, 22, 44.

volume never published; Morice was subsequently employed to prove the existence of Conan.[75]

What of the political context of La Borderie? Post-Revolutionary France had seen the inclusion of Brittany within a France-wide administrative structure of communes and *départements*, in the context of the indivisible Republic; it meant the end of the Breton États and the end of Breton law as a political instrument; government administrators arrived from beyond the former duchy and the Breton language was banned from schools. Active repression of Breton culture provoked a backlash; patriotic banquets, at which patriotic songs were sung, were a feature of intellectual culture by the 1830s;[76] journals with names like *Union bretonne* and *Indépendance bretonne* were represented at the dedication of Lobineau's monument in 1886;[77] and the political resistance movement took shape with the formation of the Union régionaliste bretonne in 1898, the year of publication of La Borderie's volume two, followed by the creation of the Parti national breton in 1911.[78] Cultural repression was a particularly sensitive issue, since academic study of language, texts and artefacts had reached new levels of expertise in the nineteenth century, sharing a movement common to many other western European countries at that time.[79] Academic interest had brought new dictionaries and new editions of texts such as early medieval Saints' Lives and the Redon charters, for example; collections of songs and (latterly) glosses; in 1843 the formation of the Association bretonne, of which La Borderie was a member (actually suspended in 1859 by the Ministry of the Interior); and the establishment of the important periodical *Annales de Bretagne* in 1885.[80] This was the immediate background to and context of La Borderie's work. The overtly national themes of La Borderie's *Histoire* thereby sit neatly within the contemporary Breton political and cultural framework, although they are also part of a much wider European

---

75 Quéniart, 'Les Mauristes', pp. 118–19; La Borderie, *Inauguration du monument*, pp. 45–55, runs through the detail of this conflict.

76 B. Tanguy, *Le Renouveau des études bretonnes au XIXe siècle*, vol. 1 of *Aux origines du nationalisme breton* (Paris, 1977), pp. 44–5; cf. p. 433: the desire for 'liberation' was manifest by the 1820s.

77 La Borderie, *Inauguration du monument*, p. 20.

78 F. Favereau, *Bretagne contemporaine: Langue, culture, identité* (Morlaix, 1993), pp. 164–80.

79 J.-Y. Guiomar, *Le Bretonisme: les historiens bretons au XIXe siècle* (Mayenne, 1987), and pp. 52–60 on French examples; Denis, 'Arthur de La Borderie', p. 152. See P. J. Geary, *Myth of Nations: The Medieval Origins of Europe* (Princeton NJ, 2001), pp. 26–33, for other parts of Europe.

80 Guiomar, *Le Bretonisme*, chapters IV, V, VII, VIII especially; Tanguy, *Le Renouveau*; Favereau, *Bretagne contemporaine*, pp. 165–7.

movement that used history, especially medieval history, to build national identities.[81] In spite of the long Breton tradition of identifying early medieval rulers as symbols of Breton nationality, and of reinforcing Breton identity by highlighting the rulers' heroic resistance against Vikings and French, La Borderie was oddly also at one with contemporary European developments. Indeed, a view of history as a 'science patriotique' was explicit in his method.[82]

And what of the political context surrounding historians of the past generation? Bretons have accepted Brittany as a region of the French state; the nationalist movement remains, but its political support is small – a newspaper poll in 1976 counted 80 per cent in favour of the status quo (a region within the French state) and 3 per cent in favour of independence. However, the value given to Breton culture (*Bretonnitude*) has if anything increased, as has knowledge of the Breton language.[83] Opposition to France is no longer appropriate, for Breton culture is celebrated within the context of the French state – as proclaimed by the French President Giscard d'Estaing at Ploërmel (in central Brittany) in 1976. Over 500 years of strong nationalist expression has become diluted in the modern world. There is also the European Union: France itself is part of a rapidly widening political framework, and of an increasingly interdependent world, one in which regional diversity and the variety of linguistic cultures are now encouraged. The recent political climate is clearly reflected in current historians' allowance of Frankish/Carolingian interpenetration within Brittany in the ninth century – 'impregnation' is one historian's word:[84] the nationalism that was once so highly valued is out of favour, and ninth-century Brittany is now seen as evidently part of a larger political framework. Perhaps there is also a touch of acceptable regional diversity in current attitudes to the Vikings: no longer the great scourge, but another culture taking its place within the European family?

I have made some rather obvious points about historiography reflecting our changing approach to primary sources, and about the influence on history-writing of the socio-political environment in which we write. They are not at all surprising, and the longevity of the exceptionally well devel-

---

81 T. Reuter, 'Modern mentalities and medieval polities', in T. Reuter, *Medieval Polities and Modern Mentalities*, ed. J. L. Nelson (Cambridge, 2006), pp. 3–18; cf. T. Reuter, 'Introduction: reading the tenth century', in T. Reuter (ed.), *NCMH* III (Cambridge, 1999), pp. 1–24; Geary, *Myth of Nations*, pp. 27–9.
82 Denis, 'Arthur de La Borderie', p. 144.
83 Favereau, *Bretagne Contemporaine*, pp. 124–40.
84 Tonnerre, 'Introduction', p. 10, n. 3.

oped Breton historiographical tradition is very well known to scholars of the early modern period. The concern with the distinctive quality of the ducal title had particular contemporary relevance in the late medieval and early modern periods because of the Bretons' unusual and particular relationship with the French state. That concern impacted on perspectives of the early Middle Ages because it was essential to demonstrate the antiquity of Breton political independence – whether by using Geoffrey's line of pre-Carolingian Breton kings, or by focusing on Nominoë's 'restoration' of ancient Breton kingship, or by emphasizing the special quality of the duchy established by Alain the Great (or Alain Barbetorte), or by dismissing Dudo's several references to the submission of Breton leaders to the Normans. Hence the considerable emphasis on sovereignty in ninth- and early tenth-century contexts – even Morice had Salomon calling his 'parlement' for advice when he wanted to make the trip to Rome at a time of Viking threat.[85] It is of considerable interest that historians chose the ducal title of the late ninth/early tenth century as the significant antecedent, rather than that of Nominoë, whose well-evidenced title of *dux in Brittannia* alternated with that of *missus imperatoris* and presumably was associated with too many connotations of dependence. Alain the Great's title *Alan rex summus Britonum dux* in a charter issued from Plessé, quoted by the Chronicle of Nantes, presumably by contrast offered a particularly suggestive and potent combination.[86] As Le Baud indicated, it was the reign of Alain the Great that was the crux.[87]

Outright hostility to the French did not have to accompany these concerns – witness Le Baud's relatively moderate language[88] – and it is not a prominent feature before the late Middle Ages. Conflict between Franks and Bretons is clear enough from the sixth century, whoever made the record, and Frankish conquest in the early ninth century is undeniable. But ninth-century Breton texts talk of French occupation and Breton resistance;[89] the language of 'oppression' by the French, the 'yoke' they imposed, and the 'servitude' and 'liberty' of the Bretons belongs with later medieval

---

85 Morice, *Mémoires pour servir de preuves*, vol. 3, col. 2; cf. *ibid.*, vol. 1, p. iii, emphasizing the importance of sovereignty, whatever the title.

86 *Chronique de Nantes*, p. 74.

87 *Histoire de Bretagne*, pp. 125–6; cf. *Chronicon Briocense* in Morice, *Preuves*, vol. 1, col. 25; Morice, *Preuves*, vol. 1, p. ii; Lobineau, *Histoire de Bretagne*, vol. 1, p. 69. As many of these historians observed, Alain the Great was sometimes *rex* and sometimes *dux* in contemporary texts.

88 Note Kerhervé's comment on the greater subtlety of Le Baud, 'Aux origines d'un sentiment national', p. 188.

89 *Gesta Sanctorum Rotonensium*, I.7 and I.11.

and modern representations – a comment in itself, of course, on changing attitudes to personal status, as it is also an obvious comment on the changing administration of the French state.[90] But, just as Carolingian conquest is undeniable, so is the fact that that conquest provoked the emergence of the Breton polity and the establishment of its historic frontiers – a state with real political significance in the later medieval and early modern periods. After all, then, ninth-century events and relationships did make a difference to the long-term development.

Historians did not merely record political attitudes; they contributed to their development. In fact, many of the differences between earlier and later historical interpretations come down to values. As we now reject the nationalism that was for many centuries a virtue, we should not lose sight of the fact that the next generation will probably be overturning our current values as well as our interpretation.[91]

90　The 'unjust' Frankish invasions of the earlier Chronicle of Nantes do not represent the perspective of that chronicler: this was the attitude he attributed to Nominoë, of whom he did not approve (*Chronique de Nantes*, p. 33), as La Borderie was well aware, *Histoire de Bretagne*, vol. 2, pp. 54–8. For the language of servitude and liberty in *Chronicon Briocense* and d'Argentré's work, see Kerhervé, 'Écriture et récriture', p. 107.

91　I am very grateful for helpful comments received when aspects of this paper were read at meetings at Southampton, Cérisy-la-Salle and Oxford during the last couple of years; and especially for the informed and judicious comments on written drafts of the whole paper made by Paul Fouracre, Michael Jones and Elizabeth Tingle.

Appendix: The estates and lordships attached to Burgheard in Domesday Book

Place-name	County	Phillimore reference number	Folio no.	Personal name of TRE landholder (normalized)	By-name, title or office	Name of lord (normalized)	Name of tenant-in-chief	Name of sub-tenant	H	V	A	C	TRE £	TRE s	TRE d	Total TRE value (£)
Demesne estates																
Shenley (Church End)	Bucks	13:2	146d	Burgheard	huscarle regis	King Edward	Earl Hugh		2				6			6.0
Shenley (Church End)	Bucks	13:3	147a	Burgheard	teignus regis	King Edward	Earl Hugh		5				4			4.0
Witham	Essex	32:3	63b	Burgheard	liber homo		Robert Gernon		4				4			4.0
Fundenhall	Norfolk	6:6	152b	Burgheard	thegn		Earl Hugh	Hugh						40		2.0
Mendlesham	Suffolk	1:76	285b	Burgheard			King William	Roger Bigot			42	2	25			25.0
Saxtead	Suffolk	4:12	299a	Burgheard			Earl Hugh				60	7				0.0
Ilketshall	Suffolk	4:24	301a	Burgheard	liber homo		Earl Hugh	Mundred				2		30		1.5
Sotterley	Suffolk	4:30	301a	Burgheard			Earl Hugh	Mundred				1.5		53	4	2.7
Croscroft	Suffolk	4:31	301b	Burgheard	liber homo		Earl Hugh					1.5		26	5	1.3
Kessingland	Suffolk	4:35	301b	Burgheard			Earl Hugh	Hugh fitz Norman				2		30		1.5
Carlton (Colville)	Suffolk	4:38	302a	Burgheard			Earl Hugh	Norman				2		30		1.5
Total									**11**	**0**	**102**	**18**	**39**	**209**	**9**	**49.5**
Commended men																
Buckingham	Bucks	B:4	143a	–	1 burgess	Burgheard of Shenley	Earl Hugh								26	0.1
Cotton	Suffolk	1:77	285b	–	18 liberi homines	Burgheard	King William				15	1		10		0.5
Wyverstone	Suffolk	1:83	286a	–	1 liber homo	Burgheard	King William				8				16	0.1
Cotton	Suffolk	1:84	286a	–	2 libere femine	Burgheard	King William				5				12	0.1
Stoke (Ash)	Suffolk	1:86	286a	–	4 liberi homines	Burgheard	King William				8				4	0.1
Cotton	Suffolk	1:95	286b	–	3 liberi homines	Burgheard	King William				8					0.1
Ilketshall	Suffolk	4:26	301a	–	1 libera femina	Burgheard	Earl Hugh				20			2		0.3
Ilketshall	Suffolk	4:28	301a	–	3 liberi homines	Burgheard	Earl Hugh				30			5		0.3
Ringsfield	Suffolk	4:29	301a	–	2 liberi homines	Burgheard	Earl Hugh	Warin son of Burnin			12			5	6	0.2
Hethburgafella	Suffolk	4:33	301b	–	3 liberi homines	Burgheard	Earl Hugh				22			4		0.2
Kessingland	Suffolk	4:35	301b	–	29 liberi homines	Burgheard	Earl Hugh					2.2	2.9			2.9
Carlton (Colville)	Suffolk	4:38	302a	–	30 liberi homines	Burgheard	Earl Hugh					2	4			4.0
Barnby	Suffolk	4:39	302a	–	5 liberi homines	Burgheard	Earl Hugh	Hugh son of Norman			44			6		0.3

Place	County	Ref	Folio	1066 holder	Holding	Antecessor	1086 tenant‑in‑chief	1086 tenant	H	V	A	C	C	s	d	£
Thornham (Magna)	Suffolk	6:215	322a	–	1 liber homo	Burgheard	Robert Malet				20			5		0.3
Willingham	Suffolk	7:42	335a	Gunnulf	liber homo	Burgheard	Roger Bigot				30			10		0.5
Willingham	Suffolk	7:43	335b	–	5 liberi homines	Burgheard	Roger Bigot				80			10		0.5
Weston	Suffolk	7:43	335b	–	5 liberi homines	Burgheard	Roger Bigot	Gannulf			18			20		1.0
Wickham (Skeith)	Suffolk	14:152	371a	Brunlocc	liber homo	Burgheard of Mendlesham	Abbot Baldwin				3			6		0.3
Wickham (Skeith)	Suffolk	14:152	371a	Hereweard	liber homo	Burgheard of Mendlesham	Abbot Baldwin	Ordgar			2.5			4		0.2
Stonham	Suffolk	16:15	374b	Sperun	liber homo	Burgheard	Odo, bishop of Bayeux	Ordgar			8			5		0.3
Helmingham	Suffolk	16:26	376a	Viking	liber homo	Burgheard	Odo, bishop of Bayeux				30			6		0.3
Willingham	Suffolk	31:21	407a	–	15 liberi homines	Burgheard	Hugh de Montfort				18	1.5		60		3.0
Weston	Suffolk	31:22	407a	–	1 liber homo	Burgheard	Hugh de Montfort				16			5		0.3
Willingham	Suffolk	31:23	407a	–	1 liber homo	Burgheard	Hugh de Montfort				3				18	0.1
Hetheburgfelda	Suffolk	31:24	407a	–	6 liberi homines	Burgheard	Hugh de Montfort				60			10		0.5
Beketuna	Suffolk	31:26	407a	–	6 liberi homines	Burgheard	Hugh de Montfort				60			4		0.2
Kessingland	Suffolk	31:27	407b	–	3 liberi homines	Burgheard	Hugh de Montfort				70			8		0.4
Rodenhala	Suffolk	31:28	407b	Aslak	liber homo	Burgheard	Hugh de Montfort				40			5		0.3
Wimundahala	Suffolk	31:29	407b	–	2 liberi homines	Burgheard	Hugh de Montfort				12			2		0.1
Gisleham	Suffolk	31:30	407b	–	3 liberi homines	Burgheard	Hugh de Montfort				17.5			7	6	0.4
Carlton (Colville)	Suffolk	31:32	407b	–	3 liberi homines	Burgheard	Hugh de Montfort				60			8		0.4
Kirkley	Suffolk	31:33	407b	–	1 liber homo	Burgheard	Hugh de Montfort				12			2		0.1
Cotton	Suffolk	31:35	408a	Seaxwine	liber homo	Burgheard	Hugh de Montfort				20					0.0
Wyverstone	Suffolk	31:36	408a	–	2 liberi homines	Burgheard	Hugh de Montfort	Hervey			18			4		0.2
Total									0	0	770	6.675	6.9	218	88	18.17
Other																
Stoke (Ash)	Suffolk	14:146	371a	Burgheard	sochemannus		Abbot Baldwin				14			3		0.2
Norwich	Norfolk	1:61	117a				Burgheard held one house in Norwich in 1086									

Abbreviations: H = hides; V = virgates; A = acres; C = carucates; TRE = tempore regis edwardi (in the time of King Edward); s = shillings; d = pence.

Professor Janet L. Nelson's publications

This list omits editorials, prefaces and DNB entries, and book reviews.

'Gelasius's doctrine of responsibility: a note', *Journal of Theological Studies* 18 (1967), pp. 154–62

'The problem of King Alfred's royal anointing', *Journal of Ecclesiastical History* 18 (1967), pp. 145–63

'National synods, kingship as office, and royal anointing: an early medieval syndrome', *Studies in Church History* 7 (1971), pp. 41–59

'Society, theodicy and the origins of heresy; towards a reassessment of the medieval evidence', *Studies in Church History* 9 (1972), pp. 65–77

'Royal saints and early medieval kingship', *Studies in Church History* 10 (1973), pp. 39–44

'Ritual and reality in the early medieval *ordines*', *Studies in Church History* 11 (1975), pp. 41–51

'Symbols in context: inauguration rituals in Byzantium and the West in the early Middle Ages', *Studies in Church History* 13 (1976), pp. 97–111

'On the limits of the Carolingian Renaissance', *Studies in Church History* 14 (1977), pp. 51–69

'Kingship, law and liturgy in the political thought of Hincmar of Rheims', *English Historical Review* 363 (1977), pp. 241–79

'Virgin territory: recent historical work on Marian belief and cult', *Religion* 7 (1977), pp. 206–25

'Inauguration rituals', in P. Sawyer and I. N. Wood (eds), *Early Medieval Kingship* (Leeds, 1977), pp. 50–71

'Queens as Jezebels: Brunhild and Balthild in Merovingian history', in D. Baker (ed.), *Medieval Women* (Oxford, 1978), pp. 31–77

'Charles the Bald and the church in town and countryside', *Studies in Church History* 16 (1979), pp. 103–17

'Religion in "histoire totale": some recent work on medieval heresy and popular religion', *Religion* 10 (1980), pp. 67–70

'The earliest royal *ordo*', in B. Tierney and P. Linehan (eds), *Authority and Power* (Cambridge, 1980), pp. 29–48

'The rites of the Conqueror', *Proceedings of the Battle Conference on Anglo-Norman Studies* 4 (1981), pp. 117–32, 210–21

with M. T. Gibson (eds), *Charles the Bald, Court and Kingdom* (Oxford, 1981)

'The Annals of St-Bertin', in Gibson and Nelson (eds), *Charles the Bald* (Oxford, 1981), pp. 15–36

'Bibliography: Anglo-Saxon England, 1970–81', *Medieval Prosopography* 3 (1982), pp. 109–12

'The Church's military service: a contemporary comparative view?', *Studies in Church History* 20 (1983), pp. 15–30

'Myths of the Dark Ages', in L. Smith (ed.), *The Making of Britain* (London, 1984), pp. 145–58

'Legislation and consensus', in P. Wormald (ed.), *Ideal and Reality* (Oxford, 1983), pp. 29–48

'Public Histories and private history in the work of Nithard', *Speculum* 60 (1985), pp. 251–93

Politics and Ritual in Early Medieval Europe (London, 1986), 17 reprinted papers

'Wealth and wisdom: the politics of Alfred', in J. Rosenthal (ed.), *Kings and Kingship*, Center for Medieval and Early Renaissance Studies, State University of New York, *Acta* 11 (1986), pp. 31–52

'Les Femmes et l'évangelisation', *Revue du Nord* 68 (1986), pp. 471–85

' "A king across the sea": Alfred in Continental perspective', *Transactions of the Royal Historical Society* 36 (1986), pp. 45–68

'Dispute settlement in Carolingian West Francia', in W. Davies and P. Fouracre (eds), *The Settlement of Disputes in Early Medieval Europe* (Cambridge, 1986), pp. 45–64

Rewriting the history of the Franks', *History* 72 (1987), pp. 69–81

'Making ends meet: wealth and poverty in the Carolingian Church', *Studies in Church History* 24 (1987), pp. 25–36

'Carolingian royal ritual', in D. Cannadine and S. Price (eds), *Rituals of Royalty: Power and Ceremonial in Traditional Societies* (Cambridge, 1987), pp. 137–80

'A tale of two princes: politics, text and ideology in a Carolingian annal', *Studies in Medieval and Renaissance History* 10 (1988), pp. 105–41

'Kingship and empire', in J. H. Burns (ed.), *The Cambridge History of Medieval Political Thought* (Cambridge, 1988), pp. 211–51

with S. Coupland, 'The Vikings on the Continent', *History Today* (December 1988), pp. 12–19

with C. Harper-Bill and C. Holdsworth (eds), *Studies in Medieval History presented to R. Allen Brown* (Woodbridge, 1989)

'Ninth-century knighthood: the evidence of Nithard', in C. Harper-Bill, C. Holdsworth and J. L. Nelson (eds), *Studies in Medieval History presented to R. Allen Brown* (Woodbridge, 1989), pp. 255–66

'Translating images of authority: the Christian Roman emperors in the Carolingian world', in M. M. Mackenzie and C. Roueché (eds), *Images of Authority: Papers presented to Joyce Reynolds on the Occasion of her 70th Birthday* (Cambridge, 1989), pp. 194–205

'The problematic in the private', *Social History* 15 (1990), pp. 355–64

with M. T. Gibson (eds), *Charles the Bald: Court and Kingdom*, 2nd edn (London, 1990)

'The reign of Charles the Bald: a survey', in Gibson and Nelson (eds), *Charles the Bald* (London, 1990), pp. 1–22

'The Annals of St Bertin', in Gibson and Nelson (eds), *Charles the Bald* (London, 1990), pp. 23–40 [reprinted from 1st edn]

'Women and the Word', *Studies in Church History* 27 (1990), pp. 53–78

'A place for medieval history in the national curriculum?', *History Workshop Journal* 29 (1990), pp. 103–6

'Commentary', in W. Affeldt (ed.), *Frauen in Spätantike und Frühmittelalter* (Sigmaringen, 1990), pp. 325–32

Contribution to J. Gardiner (ed.), *The History Debate* (London, 1990), pp. 52–60

'Zur Annahme des Herrscherrituals im Frühmittelalter', in J. Kuolt, H. Kleinschmidt and P. Dinzelbacher (eds), *Das Mittelalter: unsere fremde Vergangenheit* (Stuttgart, 1990), pp. 117–47

'Perceptions du pouvoir chez les historiennes du haut moyen-âge', in M. Rouche and J. Heuclin (eds), *La Femme au moyen âge* (Maubeuge, 1990), pp. 75–85

'The last years of Louis the Pious', in P. Godman and R. Collins (eds), *Charlemagne's Heir: New Perspectives on the Reign of Louis the Pious* (Oxford, 1990), pp. 147–60

'Hincmar of Reims on king-making: the evidence of the Annals of St. Bertin', in J. M. Bak (ed.), *Coronations* (Berkeley, 1990), pp. 16–34

'Literacy in Carolingian government', in R. McKitterick (ed.), *The Uses of Literacy in Early Medieval Europe* (Cambridge, 1990), pp. 258–96

'La Famille de Charlemagne', *Byzantion: Revue Internationale des Etudes Byzantines* 61 (1991), pp. 194–212

Ninth-Century Histories: The Annals of St-Bertin, translated, with Introduction and notes, and annotated bibliography (Manchester, 1991)

' "Not bishops' bailiffs but lords of the earth": Charles the Bald and the problem of sovereignty', in D. Wood (ed.), *The Church and Sovereignty: Essays in Honour of Michael Wilks* (Oxford, 1991), pp. 23–34

'Reconstructing a royal family: reflections on Alfred, from Asser chapter 2', in I. Wood and N. Lund (eds), *People and Places in Northern Europe 500–1600* (Woodbridge, 1991), pp. 47–66

'Charles le Chauve et les utilisations du savoir', in D. Iogna-Prat, C. Jeudy and G. Lobrichon (eds), *L'école carolingienne d'Auxerre* (Paris, 1991), pp. 37–54

'Gender and genre in women historians of the earlier Middle Ages', in J. P. Genet, *L'historiographie médiévale en Europe* (Paris, 1991), pp. 149–53

'A propos des femmes royales dans les rapports entre le monde wisigothique et le monde franc à l'époque de Reccared', in *El Concilio III de Toledo XIV Centenario* (Madrid, 1991), pp. 465–76

edited, *Richard Coeur de Lion in History and Myth* (KCLMS VII, 1992)

'Debate: trade, industry and the wealth of King Alfred, Comment 2', *Past and Present* 135 (1992), pp. 151–63

'The intellectual in politics: context, content and authorship in the Capitulary of Coulaines, November 843', in L. Smith and B. Ward (eds), *Intellectual Life in the Middle Ages* (London, 1992), pp. 1–14

Charles the Bald (London/New York, 1992); French trans. *Charles le Chauve* (Paris, 1994)

'History, women's history, and beyond history in *Lohengrin*', in Richard Wagner, *English National Opera Guide* 47 (1993), pp. 33–40

'The political ideas of Alfred of Wessex', in A. Duggan (ed.), *Kings and Kingship* (London, 1993), pp. 125–58

'Women at the court of Charlemagne: a case of monstrous regiment?', in J. Parsons (ed.), *Medieval Queenship* (New York, 1993), pp. 43–62, 203–6

'The Franks, the martyrology of Usuard and the martyrs of Córdoba', *Studies in Church History* 30 (1993), pp. 67–80

'Kingship and empire in the Carolingian world', in R. McKitterick (ed.), *Carolingian Culture* (Cambridge, 1993): a revised version of 'Kingship and empire', in *The Cambridge History of Medieval Political Thought* (1988), pp. 52–87

'Anglo-Saxon England and the Continent', in N. Saul (ed.), *England in Europe 1066–1453* (London, 1994), pp. 21–35

'Parents, children and the Church' (presidential address), *Studies in Church History*, 31 (1994), pp. 81–114

'History-writing at the courts of Louis the Pious and Charles the Bald', in A. Scharer and G. Scheibelreiter (eds), *Historiographie im Frühen Mittelalter* (Munich, 1994), pp. 435–42

'Kingship and royal government', in R. McKitterick (ed.), *The New Cambridge Medieval History*, vol. II (Cambridge, 1995), pp. 383–430

'The Frankish Kingdoms, 814–898: the West', in R. McKitterick (ed.), *The New Cambridge Medieval History*, vol. II (Cambridge, 1995), pp. 110–41

'The wary widow', in W. Davies and P. Fouracre (eds), *Property and Power in Early Medieval Europe* (Cambridge, 1995), pp. 82–113

with R. Pfaff, 'Anglo-Saxon Pontificals and Sacramentaries', in P. Szarmach (ed.), *Sources for Anglo-Saxon History and Culture* (New York, 1996), pp. 87–98

'The search for peace in a time of war: the Carolingian Brüderkrieg, 840–843', in *Vorträge und Forschungen*, 42 (Konstanzer Arbeitskreis für mittelalterliche Geschichte, 1996), pp. 87–114

The Frankish World (London, 1996): 13 reprinted papers

with J. Roberts (eds), *Alfred the Wise: Studies in Honour of Janet Bately* (Woodbridge, 1997)

'"*Sicut tunc Franci . . . nunc Angli*": Fulk's letter to Alfred revisited', in Roberts and Nelson (eds), *Alfred the Wise* (Woodbridge, 1997), pp. 135–44

'Early medieval rites of queen-making and the making of medieval queenship', in A. Duggan (ed.), *Queens and Queenship in Medieval Europe* (Woodbridge, 1997), pp. 301–15

'The Frankish Empire', in P. Sawyer (ed.), *The Oxford Illustrated History of The Vikings* (1997)

'The Anglo-Saxons', in N. Saul (ed.), *The Oxford Illustrated History of Medieval England* (1997)

'Violence in the Carolingian world and the ritualization of ninth-century warfare', in G. Halsall (ed.), *Violence in Early Medieval Society* (Woodbridge, 1997), pp. 90–107

'The siting of the Council at Frankfurt: reflections on family', in R. Berndt (ed.), *Das Konzil von Frankfurt* (Mainz, 1997), pp. 149–65

'Family, gender and sexuality', in M. Bentley (ed.), *Companion to Historiography* (1997), pp. 153–78

'Kings with justice, kings without justice: an early medieval paradox, in *La giustizia, Settimane* 44 (1997), pp. 797–823

'La Mort de Charles le Chauve', *Médiévales* (1997), pp. 53–66

'Making a difference in eighth-century politics: the daughters of Desiderius', in A. Murray (ed.), *After Rome's Fall: Narrators and Sources of early Medieval History. Essays presented to Walter Goffart* (Toronto, 1998), pp. 171–90

'A tale of two princes: politics, text and ideology in a Carolingian Annal', *Studies in Medieval and Renaissance History* 10 (1998), pp. 105–41

'Waiting for Alfred', *Early Medieval Europe*, 7 (1998), pp. 115–24

'The Franks and the English in the ninth century revisited', in J. Rosenthal and P. Szarmach (eds), *The Preservation and Transmission of Anglo-Saxon Culture* (1998), pp. 141–58

'La Cour impériale de Charlemagne', in R. Le Jan (ed.), *La Royauté et les élites dans l'Europe dans le haut moyen âge* (Lille, 1998), pp. 177–91

'Monks, secular men, and masculinity', in D. Hadley (ed.), *Masculinity in Medieval Europe* (London, 1998), pp. 121–42

'Medieval Queenship', in L. Mitchell (ed.), *Women in Western Medieval Culture* (New York and London, 1999), pp. 179–208

Rulers and Ruling Families in Early Medieval Europe: Alfred, Charles the Bald and Others, Variorum Collected Studies Series (Aldershot, 1999): 17 reprinted papers

'Bad kingship in the earlier Middle Ages', *Haskins Society Journal* 8 (1999), pp. 1–26

'Entertainments and inversions: the Ups and Downs of St-Gall', in B. Nagy and M. Sebök (eds), . . . *The Man of Many Devices Who Wandered Full Many Ways . . . Festschrift in Honor of Janos Bak* (Budapest, 1999), pp. 269–76

'Les reines carolingiennes', in S. Lebecq et al. (eds), *Femmes et pouvoirs des femmes à Byzance et en Occident* (VIe–XIe siècles) (Lille, 1999), pp. 121–32

'Kingship and Government', in T. Reuter (ed.), *New Cambridge Medieval History*, vol. III (Cambridge, 1999), pp. 95–129

'Two Exhibitions', in *History Workshop Journal*, 50 (2000), pp. 295–9

'Early medieval biography', *History Workshop Journal*, 50 (2000), pp. 129–36

'Gender, memory and social power', review article, *Gender and History*, 12 (2000), pp. 722–34

with F. Theuws (eds), *Rituals of Power from Late Antiquity to the Early Middle Ages* (Leiden, 2000)

'Viaggio, pellegrinaggi e vie di commercio', Catalogue of the Exhibition, *Il Futuro dei Longobardi*, Comune di Brescia (2000), pp. 163–71

'Nobility in the ninth century', in A. Duggan (ed.), *Nobles and Nobility in the Middle Ages* (Woodbridge, 2000), pp. 43–51

'Carolingian royal funerals', in Theuws and Nelson (eds), *Rituals of Power* (Leiden, 2000), pp. 131–84

'Epilogue', in Theuws and Nelson (eds), *Rituals of Power* (Leiden, 2000), pp. 477–85

with J. Roberts (eds), *Essays on Anglo-Saxon and Related Themes in Memory of Lynne Grundy*, King's College London Medieval Studies XVII (London, 2000)

'Power and authority at the court of Alfred', in J. Roberts and J. L. Nelson (eds), *Essays . . . in Memory of Lynne Grundy*, King's College London Medieval Studies XVII (London, 2000), pp. 311–37

with P. Stafford and J. Martindale (eds), *Law, Laity and Solidarities: Essays in Honour of Susan Reynolds* (Manchester, 2001)

'Peers in the early Middle Ages', in Stafford, Martindale and Nelson (eds), *Law, Laity and Solidarities: Essays in Honour of Susan Reynolds* (Manchester, 2001), pp. 27–46

with P. Linehan (eds), *The Medieval World* (London, 2001)

'Introduction' and Section Introductions, in Linehan and Nelson (eds), *The Medieval World* (London, 2001), pp. 1–4, 7–13, 187–8, 363–5, 555–6

'Monasticism', in Linehan and Nelson (eds), *The Medieval World* (London, 2001), pp. 576–604

'Carolingian contacts', in M. P. Brown and C. A. Farr (eds), *Mercia: An Anglo-Saxon Kingdom in Europe* (London/New York, 2001), pp. 126–43

'Aachen as a Place of Power', in M. de Jong and F. Theuws (eds), *Topographies of Power in Early Medieval Europe* (Leiden, 2001), pp. 217–41

'Charlemagne and Alcuin', pamphlet-catalogue co-authored (with M. Garrison and D. Tweddle) to accompany the Alcuin Exhibition, The Yorkshire Museum (2001), pp. 15–23

'Messagers dans l'occident et au-delà', in A. Dierkens and J.-M. Sansterre (eds), *Voyages et Voyageurs à Byzance et en Occident du VIe au XIe siècle* (Geneva, 2001), pp. 397–413

'The voice of Charlemagne', in R. Gameson and H. Leyser (eds), *Belief and Culture: Studies in the Middle Ages. Studies presented to Henry Mayr-Harting* (Oxford, 2001), pp. 76–88

'The Church and a revaluation of work in the ninth century?', *Studies in Church History* 37 (2002), pp. 35–43

'The Merovingian Church in Carolingian retrospect', in K. Mitchell and I. Wood (eds), *The Age of Gregory of Tours* (Leiden, 2002), pp. 241–59

'Charlemagne: *pater optimus?*', in J. Jarnut (ed.), *Am Vorabend der Kaiserkrönung* (Stuttgart, 2002), pp. 271–83

'Les Douaires des reines anglo-saxonnes', in F. Bougard (ed.), *Les Douaires dans le haut moyen âge* (Rome, 2002), pp. 527–34

'England and the Continent in the ninth century: I, ends and beginnings', *TRHS* 6th ser. 12 (2002), pp. 1–21

'Why study the medieval past?', *History Today* (August 2003), pp. 18–21

'England and the Continent in the ninth century: II, Vikings and others', *TRHS* 6th ser. 13 (2003), pp. 1–28

'Charlemagne and Europe', in *Quaestiones medii aevi novae* 8 (Warsaw, 2003), pp. 3–31

with D. Pelteret and H. Short, 'Medieval prosopographies and the prosopography of Anglo-Saxon England', in A. Cameron (ed.), *Fifty Years of Prosopography: The Later Roman Empire, Byzantium and Beyond* (Oxford, 2003), pp. 155–67

'Alfred and his Continental contemporaries', in T. Reuter (ed.), *Alfred the Great* (Aldershot, 2003), pp. 293–310

'Was Charlemagne's court a courtly society?', in C. Cubitt (ed.), *Court Culture in the Early Middle Ages* (Turnhout, 2003), pp. 39–57

'England and the Continent in the ninth century: III, Rights and rituals', *TRHS* 6th ser. 14 (2004), pp. 1–24

'Bertrada', in M. Becher and J. Jarnut (eds), *Der Dynastiewechsel von 751* (Münster, 2004), pp. 93–108

'Basilissai: power and its limits', in *Basilissa*, 1 (2004), pp. 124–35

'Carolingian coronations', *The Court Historian* 9 (2004), pp. 1–13

'Gendering courts in the early medieval west', in J. Smith and L. Brubaker (eds), *Gender and the Transformation of the Roman World* (Cambridge, 2004), pp. 185–97

'Tracking Einhard's *Vita Karoli*', review-article on M. Tischler, *Einharts Vita Karoli, Journal of Ecclesiastical History*, 57 (2005), pp. 301–7

'Charlemagne the man', in J. Story (ed.), *Charlemagne: Empire and Society* (Manchester, 2005), pp. 22–37

with F. Tinti, 'The aims and objectives of the prosopography of Anglo-Saxon England: 1066 and All That?', in D. Geuenich and I. Runge (eds), *Name und Gesellschaft im Frühmittelalter* (Hildesheim, 2005), pp. 241–58

'Warum es so viele Versionen von der Kaiserkrönung Karls des Grossen gibt', in B. Jussen (ed.), *Die Macht des Königs: Herrschaft in Europa vom Frühmittelalter bis in die Neuzeit* (Munich, 2005), pp. 38–54

'The queen in ninth-century Wessex', in S. Keynes and A. Smyth (eds), *Anglo-Saxons: Studies presented to Cyril Roy Hart* (Dublin, 2005), pp. 69–77

'England and the Continent in the ninth century: IV, bodies and minds', *TRHS* 6th series 15 (2005), pp. 1–23

'Did Charlemagne have a private life?', in D. Bates, S. Hamilton and J. Crick (eds), *Writing Medieval Biography, 750–1250: Essays in Honour of Frank Barlow* (Woodbridge, 2006), pp. 15–28

Sir Frank Stenton and the Vikings, Stenton Lecture (Reading, 2005)

Charlemagne and the Paradoxes of Power, Reuter Lecture (Southampton, 2006)

'European History', in A. Deyermond (ed.), *A century of British Studies* (Oxford, 2007), pp. 71–129

with Wormald (ed.), *Lay Intellectuals in the Early Middle Ages* (Cambridge, 2007)

'Dhuoda', in *Lay Intellectuals in the Early Middle Ages*, pp. 106–20

'The Dark Ages', *History Workshop Journal* 63 (2007), pp. 197–201

Courts, Elites and Gendered Power in the Early Middle Ages: Charlemagne and Others (Ashgate, 2007), 17 reprinted papers

Tabula gratulatoria

Di tibi si in qua pios respectant numina, si quid
Usquam iustitiae est, et mens sibi conscia recti
Praemia digna ferant
(Aeneid I, 603–5)

Professor Sally Alexander, Goldsmiths College, London
Professor Isabel Alfonso, CSIC, Madrid
Dr Stuart Airlie, University of Glasgow
Professor Michael I. Allen, University of Chicago
Professor Gerd Althoff, University of Münster
Dr Frances Andrews, University of St Andrews
Dr Ian Archer, Keble College, Oxford
Professor Benjamin Arnold, University of Reading
Dr Scott Ashley, University of Newcastle
Professor Hartmut Atsma, Karlsruhe, Germany
Professor Martin Aurell, University of Poitiers
Professor Bernard. S. Bachrach, University of Minnesota
Professor Sverre Bagge, University of Bergen
Dr Ross Balzaretti, University of Nottingham
Professor Janos Bak, Central European University
Professor Caroline Barron, Royal Holloway College, London
Dr Julia Barrow, University of Nottingham
Professor Dominique Barthélemy, University of Paris IV
Professor Matthias Becher, University of Bonn
Mr Matthew Bennet, Royal Military Academy, Sandhurst
Professor Michael Bentley, University of St Andrews
Professor Peter Biller, University of York
Dr James Bjork, King's College, London
Professor John Blair, The Queen's College, Oxford
Miss Brenda Bolton, University of London
Professor Nicholas Brooks, University of Birmingham

Professor Elizabeth A. R. Brown, City University of New York
Dr Giles Brown, Westminster School, London
Professor Peter Brown, Princeton University
Dr Tom Brown, University of Edinburgh
Professor Warren C. Brown, California Institute of Technology
Professor Leslie Brubaker, University of Birmingham
Professor Philippe Buc, Stanford University
Dr Arthur Burns, King's College, London
Professor James Campbell, Worcester College, Oxford
Professor David Carpenter, Kings's College, London
Dr Santiago Castellanos, University of León
Professor Celia Chazelle, The College of New Jersey
Dr Roger Collins, University of Edinburgh
Dr Kate Cooper, University of Manchester
Dr Marios Costambeys, University of Liverpool
Dr Ann Christys, Leeds
Dr Stephen Church, University of East Anglia
Professor Michael Clanchy, Oxford
Dr David Crankshaw, King's College, London
Dr Julia Crick, University of Exeter
Dr Katy Cubitt, University of York
Dr Kathleen Cushing, Keele University
Professor Martin Daunton, Trinity Hall, Cambridge
Professor David d'Avray, University College, London
Professor Mayke de Jong, University of Utrecht
Professor Philippe Depreux, University of Limoges
Dr Albrecht Diem, Syracuse University, New York
Carlotta Dionisotti, King's College, London
Dr Simon Ditchfield, University of York
Professor Saki Dockrill, King's College, London
Professor Anne Duggan, King's College, London
Professor Paul Edward Dutton, Simon Fraser University
Dr Julio Escalona, CSIC, Madrid
Dr Dominic Erdozain, King's College, London
Dr Ros Faith, Finstock, Oxon
Professor Wocjieck Falkowski, University of Warsaw
Professor Steven Fanning, University of Illinois at Chicago
Serena Ferente, King's College, London
Professor Kenneth Fincham, University of Kent
Professor Robin Fleming, Boston College
Professor Sarah Foot, University of Oxford

Professor Robert Frost, University of Aberdeen
Dr Mary Garrison, University of York
Professor Patrick Geary, University of California, Los Angeles
Professor Hans-Werner Goetz, University of Hamburg
Professor Walter Goffart, University of Toronto
Dr Anne Goldgar, King's College, London
Dr Laura Gowing, King's College, London
Professor Lindy Grant, University of Reading
Professor Eric. J. Goldberg, Williams College
Dr Dawn Hadley, University of Sheffield
Professor Christopher Harper-Bill, University of East Anglia
Dr Martina Hartmann, University of Heidelberg
Dr Wilfried Hartmann, University of Tübingen
Dr Ruth Harvey, Royal Holloway College, London
Dr Yitzhak Hen, University of Tel Aviv
Professor Judith Herrin, King's College, London
Professor Richard Hodges, University of East Anglia
Dr Anke Holdenried, University of Bristol
Professor Paul Hyams, Cornell University
Dr Charles Insley, Canterbury Christ Church University
Dr Dominique Iogna-Prat, CNRS, Paris
Professor Edward James, University College, Dublin
Professor Ludmilla Jordanova, King's College, London
Professor Martin Jones, King's College, London
Professor Brigitte Kasten, Universität des Saarlandes
Professor Derek Keene, Institute of Historical Research, London
Dr Matthew Kempshall, Wadham College, Oxford
Professor Simon Keynes, Trinity College, Cambridge
Dr David King, Lambrigg, Cumbria
Professor Geoffrey Koziol, University of California, Berkeley
Dr Lucy Kostyanovsky, King's College, London
Professor Andrew Lambert, King's College, London
Ms Sarah Lambert, Goldsmiths College, London
Professor Michael Lapidge, Cambridge
Dr M. K. Lawson, St Paul's School, London
Professor Stéphane Lebecq, Université Charles de Gaulle, Lille
Professor Régine Le Jan, Université de Paris I
Dr Conrad Leyser, University of Manchester
Dr Henrietta Leyser, St Peter's College, Oxford
Professor Felice Lifschitz, Florida International University
Dr Peter Linehan, St John's College, Cambridge

Professor Andrew Louth, University of Durham
Dr Stephen Lovell, King's College, London
Dr Chris Loveluck, University of Nottingham
Dr Ian McBride, King's College, London
Professor Michael McCormick, Harvard University
Mr Timothy McFarland, University College, London
Professor Rosamond McKitterick, University of Cambridge
Professor David McLean, King's College, London
Dr Peter Mandler, Gonville and Caius College, Cambridge
Dr Jane Martindale, London
Professor Henry Mayr-Harting, Oxford
De Rob Meens, University of Utrecht
Professor Bob Moore, University of Newcastle
Professor John Moorhead, University of Queensland
Dr Rosemary Morris, University of York
Professor Marco Mostert, University of Utrecht
Professor Lawrence Nees, University of Delaware
Professor Thomas F. X. Noble, University of Notre Dame
Professor Otto Gerhard Oexle, Max Planck Institut für Geschichte,
    Göttingen
Dr John Nightingale, Magdalen College, Oxford
Professor Andrew Orchard, University of Toronto
Professor Bruce O'Brien, University of Maryland, Washington
Professor Mark Ormrod, University of York
Dr David Pelteret, Fazely, Staffordshire
Dr Juliet Perkins, King's College, London
Professor Walter Pohl, University of Vienna
Professor Andrew Porter, King's College, London
Dr Christina Pössel, University of Birmingham
Professor Alex Potts, University of Michigan, Ann Arbor
Dr Paul Readman, King's College, London
Dr Helmut Reimitz, Institut für Mittelalterforschung University of Vienna
Mrs Georgie Reuter, Southampton
Professor Joel Rosenthal, University of New York at Stony Brook
Professor Barbara H. Rosenwein, Loyola University, Chicago
Professor Michel Rouche, University of Paris
Professor Charlotte Roueché, King's College, London
Dr Michael Rowe, King's College, London
Professor Miri Rubin, Queen Mary College, London
Dr Antonio Sennis, University College, London
Professor Toni Scharer, University of Vienna

Mr Bill Schwarz, Queen Mary College, London
Mr Barrie Singleton, Morley College, London
Dr Trish Skinner, University of Southampton
Professor Julia Smith, University of Glasgow
Professor Pauline Stafford, University of Liverpool
Professor Nikolaus Staubach, Westfälische Wilhelms-Universität, Münster
Dr Sarah Stockwell, King's College, London
Dr Joanna Story, University of Leicester
Dr Adam Sutcliffe, King's College, London
Dr Pamela Taylor, London
Professor Pat Thane, Institute of Historical Research, London
Dr Frans Theuws, University of Amsterdam
Dr Francesca Tinti, University of Bologna
Professor Richard Trainor, King's College, London
Dr Elisabeth van Houts, Emmanuel College, Cambridge
Professor Nicholas Vincent, University of East Anglia
Dr Richard Vinen, King's College, London
Professor Hannah Vollrath, Ruhr-Universität, Bochum
Dr Elizabeth Ward, Faversham, Kent
Mr Bryan Ward-Perkins, Trinity College, Oxford
Professor Marina Warner, University of Essex
Dr Teresa Webber, Trinity College, Cambridge
Dr Ann Williams, London
Dr Jon Wilson, King's College, London
Professor Herwig Wolfram, University of Vienna
Dr Jenny Wormald, University of Edinburgh
Professor Chris Wickham, All Souls College, Oxford
Dr Mark Whittow, St Peters College, Oxford
Professor Ian Wood, University of Leeds
Mr Michael Wood, London

INDEX

Note: this index is arranged around aspects of Frankish (and more generally medieval) history that have occupied Jinty Nelson in her scholarly work. The authors of the chapters in this volume have a lot to say about such matters as ritual, heresy, power, queenship, and ideology, all characteristic of Jinty's interests. The main purpose in grouping references together here is to encourage readers to pursue themes and ideas encountered in one particular essay across the rest of the volume. It is highly selective, not least in omitting most references to the people, places, and events specific to each essay, and in highlighting instead broader and more abstract aspects of the history of Frankland and its neighbours.

An outline of the main headings used in the index precedes the index itself. Although the index is designed for browsing rather than 'looking things up', the arrangement of entries under main headings is alphabetical for ease of navigation. 'n.' after a page number indicates the number of a note on that page.

INDEX